Social Media Modeling and Computing

Steven C.H. Hoi · Jiebo Luo · Susanne Boll ·
Dong Xu · Rong Jin · Irwin King

Editors

Social Media Modeling and Computing

 Springer

Editors

Asst. Prof. Steven C.H. Hoi
Nanyang Technological University
School of Computer Engineering
Singapore, Singapore
chhoi@ntu.edu.sg

Dr. Jiebo Luo
Kodak Research Laboratories
Lake Avenue 1999
14650 Rochester, NY
USA
Jiebo.luo@kodak.com

Prof. Susanne Boll
University of Oldenburg
Media Informatics and Multimedia Systems
Escherweg 2
26121 Oldenburg
Germany
susanne.boll@uni-oldenburg.de

Asst. Prof. Dong Xu
Nanyang Technological University
School of Computer Engineering
Singapore, Singapore
dongxu@ntu.edu.sg

Assoc. Prof. Rong Jin
Michigan State University
Dept. Computer Science and Engineering
Engineering Building 3115
48824 East Lansing, MI
USA
rongjin@cse.msu.edu

Prof. Irwin King
AT&T Labs Research
San Francisco
USA
and
The Chinese University of Hong Kong
Dept. Computer Science and Engineering
Shatin
Hong Kong SAR
king@cse.cuhk.edu.hk

ISBN 978-0-85729-435-7   e-ISBN 978-0-85729-436-4
DOI 10.1007/978-0-85729-436-4
Springer London Dordrecht Heidelberg New York

British Library Cataloguing in Publication Data
A catalogue record for this book is available from the British Library

Library of Congress Control Number: 2011923787

Cover design: deblik

Printed on acid-free paper

Springer is part of Springer Science+Business Media (www.springer.com)

Preface

Recent years have witnessed a growing number of user-centric multimedia applications, especially with the popularity of web 2.0. Examples include Flickr, YouTube, Facebook, Twitter, MySpace, etc. The emerging applications on social web and social networks have produced a new type of multimedia content, termed as "social media" here, as it is created by people using highly accessible and scalable publishing technologies for sharing via the web. With social media technology, images, videos and audios are generally accompanied by rich contextual information, such as tags, categories, title, metadata, comments, and ratings, etc. Massive emerging social media data offer new opportunities for solving some long-standing challenges in multimedia understanding and management, such as the semantic gap issue. These new media also introduce a number of new and challenging research problems and many exciting real-world applications.

This book presents recent advances on several aspects of emerging social media modeling and social media computing research. It is designed for practitioners and for researchers of all levels of expertise, from novice to expert. It targets various groups of people who need information on social media modeling and social media computing. They include:

- People who need a general understanding of social media. They are high-level managers and professional engineers who are interested in emerging social media modeling and computing technologies.
- Software developers who apply social media modeling and computing techniques. It also includes practitioners in related disciplines such as multimedia content management, information retrieval, web search, data mining, and machine learning.
- Researchers and students who are working on social media, multimedia, web search, data mining, and machine learning, and related disciplines, as well as anyone who wants a deep understanding of techniques for social media modeling and computing.

Regarding the contents and organization, this book consists of 12 chapters that present a variety of emerging technologies on social media modeling and computing. In particular, these book chapters can be summarized in the following three major aspects:

- *Social media content analysis*: The first part of the book is related to the application of multimedia content analysis techniques to the emerging social media data. It includes social image tag analysis (chapter "Quantifying Visual-Representativeness of Social Image Tags using Image Tag Clarity"), social image tag ranking (chapter "Tag-Based Social Image Search: Towards Relevant and Diverse Results"), and tag-based social image search (chapter "Social Image Tag Ranking by Two-View Learning"), social media content analysis by combining multimodal features (chapter "Combining Multimodal Features for Social Media Analysis"), and multi-label social image annotation by exploring group structures (chapter "Multi-label Image Annotation by Structural Grouping Sparsity").
- *Social media system design and analysis*: The second part of the book is devoted to social media system design and analysis. It includes the design of effective social media mechanism for incentivizing social media contributions (chapter "Mechanism Design for Incentivizing Social Media Contributions"), the design of efficient access control for privacy and security issues in multimedia social networks (chapter "Efficient Access Control in Multimedia Social Networks"), the analysis of users and their online behaviors in social video sharing portals (chapter "Call Me Guru: User Categories and Large-Scale Behavior in YouTube"), and visual analytic tools for social event analysis (chapter "Social Media Visual Analytics for Events").
- *Social media applications*: The last part of the book is related to the development of emerging social media applications by exploring emerging user-contributed social media data. It includes the application of social media information to music recommendation (chapter "Using Rich Social Media Information for Music Recommendation via Hypergraph Model"), the application of user-contributed Geotag information to automatic image annotation (chapter "Using Geotags to Derive Rich Tagclouds for Image Annotation"), and the application of social media techniques to analyze and improve real-world photobooks (chapter "Social Aspects of Photobooks: Improving Photobook Authoring from Large-scale Multimedia Analysis").

Each of the above book chapters can be considered as a compact, self-contained mini-book in its own right under its title. They are, however, organized and presented in relation to the basic principles and practice of social media modeling and computing. We also note that this book can be used as advanced materials by graduate students of information technology related subjects, such as computer science, computer engineering, and information systems, either in a classroom or for self-study.

Finally, this book was first initialized during the organization of the first international workshop on social media (WSM2009). It was later developed by soliciting contributions from a number of international experts on social media modeling and computing to present their best knowledge and practice on specific social media related topics. Some chapters of this book were originated from recent studies in international conferences and workshops, including the SIGMM international Workshop on Social Media (WSM), and ACM International Conference on Multimedia (ACM Multimedia), and ACM International conference on Web Search and Data Mining (WSDM). As co-editors of this book, we would like to thank all the authors of the book chapters for their great efforts in providing the high quality contents to this book, and our colleagues who helped us during the organization of the WSM workshops and the book editing process.

Singapore	Steven C.H. Hoi
USA	Jiebo Luo
Germany	Susanne Boll
Singapore	Dong Xu
USA	Rong Jin
USA	Irwin King

Contents

Part III   Social Media Applications

Contributors

Sourav S. Bhowmick School of Computer Engineering, Nanyang Technological University, Singapore, Singapore, assourav@ntu.edu.sg

Joan-Isaac Biel Idiap Research Institute, Ecole Polytechnique Fédérale de Lausanne (EPFL), Lausanne, Switzerland, jibiel@idiap.ch

Susanne Boll University of Oldenburg, Oldenburg, Germany, susanne.boll@uni-oldenburg.de

Jiajun Bu Zhejiang Key Laboratory of Service Robot, College of Computer Science, Zhejiang University, Hangzhou 310027, China, bjj@zju.edu.cn

Chun Chen Zhejiang Key Laboratory of Service Robot, College of Computer Science, Zhejiang University, Hangzhou 310027, China, chenc@zju.edu.cn

Nicholas Diakopoulos School of Communication and Information, Rutgers University, 4 Huntington St., New Brunswick, NJ 08901, USA, nicholas.diakopoulos@gmail.com

Sabu Emmanuel School of Computer Engineering, Nanyang Technological University, Singapore, Singapore, asemmanuel@ntu.edu.sg

Andrew Gallagher Corporate Research and Engineering, Eastman Kodak Company, Rochester, USA

Daniel Gatica-Perez Idiap Research Institute, Ecole Polytechnique Fédérale de Lausanne (EPFL), Lausanne, Switzerland, gatica@idiap.ch

Eirini Giannakidou Informatics & Telematics Institute, Thermi, Thessaloniki, Greece, igiannak@iti.gr; Department of Computer Science, Aristotle University of Thessaloniki, Thessaloniki, Greece

Yahong Han College of Computer Science, Zhejiang University, Hangzhou, China, yahong@zju.edu.cn

Xiaofei He State Key Laboratory of CAD&CG, College of Computer Science, Zhejiang University, Hangzhou 310027, China, xiaofeihe@cad.zju.edu.cn

Steven C.H. Hoi School of Computer Engineering, Nanyang Technological University, Singapore, Singapore, chhoi@ntu.edu.sg

Xian-Sheng Hua Media Computing Group, Microsoft Research Asia, Beijing 100080, China, xshua@microsoft.com

Ramesh Jain University of California, Irvine, Irvine, USA, jain@ics.uci.edu

Dhiraj Joshi Corporate Research and Engineering, Eastman Kodak Company, Rochester, USA, dhiraj.joshi@kodak.com

Mohan Kankanhalli National University of Singapore, Singapore, Singapore, mohan@comp.nus.edu.sg

Funda Kivran-Swaine School of Communication and Information, Rutgers University, 4 Huntington St., New Brunswick, NJ 08901, USA

Ioannis Kompatsiaris Informatics & Telematics Institute, Thermi, Thessaloniki, Greece, ikom@iti.gr

Phoury Lei Corporate Research and Engineering, Eastman Kodak Company, Rochester, USA

Jiebo Luo Corporate Research and Engineering, Eastman Kodak Company, Rochester, USA

Mor Naaman School of Communication and Information, Rutgers University, 4 Huntington St., New Brunswick, NJ 08901, USA

Spiros Nikolopoulos Informatics & Telematics Institute, Thermi, Thessaloniki, Greece, nikolopo@iti.gr; School of Electronic Engineering and Computer Science, Queen Mary University of London, E1 4NS, London, UK

Ioannis Patras School of Electronic Engineering and Computer Science, Queen Mary University of London, E1 4NS, London, UK, i.patras@eecs.qmul.ac.uk

Amit Sachan School of Computer Engineering, Nanyang Technological University, Singapore, Singapore, amit0009@ntu.edu.sg

Philipp Sandhaus OFFIS – Institute for Information Science, Oldenburg, Germany, sandhaus@offis.de

Vivek K. Singh University of California, Irvine, Irvine, USA, singhv@uci.edu

Aixin Sun School of Computer Engineering, Nanyang Technological University, Singapore, Singapore, axsun@ntu.edu.sg

Shulong Tan Zhejiang Key Laboratory of Service Robot, College of Computer Science, Zhejiang University, Hangzhou 310027, China, shulongtan@zju.edu.cn

Athena Vakali Department of Computer Science, Aristotle University of Thessaloniki, Thessaloniki, Greece, avakali@csd.auth.gr

Meng Wang AKiiRA Media Systems Inc, Palo Alto, CA 94301, USA,
eric.mengwang@gmail.com

Fei Wu College of Computer Science, Zhejiang University, Hangzhou, China,
wufei@zju.edu.cn

Kuiyuan Yang Department of Automation, The University of Science and Technology of China, Hefei, Anhui 230027, China, yky@ustc.edu

Tayebeh Yazdani School of Communication and Information, Rutgers University,
4 Huntington St., New Brunswick, NJ 08901, USA

Jie Yu Corporate Research and Engineering, Eastman Kodak Company, Rochester,
USA

Hong-Jiang Zhang Microsoft Advanced Technology Center, Beijing 100080,
China, hjzhang@microsoft.com

Jinfeng Zhuang School of Computer Engineering, Nanyang Technological University, Singapore, Singapore, zhua0016@ntu.edu.sg

Yueting Zhuang College of Computer Science, Zhejiang University, Hangzhou,
China, yzhuang@zju.edu.cn

Part I
Social Media Content Analysis

Quantifying Visual-Representativeness of Social Image Tags Using Image Tag Clarity

Aixin Sun and Sourav S. Bhowmick

Abstract Tags associated with images in various social media sharing web sites are valuable information source for superior image retrieval experiences. Due to the nature of tagging, many tags associated with images are not visually descriptive. In this chapter, we propose *Image Tag Clarity* to evaluate the effectiveness of a tag in describing the visual content of its annotated images, which is also known as the image tag visual-representativeness. It is measured by computing the zero-mean normalized distance between the *tag language model* estimated from the images annotated by the tag and the *collection language model*. The tag/collection language models are derived from the bag of visual-word local content features of the images. The visual-representative tags that are commonly used to annotate visually similar images are given high tag clarity scores. Evaluated on a large real-world dataset containing more than 269K images and their associated tags, we show that the image tag clarity score can effectively identify the visual-representative tags from all tags contributed by users. Based on the tag clarity scores, we have made a few interesting observations that could be used to support many tag-based applications.

1 Introduction

With the advances in digital photography (e.g., digital cameras and mobile phones) and social media sharing web sites, a huge number of multimedia content is now available online. Most of these sites enable users to annotate web objects including images with free tags (e.g., aircraft, lake, sky). For instance, most images accessible through Flickr[1] are annotated with tags from their uploaders as well as

---

[1]http://www.flickr.com.

This chapter is an extended version of the paper [11] presented at the first ACM SIGMM Workshop on Social Media (WSM), held in conjunction with ACM Multimedia, 2009.

A. Sun (✉) · S.S. Bhowmick
School of Computer Engineering, Nanyang Technological University, Singapore, Singapore
e-mail: axsun@ntu.edu.sg

S.S. Bhowmick
e-mail: assourav@ntu.edu.sg

S.C.H. Hoi et al. (eds.), *Social Media Modeling and Computing*,
DOI 10.1007/978-0-85729-436-4_1, © Springer-Verlag London Limited 2011

other users. A key consequence of the availability of such tags as meta-data is that it has significantly facilitated web image search and organization as this rich collection of tags provides more information than we can possibly extract from content-based algorithms.

Due to the popularity of tags, there have been increasing research efforts to better understand and exploit tag usage patterns for information retrieval and other related tasks. One such effort is to make better use of the tags associated with images for superior image retrieval experiences. However, this is still a challenging research problem, as it is well known that tags are noisy and imprecise [1]. As discussed in [4], tags are created by users more for their personal use than for others' benefit. Consequently, two similar images may be associated with significantly different sets of tags from different users, especially when images can only be annotated by users with *tagging permissions* (e.g., in Flickr, only the uploader and his/her contacts can tag an image). Further, tags associated with an image may describe the image from significantly different perspectives. For example, consider a photo uploaded by Sally which she took using her Canon 40D camera at Sentosa when she traveled to Singapore in 2008. This image may be annotated by different tags such as Canon, 40D, 2008, Singapore, travel, beach, Sentosa, and many others. Notice that tags like 2008 and Canon do not effectively describe the visual content of the image, but more on providing contextual information about the image. Consequently, these tags maybe considered as noise in many applications (e.g., content-based tag recommendation). As the presence of such noise may reduce the usefulness of tags in image retrieval, "de-noising" tags has been recently identified as one of the key research challenges in [1]. Such de-noising of tags also enables us to build more effective tag ranking and recommendation services [8].

In this chapter, we take a step toward addressing the above challenge. We focus on identifying and quantifying *visual-representative* tags from all tags assigned to images so that less visually representative tags can be eliminated. Intuitively, a tag is *visual-representative* if it effectively describes the *visual content* of the images. A visual-representative tag (such as sky, sunset, and tiger) easily suggests the scene or object that an image may describe even before the image is presented to a user. On the other hand, tags like 2008 and Asia often fail to suggest anything meaningful with respect to the visual content of the annotated image as any image taken in 2008 or in Asia could be annotated by the two tags.

We propose the notion of *image tag clarity* to identify visual-representative tags. It is inspired by the *clarity score* proposed for query performance prediction in ad-hoc information retrieval for textual documents [2]. Note that clarity score cannot be directly applied to annotated images as keywords of a query literally appears in the retrieved text documents whereas the tags associated with an image do not explicitly appear in it. Informally, the *image tag clarity* is computed by the Kullback–Leibler (KL) divergence between the tag language model and collection language model and further normalized with zero-mean normalization. The tag/collection language models are derived from the local content features (i.e., bag of visual-words) of the images. Our experimental study with the NUS-WIDE dataset [1], containing 269,648 images from Flickr, demonstrates that the proposed clarity score measure can effectively identify the visually representative tags.

Based on the experimental results, we further investigated the relationships between tag visual-representativeness and tag frequency. Our study revealed that they are weakly correlated. That is, frequently used tags are more likely to be visually representative. We also observed that for images having three to 16 tags, the percentage of visually representative tags increases with the increase in number of tags. Furthermore, the visual-representativeness of a tag and its *position* with respect to other tags for a given image are correlated. That is, the first few tags assigned to an image are more likely to be visually representative compared to tags assigned later. This probably reflects the phenomenon that users tend to first tag an image based on its visual content and later add other tags to describe it from different perspectives. Lastly, the visually (resp. non-visually) representative tags have higher chance of *co-occurring* strongly with other visually (resp. non-visually) representative tags. These interesting observations could be very useful in supporting a wide range of tag-based applications such as tag recommendation and social image retrieval.

The rest of the chapter is organized as follows. In Sect. 2, we review the related work with emphasis on clarity score for query performance prediction as well as image tagging. Section 3 discusses the notion of image tag clarity. The details of the dataset and experimental results are reported in Sect. 4. The observations are presented in Sect. 5 and we conclude this chapter in Sect. 6.

2 Related Work

Recall that our proposed image tag clarity measure is inspired by the notion of clarity score proposed for query performance prediction in ad-hoc retrieval. Hence, we begin by reviewing the clarity score measure. Next, we discuss relevant research efforts in annotating web objects with tags.

2.1 Clarity Score

Query performance prediction is to predict the effectiveness of a keyword query in retrieving relevance documents from a document collection [2]. The prediction enables a search engine to answer poorly performing queries more effectively through alternative retrieval strategies (e.g., query expansion) [5, 15, 19, 20]. Depending on whether documents need to be retrieved for the query, the query performance prediction algorithms can be classified into two types: *pre-retrieval* and *post-retrieval* algorithms. Pre-retrieval algorithms rely on the statistics of the words in both the query and the collection. For instance, queries consisting of words with low document frequencies in the collection tend to perform better than queries with high document frequency words. Post-retrieval algorithms predict query performance based on the properties of the retrieved documents from the collection using the query. Among various post-retrieval algorithms, one significant contribution is the *clarity score* [2].

The *clarity score* of a query is computed as the *distance* between the *query language model* and the *collection language model*. If a query is effective in retrieving topically cohesive documents, then the query language model contains unusually large probabilities of words specific to the topic covered by the retrieved documents. Consequently, the distance between the query and the collection language models is large. If a query is ambiguous, then the documents covering various topics are likely to be retrieved. That is, the retrieved set of documents is similar to a set of documents through random sampling. As the word distribution in the retrieved documents is similar to that in the collection, the distance between them is small.

Formally, let Q be a query consisting of one or more query words $\{q|q \in Q\}$ and R be the set of top-K documents retrieved by Q from the collection $\mathscr{D}$. The value of K is predefined and set to 500 in [2]. Let w be an arbitrary word in the vocabulary. Then, the query language model $P(w|Q)$ is estimated by Eq. (1), where $P(d|Q)$ is estimated using Bayes' theorem as shown in Eq. (2).

$$P(w|Q) = \sum_{d \in R} P(w|d)P(d|Q), \tag{1}$$

$$P(Q|d) = \prod_{q \in Q} P(q|d). \tag{2}$$

Observe that in both Eqs. (1) and (2), $P(w|d)$ (resp. $P(q|d)$) is the relative frequency of word w (resp. q) in the document d linearly smoothed by w's relative frequency in the collection. The collection language model, $P(w|\mathscr{D})$, is estimated by the relative frequency of w in $\mathscr{D}$. Then, the clarity score of Q is the Kullback–Leibler (KL) divergence between $P(w|Q)$ and $P(w|\mathscr{D})$, and is given by the following equation.

$$KL(Q\|\mathscr{D}) = \sum_{w} P(w|Q) \log_2 \frac{P(w|Q)}{P(w|\mathscr{D})}. \tag{3}$$

Tagging is a popular technique for annotating objects on the web. In our previous work [13], we introduced the notion of *tag clarity* in the context of user behavior study in self-tagging systems, i.e., blogs. The clarity score of a tag is defined by the KL divergence between the tag language model (estimated from the blog posts associated with the tag) and the collection language model estimated from all blog posts. As blogs are self-tagging, i.e., only the blogger could annotate his/her blog posts, the tag clarity was proposed to study whether users implicitly develop consensus on the semantic of the tags. We observed that frequently used tags are topic discriminative. This finding is partially consistent with the findings in this proposed work although the object (text vs. image) of annotation and tagging rights (self-tagging vs. permission-based tagging) are different.

2.2 Tagging Images

Recent years have witnessed increasing research efforts to study images annotated with tags in social media sharing web sites like Flickr. Tag recommendation, tag ranking, and tag-based classification are identified as key research tasks in this context [1]. Only few works exploit the relationship between a tag to the content of its annotated images. For a given image and its annotated tags, the *relevance* between the image and each tag is estimated through kernel density estimation in [8] and through k-nearest neighbor voting in [7]. In simple words, a tag is relevant to an image I if the tag has been used to annotate many images similar to I. The relevance score for a tag is therefore image-specific, whereas in our case the tag clarity score is *global*. For a given tag, the score reflects its effectiveness in visually describing all its annotated images. In this context, our work is also related to [10] where the main focus is on searching for high-level concepts (e.g., sunset) with little semantic gaps with respect to image representation in visual space. In [10], for a given image I, its confidence score is derived based on the coherence degree of its nearest neighbors in both visual and textual spaces, assuming that each image is surrounded by textual descriptions. The high-level concepts are then derived through clustering those images with high confidence scores. In contrast, our work differs in the following ways: (i) the computation of clarity score of a tag is purely based on its annotated images represented in visual space only; (ii) our task is to measure the visual-representativeness of a tag (i.e., a given concept) and not to mine concepts from textual descriptions; and (iii) our work does not rely on neighborhood relationships between images.

Very recently, *Flickr distance* was proposed to model two tags' similarity based on their annotated images [17]. For each tag, a visual language model is constructed from 1000 images annotated with the tag and the Flickr distance between the two tags is computed using the Jensen–Shannon divergence. Our work is significantly different from [17] in three aspects. First, our main research objective is to measure the visual-representativeness of a single tag and not the relationship between tag pairs. Second, the language models are estimated from different image representations. Our language models are estimated on top of the widely adopted bag of visual-words representation [9] while visual language model has its own definition in [17]. Third, we analyze the impact of tag frequency on its language modeling. In their work, a fixed number (i.e., 1000) of images for each tag were sampled for estimating its language model.

In [16], a probabilistic framework was proposed to resolve *tag ambiguity* in Flickr by suggesting semantic-orthogonal tags from those tags that co-occurred with the given set of tags. Although tag ambiguity is highly related to tag clarity, the approach in [16] was purely based on tag co-occurrence without considering the content of annotated images.

3 Image Tag Clarity

Intuitively, a tag is visually representative if all the images annotated with the tag are visually similar to each other. In this sense, we heuristically consider the assignment of a tag t to an image I as a sampling process. We assume that a user samples images from a large collection and decides whether t shall be assigned to some images. Based on this setting, if all users have an implicit common understanding on the sampling process with respect to the visual content of the images, then the assignment of the visual-representative tags is a biased sampling process such that only those images that contain certain visual concepts (e.g., sunset scene) will be assigned as a visual-representative tag (e.g. `sunset`). On the other hand, the assignment of a non-visually representative tag is an unbiased sampling process to images regardless of their visual content. Most contextual tags describing the time and location in general (e.g., the country where the photo was taken) belong to the latter case. For instance, any image taken in Singapore during year 2008 can be tagged by `Singapore` and `2008` and either tag hardly describes the visual content of the tagged images. Based on this heuristic, for a given tag t, we can consider the set of images I_t annotated by t and compare this set to a randomly drawn set of images of similar size, denoted by I_t' ($|I_t| \simeq |I_t'|$), where t' denotes a dummy tag randomly assigned to images. If I_t is similar to any I_t', randomly drawn from a large collection of images in terms of visual content, then t is unlikely to describe any specific visual concepts. Otherwise, if I_t is significantly different from I_t', demonstrating common visual content features, then we consider t to be visually representative. In the following, we present image tag clarity measure to quantify tag visual-representativeness.

The image tag clarity score is based on the following framework. We consider a tag to be a keyword query and the set of images annotated with the tag are the retrieved documents based on a boolean retrieval model (returns an image as long as the image is annotated with the tag with equal relevance score). Then the clarity score proposed for query performance prediction can be adopted to measure tag clarity if the visual content of the images can be represented by "word" vectors similar to that for representing textual documents. That is, if all images associated with the tag are visually similar, then the language model estimated from the set of retrieved images (or the tag language model) shall contain some "words" with unusually high probabilities specific to the tag making the distance between the tag and the collection language models large. Among the various low-level features that are commonly used to represent images, the *bag of visual-words* feature represents images very much like textual documents [9]. In the sequel, we assume that a bag of visual-words has been extracted to represent each image.[2] We also use "image" and "document" interchangeably due to this representation.

3.1 Image Tag Clarity Score

Let I_t be the set of images annotated by a tag t and $\mathscr{I}$ be the image collection. Based on the clarity score definition in Eq. (3), the *image tag clarity* score of t, denoted by $\tau(t)$, is defined as the *KL* divergence between the *tag language model* ($P(w|I_t)$)

---

[2]Nevertheless, we believe that the image tag clarity score is generic and can be computed using other feature representations.

and the *collection language model* ($p(w|\mathscr{I})$), where w denotes a visual-word. It is expressed by the following equation.

$$\tau(t) = KL(I_t \| \mathscr{I}) = \sum_w P(w|I_t) \log_2 \frac{P(w|I_t)}{P(w|\mathscr{I})}. \tag{4}$$

As a collection language model is often estimated by the relative word frequency in the collection, our main focus in this section is to estimate the tag language model $P(w|I_t)$. This is a challenging issue for the following reason. In textual documents, keywords in a query Q literally appear in the retrieved documents. Hence, the degree of relevance between a document d and query Q (i.e., $P(d|Q)$) can be estimated using Eq. (2). However, in a bag of visual-words representation, the tag and the words are from two different feature spaces. As a tag does not literally appear in images, the degree of relevance of an image to a tag is unknown. That is, $P(d|Q)$ in Eq. (1) (or $P(I|I_t)$ in our setting) has to be estimated differently, as Eq. (2) cannot be directly applied.

Intuitively, there are at least two approaches to estimate the tag language model. First, we can simply treat all images equally representative of a tag t, so all the images annotated with t have uniform probability to be sampled. Second, we can estimate the representativeness of images based on their distances to I_t's centroid. Images that are more close to the centroid of I_t are considered more representative and shall contribute more to the estimation of the tag language model.

- The first approach estimates the tag language model as the average relative visual-word frequency in the images with equal importance $\frac{1}{|I_t|}$. Hence, the tag language model, denoted by $P_s(w|I_t)$, is given by the following equation.

$$P_s(w|I_t) = \sum_{I \in I_t} \frac{1}{|I_t|} P_{ml}(w|I). \tag{5}$$

Observe that it is consistent with the *small document model* used in [3] for blog feed search. Similar approach has also been used in modeling blog tag clarity in our earlier work [13].
- In the second approach, also known as the *centrality document model*, the tag language model $P_c(w|I_t)$ is estimated using Eq. (6), where $P(I|I_t)$ reflects the relative closeness of the image I to I_t's centroid defined in Eq. (7).

$$P_c(w|I_t) = \sum_{I \in I_t} P_{ml}(w|I) P(I|I_t), \tag{6}$$

$$P(I|I_t) = \frac{\varphi(I, I_t)}{\sum_{I \in I_t} \varphi(I, I_t)}, \tag{7}$$

$$\varphi(I, I_t) = \prod_{w \in I} P_s(w|I_t)^{P_{ml}(w|I)}. \tag{8}$$

In Eq. (7), $\varphi(I, I_t)$ is a *centrality function* which defines the similarity between an image I to the tagged collection I_t. Let $P_s(w|I_t)$ be the tag language model estimated with small document model in Eq. (5) and $P_{ml}(w|I)$ be the relative

Fig. 1 Tag language models against collection language model. The x-axis is the visual-words ordered according to $P(w|\mathscr{I})$ in descending order, and the y-axis shows the $P(w|I_t)$ and $P(w|\mathscr{I})$ for each tag

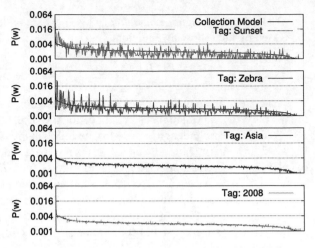

visual-word frequency of w in image I. Then based on [3], $\varphi(I, I_t)$ is defined to be the weighted geometric mean of word generation probabilities in I_t as shown in Eq. (8). The weight of each visual-word is its likelihood in image I.

The estimated tag language model is further smoothed using the Jelinek–Mercer smoothing with $\lambda = 0.99$.

$$P_{\text{smoothed}}(w|I_t) = \lambda P_c(w|I_t) + (1 - \lambda)P(w|\mathscr{I}). \tag{9}$$

Intuitively the centrality document model better simulates the clarity score compared to the small document model. However, the distance between an image I to the tagged collection I_t is an estimation which may not necessarily reflect the relevance between the image I and the tag t. Our experimental study revealed that the two models deliver nearly identical results. Hence in this chapter, we report the results based on the small document model due to its simplicity.

Figure 1 illustrates four example tag language models against the collection language model derived from the NUS-WIDE dataset (see Sect. 4). The x-axis is the visual-words ordered according to $P(w|\mathscr{I})$ in descending order; and the y-axis shows the $P(w|I_t)$ and $P(w|\mathscr{I})$, respectively. Clearly, the tag language models for Sunset and Zebra are significantly different from the collection language model, while the models for Asia and 2008 are very similar to that of the collection model. That is, the images tagged by either Asia or 2008 are similar to a randomly sampled set of images from the collection. For either Sunset or Zebra, one may expect the annotated image contains or describes the scene or object expressed by the semantic of the tag, making these images similar to each other and distinctive from the entire collection. Table 1 reports the tag clarity scores of these four tags. Observe that $\tau(Sunset)$ and $\tau(Zebra)$ are much larger than $\tau(Asia)$ and $\tau(2008)$.

Table 1 Clarity scores, normalized clarity scores and tag frequencies for the four example tags

Tag	Tag clarity $\tau(t)$	Normalized tag clarity $\tau_z(t)$	Tag frequency $|I_t|$
Sunset	0.294	285.3	10962
Zebra	0.412	97.9	627
Asia	0.004	−2.5	3878
2008	0.005	−1.9	4388

3.2 Normalized Image Tag Clarity Score

The aforementioned example demonstrates that Sunset and Zebra are more visually representative than Asia and 2008. However, it is hard to determine a *threshold* for tag clarity $\tau(t)$ such that if a tag t has its clarity score above the threshold value then it is considered visually representative. Recall from Sect. 2.1, the query language model is estimated from a fix number of top-K documents (e.g., $K = 500$ in [2]). The clarity scores for all queries are therefore computed based on the same number of documents. However in tagging, the tag distribution follows power-law distribution where a small set of tags are much more frequently used than other tags (see Sect. 4). The sizes of the I_t for different tags can therefore be significantly different. We address this issue by *normalizing* the image tag clarity score.

Reconsider the task of assigning a tag to an image as a sampling process of picking up images from a large collection (i.e., $\mathscr{I}$). If the sampling is unbiased (i.e., uniform sampling), then the language model of the sampled images $P(w|I_t)$ naturally gets closer to $P(w|\mathscr{I})$ as I_t gets larger. Hence, the distance $KL(I_t\|\mathscr{I})$ becomes smaller. Therefore, $KL(I_t\|\mathscr{I})$ may not accurately reflect the clarity of a tag as it is expected that $KL(I_{t1}\|\mathscr{I}) < KL(I_{t2}\|\mathscr{I})$ if $|I_{t1}| > |I_{t2}|$ when both t_1 and t_2 are uniformly sampled, i.e., not visually representative.

To determine whether a tag t is visually representative, its tag clarity score $\tau(t)$ is compared with the clarity score of a dummy tag t' which is randomly assigned to images in $\mathscr{I}$ such that t and t' have the same tag frequency. That is, if a tag t is visually representative, then its image tag clarity score $\tau(t)$ is expected to be significantly larger than $\tau(t')$ where t' is a dummy tag randomly assigned to the same number of images as of t (or $|I_{t'}| = |I_t|$).[3] In our experiments, we observed that $\tau(t')$ follows a normal distribution for all dummy tags having the same tag frequency $|I_{t'}|$. Hence we apply zero-mean normalization and the normalized image tag clarity score $\tau_z(t)$ is given in Eq. (10), where $\mu(t')$ and $\sigma(t')$ are the *expected tag clarity score* and its *standard deviation* derived from multiple dummy tags, respectively.

$$\tau_z(t) = \frac{\tau(t) - \mu(t')}{\sigma(t')}. \tag{10}$$

---

[3] Recall that both $\tau(t)$ and $\tau(t')$ are computed purely from visual content features of their tagged images.

Fig. 2 The expected tag
clarity scores and their
standard deviations derived
from 500 dummy tags with
respect to the tag frequency
on the *x*-axis. The four
example tags are also plotted
with their frequencies and
clarity scores

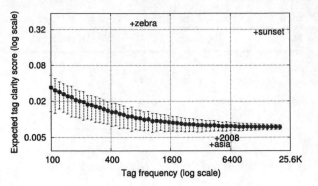

The normalized image tag clarity score is the number of standard deviations a tag is observed with respect to a randomly assigned dummy tag with the same tag frequency. Note that tag frequency is an important measure here as both $\mu(t')$ and $\sigma(t')$ are heavily affected by it. As discussed earlier, the larger is $|I_{t'}|$ the closer its language model to the collection model. This is illustrated by Fig. 2, which reports the expected tag clarity scores and their standard deviations derived from 500 dummy tags with respect to the tag frequencies on the *x*-axis. The four example tags are also plotted with their frequencies and clarity scores. Observe that although $\tau(Sunset) < \tau(Zebra)$, $\tau_z(Sunset) > \tau_z(Zebra)$ after the normalization process (Table 1).

3.3 Time Complexity

The proposed tag language model can be estimated in $O(N)$ time for a tag associated with N images. Note that the expected tag clarity scores and standard deviation need to be computed only once for all tags with tag frequency N in a given dataset. Moreover, the computation of expected tag clarity scores and standard deviation can be further reduced by binning the tag frequencies and computing the expected tag clarity scores and standard deviations for each frequency bin.

In our experiments, we are interested in the tags that have been used to tag at least 100 images. We set our first frequency bin to cover tag frequency from $b_0 = 100$ to $b_1 = 110$. Subsequently, we set $b_{n+1} = (1 + 10\%) \times b_n$ $(n \geq 0)$ until the last bin covers the tag with highest tag frequency in our dataset. For each bin starting with b_n, 500 dummy tags with tag frequency randomly generated within $[b_n, b_{n+1})$ are used to derive the expected tag clarity and standard deviation (shown in Fig. 2). A given tag clarity score is then normalized by $\mu(b_n)$ and $\sigma(b_n)$ where b_n is the bin $|I_t|$ belongs to. Observe that in this setting every tag is normalized using dummy tags generated with frequencies within 10% of its frequency.[4]

---

[4]Note that the way we bin the tag frequencies and the number of dummy tags used for estimation of the expected tag clarity scores and their standard deviations are different from that in [11]. This leads to differences in the normalized tag clarity scores reported in Sects. 4 and 5.

4 Performance Evaluation

Evaluation of the techniques for quantifying tag visual-representativeness is a challenging research issue for two reasons. Firstly, there is a lack of widely adopted metric for the performance evaluation. Secondly, there is a lack of benchmark data for the evaluation. In the following, we present a summary of the evaluations conducted in our earlier work [12] and then report the observations from the experimental results. The technical details of the evaluation can be found in [12].

We used the NUS-WIDE dataset[5] containing 269,648 images from Flickr [1]. The images are assigned with zero, one or more categories (or concepts) from a pre-defined list of 81 categories. The dataset provides six types of low-level features including both global features (e.g., color histogram, edge direction histogram, wavelet texture features and others) and local features (500-D bag of visual-words). The normalized image tag clarity score discussed in this chapter is also known as *SClarL* method in [12] and the method is compared against another six methods for quantifying image tag visual-representativeness using either global features or local features. In our evaluation, we formulate the task of quantifying tag visual-representativeness as a classification task to distinguish visual-representative tags (i.e., positive tags) from non-visual-representative tags (i.e., negative tags).

Two sets of labeled tags were used in the experiments. In the first set of labeled tags, the 81 categories (which also appear as tags) in the NUS-WIDE dataset were used as positive tags and another 78 frequently used tags in the dataset were identified as negative tags. These 78 tags include 17 tags related to time (e.g., 2004–2008, January–December) and 61 location tags related to continent and country names (e.g., Europe, Japan). In the second set of labeled tags, 1576 frequently used tags were manually labeled including 814 positive tags (for object, scene, activity, color, and picture type) and 762 negative tags (for location, self-reference, opinion, camera model, and time).

The experimental evaluation adopted three performance metrics, namely, Average Precision, Precision@N, and Coverage@N. Among the seven methods evaluated, image tag clarity performed very well, with very good precision and fairly good coverage. In particular, the average precisions for the first and second sets of labeled tags were 0.89 and 0.74, respectively. The detailed results are reported in [12].

5 Observations Related to Image Tag Clarity Scores

In the NUS-WIDE dataset, there are more than 420K distinct tags that appear at least once. The tag distribution is reported in Fig. 3. Similar to statistics related to many studies on user-generated content, the tag frequency distribution follows a power-law distribution. Among the 420K distinct tags, 5981 tags have been used

---

[5]http://lms.comp.nus.edu.sg/research/NUS-WIDE.htm Accessed June 2009.

Fig. 3 Tag frequency distribution

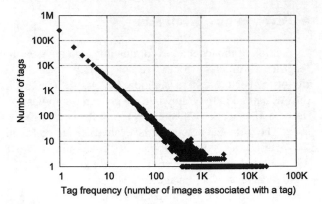

Fig. 4 Normalized image tag score distribution. Tags are binned by $floor(\tau_z(t))$ shown on the x-axis and the y-axis plots the corresponding number of tags in each bin

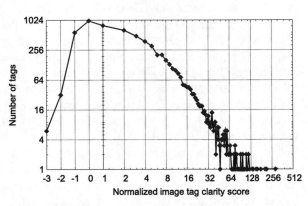

to annotate at least 100 images each.[6] We consider these tags as *popular* tags and report the observations made on their image tag clarity scores. In the sequel, all tag clarity scores refer to the normalized scores.

5.1 Image Tag Clarity Score Distribution

We first report the image tag clarity score distribution as well as the top-25 most and least visual-representative tags identified through our experiments.

The relationship between the number of tags (tags are binned by $floor(\tau_z(t))$) with their image tag clarity scores is shown in Fig. 4. Observe that among 5981 popular tags, 2950 tags (or about 49.3%) have tag clarity scores greater than 3. Recall that the normalized image tag clarity score is the number of standard deviations a tag is observed with respect to a randomly assigned dummy tag with the same tag frequency. If $\tau(t) \geq \mu(t') + 3\sigma(t')$, then the chance of t being randomly assigned

---

[6]The number reported here is slightly different from that reported in [1] probably due to different pre-processing. Nevertheless, the tag distribution remains similar.

Table 2 The top-25 most and least visual-representative tags with their image tag clarity scores $\tau_z(t)$ and frequency percentile $P_f(t)$. The tags that match the category labels in the NUS-WIDE dataset are shown in bold

	Tag	$\tau_z(t)$	$P_f(t)$	Tag	$\tau_z(t)$	$P_f(t)$
1	**sunset**	285.3	100	people	−2.8	100
2	fog	215.4	97	brown	−2.7	97
3	**sky**	206.4	100	asia	−2.5	98
4	silhouette	178.5	98	japan	−2.4	98
5	sunrise	160.3	98	france	−2.1	98
6	charts	153.4	78	washington	−2.1	97
7	**sun**	138.3	99	2008	−1.9	99
8	mist	137.4	95	china	−1.8	97
9	sea	134.2	100	photograph	−1.6	89
10	**clouds**	122.3	100	july	−1.6	86
11	lightning	118.4	74	picture	−1.5	92
12	**beach**	118.3	99	virginia	−1.5	87
13	landscape	114.7	100	religion	−1.3	95
14	minimalism	111.4	78	india	−1.3	97
15	dunes	110.0	83	ohio	−1.3	87
16	blue	109.9	100	august	−1.2	80
17	dawn	108.8	91	photographers	−1.2	86
18	horizon	102.0	92	royal	−1.2	73
19	moon	99.1	95	finepix	−1.2	65
20	**ocean**	98.7	99	pic	−1.2	59
21	**zebra**	97.9	82	smorgasbord	−1.2	61
22	storm	97.5	96	world	−1.2	95
23	sketches	95.7	82	may	−1.2	84
24	**lake**	94.4	99	global	−1.1	66
25	windmills	93.7	76	2005	−1.1	96

to the images (independent of their visual content) is less than 0.1%, and we consider t to be visually representative. Here, we use three standard deviations as the threshold as it is often used as threshold to determine outliers statistically for normal distributions [6]. Nevertheless, this threshold value is only used in this chapter for analysis and can be adjusted according to a specific application. For brevity, we refer to tags that are visually representative (e.g., $\tau_z(t) \geq 3$) as *visual tags* and others as *non-visual tags*. There are 2950 visual tags and 3031 non-visual tags, respectively.

The top-25 most and least visual-representative tags are listed in Table 2 together with their normalized tag clarity score $\tau_z(t)$ and frequency percentiles (denoted by $P_f(t)$). Observe that many of the top-25 most visual-representative tags describe common scenes (e.g., sunset, lightning, sea, and sky) or objects (e.g., zebra and moon). As these are commonly used words, most users could easily use them to describe images containing the scenes or objects. Consequently, it creates strong connection between the user-specified tags and the images demonstrating the

(a) Images for tag search: people (least visual-representative tag)

(b) Images for tag search: sunset (most visual-representative tag)

Fig. 5 Images returned by Flickr for search tags people and sunset

aforementioned scenes and objects, making these tags highly visual-representative. Further, the frequency percentile values associated with the tags suggest that a large user group indeed develops consensus implicitly to use a relatively small set of common tags to describe a large number of images. Specifically, among the top 25 most visually representative tags, 18 tags have frequency percentile above 90, indicating that these are extremely popular tags.

Observe that most of the least visual-representative tags are locations (e.g., asia, washington, japan, france, china), or temporal such as 2008, july, august, may, or high-level descriptions including pic, photograph, picture. All these tags do not convey much information related to the visual content of the images. For instance, images accompanied with the asia tag are very diverse and can range from the busy street scenes in Bangkok to images of Gobi desert in Mongolia. Such results show that the proposed image clarity score seems to be a good measure reflecting the semantic relationship of an assigned tag to the visual content of the image.

An interesting observation is that people is rated as a least visually representative tag. A tag search of people on Flickr showed that most of the returned images indeed contained people in their visual content (see Fig. 5(a)). However, the images demonstrated a great variety especially with respect to the background settings. Hence the proposed technique may wrongly identify the tags that are indeed related to some visual content as non-visual tags when the visual pattern is not clear from the feature representation. That is, such visual pattern may require a certain high-level recognition. This calls for further study on how to detect visual tags related to complicated visual patterns like people. On the other hand, images returned in response to the tag sunset indeed show similar visual scenes (see Fig. 5(b)).

5.2 Tag Usage Pattern

5.2.1 Tag Visual-Representativeness vs. Tag Frequency

It is often assumed that extremely popular tags, like stop-words in textual documents, contain little information in image tagging [18]. However, as demonstrated

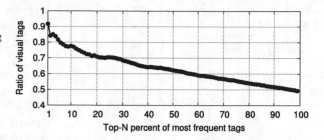

Fig. 6 Ratio of visual tags against the tag frequency at top N percent indicated along the x-axis

in our empirical study, many of the highly representative tags (e.g., the top-25 most representative tags) have frequency percentile above 90. One example is sky which is the third most popular tag in the dataset. It is also the third most visually representative tag and been used as a category label in the NUS-WIDE dataset. Using the notion of image tag clarity, we aim to have a deeper understanding on the relationship between tag clarity and its frequency.

Our study showed that the 2950 visual tags are used 2,225,239 times to annotate images in the dataset[7]; while the 3031 non-visual tags are used 997,014 times only. That is, the visual tags are 2.23 times more frequently used than the non-visual tags. In other words, users are more likely to annotate images using tags related to the visual content of the images.

To further study the relationship between tag visual-representativeness and tag frequency, we sorted 5981 tags of interests according to their tag frequency in descending order. Figure 6 plots the ratio of visual tags among the top $N\%$ most frequent tags ($1 \leq N \leq 100$). The figure clearly indicates that the highly frequently used tags are more likely to be visual tags. For instance, more than 90% of the 60-most frequently used tags (or 1% of the 5981 tags) are visual tags. This is consistent with that listed in Table 2, where many of the most visually representative tags have high frequency percentiles. The Pearson's correlation coefficient between tag frequency and tag clarity score is 0.35. That is, they are weakly correlated and more frequent tags are in general more likely to be visually representative. This is not surprising as tags are in general considered resource annotations and the resource in this setting is images. The aforementioned observation also supports tag-based approach for social image retrieval as most frequently used tags are indeed visual tags.

5.2.2 Visual Tags vs. Non-visual Tags

In this section, we study the distribution of visual and non-visual tags with respect to the number of tags associated with images as well as their positions. We first plot the tag distribution among images in the dataset in Fig. 7(a). In this plot, the x-axis is the number of tags per image and y-axis plots the number of images having that

---

[7]One image may be annotated by multiple visual or non-visual tags, respectively.

Fig. 7 Tag usage patterns between tag visual-representativeness, tag frequency and tag position

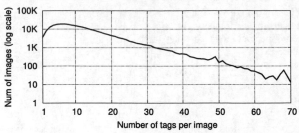

(a) The number of images against the number of tags per image.

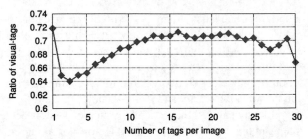

(b) Average ratio of visual tags among all images having the number of tags specified on x-axis.

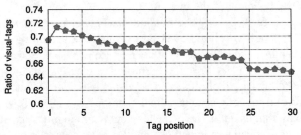

(c) Ratio of visual-tags at different tag positions.

number of tags. Among the 269K images in the dataset, nearly 74% of images are associated with three to 16 tags (from the domain of 5981 tags of interest). Fewer than 5% of images have more than 30 tags each. Hence, we only focus on those images with no more than 30 tags for the study of tag position distribution.

Figure 7(b) plots the average ratio of visual tags among each image having K tags ($1 \leq K \leq 30$). The ratio of visual tags gradually increases from 0.64 to 0.72 with the increase of the number of tags from three to 16. Subsequently, the ratio remains relatively stable for images having 17 to 25 tags each. Figure 7(b) shows that the chance of an image being annotated by visual tags increases with the number of tags received. As many tags are received from the contacts of the image uploader in Flickr, these users may not know much about the image other than its visual content. The tags contributed by these users are more likely to be visual tags. Overall, the results also show that in general more visual tags are associated with images than non-visual tags with the ratio of visual tags well above 0.6. This is consistent with

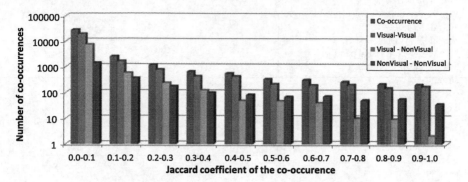

Fig. 8 Tag co-occurrence distribution with respect to the co-occurrence strength computed using Jaccard coefficient. The legend "co-occurrence" refers to the distribution of all co-occurrence pairs; "Visual–Visual" means that both tags in a co-occurrence pair are visual tags; and "Visual–NonVisual" means only one tag in the co-occurrence pair is visual tag and the other one is non-visual tag regardless of the order

our earlier observation where the visual tags are used much more frequently than non-visual tags.

Figure 7(c) plots the ratio of visual tags among the tags annotated at position K, varying K from 1 to 30. We assume that the dataset preserves the tag order. Observe that the ratio of visual tags gradually declines with the increase in K. That is, users typically use visual tags first to describe the images rather than non-visual tags.

5.3 Tag Co-occurrence Pattern

In this section, we look at the co-occurrence patterns among tags with respect to their visual-representativeness. Among the 5981 tags of interests, we have in total 33,884 pairs of tags which co-occur at least 100 times. In this work, we use Jaccard coefficient to measure the strength of the co-occurrence between a pair of tag t_a and t_b. The Jaccard coefficient is defined in Eq. (11) where I_{t_a} denotes the set of images tagged by t_a. Note that as the Jaccard coefficient is bidirectional, we do not distinguish the order of tags in a co-occurrence pair.

$$Jaccard(t_a, t_b) = \frac{|I_{t_a} \cap I_{t_b}|}{|I_{t_a} \cup I_{t_b}|}. \tag{11}$$

Figure 8 plots the distribution of co-occurrence pairs against the co-occurrence strength. We also plot the distributions of co-occurrence of tag pairs distinguished by their visual-representativeness. For instance, the legend "Visual–Visual" means that both tags in a co-occurrence pair are visual tags, whereas "Visual–NonVisual" means only one tag in the co-occurrence pair is a visual tag and the other is non-visual tag regardless of the order. Observe that most co-occurrence pairs are formed by two visual tags especially when the co-occurrence strength is strong.

Fig. 9 Percentages of
Visual–Visual,
Visual–NonVisual, and
NonVisual–NonVisual pairs
against the co-occurrence
strength

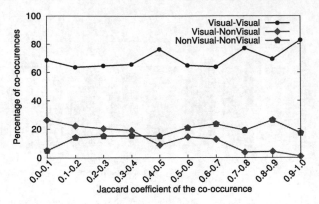

Fig. 10 Percentage of visual
tags against the tag frequency

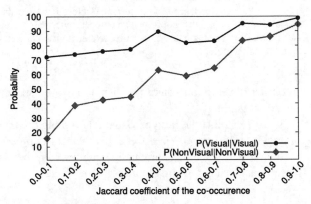

Figure 9 reports the percentages of various co-occurrence pairs (e.g., Visual–Visual, Visual–NonVisual, and NonVisual–NonVisual) against the co-occurrence strength. Observe that about 70% of the co-occurrence are from visual tag pairs and the remaining two types of co-occurrences are only about 30%. More interestingly, as the co-occurrence strength increases, the percentage of NonVisual–NonVisual pairs increases but the percentage of Visual–NonVisual pairs decreases. This suggests that the strong co-occurrence relationships are often formed by tags in the same category (e.g., visual or non-visual). For instance, a location or time tag such as `Japan` and `2008` may often co-occur with another location and time tag like `Asia` or `January`, respectively. On the other hand, visual tags such as `sunset`, `water`, and `beach` often co-occur together to describe the scene in an image.

To further support the above claim, we plot the probability of co-occurrence between the visual and non-visual tags as depicted in Fig. 10. In this figure, $P(Visual|Visual)$ denotes the probability of observing the Visual–Visual co-occurring pairs among all co-occurring pairs having at least one visual tag in a pair. Similarly, $P(NonVisual|NonVisual)$ is the probability of observing NonVisual–NonVisual co-occurring pairs among pairs with at least one non-visual tag. The plot shows that both $P(Visual|Visual)$ and $P(NonVisual|NonVisual)$ increase with the increase of co-occurrence strength. In particular, both probabilities reach 80% and above when the Jaccard coefficient is above 0.7.

Fig. 11 (Color online) Tag co-occurrence graphs of the four tags containing the top-10 most co-occurring tags. *Green colored nodes* are tags with low visual-representativeness and *purple colored nodes* are tags with high visual-representativeness

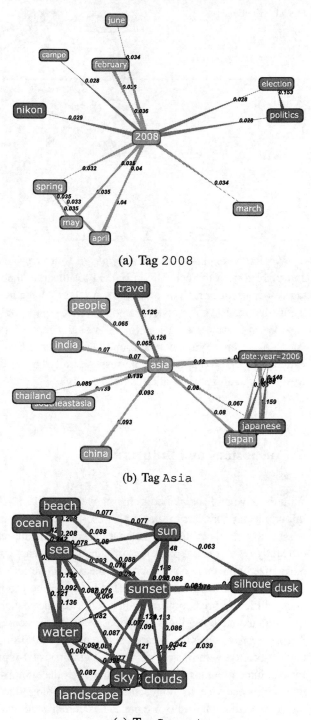

(a) Tag 2008

(b) Tag Asia

(c) Tag Sunset

Fig. 11 (Continued)

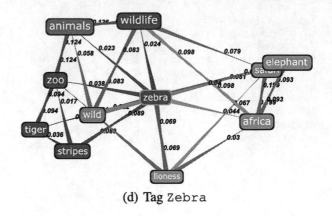

(d) Tag Zebra

We plot the *tag co-occurrence graphs* of four tags (i.e., Asia, 2008, sunset, and zebra used in Sect. 3.1) in Fig. 11 to illustrate the above phenomenon. Each tag co-occurrence graph involves the top-10 tags that co-occur most frequently with the given tag. The color code of a node denotes the visual-representativeness of the tags, green (purple) being less (more) visually representative. More details on the tag co-occurrence graph can be found in [14]. These four tag co-occurrence graphs validate our claim that non-visual (resp. visual) tags are likely to co-occur strongly with non-visual (resp.visual) tags.

6 Conclusions and Future Work

With the advent of social media sharing web sites like Flickr, tagging has become an important way for users to succinctly describe content of images. However, the huge volume of tags contributed by ordinary users can be imprecise and hence it may significantly restrict the applications of tags. In this chapter, we propose the notion of normalized image tag clarity score to measure the effectiveness of a tag in describing the visual content of its annotated images. The proposed approach bridge the query difficulty prediction in ad-hoc retrieval and visual-representativeness quantification in image tagging. Our proposed tag clarity score can be effectively used to further improve several tag-based applications. For example, it can be used to rank tags associated with images according to their visual-representativeness as well as for recommending tags. Our experimental results demonstrate that most of popular tags are indeed visually representative in describing their annotated images. Based on the experimental results, we present a detailed study on the relationships between tag visual-representativeness and tag frequency, tag position, and tag co-occurrence.

References

1. Chua, T.-S., Tang, J., Hong, R., Li, H., Luo, Z., Zheng, Y.-T.: Nus-wide: A real-world web image database from National University of Singapore. In: Proc. of ACM CIVR, Santorini, Greece, July 2009
2. Cronen-Townsend, S., Zhou, Y., Croft, W.B.: Predicting query performance. In: Proc. of SIGIR, Tampere, Finland, pp. 299–306 (2002)
3. Elsas, J.L., Arguello, J., Callan, J., Carbonell, J.G.: Retrieval and feedback models for blog feed search. In: Proc. of SIGIR, Singapore, pp. 347–354 (2008)
4. Golder, S.A., Huberman, B.A.: Usage patterns of collaborative tagging systems. J. Inf. Sci. **32**(2), 198–208 (2006)
5. Hauff, C., Murdock, V., Baeza-Yates, R.: Improved query difficulty prediction for the web. In: Proc. of CIKM, Napa Valley, CA, pp. 439–448 (2008)
6. Knorr, E.M., Ng, R.T.: Algorithms for mining distance-based outliers in large datasets. In: Proc. of VLDB, pp. 392–403. Morgan Kaufmann, San Mateo (1998)
7. Li, X., Snoek, C.G.M., Worring, M.: Learning tag relevance by neighbor voting for social image retrieval. In: Proc. of MIR, pp. 180–187 (2008)
8. Liu, D., Hua, X.-S., Yang, L., Wang, M., Zhang, H.-J.: Tag ranking. In: Proc. WWW, Madrid, Spain, pp. 351–360 (2009)
9. Lowe, D.G.: Distinctive image features from scale-invariant keypoints. Int. J. Comput. Vis. **60**(2), 91–110 (2004)
10. Lu, Y., Zhang, L., Tian, Q., Ma, W.-Y.: What are the high-level concepts with small semantic gaps. In: Proc. of CVPR, Alaska, USA (2008)
11. Sun, A., Bhowmick, S.S.: Image tag clarity: In search of visual-representative tags for social images. In: Proc. of ACM SIGMM Workshop on Social Media (WSM) with ACM Multimedia, Beijing, China, Oct 2009
12. Sun, A., Bhowmick, S.S.: Quantifying tag representativeness of visual content of social images. In: Proc. of ACM Multimedia (MM), Firenze, Italy, Oct 2010
13. Sun, A., Datta, A.: On stability, clarity, and co-occurrence of self-tagging. In: Proc. of ACM WSDM (Late Breaking-Results) (2009)
14. Sun, A., Bhowmick, S.S., Liu, Y.: iavatar: An interactive tool for finding and visualizing visual-representative tags in image search. In: Proceedings of the VLDB Endowment (PVLDB) 3(2), Sep 2010
15. Teevan, J., Dumais, S.T., Liebling, D.J.: To personalize or not to personalize: modeling queries with variation in user intent. In: Proc. of SIGIR, Singapore, pp. 163–170 (2008)
16. Weinberger, K., Slaney, M., van Zwol, R.: Resolving tag ambiguity. In: Proc. of ACM Multimedia (MM), Vancouver, Canada (2008)
17. Wu, L., Hua, X.-S., Yu, N., Ma, W.-Y., Li, S.: Flickr distance. In: Proc. of ACM Multimedia (MM), Vancouver, Canada, pp. 31–40 (2008)
18. Wu, L., Yang, L., Yu, N., Hua, X.-S.: Learning to tag. In: Proc. WWW, Madrid, Spain, pp. 361–370 (2009)
19. Yom-Tov, E., Fine, S., Carmel, D., Darlow, A.: Learning to estimate query difficulty: including applications to missing content detection and distributed information retrieval. In: Proc. of SIGIR, Salvador, Brazil, pp. 512–519 (2005)
20. Zhou, Y., Croft, W.B.: Query performance prediction in web search environments. In: Proc. of SIGIR, Amsterdam, pp. 543–550 (2007)

Tag-Based Social Image Search: Toward Relevant and Diverse Results

Kuiyuan Yang, Meng Wang, Xian-Sheng Hua, and Hong-Jiang Zhang

Abstract Recent years have witnessed a great success of social media websites. Tag-based image search is an important approach to access the image content of interest on these websites. However, the existing ranking methods for tag-based image search frequently return results that are irrelevant or lack of diversity. This chapter presents a diverse relevance ranking scheme which simultaneously takes relevance and diversity into account by exploring the content of images and their associated tags. First, it estimates the relevance scores of images with respect to the query term based on both visual information of images and semantic information of associated tags. Then semantic similarities of social images are estimated based on their tags. Based on the relevance scores and the similarities, the ranking list is generated by a greedy ordering algorithm which optimizes Average Diverse Precision (ADP), a novel measure that is extended from the conventional Average Precision (AP). Comprehensive experiments and user studies demonstrate the effectiveness of the approach.

1 Introduction

There is an explosion of social media content available online, such as Flickr, Youtube and Zooomr. Such media repositories promote users to collaboratively cre-

K. Yang (✉)
Department of Automation, The University of Science and Technology of China, Hefei, Anhui 230027, China
e-mail: yky@ustc.edu

M. Wang
AKiiRA Media Systems Inc, Palo Alto, CA 94301, USA
e-mail: eric.mengwang@gmail.com

X.-S. Hua
Media Computing Group, Microsoft Research Asia, Beijing 100080, China
e-mail: xshua@microsoft.com

H.-J. Zhang
Microsoft Advanced Technology Center, Beijing 100080, China
e-mail: hjzhang@microsoft.com

S.C.H. Hoi et al. (eds.), *Social Media Modeling and Computing*,
DOI 10.1007/978-0-85729-436-4_2, © Springer-Verlag London Limited 2011

Fig. 1 An example of a social image with its associated tags

ate, evaluate and distribute media information. They also allow users to annotate their uploaded media data with descriptive keywords called tags. As an example, Fig. 1 illustrates a social image and its associated user-provided tags. These valuable metadata can greatly facilitate the organization and search of the social media. By indexing the images with associated tags, images can be easily retrieved for a given query. However, since user-provided tags are usually noisy and incomplete, simply applying text-based retrieval approach may lead to unsatisfactory results. Therefore, a ranking approach that is able to explore both the tags and images' content is desired to provide users better social image search results.

Currently, Flickr provides two ranking options for tag-based image search. One is "most recent", which orders images based on their uploading time, and the other is "most interesting", which ranks the images by "interestingness", a measure that integrates the information of click-through, comments, etc. In the following discussion, we name these two methods time-based ranking and interestingness-based ranking, respectively. They both rank images according to measures (interestingness or time) that are not related to relevance and it results in many irrelevant images in the top search results. As an example, Fig. 2 illustrates the top results of query "waterfall" with the two ranking options, in which we can see that many images are irrelevant to the query, such as those marked with red boxes. In addition to relevance, lack of diversity is also a problem. Many images from social media websites are actually close to each other. For example, several users get used to upload continuously captured images in batch, and many of them are visually and semantically close. When these images appear simultaneously as top results, users will get only limited information. From Fig. 2 we can also observe this fact, the images marked with blue or green boxes are very close to at least one of the other images.

Therefore, a ranking scheme that can generate relevant and diverse results is highly desired. This problem is closely related to a key scientific challenge that is recently released by Yahoo research: *"how do we combine both content-based retrieval with tags to do something better than either approach alone for multimedia retrieval"* [33].

The importance of relevance is clear. In fact, this is usually regarded as the bedrock of information retrieval: *if an IR system's response to each query is a ranking of documents in order of decreasing probability of relevance, the overall effectiveness of the system to its user will be maximized* [22]. The time-based and interestingness-based ranking options are of course useful. For example, users can easily browse the images that are recently uploaded via the time-based ranking. But

(a) Ranking by uploading time   (b) Ranking by interestingness

Fig. 2 (Color online) The top 20 search results of the query "waterfall" with the two ranking options. (**a**) Time-based ranking. (**b**) Interestingness-based ranking. We can see that many images are irrelevant to the query (marked with *red* border) or close to others (marked with *blue* or *green* border)

when users perform search with the intention of finding specific images, relevance will be more important than time and interestingness.

The necessity of diversity may seem less intuitive than relevance, but its importance has also been long acknowledged in information retrieval [9, 28]. One explanation is that the relevance of a document (can be a web page, image or video) with respect to the query should depend on not only the document itself but also its difference with the documents appearing before it. Now we observe this issue from another perspective. In many cases users cannot accurately and exhaustively describe their requests, and thus keeping diversity of the search results will provide users more chances to find the desired content quickly. For example, we can consider the following cases in image search:

(1) The users only provide an ambiguous query [1]. For example, the query "apple" may refer to different topics, such as fruit, computer and mobile. Thus, it is better to provide diverse results to cover multiple topics.
(2) The users cannot fully describe their requests by simple words. For example, although a user only provides a simple query "car", he/she may actually want to

find a picture of a red car on grass. In this case, the hit probability of a diverse image set should be greater than a set of images that are quite close.

Therefore, diversity of results is also important for users [25, 28]. This fact can also be explained in the information theoretic point of view. If the returned images are all identical for a query, the information gained by the user is actually equivalent to only returning one image.

In this chapter, we will first review recent some research efforts related to the relevance and diversity problems of image search, and then introduce the Diverse Relevance Ranking (DRR) scheme. The organization of the rest of this chapter is as follows. In Sect. 2, we provide a review on the related work. In Sect. 3, we present DRR as a general ranking algorithm. In Sect. 4, we detail the relevance and semantic similarity estimation of social images. Empirical results is presented in Sect. 5. Finally, we conclude the chapter in Sect. 6.

2 Related Work Review

2.1 Social Image Search

The last decade has witnessed a great advance of image search technology [10, 17, 23, 34]. Different from general web images, social images are usually associated with a set of user-provided descriptors called tags, and thus tag-based image search can be easily accomplished by using these descriptors as index terms. Since user-provided tags are usually very noisy [14, 18] and it frequently results in unsatisfactory search results. In comparison with the extensive studies on how to help users better perform tagging or mining tags for other applications, the literature regarding tag-based image search is still very sparse. Most of such efforts focus on how to refine the image's tags or measure their relevance levels. Li et al. proposed a tag relevance learning method which is able to assign each tag a relevance score, and they have shown its application in tag-based image search [18]. Kennedy et al. [15] proposed a method to establish reliable tags by investigating highly similar images that are annotated by different photographers. Liu et al. [19] proposed an optimization scheme for tag refinement based on the visual and semantic connection between images. Sun and Bhowmick [27] proposed a method to measure the tag clarity score based on the query language model and the collection language model. These methods can help tag-based image search by improving the tags' quality, but they cannot deal with the aforementioned lack-of-diversity problem.

2.2 Diversifying Image Search Result

It has been long acknowledged that diversity plays an important role in information retrieval. In 1964, Goffman recognized that the relevance of a document must be determined with respect to the documents appearing before it [9]. Carbonell et al.

propose a ranking method named Maximal Marginal Relevance, which attempts to maximize relevance while minimizing similarity to higher ranked documents [4]. Zhai et al. propose a subtopic search method, which aims to return results that cover more subtopics [35, 36]. Santos et al. propose an approach to enhance diversity by explicitly modeling the query aspects and then actively seeking to maximize the coverage of the selected documents with respect to these aspects [24].

The diversity problem is actually more challenging in an image search, as it involves not only the semantic ambiguity of queries but also the visual similarity of search results [28]. Currently there are two typical approaches to enhancing the diversity in image search: search results clustering and duplicates removing. When performing search results clustering, a representative image can be selected from each cluster. Then we can either only present these representatives or put other images behind them in the ranking list. In [3], Cai et al. propose a method to cluster web image search results into different semantic clusters to facilitate users' browsing. Jing et al. [13] have proposed an IGroup system for clustering image search results. Song et al. have studied the topic coverage of image search diversification method [25]. Recently, Leuken et al. have investigated different clustering methods for visual diversification of image search results [28]. Different from clustering, the duplicates removing approach directly eliminates the duplicates or near-duplicates detected in image search results. Many different duplicate detection methods have been proposed, such as pair-wise image comparison [11], approximate search [29], and fingerprint-based algorithms [26]. Recent progress of image duplicate detection can be found in [37, 38].

Although encouraging results have been demonstrated, the clustering and duplicates removing techniques have their limitations due to the involved heuristics. For clustering, how to establish the number of clusters is a problem. If too many clusters are generated, then the diversity of search results cannot be guaranteed, and contrarily if the clusters are too few, then the search relevance may degrade. In addition, how to take images' relevance levels into the clustering process is also a problem. For duplicates removing, if we set a low threshold for near-duplicate detection, then the diversity of search results cannot be guaranteed, and contrarily if we set a high threshold for near-duplicate detection, many informative images will be removed.

2.3 Performance Evaluation Metric

To quantitatively evaluate different ranking schemes, many performance evaluation metrics are proposed in literature. The classical IR metrics such as AP [2] and NDCG [12] are widely used for measuring search quality. However, they only care about relevance but do not take diversity into account. Several metrics have been proposed for evaluating the diversity of search results, including α-NDCG [7], k-call metric [5] and Intent-Aware measures (NDCG-IA, MAP-IA, MRR-IA) [1]. In this chapter, we present a new performance metric which takes both relevance and diversity into account, and thus the images for a query can be ordered by directly optimizing the performance metric.

3 Diverse Relevance Ranking

We introduce the Diverse Relevance Ranking (DRR) approach in this section. Here we present it as a general ranking algorithm and leave the two flexible components, i.e., relevance score and similarity estimation of images, to the next section. We first prove that ranking by relevance scores can be viewed as a process of optimizing the mathematical expectation of the conventional Average Precision (AP) measure. Then we analyze the limitation of AP and generalize it to an Average Diverse Precision (ADP) measure to integrate diversity. The DRR algorithm is then derived by greedily optimizing the mathematical expectation of ADP measurement.

3.1 Average Precision

AP is a widely-applied performance evaluation measure in information retrieval. Given a collection of images $\mathscr{D} = \{x_1, x_2, \ldots, x_n\}$, we denote the binary relevance label of x_i with respect to the given query as $y(x_i)$, i.e., $y(x_i) = 1$ if x_i is relevant and otherwise $y(x_i) = 0$. Denote by τ an ordering of the images, and let $\tau(i)$ be the image at the position of rank i (a lower number indicates image with a higher rank). Let R be the number of true relevant images in the set $\mathscr{D}$. Then the non-interpolated AP is defined as

$$AP(\tau, \mathscr{D}) = \frac{1}{R} \sum_{j=1}^{n} y(\tau(j)) \frac{\sum_{k=1}^{j} y(\tau(k))}{j}. \tag{1}$$

Thereby, ranking images with their relevance scores in decreasing order is the most intuitive approach. Now we prove that the ranking list generated in this way actually maximizes the mathematical expectation of AP measurement.

Denote by $r(x_i)$ the relevance score of x_i (how to estimate it will be introduced in the next section), and it is reasonable for us to assume that $r(x_i) = P(y(x_i) = 1)$, i.e., we regard the relevance score $r(x_i)$ as the probability that x_i is relevant. Since R can be regarded as a constant, we do not take it into account in the expectation estimation. We also assume that the relevance of an image is independent with other images, and hence the expected value of $AP(\tau, \mathscr{D})$ can be computed as follows

$$E\{AP(\tau, \mathscr{D})\} = \frac{1}{R} \sum_{j=1}^{n} \sum_{k=1}^{j} \frac{E\{y(\tau(k))y(\tau(j))\}}{j}$$

$$= \frac{1}{R} \sum_{j=1}^{n} \frac{1}{j} \left(r(\tau(j)) + \sum_{k=1}^{j-1} r(\tau(k))r(\tau(j)) \right). \tag{2}$$

Then we have the following theorem:

Theorem 1 *Ranking the images in $\mathscr{D}$ with relevance scores $r(x_i)$ in non-increasing order maximizes $E\{AP(\tau, \mathscr{D})\}$.*

Proof Denote by τ^* the ranking of images in $\mathscr{D}$ with relevance scores in non-increasing order, i.e., $r(\tau^*(i)) \geq r(\tau^*(i+1))$. Then we only need to prove $E\{AP(\tau^*, \mathscr{D})\} \geq E\{AP(\tau, \mathscr{D})\}$ for every possible τ.

Without loss of generality, we consider an ordering τ' that has exchange the documents at the positions of rank i and $i+1$ in τ^*, i.e., $\tau'(i) = \tau^*(i+1)$ and $\tau'(i+1) = \tau^*(i)$. Actually it is not difficult to find that any change on the τ^* can be decomposed into a series of such adjacent exchanges. So, our task is simplified to prove $E\{AP(\tau^*, \mathscr{D})\} \geq E\{AP(\tau', \mathscr{D})\}$.

For simplicity, we denote $r_i = r(\tau^*(i))$ and $r'_i = r(\tau'(i))$. Since $r'_i = r_{i+1}, r'_{i+1} = r_i$, and $r'_k = r_k$ when $k \neq i$ and $i+1$, we have

$$
\Delta = E\{AP(\tau^*, \mathscr{D})\} - E\{AP(\tau', \mathscr{D})\}
$$

$$
= \frac{1}{R}\left(\sum_{1 \leq j \leq n, j \neq i, j \neq i+1} \frac{r_j + \sum_{k=1}^{j-1} r_k r_j}{j} + \frac{r_i + \sum_{k=1}^{i-1} r_k r_i}{i} \right.
$$

$$
\left. + \frac{r_{i+1} + \sum_{k=1}^{i} r_k r_{i+1}}{i+1} \right)
$$

$$
- \frac{1}{R}\left(\sum_{1 \leq j \leq n, j \neq i, j \neq i+1} \frac{r'_j + \sum_{k=1}^{j-1} r'_k r'_j}{j} + \frac{r'_i + \sum_{k=1}^{i-1} r'_k r'_i}{i} \right.
$$

$$
\left. + \frac{r'_{i+1} + \sum_{k=1}^{i} r'_k r'_{i+1}}{i+1} \right)
$$

$$
= \frac{r_i - r_{i+1} + \sum_{k=1}^{i-1} r_k(r_i - r_{i+1})}{i} - \frac{r_i - r_{i+1} + \sum_{k=1}^{i-1} r_k(r_i - r_{i+1})}{i+1}
$$

$$
= \left(1 + \sum_{k=1}^{i-1} r_k \right)(r_i - r_{i+1})\left(\frac{1}{i} - \frac{1}{i+1} \right). \tag{3}
$$

Since $r_i \geq r_{i+1}$, we have $\Delta \geq 0$, i.e., $E\{AP(\tau^*, \mathscr{D})\} \geq E\{AP(\tau', \mathscr{D})\}$, which completes the proof. $\square$

This demonstrates that the AP performance evaluation measure encourages prioritizing images with high relevance. However, the measure may not be consistent with users' experience due to the neglect of diversity. Figure 3 illustrates an example to demonstrate this fact. In Fig. 3(a), all images are relevant and several images in (b) are irrelevant. Therefore, most probably illustrating images in (a) on the top of the ranking list will introduce higher AP measurement than (b), but clearly it provides little information for users because the images are just duplicates. Therefore, the conventional AP measure can be improved to be more consistent with user experience by integrating diversity.

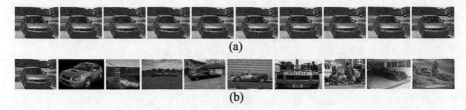

(a)

(b)

Fig. 3 An extreme example to illustrate the limitation of the conventional AP measure that only considers relevance. In (**a**), all the top 10 results are highly relevant to "car" and in (**b**) several images are irrelevant. Therefore, illustrating the images in (**a**) on top in the ranking list will most probably introduce higher AP measurement than (**b**), but clearly the images in (**b**) are more informative because (**a**) only illustrates duplicates

3.2 Average Diverse Precision

Here we generalize the existing AP measure to Average Diverse Precision (ADP) to take diversity into account, which is defined as

$$ADP(\tau, \mathscr{D}) \triangleq \frac{1}{R} \sum_{j=1}^{n} y(\tau(j)) Div(\tau(j)) \left(\frac{\sum_{k=1}^{j} y(\tau(k)) Div(\tau(k))}{j} \right), \quad (4)$$

where $Div(\tau(k))$ indicates the diversity score of $\tau(k)$. We define $Div(\tau(k))$ as its minimal difference with the images appearing before it, i.e.,

$$Div(\tau(k)) = \min_{1 \le t < k} \left(1 - s(\tau(t), \tau(k)) \right), \quad (5)$$

where $s(\cdot, \cdot)$ is a similarity measure between two images. Comparing the definition of AP and ADP (see Eq. (1) and Eq. (4)), we can see that the only difference is that we have changed $y(\tau(k))$ to $y(\tau(k)) Div(\tau(k))$. For an image in the ranking list, its contribution to the ADP measure is not only determined by its relevance with respect to the query but also its difference with the images appearing before it. If an image is identical to one of the images that have previously appeared, it will add no contribution to the ADP measurement. Thus the ADP measure takes both relevance and diversity into account. Denote by τ^* the optimal ranking list under the ADP performance evaluation measure, i.e., the list that achieves the highest ADP measurement, we can prove that $y(\tau(i)) Div(\tau(i)) \ge y(\tau(j)) Div(\tau(j))$ for any $i \le j$. This indicates that the top images will tend to be more relevant and diverse. Here we omit its proof since it is analogous to Theorem 1.

3.3 Diverse Relevance Ranking

The DRR algorithm is actually a greedy approach to optimizing the expected value of the ADP measurement. Analogous to AP, we can estimate the expected value of ADP as

$$E\{ADP(\tau, \mathscr{D})\}$$

$$= \frac{1}{R}\sum_{j=1}^{n}\sum_{k=1}^{j}\frac{E\{y(\tau(k))y(\tau(j))Div(\tau(k))Div(\tau(j))\}}{j}$$

$$= \frac{1}{R}\sum_{j=1}^{n}r\big(\tau(j)\big)Div\big(\tau(j)\big)\left(\frac{Div(\tau(j)) + \sum_{k=1}^{j-1}r(\tau(k))Div(\tau(k))}{j}\right). \quad (6)$$

The direct optimization of $E\{ADP(\tau, \mathscr{D})\}$ is a permutation problem and the solution space scales is $O(n!)$. Thus here we propose a greedy method to solve it. Considering the top $i - 1$ documents have been established, based on Eq. (6) we can derive that the ith image should be decided as follows

$$\tau(i) = \arg\max_{x \in \mathscr{D} - \mathscr{S}_i}\frac{r(x)}{i}Div(x)\big(C + Div(x)\big), \quad (7)$$

where

$$\mathscr{S}_i = \big\{\tau(1), \tau(2), \ldots, \tau(i-1)\big\}, \quad (8)$$

$$C = \sum_{k=1}^{i-1}r\big(\tau(k)\big)Div\big(\tau(k)\big). \quad (9)$$

Figure 4 illustrates implementation process of the DRR algorithm. Note that C can be viewed as constant in Eq. (7). So we can clearly see that the selection of the ith image will be determined by two factors: the relevance of the image and its difference with the previously selected images.

4 Relevance and Similarity of Social Images

In this section, we introduce the estimation of relevance scores and similarities of social images, which are the two necessary components of the DRR algorithm (see Fig. 4). The following notations will be used. Given a query tag t_q, denote by $\mathscr{D} = \{x_1, x_2, \ldots, x_n\}$ the collection of images that are associated with the tag. For image x_i, denote by $\mathscr{T}_i = \{t_1^i, t_2^i, \ldots, t_{|\mathscr{T}_i|}^i\}$ the set of its associated tags. The relevance scores of all images in $\mathscr{D}$ are represented in a vector $\mathbf{r} = [r(x_1), r(x_2), \ldots, r(x_n)]^T$, whose element $r(x_i) > 0$ denotes the relevance score of image x_i with respect to query tag t_q. Denote by $\mathbf{W}$ a similarity matrix whose element W_{ij} indicates the visual similarity between images x_i and x_j.

4.1 Relevance Estimation

Our relevance estimation approach is accomplished by leveraging both the visual information of images and the semantic information of tags. Our first assumption is

Input:
$\mathcal{D} = \{x_1, x_2, \ldots, x_n\}$;   /*image collection*/
$\mathcal{S} = \phi$;   /*selected set*/
$r(x_i), 1 \leq i \leq n$;   /* relevance scores*/
$s(x_i, x_j)$;   /*the semantic similarity between two images*/
$C = 0$

Output:
τ /*an order of the images*/

Begin:
$\tau(1) = \arg\max_{x \in \mathcal{D}} r(x)$;
$\mathcal{S} = \mathcal{S} \cup \tau(1)$;
for $i = 2, 3, \ldots, n$
    /*decide the ith sample*/
    $\tau(i) = \arg\max_{x \in \mathcal{D} - \mathcal{S}} \frac{r(x)}{i} Div(x)(C + Div(x))$
    $\mathcal{S} = \mathcal{S} \cup \tau(i)$;
    $C = C + r(\tau(i))Div(\tau(i))$;
    for each $x \in \mathcal{D} - \mathcal{S}$ /*update $Div(x)$*/
        $Div(x) = \min\{Div(x), 1 - s(x, \tau(i))\}$
    end
end

Fig. 4 Pseudo-code of the proposed DRR algorithm

that the relevance of an image should depend on the "closeness" of its tags to the query tag. Thus we first have to define the similarity of tags. Different from images, which can be represented as sets of low-level features, tags are textual words and their similarity exists only in semantics. Recently, there are several works aim to address this issue [6, 32]. Here we adopt an approach that is analogous to Google distance [6], in which the similarity between tag t_i and t_j is defined as

$$sim(t_i, t_j) = \exp\left(-\frac{\max(\log c(t_i), \log c(t_j)) - \log c(t_i, t_j)}{\log M - \min(\log c(t_i), \log c(t_j))}\right), \qquad (10)$$

where $c(t_i)$ and $c(t_j)$ are the numbers of images associated with t_i and t_j on Flickr, respectively, $c(t_i, t_j)$ is the number of images associated with both t_i and t_j simultaneously, and M is the total number of images on Flickr. Therefore, the similarity of the query tag t_q and the tag set of image x_i can be computed as

$$sim(t_q, \mathcal{T}_i) = \frac{1}{|\mathcal{T}_i|} \sum_{t \in \mathcal{T}_i} sim(t_q, t). \qquad (11)$$

Figure 5 illustrates two examples to demonstrate the rationality of this approach. Figure 5(a) and (b) show two images associated with query tags "dolphin" and "eagle", respectively. Intuitively, we can see that the images on the left are much more relevant than the images on the right. Then we can see that actually this fact can

Fig. 5 (a) Two images tagged with "dolphin". (b) Two images tagged with "eagle". We can see that the images on the left are more relevant with respect to the query tags, and their associated tags are also closer to the query tags

ocean water mammal
dolphin bottlenose flying

sky cloud hotel orlando
florida dolphin

(a)

bird nature eagle
wildlife raptor

park eagle farm
idaho prison

(b)

be inferred from the associated tag sets of the images. The tags of the left images are obviously closer to the query tags (for example, "dolphin" is strongly correlated with "ocean" and "water", and this correlation can be reflected on their Google distance [6]).

Our second assumption is that the relevance scores of visually similar images should be close. The visual similarity between two images can be directly computed based on Gaussian kernel function with a radius parameter σ, i.e.,

$$W_{ij} = \exp\left(-\frac{\|x_i - x_j\|^2}{\sigma^2}\right). \tag{12}$$

But it is worth mentioning that we can also adopt other similarity measures here, such as those proposed in [21, 30]. Note that this assumption may not hold for several images, but it is still reasonable in most cases. Based on the two assumptions, we formulate a regularization framework as follows

$$Q(\mathbf{r}) = \sum_{i,j=1}^{n} W_{ij} \left(\frac{r(x_i)}{\sqrt{D_{ii}}} - \frac{r(x_j)}{\sqrt{D_{jj}}}\right)^2 + \lambda \sum_{i=1}^{n} \left(r(x_i) - sim(t_q, \mathcal{T}_i)\right)^2, \tag{13}$$

$$\mathbf{r}^* = \arg\min Q(\mathbf{r}),$$

where $r(x_i)$ is the relevance score of x_i, and $D_{ii} = \sum_{j=1}^{n} W_{ij}$. We can see that the above regularization scheme contains two terms. The first term is a smoothness term which means that the relevance scores between two visually similar images should be close (i.e., $r(x_i)$ and $r(x_j)$ should be close if W_{ij} is large), and the second term is a consistency term which means that the relevance score should be consistent with the relevance of the tag set (i.e., $r(x_i)$ should be great if $sim(t_q, \mathcal{T}_i)$ is great. The above equation can be written in matrix form as

$$Q(\mathbf{r}) = \mathbf{r}^T \left(\mathbf{I} - \mathbf{D}^{-1/2}\mathbf{W}\mathbf{D}^{-1/2}\right)\mathbf{r} + \lambda \|\mathbf{r} - \mathbf{v}\|^2, \tag{14}$$

where $\mathbf{D} = \mathrm{Diag}(D_{11}, D_{22}, \ldots, D_{nn})$ and $\mathbf{v} = [sim(t_q, \mathcal{T}_1), sim(t_q, \mathcal{T}_2), \ldots, sim(t_q, \mathcal{T}_n)]^T$.

Taking derivative of Eq. (14) with respect to $\mathbf{r}$, we obtain

$$\left.\frac{\partial Q}{\partial \mathbf{r}}\right|_{\mathbf{r}=\mathbf{r}^*} = 2\left(\mathbf{I} - \mathbf{D}^{-1/2}\mathbf{W}\mathbf{D}^{-1/2}\right)\mathbf{r}^* + 2\lambda(\mathbf{r}^* - \mathbf{v}) = 0 \tag{15}$$

and we can derive

$$\mathbf{r}^* = \frac{\lambda}{\lambda+1}\left(\mathbf{I} - \frac{1}{1+\lambda}\mathbf{D}^{-1/2}\mathbf{W}\mathbf{D}^{-1/2}\right)^{-1}\mathbf{v}. \tag{16}$$

This is the closed-form solution of our optimization framework. However, we can see that the above solution involves the inversion of an $n \times n$ matrix, of which the computational cost scales as $O(n^3)$. Here we present a more efficient algorithm to solve $\mathbf{r}$ in an iterative way:

(1) Construct the image affinity matrix $\mathbf{W}$ by Eq. (11) if $i \neq j$ and otherwise $W_{ii} = 0$.
(2) Initialize $\mathbf{r}^{(0)}$. The initial values will not influence the final results.
(3) Iterate $\mathbf{r}^{(t+1)} = \frac{1}{1+\lambda}\mathbf{D}^{-1/2}\mathbf{W}\mathbf{D}^{-1/2}\mathbf{r}^{(t)} + \frac{\lambda}{1+\lambda}\mathbf{v}$ until convergence.

The method can be viewed as a random walk process, and it will converge to a fixed point, i.e.,

Theorem 2 *The iterative process converges to the optimal* $\mathbf{r}^*$ *in Eq. (16).*

Proof According to the iterative function

$$\mathbf{r}^{(t+1)} = \frac{1}{1+\lambda}\mathbf{D}^{-1/2}\mathbf{W}\mathbf{D}^{-1/2}\mathbf{r}^{(t)} + \frac{\lambda}{1+\lambda}\mathbf{v} \tag{17}$$

we have

$$\mathbf{r}^* = \lim_{t \to \infty}\left(\frac{1}{1+\lambda}\mathbf{D}^{-1/2}\mathbf{W}\mathbf{D}^{-1/2}\right)^t\mathbf{v}$$

$$+ \frac{\lambda}{1+\lambda}\left(\sum_{m=1}^{t}\left(\frac{1}{1+\lambda}\mathbf{D}^{-1/2}\mathbf{W}\mathbf{D}^{-1/2}\right)^m\right)\mathbf{v}. \tag{18}$$

Based on the fact that $0 < \frac{1}{1+\lambda} < 1$ and that the eigenvalues of matrix $\mathbf{D}^{-1/2}\mathbf{W}\mathbf{D}^{-1/2}$ are in $(0, 1)$, we have

$$\lim_{t \to \infty}\left(\frac{1}{1+\lambda}\mathbf{D}^{-1/2}\mathbf{W}\mathbf{D}^{-1/2}\right)^t = 0 \tag{19}$$

and

$$\lim_{t\to\infty} \sum_{m=1}^{t} \left(\frac{1}{1+\lambda}\mathbf{D}^{-1/2}\mathbf{W}\mathbf{D}^{-1/2}\right)^m = \left(\mathbf{I} - \frac{1}{1+\lambda}\mathbf{D}^{-1/2}\mathbf{W}\mathbf{D}^{-1/2}\right)^{-1}. \quad (20)$$

Hence,

$$\mathbf{r}^* = \frac{\lambda}{1+\lambda}\left(\mathbf{I} - \frac{1}{1+\lambda}\mathbf{D}^{-1/2}\mathbf{W}\mathbf{D}^{-1/2}\right)^{-1}\mathbf{v}. \quad (21)$$

This is the same as the closed-form solution in Eq. (16).   □

4.2 Similarity Estimation

We define a semantic similarity for social images, which is estimated based on their associated tag sets. Note that we have obtained the similarity of tag pair in Eq. (10). Consequently, we estimate the semantic similarity of images x_i and x_j as

$$s(x_i, x_j) = \frac{1}{2|\mathscr{T}_i|} \sum_{k=1}^{|\mathscr{T}_i|} \max_{t\in\mathscr{T}_j} sim(t_k^i, t) + \frac{1}{2|\mathscr{T}_j|} \sum_{k=1}^{|\mathscr{T}_j|} \max_{t\in\mathscr{T}_i} sim(t_k^j, t). \quad (22)$$

We can see that the above definition satisfies the following properties:

(1) $s(x_i, x_j) = s(x_j, x_i)$, i.e., the semantic similarity is symmetry.
(2) $s(x_i, x_j) = 1$ if $\mathscr{T}_i = \mathscr{T}_j$, i.e., the semantic similarity of two images is 1 if their tag sets are identical.
(3) $s(x_i, x_j) = 0$ if and only if $sim(t', t'') = 0$ for every $t' \in \mathscr{T}_i$ and $t'' \in \mathscr{T}_j$, i.e., the semantic similarity is 0 if and only if every pair formed by the two tag sets has zero similarity.

This method is close to Song et al.'s approach [25], which estimates the similarity of images based on their annotated semantic concepts. However, their method simply counts the overlapped concepts of two images and our approach further takes the relationship between different concepts into consideration. Now we explain why we do not use visual similarity which should be the most straightforward approach. First we emphasize that visual diversity and semantic diversity have both been investigated in many research works [25, 28, 31] and both have their own rationality. However, in our scheme search relevance will significantly degrade if we adopt visual similarity. This is because the relevant images are more aggregated in visual space in comparison with semantic space. To quantitatively demonstrate this fact, we first define the aggregation score of relevant images for a query as follows

$$A = \frac{\frac{1}{|\mathscr{R}|^2} \sum_{x_i, x_j \in \mathscr{R}} s(x_i, x_j)}{\frac{1}{|\mathscr{R}||\bar{\mathscr{R}}|} \sum_{x_i \in \mathscr{R}} \sum_{x_j \in \bar{\mathscr{R}}} s(x_i, x_j)}, \quad (23)$$

where $\mathscr{R}$ and $\bar{\mathscr{R}}$ are the sets of relevant and irrelevant images, respectively.

Table 1 The aggregation score comparison of using visual similarity and using semantic similarity for several queries. Higher aggregation score indicates that relevant samples are more aggregated in the space and the diversifying process is more likely to degrade the search relevance

	Using Visual Similarity	Using Semantic Similarity
Car	1.466	1.112
Forest	1.324	1.048
Hairstyle	1.960	1.013
Jaguar	1.333	1.074
Shark	1.588	1.296
Waterfall	1.097	1.052

Then we compare the aggregation scores using visual similarity and semantic similarity for several queries. The dataset and parameter settings will be described in the next section. Table 1 illustrates the results. From the table we can see that the obtained aggregation scores with visual similarity are much higher than those obtained with semantic similarity. This indicates that relevant images are more aggregated in visual space than semantic space (now we can revisit our second assumption in relevance estimation and see its rationality: the relevance scores of visually similar images should be close). Therefore, in our diverse relevance ranking approach it will be difficult to simultaneously maintain high relevance level and visual diversity. For example, in the process in Fig. 4 if previous images are relevant, then the next image will have high probability to be irrelevant as we enforce it to be visually different with the previous images. Empirical results in the next section will demonstrate this fact and user study will show the superiority of semantic similarity over visual similarity.

5 Empirical Study

5.1 Flickr Dataset

We evaluate our approach on a set of social images that are collected from Flickr. We first select a diverse set of popular tags from the tag list of [32], including *airshow, apple, beach, bird, car, cow, dolphin, eagle, flower, fruit, jaguar, jellyfish, lion, owl, panda, starfish, triumphal, turtle, watch, waterfall, wolf, chopper, fighter, flame, hairstyle, horse, motorcycle, rabbit, shark, snowman, sport, wildlife, aquarium, basin, bmw, chicken, decoration, forest, furniture, glacier, hockey, matrix, Olympics, palace, rainbow, rice, sailboat, seagull, spider, swimmer, telephone,* and *weapon*. We then perform tag-based image search with "ranking by most recent" option, and the top 2,000 returned images for each query are collected together with their associated information, including tags, uploading time, user identifier, etc. In this way, we obtain a social image collection consisting of 104,000 images and 83,999 unique tags. But many of the raw tags are misspelling and meaningless. Hence, we adopt a pre-filtering process on these tags. Specifically, we match each tag with the entries in a Wikipedia thesaurus and only the tags that have a coordinate in Wikipedia are kept. In this way, 12,921 unique tags are kept for our experiment, and there are 7.74 tags associated with an image in average.

For each image, we extract 428-dimensional features, including 225-dimensional block-wise color moment features generated from 5-by-5 fixed partition of the image, 128-dimensional wavelet texture features, and 75-dimensional edge distribution histogram features. The ground truth of the relevance of each image is voted by three human labelers. The radius parameter σ in Eq. (12) is empirically set to the median value of all the pair-wise Euclidean distances between images, and the weighting parameter λ is empirically set to 0.1 for all queries.

5.2 Empirical Results

We first compare the following six ranking methods:

(1) Time-based ranking, i.e., order the images according to their uploading time.
(2) Relevance-based ranking, i.e., order the images according to their estimated relevance scores $r(x_i)$.
(3) We cluster the images with Affinity Propagation [8], and the cluster exemplars are put forward in the ranking list and they are ordered according to their relevance scores. The non-exemplars are also ordered based on their relevance scores.
(4) We first rank images according to their relevance scores and then perform the folding method proposed in [28]. The parameter ϵ is set to the mean value of pair-wise distances among all images.
(5) Diverse Relevance Ranking (DRR) with visual similarity.
(6) Diverse Relevance Ranking (DRR) with semantic similarity, i.e., the method proposed in this work.

For simplicity, these methods are denoted as "Time-Based Ranking", "Relevance-Based Ranking", "AP-Based Diversifying", "Folding-Based Diversifying", "DRR with Visual Similarity" and "DRR with Semantic Similarity", respectively. The first two methods are baseline and the next two methods diversify search results with clustering approach on a relevance-based ranking list. Figure 6 illustrates the top results of exemplary query "waterfall" and "triumphal", from which we can see that the results of our method are both relevant and diverse, whereas the results of the other methods are not satisfying in terms of either relevance or diversity. Figure 7(a) and Fig. 7(b) illustrate the AP and ADP measurements obtained by different methods, respectively. We also illustrate the mean AP (MAP) and mean ADP (MADP) measurements that are averaged over all queries. The MAP measurements of the six methods are 0.583, 0.684, 0.646, 0.621, 0.577 and 0.664, respectively, and their MADP measurements are 0.308, 0.361, 0.374, 0.334, 0.331 and 0.411, respectively. It can found that relevance-based ranking achieves the highest AP measurement, but its ADP measurement is rather low. This indicates that it suffers from the lack-of-diversity problem. Although the AP-Based Diversifying, Folding-Based Diversifying and DRR with Visual Similarity methods can enhance the diversity, they

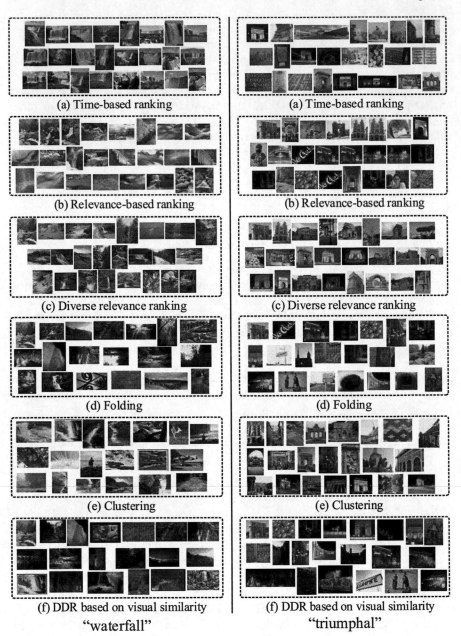

(a) Time-based ranking

(b) Relevance-based ranking

(c) Diverse relevance ranking

(d) Folding

(e) Clustering

(f) DDR based on visual similarity

"waterfall"

(a) Time-based ranking

(b) Relevance-based ranking

(c) Diverse relevance ranking

(d) Folding

(e) Clustering

(f) DDR based on visual similarity

"triumphal"

Fig. 6 The top results of different ranking methods of query "waterfall" and "triumphal"

degrade search relevance much in comparison with relevance-based ranking (we have analyzed why DRR with Visual Similarity will degrade search relevance in Sect. 4.2) and thus we can see that their ADP measurements are not high. The DRR

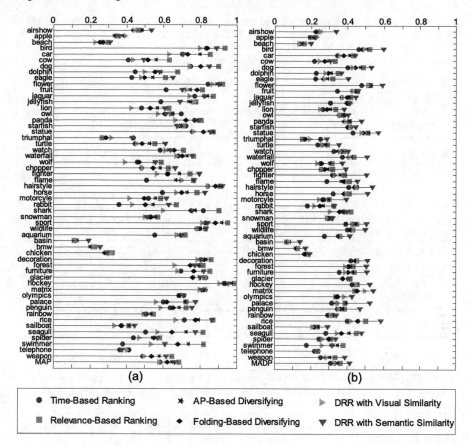

Fig. 7 (a) The comparison of AP measurements of different approaches. (b) The comparison of ADP measurements of different approaches

with Semantic Similarity achieves the best ADP measurements and it only performs slightly worse than Relevance-Based Ranking in terms of AP. This shows that it is able to achieve a good trade-off between relevance and diversity.

We then conduct a user study to compare the six ranking schemes. To avoid bias, a third-party data management company is involved. The company invited 30 anonymous participants, who declare they are regular users of Internet and familiar with image search and media sharing websites. They were asked to freely choose queries and observe image ranking lists. They compared DRR with Semantic Similarity, i.e., our proposed approach, with each of the other five ranking approaches in terms of search relevance and diversity.[1] The users are asked to give the com-

---

[1] It is worth noting that diversity is not directly related to a user's search requirements. Therefore, actually the users are asked to take search relevance and comprehensiveness into account. For search comprehensiveness, we asked them to imagine different search intentions when they posed these queries for themselves, and then it is better if the top results in a list cover more possibilities.

Table 2 The left part illustrates the average rating scores and variances converted from the users study on the comparison of "DRR with Semantic Similarity" and "Time-Based Ranking". The right part illustrates the ANOVA test results. The p-values show that the difference of the two ranking schemes is significant, and the difference of users is insignificant

DRR with Semantic Similarity vs. Time-Based ranking		The factor of ranking schemes		The factor of users	
DRR with Semantic Similarity	Time-Based ranking	F-statistic	p-value	F-statistic	p-value
2.40 ± 0.386	1.03 ± 0.033	108.57	2.58×10^{-11}	0.656	0.894

Table 3 The left part illustrates the average rating scores and variances converted from the user study on the comparison of "DRR with Semantic Similarity" and "Relevance-Based Ranking". The right part illustrates the ANOVA test results

DRR with Semantic Similarity vs. Relevance-Based ranking		The factor of ranking schemes		The factor of users	
DRR with Semantic Similarity	Relevance-Based Ranking	F-statistic	p-value	F-statistic	p-value
2.40 ± 0.455	1.133 ± 0.189	46.74	2.5×10^{-11}	0.25	0.999

Table 4 The left part illustrates the average rating scores and variances converted from the user study on the comparison of "DRR with Semantic Similarity" and "AP-Based Diversifying". The right part illustrates the ANOVA test results

DRR with Semantic Similarity vs. AP-Based Diversifying		The factor of ranking schemes		The factor of users	
DRR with Semantic Similarity	AP-Based Diversifying	F-statistic	p-value	F-statistic	p-value
2.43 ± 0.392	1.10 ± 0.162	62.7	9.85×10^{-9}	0.3	0.999

parison results using ">", "≫" and "=", which mean "better", "much better" and "comparable". To quantify the results, we convert the results into ratings. We assign score 1 to the worse scheme and the other scheme is assigned a score 2, 3 and 1 if it is better, much better and comparable than this one, respectively. Since there will be disagreements among the evaluators, we perform an ANOVA test [16] to statistically analyze the comparison. The five comparison results are illustrated in Table 2, 3, 4, 5 and 6, respectively. The results demonstrate the superiority of our approach over the other methods. ANOVA test shows that the superiority is statistically significant and the difference of the evaluators is not significant. This further confirms the effectiveness of our approach.

In the user study we also found several failure cases of our approach, such as the top images are irrelevant or not diverse enough. One major reason is the noises of

Table 5 The left part illustrates the average rating scores and variances converted from the user study on the comparison of "DRR with Semantic Similarity" and "Folding-Based Diversifying". The right part illustrates the ANOVA test results

DRR with Semantic Similarity vs. Folding-Based Diversifying		The factor of ranking schemes		The factor of users	
DRR with Semantic Similarity	Folding-Based Diversifying	F-statistic	p-value	F-statistic	p-value
1.97 ± 0.240	1.13 ± 0.195	33.26	3.02×10^{-6}	0.15	1.0

Table 6 The left part illustrates the average rating scores and variances converted from the user study on the comparison of "DRR with Semantic Similarity" and with "DRR with Visual Similarity". The right part illustrates the ANOVA test results

DRR with Semantic Similarity vs. DRR with Visual Similarity		The factor of ranking schemes		The factor of users	
DRR with Semantic Similarity	DRR with Visual Similarity	F-statistic	p-value	F-statistic	p-value
2.20 ± 0.441	1.10 ± 0.093	46.37	1.77×10^{-7}	0.37	0.996

tags which result in inaccurate relevance and semantic similarity estimation. Performing a tag refinement step [15, 18, 19] to reduce the noisy tags should further benefit our approach.

5.3 Complexity Analysis

According to the introduction in Sect. 3 and Sect. 4, we can see that the computational costs of relevance estimation, semantic similarity computation and the DRR algorithm all scale as $O(n^2)$. However, the relevance and similarity estimation can be accomplished off-line (an image-tag relevance matrix and a sparse image similarity matrix can be stored). We also do not need to generate the full ranking list using DRR. Actually, we can only generate the list of the first k images with the proposed algorithm, and then the rest images are simply ranked by relevance scores. In our experiments, it needs about 1.2 seconds to accomplish the ranking with 2000 images (Pentium4 3.0G CPU and 2 G memory), and a study on web users shows that the tolerable waiting time for web information retrieval is about 2 seconds [20]. The process can still be speeded up by adopting several strategies. For example, we can rank the images in a piecewise manner, such as first ranking the most relevant 500 images with DRR and put them on the top, and then rank the next most relevant 500 images with DRR, and so forth.

6 Conclusion

This chapter presents a diverse relevance ranking scheme for social image search, which is able to simultaneously take relevance and diversity into account. It leverages both visual information of images and semantic information of the associated tags. The ranking algorithm optimizes an Average Diverse Precision (ADP) measure, which is generalized from the conventional AP measure by integrating with diversity. Experimental results have demonstrated the effectiveness of the approach.

References

1. Agrawal, R., Gollapudi, S., Halverson, A., Leong, S.: Diversifying search results. In: Proceedings of ACM International Conference on Web Search and Data Mining (2009)
2. Buckley, C., Voorhees, E.M.: Retrieval evaluation with incomplete information. In: SIGIR (2004)
3. Cai, D., He, X., Li, Z., Ma, W.-Y., Wen, J.-R.: Hierarchical clustering of WWW image search results using visual, textual and link information. In: Proceedings of ACM Multimedia, pp. 952–959 (2004)
4. Carbonell, J., Goldstein, J.: The use of MMR, diversity-based reranking for reordering documents and producing summaries. In: Proceedings of SIGIR, pp. 335–336 (1998)
5. Chen, H., Karger, D.R.: Less is more: probabilistic models for retrieving fewer relevant documents. In: Proceedings of the 29th Annual International ACM SIGIR Conference on Research and Development in Information Retrieval, p. 436. ACM, New York (2006)
6. Cilibrasi, R., Vitanyi, P.M.B.: The google similarity distance. IEEE Trans. Knowl. Data Eng. **19**, 370–383 (2007)
7. Clarke, C.L.A., Kolla, M., Cormack, G.V., Vechtomova, O., Ashkan, A., Büttcher, S., MacKinnon, I.: Novelty and diversity in information retrieval evaluation. In: Proceedings of the 31st Annual International ACM SIGIR Conference on Research and Development in Information Retrieval, pp. 659–666. ACM, New York (2008)
8. Frey, B.J., Dueck, D.: Clustering by passing messages between data points. Science **315**, 972–976 (2007)
9. Goffman, W.: A searching procedure for information retrieval. In: Information Storage and Retrieval, vol. 2, pp. 73–78 (1964)
10. Hsu, W.H., Kennedy, L.S., Chang, S.-F.: Video search reranking via information bottleneck principle. In: Proceedings of ACM Multimedia, pp. 35–44 (2006)
11. Jaimes, A., Chang, S.-F., Loui, A.C.: Detection of non-identical duplicate consumer photographs. In: Proceedings of ACM Multimedia, pp. 16–20 (2003)
12. Järvelin, K., Kekäläinen, J.: Cumulated gain-based evaluation of IR techniques. ACM Trans. Inf. Syst. **20**(4), 446 (2002)
13. Jing, F., Wang, C., Yao, Y., Deng, K., Zhang, L., Ma, W.-Y.: IGroup: web image search results clustering. In: Proceedings of ACM Multimedia, pp. 587–596 (2006)
14. Kennedy, L.S., Chang, S.F., Kozintsev, I.V.: To search or to label? predicting the performance of search-based automatic image classifiers. In: Proceedings of MIR, pp. 249–258 (2006)
15. Kennedy, L., Slaney, M., Weinberger, K.: Reliable tags using image similarity: mining specificity and expertise from large-scale multimedia databases. In: WSMC '09: Proceedings of the 1st Workshop on Web-scale Multimedia Corpus, pp. 17–24. ACM, New York (2009)
16. King, B.M., Minium, E.W.: Statistical reasoning in psychology and education. Wiley, New York (2003)
17. Li, J., Wang, J.: Real-time computerized annotation of pictures. IEEE Trans. Pattern Anal. Mach. Intell. **30**(6), 985–1002 (2008)

18. Li, X.R., Snoek, C.G.M., Worring, M.: Learning tag relevance by neighbor voting for social image retrieval. In: Proceedings of MIR, pp. 180–187 (2008)
19. Liu, D., Wang, M., Yang, L., Hua, X.-S., Zhang, H.-J.: Tag quality improvement for social images. In: Proceedings of ICME, pp. 350–353 (2009)
20. Nah, F.F.-H.: A study on tolerable waiting time: how long are web users willing to wait. Behav. Inf. Technol. 23(3), 153–163 (2004)
21. Qi, G.J., Hua, X.S., Rui, Y., Tang, J.H., Zha, Z.J., Zhang, H.J.: A joint appearance-spatial distance for kernel-based image categorization. In: Proceedings of CVPR, pp. 1–8 (2008)
22. Robertson, S.: The probability ranking principle in IR. J. Doc. 33(294), 294–304 (1977)
23. Rui, Y., Huang, T.S.: Relevance feedback: a power tool for interactive content-based image retrieval. IEEE Trans. Circuits Syst. Video Technol. 8(5), 644–655 (1999)
24. Santos, R.L.T., Macdonald, C., Ounis, I.: Exploiting query reformulations for Web search result diversification. In: Proceedings of the 19th International Conference on World Wide Web, pp. 881–890. ACM, New York (2010)
25. Song, K., Tian, Y., Huang, T., Gao, W.: Diversifying the image retrieval results. In: Proceedings of ACM Multimedia, pp. 707–710 (2006)
26. Srinivasan, S.H., Sawant, N.: Finding near-duplicate images on the web using fingerprints. In: Proceedings of ACM Multimedia, pp. 881–884 (2008)
27. Sun, A., Bhowmick, S.S.: Image tag clarity: in search of visual-representative tags for social images. In: WSM '09: Proceedings of the First SIGMM Workshop on Social Media, pp. 19–26. ACM, New York (2009)
28. Van Leuken, R.H., Garcia, L., Olivares, X., Zwol, R.: Visual diversification of image search results. In: Proceedings of WWW, pp. 341–350 (2009)
29. Wang, B., Li, Z., Li, M., Ma, W.-Y.: Large-scale duplicate detection for web image search. In: Proceedings of ICME, pp. 353–356 (2006)
30. Wang, M., Hua, X.-S., Tang, J., Hong, R.: Beyond distance measurement: constructing neighborhood similarity for video annotation. IEEE Trans. Multimed. 11(3), 465–476 (2009)
31. Weinberger, K.Q., Slaney, M., Van Zwol, R.: Resolving tag ambiguity. In: MM '08: Proceeding of the 16th ACM International Conference on Multimedia, pp. 111–120. ACM, New York (2008)
32. Wu, L., Hua, X.-S., Ma, W.-Y., Yu, N., Li, S.: Flickr distance. In: Proceedings of ACM Multimedia, pp. 31–40 (2008)
33. Yahoo key scientific challenges program. http://research.yahoo.com/ksc/multimedia
34. Yang, K., Wang, M., Hua, X.-S., Zhang, H.-J.: Social image search with diverse relevance ranking. In: International MultiMedia Modeling Conference (MMM) (2010)
35. Zhai, C., Cohen, W.W., Lafferty, J.: Beyond independent relevance: methods and evaluation metrics for subtopic retrieval. In: Information Processing and Management, pp. 10–17 (2006)
36. Zhai, C., Lafferty, J.: A risk minimization framework for information retrieval. Inf. Process. Manag. 31–55 (2006)
37. Zhao, W.L., Ngo, C.W.: Scale-rotation invariant pattern entropy for keypoint-based near-duplicate detection. IEEE Trans. Image Process. 18(2), 412–423 (2009)
38. Zhu, J., Hoi, S.C.H., Lyu, M.R., Yan, S.: Near-duplicate keyframe retrieval by nonrigid image matching. In: Proceedings of ACM Multimedia, pp. 41–50 (2008)

Social Image Tag Ranking by Two-View Learning

Jinfeng Zhuang and Steven C.H. Hoi

Abstract Tags play a central role in text-based social image retrieval and browsing. However, the tags annotated by web users could be noisy, irrelevant, and often incomplete for describing the image contents, which may severely deteriorate the performance of text-based image retrieval models. In order to solve this problem, researchers have proposed techniques to rank the annotated tags of a social image according to their relevance to the visual content of the image. In this paper, we aim to overcome the challenge of *social image tag ranking* for a corpus of social images with rich user-generated tags by proposing a novel two-view learning approach. It can effectively exploit both textual and visual contents of social images to discover the complicated relationship between tags and images. Unlike the conventional learning approaches that usually assumes some parametric models, our method is completely data-driven and makes no assumption about the underlying models, making the proposed solution practically more effective. We formulate our method as an optimization task and present an efficient algorithm to solve it. To evaluate the efficacy of our method, we conducted an extensive set of experiments by applying our technique to both text-based social image retrieval and automatic image annotation tasks. Our empirical results showed that the proposed method can be more effective than the conventional approaches.

1 Introduction

In the web 2.0 era, along with the popularity of various digital imaging devices and the advances of Internet technologies, we have witnessed a growing number of user-centric multimedia applications in social web and social networking portals, such as Flickr, Facebook, MySpace, etc. These emerging applications enable digital images

---

This book chapter is an extended version of the paper [35], which will appear at the fourth ACM Conference on Web Search and Data Mining (WSDM), Hong Kong, 2011.

J. Zhuang (✉) · S.C.H. Hoi
School of Computer Engineering, Nanyang Technological University, Singapore, Singapore
e-mail: zhua0016@ntu.edu.sg

S.C.H. Hoi
e-mail: chhoi@ntu.edu.sg

S.C.H. Hoi et al. (eds.), *Social Media Modeling and Computing*,
DOI 10.1007/978-0-85729-436-4_3, © Springer-Verlag London Limited 2011
47

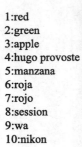

1:red
2:green
3:apple
4:hugo provoste
5:manzana
6:roja
7:rojo
8:session
9:wa
10:nikon

1:apple
2:red
3:manzana
4:hugo provoste
5:nikon
6:roja
7:rojo
8:green
9:session
10:wa

Fig. 1 Illustration of the efficacy of the proposed social image tag-ranking technique. The original annotations contain irrelevant tags, e.g. "green" is apparently a noisy tag. After the tag ranking, the most relevant tags "apple" and "tag" are ranked at the top 2 positions. The irrelevant tag "green" dropped to the 8th position

and photos to be easily created, uploaded, shared and distributed over the Internet, which have produced a new type of images, "social images", which are created by people using highly accessible and scalable publishing technologies for sharing via the Internet. Social images are nowadays playing a more and more important role in web search and data mining as well as multimedia semantic understanding [7].

One emerging research challenge in this area is social image search [34]. For regular web image search, a major difficulty is that traditional web images are usually not annotated with proper tags, and many of them are even completely unlabeled. In addition, even for the annotated images, their associated tags could be noisy, irrelevant, and often incomplete for describing the contents of the images. Although this issue is less serious for social images that often have better quality user-contributed tags, noisy and irrelevant tags remain a key challenge. For example, according to the empirical study [14] conducted on Flickr,[1] a popular social image sharing portal, only 50% of tags are actually related to the image content. This poses a great challenge for regular web image search paradigms, which often simply apply regular text-based retrieval techniques on the web image search domain.

To address the emerging social image search challenge, one approach is to study social image tag refinement techniques, which have been proposed by many researchers recently [10, 12, 14, 22, 23, 28]. Although tag refinement techniques can generally improve the quality of the tags, they do not explicitly answer which tag is more relevant than the other for a specific image. Very recently, *tag ranking* [14] has emerged as an alternative solution to address the social tag improvement issue. In general, the goal of social image tag ranking is to rank the tags of a social image according to their relevance to the semantic/visual content of the image. Figure 1 shows an example with the two lists of tags before and after the proposed social tag-ranking technique, in which relevant tags can be ranked in the top positions by our social tag-ranking technique.

---

[1]http://www.flickr.com/.

Social tag ranking is important as it can facilitate a lot of real-world multimedia applications, including social image retrieval, browsing, and annotation tasks. Despite the encouraging results reported by the study in [14], there remains some limitations for the existing work. First of all, the existing approaches usually assume some parametric functions to model the tag generation process. The probabilistic approaches often limit the capability of fitting the complicated image and tag relationship as such parametric probabilistic model assumptions seldom hold in practice. In addition, the existing studies often adopt heuristic methods for tag ranking, which usually lead to suboptimal performance.

Unlike the existing work, this paper proposes a novel two-view learning approach for social image tag ranking, which is purely data-driven by exploring large-scale social image data, and does not assume any parametric relevance models between tags and images. Specifically, we formulate the tag-ranking task as a problem of learning a *nonparametric* tag weighting matrix that encodes the relevance relationship between images and tags. We then present an effective algorithm to optimize the weight matrix by exploiting both local visual geometry in image space and local textual geometry in tag space.

In sum, the main contributions of our work include:

- We propose a novel two-view learning framework for social image tag ranking, which is purely data-driven without making any assumption on modeling the relationship between images and tags. Thus it is more flexible and powerful to learn the complicated relationship in real-world social image data.
- We formulate the two-view tag weighting problem as an optimization task, and present an effective stochastic coordinate descent algorithm, which can solve the optimization problem efficiently.
- We conduct an extensive set of experiments to examine the empirical performance of the proposed tag-ranking technique and apply our technique to several applications, including social image retrieval and tag recommendation for web photo tagging.

The rest of this book chapter is organized as follows. Section 2 discusses the related work. Section 3 presents the proposed two-view learning approach for social image tag ranking. Section 4 conducts an extensive set of experiments to evaluate the proposed methods. Section 5 discusses some limitations of our study, and Sect. 6 concludes this work.

2 Related Work

The quality of tags play a crucial role in social image retrieval. A number of recent studies aim to address the tag quality issues. In this section, we summarize and analyze some representative methods that are closely related to the techniques presented in this paper.

The first category of related techniques refers to *tag annotation*. Annotating an image automatically by machine learning methods enables large amounts of unlabeled images to be indexed and searchable by existing text-based image search engines. A variety of techniques have been proposed for auto-image annotation in recent years [4, 6, 15, 17, 19, 24, 26, 27, 29, 32]. In general, auto-image annotation can be viewed as an intermediate task for a generic web image retrieval task. Most of these methods try to model the probabilistic relationship between tags and images. How to produce highly accurate annotations remains an unsolved long-term challenge.

An alternative approach to auto-annotation is *tag refinement* [10, 13, 22, 23], which aims to model the relevance of the associated tags to an image. Jin et al. [10] proposed the pioneering work on annotation refinement by a generic data-based WordNet. The assumption is that highly correlated annotation tends to be correct and non-correlated tags tend to be noisy. With a large collection of social images, one could build the correlation matrix among the tags. The main drawback of this method simply ignores the specific content information of individual images.

To address the limitation of WordNet, Wang et al. [22] proposed the Random Walk with Restarts (RWR) algorithm. The key idea is to leverage the information of the original annotated order of tags besides the correlation among tags. Further, Wang et al. [23] proposed the Content-based Image Annotation Refinement (CIAR) algorithm that formulates the tag refinement problem as a Markov process and the candidate tags are defined as the states of a Markov chain. The transition matrix is constructed based on the query image using both visual features of the query image and the corpus information. The CIAR algorithm focuses on refining the automatic annotation results for query image. It is however difficult to apply this approach to refine the existing tags for a large corpus due to the high computational cost. Weinberger et al. [25] proposed a probabilistic approach to model the ambiguity of tags. Different from the previous methods, it can suggest tags that are not included in the user-generated tag list. Li et al. [12] proposed a voting method in which the relevance of a tag to a test image is determined based on the number of such votes from the nearest neighbors.

Very recently, researchers are interested in a specific tag refinement task, known as "tag ranking" [14], which aims to generate a permutation of the associated tags for an image, in which the resulting order indicates the tags' relevance or importance to the image. Although existing tag refinement methods might be adapted to the tag-ranking task, the *tag-ranking* problem is explicitly addressed very recently in [14]. In their algorithm, they first model the generating probability of tags from an image with some exponential function. After that they refine the ranking score by random walk over a similarity matrix between tags constructed by incorporating both the representative image of that tag and the Google distance between pairs of tags. Despite encouraging results reported, their method assumes some parametric models, which may limit their capability of modeling complicated tag–image relationships.

The importance of tag ranking calls for further study on this problem. In this contribution, we propose a novel two-view learning approach without assuming any parametric models between images and tags, which distinguishes our work from the existing model-based methods. Finally, we formally formulate our method as an optimization task, which differs from the other heuristic tag-ranking methods.

3 Two-View Learning for Social Tag Ranking

In this section we present a novel two-view learning approach for social tag ranking. We first give some preliminaries to introduce our problem setting and present the two-view representation for modeling social images. We then present the proposed learning framework and an efficient algorithm to solve the optimization followed by the discussion on some practical implementation issues.

3.1 Preliminaries

Consider a social image z is represented as a pairwise example (x, t), which consists of an image $x \in \mathcal{X}$ and its associated set of tags $t \subseteq \mathcal{T}$, where $\mathcal{X}$ and $\mathcal{T}$ are referred to the image and tag spaces, respectively. In the sequel, we let n denote the number of social images in the corpus, and $m = |\mathcal{T}|$ denote the number of unique tags in the corpus. For a positive integer d, we define $\mathbb{N}_d = \{1, \ldots, d\}$ as a series of d. For any matrix M, we use the following notation:

- M_i denotes the ith row vector of M;
- M_i^c denotes the ith column vector of M;
- M_{ij} denotes the (i, j)th entry of M;
- $M^\top$ denotes the transpose of M;
- $\|M\|_F = \sqrt{\sum_{ij} M_{ij}^2}$ is the Frobenius norm of M;
- $\operatorname{tr} M = \sum_i M_{ii}$ is the trace of M if M is square.

For every social image $z_i = (x_i, t_i)$, the set of associated tags is assigned to z_i provided by web users. Without further information, we treat all the assigned tags equally important. Therefore, we indicate the initial annotation of z_i by a vector $t_i \in \mathbb{R}^m$, where $t_{ij} = 1/|t_i|$ if the jth tag is assigned to z_i; $t_{ij} = 0$ otherwise. We tile all t_i values into a tag indicator matrix T such that $T_{ij} := t_{ij}$.

Based on the above definitions, for a given social image $z_i = (x_i, t_i)$, social tag ranking in general is to find an optimal permutation of the tag list t_i by learning from a corpus of social images $\{z_i = (x_i, t_i), i \in \mathbb{N}_n\}$. It is, however, hard to directly optimize the permutation of the tag list t_i. In this paper, we consider an alternative approach by learning a nonparametric tag weighing matrix $W \in \mathbb{R}_+^{n \times m}$, where entry $w_{ij}, i \in \mathbb{N}_n, j \in \mathbb{N}_m$, indicates the relevance of tag t_{ij} with respect to image x_i.

As a result, the problem of *social tag ranking* is equivalent to looking for the optimal tag weighting matrix from mining the hidden knowledge from the social image corpus $\{z_i = (x_i, t_i), i \in \mathbb{N}_n\}$. Below we propose a purely data-driven approach to learning the optimal tag weighting matrix W. Our method does not make explicit parametric assumptions on any generative models between $\mathcal{T}$ and $\mathcal{X}$.

Fig. 2 Illustration of the two views of the weight matrix of social images. Each W_{ij} is the weight of the jth tag for the ith image. The weights in the vertical blue ellipse provides an exemplar representation of "fruit". The weights in the horizontal yellow ellipse provides a semantic representation of the image strawberry

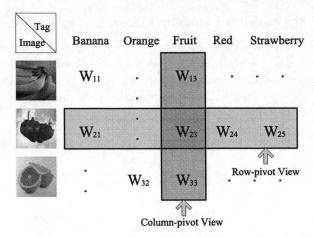

3.2 Two-View Representation for Social Tags

The social image data Z consists of two views: the visual view ($\mathcal{X}$) and the tag or concept view ($\mathcal{T}$). As mentioned above, to model the relationship between images and tags, we employ a nonparametric tag weighting matrix W, which has a natural interpretation for the two-view representation of social images:

- *Row-Pivot* view: Each row vector of W, denoted as W_i, is a weighting vector over a set of user-generated tags, which forms a semantic summarization for describing the semantic content of the visual image x_i. From this point of view, we can represent a visual image as a weighted combination of a set of relevant tags via specifying the row of W in tag space.
- *Column-Pivot* view: Each column vector of W, denoted as W_i^c, is a weighting vector over a set of images, which actually forms an exemplar of the corresponding tag. From this point of view, we can represent a tag / a semantic concept as a weighted combination of a set of most representative images via specifying the column of W in visual space.

To better understand the idea, we give a visual example to illustrate the two-view representation as shown in Fig. 2. For the highlighted row and column in this figure, the weights in the vertical (blue) zone provides an exemplar representation of the tag "fruit", and the weights in the horizontal (yellow) zone provides a semantic representation of the image "strawberry". From the above observation, we can see that the relevance weighing matrix W plays a central role for modeling the relationship between $\mathcal{X}$ and $\mathcal{T}$.

3.3 Two-View Learning for Tag Weighting

The basic idea of learning the optimal W is twofold: (1) we aim to make the above two-view representations coincide with the local geometry in both visual space and concept space; (2) we shall preserve the user annotation results to some extent. Motivated by these two considerations, we propose to devise the following learning scheme.

For the first purpose, we have to make use of the similarity graph S^x in $\mathscr{X}$ and S^t in $\mathscr{T}$ (we assume that both S^x and S^t are symmetric). We take S^x to sketch the details. For any two images x_i and x_j, the entry S_{ij}^x computes the visual similarity between x_i and x_j. With the row-pivot view of W, the Euclidean distance between image x_i and x_j is computed by $\|W_i - W_j\|_2$. Thus the distortion between W and prior similarity S^x can be computed by

$$\Omega\left(W, S^x\right) = \frac{1}{2} \sum_{i,j=1}^{n} S_{ij}^x \left\| \frac{W_i}{\sqrt{d_i}} - \frac{W_j}{\sqrt{d_j}} \right\|_2^2 = \mathrm{tr}\left(W^\top L^x W\right) = \mathrm{tr}\, L^x\left(W W^\top\right), \quad (1)$$

where $d_i = \sum_{j=1}^n S_{ij}^x$ is engaged for the normalization purpose, L^x is the normalized graph Laplacian defined as

$$L^x = I - D^{-1/2} S^x D^{-1/2}, \quad (2)$$

where $D = \mathrm{diag}(d_1, d_2, \ldots, d_n)$ is a diagonal matrix. The above formulation was partially inspired by some previous work on nonparametric kernel learning with side information [8].

Similarly, we also compute the graph Laplacian L^t in concept space, and calculate the distortion between W and the textual similarity S^t:

$$\Omega\left(W, S^t\right) = \frac{1}{2} \sum_{i,j=1}^{n} S_{ij}^t \left\| \frac{W_i^c}{\sqrt{d_i}} - \frac{W_j^c}{\sqrt{d_j}} \right\|_2^2 = \mathrm{tr}\left(W L^t W^\top\right) = \mathrm{tr}\, L^t\left(W^\top W\right). \quad (3)$$

In the above, unlike the row-pivot view where the similarity induced by W in visual space is computed by $W W^\top$, the similarity in concept space is computed by $W^\top W$ under the column-pivot view.

Combining the above two-view formulations, we are ready to expose the objective function to address the first motivation, i.e., we should minimize the overall distortion between W and the two-view data:

$$\min_{W \in \mathbb{R}_+^{n \times m}} \lambda_x \, \mathrm{tr}\, L^x\left(W W^\top\right) + \lambda_t \, \mathrm{tr}\, L^t\left(W^\top W\right) \quad : \quad W_{ij} \geq 0, \quad (4)$$

where λ_x and λ_t controls the trade-off between visual information and concept information.

For the second motivation, we bound the difference between W and some initial relevance score T. Here we employ the Frobenius norm:

$$\min_{W \in \mathbb{R}_+^{n \times m}} \|W - T\|_F^2 \quad : \quad W_{ij} \geq 0, W_{ij} = 0, \forall (i, j) \notin \mathscr{M}, \quad (5)$$

where T is the initial weight matrix determined by users or some other ranking model, $\mathscr{M}$ denotes the indices of non-zeros in T, i.e., $M := \{(i, j) | T_{ij} \neq 0, i \in \mathbb{N}_n, m \in \mathbb{N}_m\}$.

Therefore, we obtain the following optimization by combining (4) and (5):

$$\min_{W} \quad \lambda_x \operatorname{tr} L^x (W W^\top) + \lambda_t \operatorname{tr} L^t (W^\top W) + \|W - T\|_F^2 \tag{6}$$

$$\text{s.t.} \quad W \in \mathbb{R}_+^{n \times m}, \quad W_{ij} \geq 0, \forall i \in \mathbb{N}_n, j \in \mathbb{N}_m,$$

$$W_{ij} = 0, \quad \forall (i, j) \notin \mathcal{M}.$$

So far we have the unified two-view framework. It is similar to two-view learning algorithms (see [5]) in the sense that the learning in the two views regularize each other such that the resultant solution is more robust. Comparing with previous work (for example, [14, 23]) on tag ranking/refinement, it does not involve any probabilistic models. Probably it has more flexibility to fit the diverse data and avoids the difficulty in model selection.

3.4 Algorithm

There is no off-the-shelf optimization tools to solve (6) directly. Inspired by the ideas of sequential minimization [30], we propose to resolve (6) by an iterative projection algorithm, which is a variant of stochastic coordinate descent optimization [20].

In particular, in each optimization step, we randomly choose one row W_i to optimize and fix the rest $n - 1$ rows. Consequently, the objective is simplified to be:

$$\min_{W_i} \quad W_i \big(\lambda_t L^t + (\lambda_x L_{ii}^x + 1) I \big) W_i^\top + 2 \lambda_x \sum_{j=1, j \neq i}^{m} L_{ij}^x W_j W_i^\top - 2 T_i W_i^\top, \tag{7}$$

where the constraints are omitted in the above formulation. This is a standard quadratic program [2] over vector W_i, which can be solved by the interior-point algorithm with typical polynomial time complexity of $O(m^3)$. Fortunately, we can derive the closed-form solution of (7) by dropping the constraints. Let J abbreviate the objective function (7), by taking its derivatives w.r.t. W_i, we have

$$\nabla J = W_i \big(\lambda_t L^t + (\lambda_x L_{ii}^x + 1) I \big) + \lambda_x \sum_{j=1, j \neq i}^{n} L_{ij}^x W_j^\top - T_i.$$

Setting ∇J to 0 yields the following:

$$W_i = \left(T_i - \lambda_x \sum_{j=1, j \neq i}^{n} L_{ij}^x W_j^\top \right) \big(\lambda_t L^t + (\lambda_x L_{ii}^x + 1) I \big)^{-1}, \tag{8}$$

which is the optimal solution of current W_i. Therefore we are making progress towards a local optimal objective value at each iteration step.

Despite the nice closed-form solution above, in practice, it remain challenging to directly compute the matrix inverse, which often has the time complexity of $O(m^3)$ for a dense matrix. This is because the size of tag vocabulary could be potentially very large in a real application; as a result, the computation of matrix inverse is prohibitive for large-scale applications. To overcome this obstacle, we use the Taylor approximation for the matrix inverse problem $(I + A)^{-1}$:

$$(I + A)^{-1} = I + \sum_{i=1}^{\infty} (-1)^i A^i.$$

As a result, we arrive at the approximate solution:

$$\left(\lambda_t L^t + (\lambda_x L_{ii}^x + 1)I\right)^{-1} \approx \frac{1}{\lambda_x L_{ii}^x + 1}\left(I + \sum_{j=1}^{p}(-1)^j\left(\frac{\lambda_t}{\lambda_x L_{ii}^x + 1}L^t\right)^j\right),$$

where p is the order of approximation. In practice, we can pre-compute the power of L^t and cache it for improving the time efficiency.

The solution (8) may violate the constraints over W. We project the solution into the feasible domain at each step:

$$W_{ij} = 0 \quad \text{if } W_{ij} < 0 \text{ or } (i, j) \notin \mathcal{M}.$$

It implies we only need to consider the nonzero indices of W. Since each image is annotated by a very limited number of tags on average, W is essentially very sparse. Therefore the computation in (8) could be very efficient. Finally, we summarize the iterative projection solution in Algorithm 1.

Once the optimal tag weighting matrix W is obtained by the proposed algorithm, we rank the tags for an image x_i according to their relevance scores W_i's. For any two tags t_{ij} and t_{ik}, tag t_{ij} ranks on top of tag t_{ik} i.f.f $W_{ij} \geq W_{ik}$.

Algorithm 1: The Two-View Tag Weighing Algorithm

Input: Social image corpus Z;
kernel function $k_x : \mathcal{X} \times \mathcal{X} \to \mathbb{R}_+$ and $k_t : \mathcal{T} \times \mathcal{T} \to \mathbb{R}_+$;
parameters λ_x, λ_t, p;
Output: Weighting matrix W.

1: Cluster the images into k groups;
2: **for** each group **do**
3:     Construct graph Laplacian L_t and L_x using k_t and k_x, respectively;
4:     Initialize $W^0 = T$
5:     **repeat**
6:         Randomly choose a row index i to update
7:         Compute $U^j = (\frac{\lambda_t}{\lambda_x L_{ii}^x + 1}L^t)^j$
8:         $W_i = (T_i - \lambda_x \sum_{j=1, j\neq i}^{n} L_{ij}^x W_j^\top)(I + \sum_{j=1}^{p}(-1)^j U^j)/(\lambda_x L_{ii}^x + 1)$
9:     **until** convergence criterion satisfied
10: **end for**
11: Tile the W in all groups to obtain W;

3.5 Similarity Measure for Building Graphs

The graph Laplacian L^x and L^t encode the local geometric information in visual space and concept space, respectively. It is our prior knowledge about the data distribution. With a proper similarity matrix S, the graph Laplacian can be computed immediately from (2). Therefore we just focus on S^x and S^t.

3.5.1 Similarity in Visual Space

Let $[S^x]_{ij} := k_x(x_i, x_j)$ be the similarity matrix of images computed from some function $k_x : \mathscr{X} \times \mathscr{X} \to \mathbb{R}_+$. Depending on the features employed to represent a feature, one can adopt different kinds of similarity functions to define k_x. How to extract features for representing an image remains a very challenging problem itself. We will discuss our approach in the experimental section. Here we discuss how to compute the similarity between two images for two major types of features: global and local features.

For global features, a typical approach for similarity measure is based on a Gaussian kernel:

$$k_x^g(x_i, x_j) = \exp\left(-\frac{\|x_i - x_j\|^2}{\sigma^2}\right). \tag{9}$$

In this case the visual space $\mathscr{X}$ can be deemed as a subset of $\mathbb{R}^d$, where d is the number of extracted features. We present a set of global features in Sect. 4.

For local features (such as SIFT [16]), each image is represented by a bag of descriptors. To measure similarity between two images given the two bags of descriptors, we employ a simple yet effective matching kernel [21]:

$$k_x^l(x_i, x_j) = \frac{1}{2}\left(\hat{k}(x_i, x_j) + \hat{k}(x_j, x_i)\right), \tag{10}$$

where $\hat{k}(x_i, x_j)$ is defined as

$$\hat{k}(x_i, x_j) = \frac{1}{|x_i|} \sum_{s=1}^{|x_i|} \max_t \tilde{k}(d_{i,s}, d_{j,t}), \tag{11}$$

where $\tilde{k}(d_{i,s}, d_{j,t})$ measures similarity between two descriptors. Finally, we combine both the global and the local similarity functions for computing similarity in visual space.

3.5.2 Similarity in Concept Space

Given a collection of social images, we can mine the relationship among tags by carefully studying the related statistics. For example, if two tags appear together frequently, the distance between them should be reasonably small. Here we adopt the Google distance [3]:

$$d(t_i, t_j) = \frac{\max(\log f(t_i), \log f(t_j)) - \log f(t_i, t_j)}{\log n - \min(\log f(t_i), \log f(t_j))},$$

where $f(t_i)$ is the number of images containing tag t_i, $f(t_i, t_j)$ is the number of images containing both t_i and t_j.

Our target is the similarity matrix S^t. With the Google distance function, we compute the similarity among tags by

$$k_t(t_i, t_j) = \exp(-d(t_i, t_j)). \tag{12}$$

For more other methods to explore the correlation among tags, please refer to [10] for more examples.

3.6 Speedup by Clustering

The updating of W is benefited from the sparseness of the annotated tags. However, in real application, the corpus size n and the vocabulary size m could be very large, which makes the algorithm slow. We stress the fact that social images form meaningful groups. Images from different groups share little similarity. Thus we can employ some clustering algorithm to separate the images into g visual groups. The inter-group similarity is simply set to zero.

In order to upper bound the size of each cluster effectively, we employ a bisecting clustering algorithm [31]. At each iteration, the largest group is chosen to split. The clustering objective function is to maximize the overall inner-cluster similarity [31], i.e.,

$$I_2 = \sum_{k=1}^{g} \sum_{x_i \in S_k} \cos(x_i, C_k),$$

where g is the target number of groups, S_k is the kth group, and C_k is the centroid of S_k. By this strategy, the size of the Laplacian L^x reduces from n to a small number, and thus the overall computational cost can be reduced.

4 Experiments

We conduct an extensive set of experiments to verify our tag-ranking algorithm, and apply our technique to two important applications: text-based social image retrieval and automatic tag recommendation.

4.1 Experimental Testbed and Setup

We crawled a data set consisting of about 1,000,000 social images from Flickr.[2]
To evaluate the proposed algorithm, we form the evaluation testbed by choosing
a number of query images that are related to a wide range of tags, including ani-
mals, plants, humans, landmarks, natural sceneries, and some daily objects. Some
examples are shown in Fig. 3.

For feature representation, we extract four kinds of effective global features
by [33]. These features include: (1) 81-dimensional grid color moment features,
(2) 59-dimensional Local Binary Pattern (LBP) texture features [18], (3) 120-
dimensional Gabor wavelets texture features [11], and (4) 37-dimensional edge direction histogram features. In total, a 297-dimensional vector is used to represent an
image in the data sets. The similarity of global features in visual space in computed
by the Gaussian kernel in Eq. (9). For local features, we employ SIFT feature descriptors [16] to extract local features and employ the kernel function in Eq. (10) to
define the similarity of local features in visual space. A simple linear combination
is adopted to combine the similarity of both global and local features.

For the preprocess on tags, we first filter out the extremely unpopular tags. Then
we adopt the Gaussian with Google distance to calculus the similarity in concept
space (12).

For experimental setting, there are several hyper-parameters used in our two-view
tag-ranking algorithm. For most of our results, these parameters are set below:

- σ: the band-width parameter of Gaussian kernel. We set it to be the average square
  Euclidean distance among all the images;
- λ_x and λ_t: the trade-off parameters in (6). We set $\lambda_x = 0.5$ and $\lambda_t = 1.0$ empirically;
- g: the number of groups in the clustering process. We set it to 120. We employ
  the *CLUTO* toolkit[3] to help to do clustering.
- p: the approximation order when computing the matrix inverse. We use $p = 5$.
- T: the initial tag weight matrix. For an image x_i, we set its tags the uniform
  weight $1/|t_i|$, where $|t_i|$ is the number of tags annotated to x_i.

4.2 Performance Evaluation on Tag-based Social Image Retrieval

We focus on the *query-by-text* setting. We assume that ground-truth rankings have
two grades, *relevant* and *irrelevant*. In order to make the results reliable, we selected
20 queries and requested six staff to label the images by examining if the contents
of the images are relevant to the queries, which sometimes may be subjective for
different persons. In our study, we considered those queries that are popular and
diverse. The complete list of the engaged queries are shown in Table 1.

---

[2]http://www.flickr.com/.

[3]http://glaros.dtc.umn.edu/gkhome/views/cluto/.

Fig. 3 Illustration of sample figures related to the queries in our experiments

Table 1 The statistics of the queries in the data set

TestQuery	Eiffel tower	Barack Obama	great wall	Big Ben	red car	pyramid	airplane	Ferrari	lily	bicycle
#RelDoc	919	88	57	200	477	229	771	401	452	1475
TestQuery	banana	fruit orange	sunflower	strawberry	singing	panda	lion	sheep	eagle	elephant
#RelDoc	124	266	798	715	945	1512	1308	487	664	739

4.2.1 Ranking Schemes and Evaluation Metric

For an input query q, we only consider the social images containing q as candidate relevant images. For an image x_i, let π_i denote the position of q in the ranked tag list of x_i. We define the relevance score in the way of [14]:

$$r(x_i) = -\pi_i + \frac{1}{n_i}. \tag{13}$$

Note two key properties of this scheme: (1) if $\pi_i < \pi_j$, we always have $r(x_i) > r(x_j)$, which means we assign higher relevance score to the image containing the query tag at more advanced positions in its ranked tag list; (2) if $\pi_i = \pi_j$, the image having fewer tags is assigned larger relevance score. The motivation is that the more tags an image possesses, the more noisy of its visual content.

To our knowledge, [14] is the first and only paper aiming to attack the tag-ranking problem. However, we are aware that some existing image annotation or annotation refinement works can be easily adapted to generate a permutation over the tags. For example, CMRM [9], WNM [10], RWRM [22] and CIAR [23]. One can always rank the tags according to their relevance score to the image. Since it has been shown that CIAR outperforms the other annotation methods, we evaluate it specifically for comparison purpose. To summarize, we evaluate the following tag-ranking schemes:

- **Baseline**: the original order of the tags is maintained, i.e., the tag position is determined by some web users;
- **CIAR**: adaption of the Content-Based image Annotation Refinement algorithm in [23]. They estimate the condition probability $p(t_j|x_i)$ of generating tag t_j by image x_i by Gaussian kernel density. We use this score to rank tags;
- **GM-RW**: the method proposed by [14]. The tag-ranking score is first computed by a Generative Model $p(x_i|t_j)$ and then perform Random Walk over a similarity graph on tags to refine the score;
- **KNN**: the method proposed by [12]. The tag-ranking score is the total number of votes received from its visual nearest neighbors. It is shown in [12] that this voting method could be better than model-based methods in [23];
- **TW-TV**: the proposed two-view Tag Weighing method that combines the local information both in Tag space and in Visual space. The objection function is (6). All the hyper-parameters are described in Sect. 4.1. The solution is obtained from Algorithm 1;
- **TW-V**: the proposed two-view Tag Weighing method in Visual space, that is, $\lambda_t = 0$ in objective (6);
- **TW-T**: the proposed model-free Tag Weighting method in Tag space, that is, $\lambda_x = 0$ in objective (6).

To evaluate the performance, we use the standard *mean average precision* (MAP) measure [1]: Let π^* be the ground-truth ranking and π be the ranking result by some relevance score r, the average precision score is defined as

$$MAP(\pi^*, \pi) = \frac{1}{rel} \sum_{j:\pi_j^*=1} Prec@j,$$

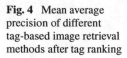
Fig. 4 Mean average precision of different tag-based image retrieval methods after tag ranking

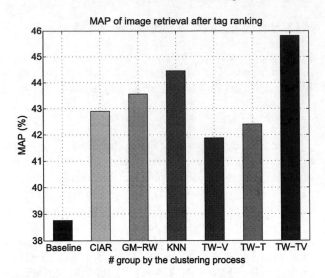

where $rel = |\{i : \pi_i^* = 1\}|$ is the number of relevant documents, and $Prec@j$ is the percentage of relevant documents in the top j documents n predicted ranking r. MAP is the mean of the average precision scores of a group of queries.

4.2.2 Results of Image Retrieval Accuracy

The MAP measure results were shown in Fig. 4. We can draw some observations from the results.

First we observe that all the tag-ranking methods outperform the baseline method significantly. This verifies the necessity of tag ranking. It also coincides with the statements of [14] that the relevant tags may not be ranked at the top positions. Thus the ranking score computed by (13) cannot reflect the relevance of the image to the query tag effectively.

Second, we observe that our two-view tag-ranking scheme works well. It produces very competitive results with CIAR, GM-RW, and KNN (actually TW-TV is the best on our data set). Both CIAR and GM-RW involves generative models and performs a random walk over the similarity graph S^t over tags. We observe that GM-RW is better than CIAR. GM-RW makes use of both exempler-based visual information and statistical information of tags when constructing S^t, while CIAR only uses visual information. This probably explains the advantage of GM-RW. However, a simple k nearest neighbor voting method outperforms model-based CIAR and GM-RW. This implies that when large amount of data is accessible, we should pay more effort to data-driven approaches. The best algorithm TW-TV in Fig. 4 is a model-free learning scheme. Without assume any parametric model between visual and tag spaces, it has more flexibility to fit the diverse data, which is our motivation of the two-view learning algorithm. We also stress that both TW-TV and GM-RW explores the same source of information. However, our method is conceptually simple and purely data-driven. It has fewer hyper-parameters and can be easily applied on a large scale. We show this computation merit of TW-TV in next section.

At last, the combination of two view is better than using single view. The membership between images and tags connects the visual view to concept view. The learning in each view regularizes each other such that the resultant solution is more robust. The essential complementary property of visual and tag space makes TW-TV more effective than the other data-driven method KNN.

Finally, Fig. 5 shows some examples to examine the qualitative performance of the retrieval results achieved by different methods.

4.3 Evaluation of Computation Efficiency

In this section, we examine the time complexity of the TW-TV and GM-RW tag-ranking methods over a randomly chosen subset consisting of 10,000 images. For both methods, we pre-compute the similarity matrix in visual space. The tag similarity based on Google distance is also pre-computed and is excluded from the running time reported here. For the proposed TW-TV method, we cluster the images into groups such that the resultant maximal group has no more than 2,000 images. Our goal is to test the time complexity with the increment of image number n.

We plot the CPU time in Fig. 6. We observe that GM-RW is significantly slower than TW-TV for all n values. When $n = 10,000$, GM-RW cost about 20 minutes, while TW-TV takes only about 3 minutes. More importantly, the curve of GM-RW shows that it has polynomial empirical complexity on n. On the other hand, TW-TV exhibits linear asymptotic time cost. To measure this quantitatively, we fit the curves in Fig. 6 by least squares. The empirical complexity of TW-TV and GM-RW are $O(n^{0.48})$ and $O(n^{0.63})$, respectively. This efficiency gain is crucial for real systems dealing with a large-scale data set.

The linear time complexity of TW-TV can be interpreted by the clustering process in Sect. 3.6. By dividing the data into small groups, n drops to the size of some single cluster, which is a much smaller value. Therefore, the overall time cost is linear on the number of clusters, even though the total number of images could be large.

4.4 Evaluation of Hyper-parameters

The proposed TW-TV tag-ranking algorithm has a few free parameters. The most important ones may be λ_x and λ_t, which control the trade-off between the importance of visual information and tag statistics. Note that we deem all the annotated tags have identical prior weight for any image. Thus T would not affect the tag

Fig. 5 The top 5 tag-base retrieval results on the query Eiffel tower after different tag-ranking algorithms. One can see that the result of TW-TV is visually more pure

weighing result. If we scale λ_x and λ_t by the same value, the final weight W remains the same. Only the ratio $\frac{\lambda_x}{\lambda_t}$ affects the performance. So we restrict λ to the range [0, 1]. The MAP results are plotted in Fig. 7.

First of all, we see that the retrieval performance is not sensitive to λ in the range [0.4, 0.8]. The fluctuation of MAP is bounded by 2 percent. Moreover, the MAP measure varies smoothly with λ. This shows the robustness of our method, which is

Fig. 6 Time cost of TW-TV
and GM-RW tag-ranking
algorithms with the number
of social images. The results
are averaged over 10 times
run

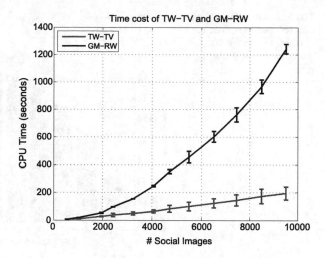

Fig. 7 MAP of tag-based
image retrieval after TW-TV
with different
hyper-parameter λ_x and λ_t.
T is set to be uniform value
for each image. Only the ratio
λ_x/λ_t affects the performance

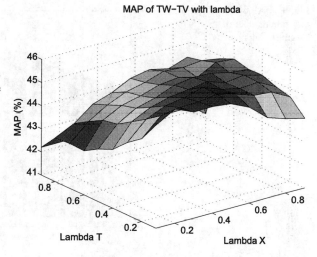

probably induced by the complementary information in both spaces. At the center of
the surface, TW-TV produces the best MAP. This is somewhat surprising because
empirically visual information is more important. For example, Liu et al. [14] set
the ratio of visual and tag importance as 4:1. We conjecture that maybe this is resulted by the image representations. We extract different visual features with [14]. It
also suggests that there are potentials to improve the performance of TW-TV. When
λ_x/λ_t is skew, that is, the left-most and the right-most square of the surface, the
performance is poor. It means that single view cannot result in satisfactory solution.

The success of TW-TV relies on the local geometric information of image and
tag similarity graphs. We take the following three steps to build the Laplacian in
visual space: for each image, (1) using global and local features to locate the k
nearest neighbors; (2) in the similarity graph, set the value at these k-NN indices
to 1, otherwise 0; (3) compute the normalized Laplacian by (2). The similarity in tag

Fig. 8 MAP of TW-TV with
different number of nearest
neighbors when building
graph Laplacian in visual
space

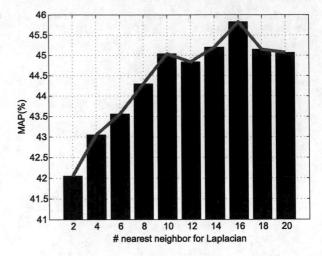

Fig. 9 MAP of TW-TV with
different number of groups in
the clustering process

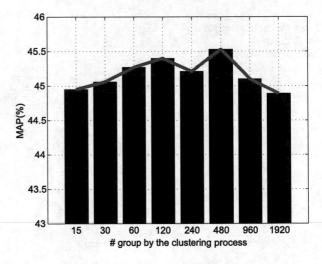

space is constructed using Google distance. We present the influence of the value k in Fig. 8.

We observe that the MAP increases with k when k is small. When k is larger than 10, the increment in MAP is marginal. The most possible reason is that the local geometry is already preserved for reasonably large k. Moreover, we see when $k = 20$, the performance actually starts to drop. In this case, the images that do not share much similarity is considered as neighbors. Therefore, such images are essentially noise and misleads the learning. The MAP measure is not too sensitive to k.

The clustering process plays an important role to make the whole weighting method practical. We evaluate the MAP with different group number g in Fig. 9.

From Eq. (8), we see the quadratic complexity over n. Therefore, for a fixed image corpus, the more groups we have, the faster of TW-TV. On the other hand,

Annotated Tags:	Annotated Tags:	Annotated Tags:	Annotated Tags:	Annotated Tags:
lion animal zoo	bird sky blue eagle	flower plant lily	sunset yellow	flower sunflower
bigcat Nikon wild	sea tree tree	botanic garden	orange car sunrise	yellow color sun
wildlife tree		nature	supercar white	summer tree

Fig. 10 An illustration of image annotation results with the TW-TV tag-ranking scheme

inter-group similarity is ignored in our algorithm. Therefore we should be aware of the granularity of the groups. If g is too small, we could loss the local similarity information. The above figure shows the trend of MAP with the number of groups g. It is shown that MAP is not sensitive to g. For g range from 15 to 2000, the MAP value fluctuates within 1 percent. Thus we conclude that the clustering process is reasonable and effective for TW-TV. When g is greater than 480, MAP starts to drop. This verifies our conjecture about the granularity of the clustering.

4.5 Application to Auto Tag Recommendation

After we have the tag-ranking results, we can use the images with properly ordered tags to annotate a given image automatically. We need not require users to provide any initial candidate tags. We implement this by a simple nearest neighbor voting method, first proposed in [14]. For an input image, we first locate its k nearest neighbors in the corpus. Then we extract the top h tags of each of these neighbors. So have a collection of size $k \times h$. Then we remove the redundant ones in this collection and recommend the resulting tag set to the image. For each tag in this collection, we can indicate its weight by this redundancy number. Accordingly we obtain a rank of the annotated tags.

Figure 10 shows some examples by applying the proposed TW-TV tag-ranking method. It is clear to observe that most of the top ranked tags are quite relevant to the semantic concepts of the query images.

We use the precision of the top l annotated tags to measure the performance. We evaluate CIAR, GM-RW, and TW-TV for annotation in this section.

We randomly choose 1,000 images from our data set to annotate. We employ several staff to label the annotated tags as "relevant" or "irrelevant". We use precision as the performance evaluation measure. Figure 11 shows the evaluation results. One can see that all the tag-ranking algorithms outperform baseline in all three cases. The proposed TW-TV algorithm produces the best precision. For the top 1 annotated tag, TW-TV outperforms CIAR and GM-RW by more than 5 percent in precision. However, for top 5, the precision gain of TW-TV becomes limited. Another interesting observation is that CIAR can be better than GM-RW in our data set.

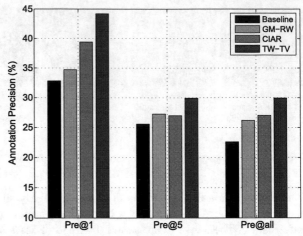

Fig. 11 Annotation precision of TW-TV, CIAR and GM-RW at the top l position. We set $k = 5$, $m = h$

5 Limitations and Discussions

Despite the encouraging results achieved above, there are still several limitations for our study in this book chapter. First of all, we only exploit textual tags and visual contents of social images for ranking the tags of social images. However, for real-world social images, there often exists other user-generated contents, such as descriptions, user info, rating, and geo-tags, etc. In future work, we plan to extend our method by adding the extra information, which could further improve the performance of the tag-ranking scheme. Moreover, in the proposed scheme, we apply a simple clustering processing step to speed up the solution in order to handle large data, which may lose some information in some situations. In future work, we plan to investigate more sophisticated techniques to improve both the efficiency and efficacy of our method.

6 Conclusions

In this book chapter, we proposed a novel two-view learning approach to address the tag-ranking problem in this paper. Our method does not assume any parametric model on the relevance between images and tags. It is purely data-driven, which distinguishes it from previous generative model-based works on this topic. It thus enjoys better flexibility to fit diverse patterns in real-world image data. The key idea of our technique was inspired by a two-view learning methodology. In particular, when the representation of data has two complementary views, we can make use of the information of each to regularize the other such that the resultant solution is more robust. We also devised an efficient algorithm and practical strategies to speed up the learning process. Empirical results on a real data set validated both the efficacy and efficiency of our methods. Future work will extend our method to exploit other rich contents of social images for tag ranking.

References

1. Baeza-Yates, R.A., Ribeiro-Neto, B.A.: Modern Information Retrieval. ACM Press/Addison-Wesley, New York (1999)
2. Boyd, S., Vandenberghe, L.: Convex Optimization. Cambridge University Press, Cambridge (2004)
3. Cilibrasi, R., Vitányi, P.M.B.: The google similarity distance. IEEE Trans. Knowl. Data Eng. **19**(3), 370–383 (2007)
4. Datta, R., Ge, W., Li, J., Wang, J.Z.: Toward bridging the annotation-retrieval gap in image search by a generative modeling approach. In: ACM Multimedia, pp. 977–986 (2006)
5. Farquhar, J.D.R., Hardoon, D.R., Meng, H., Shawe-Taylor, J., Szedmák, S.: Two view learning: Svm-2k, theory and practice. In: NIPS, 2005
6. Golder, S.A., Huberman, B.A.: The structure of collaborative tagging systems. J. Inf. Sci. **32**, 198–208 (2005)
7. Hoi, S.C., Lyu, M.R.: Web image learning for searching semantic concepts in image databases. In: Proceedings of the 13th International World Wide Web Conference (WWW2004), New York City, US, May 17–22 2004
8. Hoi, S.C.H., Jin, R., Lyu, M.R.: Learning nonparametric kernel matrices from pairwise constraints. In: Proceedings of the 24th International Conference on Machine Learning. ICML'07, Corvalis, Oregon, pp. 361–368. ACM, New York (2007)
9. Jeon, J., Lavrenko, V., Manmatha, R.: Automatic image annotation and retrieval using cross-media relevance models. In: Proceedings of ACM Special Interest Group on Information Retrieval, pp. 119–126 (2003)
10. Jin, Y., Khan, L., Wang, L., Awad, M.: Image annotations by combining multiple evidence & wordnet. In: ACM Multimedia, pp. 706–715 (2005)
11. Lades, M., Vorbrüggen, J.C., Buhmann, J.M., Lange, J., von der Malsburg, C., Würtz, R.P., Konen, W.: Distortion invariant object recognition in the dynamic link architecture. IEEE Trans. Comput. **42**(3), 300–311 (1993)
12. Li, X., Snoek, C.G.M., Worring, M.: Learning tag relevance by neighbor voting for social image retrieval. In: Multimedia Information Retrieval, pp. 180–187 (2008)
13. Liu, D., Wang, M., Yang, L., Xua, X.-S., Zhang, H.J.: Tag quality improvement for social images. In: Multimedia and Expo, pp. 350–353 (2009)
14. Liu, D., Hua, X.-S., Yang, L., Wang, M., Zhang, H.-J.: Tag ranking. In: WWW, pp. 351–360 (2009)
15. Liu, X., Ji, R., Yao, H., Xu, P., Sun, X., Liu, T.: Cross-media manifold learning for image retrieval & annotation. In: Multimedia Information Retrieval, pp. 141–148 (2008)
16. Lowe, D.G.: Distinctive image features from scale-invariant keypoints. Int. J. Comput. Vis. **60**(2), 91–110 (2004)
17. Marlow, C., Naaman, M., Boyd, D., Davis, M.: Ht06, tagging paper, taxonomy, flickr, academic article, to read. In: HYPERTEXT '06: Proceedings of the Seventeenth Conference on Hypertext and Hypermedia, pp. 31–40 (2006)
18. Ojala, T., Pietikäinen, M., Harwood, D.: A comparative study of texture measures with classification based on featured distributions. Pattern Recognit. **29**(1), 51–59 (1996)
19. Sigurbjörnsson, B., van Zwol, R.: Flickr tag recommendation based on collective knowledge. In: WWW, pp. 327–336 (2008)
20. Spall, J.C.: Introduction to Stochastic Search and Optimization. Wiley, New York (2003)
21. Wallraven, C., Caputo, B., Graf, A.: Recognition with local features: the kernel recipe. In: ICCV '03: Proceedings of the Ninth IEEE International Conference on Computer Vision, p. 257. IEEE Computer Society, Washington (2003)
22. Wang, C., Jing, F., Zhang, L., Zhang, H.: Image annotation refinement using random walk with restarts. In: ACM Multimedia, pp. 647–650 (2006)
23. Wang, C., Jing, F., Zhang, L., Zhang, H.-J.: Content-based image annotation refinement. In: CVPR, 2007

24. Wang, C., Zhang, L., Zhang, H.-J.: Learning to reduce the semantic gap in web image retrieval and annotation. In: Proceedings of ACM Special Interest Group on Information Retrieval, pp. 355–362 (2008)
25. Weinberger, K.Q., Slaney, M., van Zwol, R.: Resolving tag ambiguity. In: ACM Multimedia, pp. 111–120 (2008)
26. Wu, L., Hoi, S.C., Zhu, J., Jin, R., Yu, N.: Distance metric learning from uncertain side information with application to automated photo tagging. In: Proceedings of ACM International Conference on Multimedia (MM2009), Beijing, China, Oct. 19–24 2009
27. Wu, L., Hoi, S.C., Zhu, J., Jin, R., Yu, N.: Distance metric learning from uncertain side information for automated photo tagging. ACM Trans. Intell. Syst. Technol. 2(2), 13:1–13:28 (2011)
28. Wu, L., Yang, L., Yu, N., Hua, X.-S.: Learning to tag. In: WWW, pp. 361–370 (2009)
29. Wu, P., Hoi, S.C., Zhao, P., He, Y.: Mining social images with distance metric learning for automated image tagging. In: Fourth ACM International Conference on Web Search and Data Mining (WSDM2011), Hong Kong, 2011
30. Zhang, T.: Sequential greedy approximation for certain convex optimization problems. IEEE Trans. Inf. Theory 49(3), 682–691 (2003)
31. Zhao, Y., Karypis, G.: Empirical and theoretical comparisons of selected criterion functions for document clustering. Mach. Learn. 55(3), 311–331 (2004)
32. Zhu, J., Hoi, S.C., Lyu, M.R.: Face annotation by transductive kernel fisher discriminant. IEEE Trans. Multimed. 10(01), 86–96 (2008)
33. Zhu, J., Hoi, S.C.H., Lyu, M.R., Yan, S.: Near-duplicate keyframe retrieval by nonrigid image matching. In: ACM Multimedia, pp. 41–50 (2008)
34. Zhuang, J., Hoi, S.C.: Non-parametric kernel ranking approach for social image retrieval. In: ACM International Conference on Image and Video Retrieval (CIVR2010), Xian, PR China, 2010
35. Zhuang, J., Hoi, S.C.: A two-view learning approach for image tag ranking. In: Fourth ACM International Conference on Web Search and Data Mining (WSDM2011), Hong Kong, 2011

Combining Multi-modal Features for Social Media Analysis

Spiros Nikolopoulos, Eirini Giannakidou, Ioannis Kompatsiaris,
Ioannis Patras, and Athena Vakali

Abstract In this chapter we discuss methods for efficiently modeling the diverse information carried by social media. The problem is viewed as a multi-modal analysis process where specialized techniques are used to overcome the obstacles arising from the heterogeneity of data. Focusing at the optimal combination of low-level features (i.e., early fusion), we present a bio-inspired algorithm for feature selection that weights the features based on their appropriateness to represent a resource. Under the same objective of optimal feature combination we also examine the use of pLSA-based aspect models, as the means to define a latent semantic space where heterogeneous types of information can be effectively combined. Tagged images taken from social sites have been used in the characteristic scenarios of image clustering and retrieval, to demonstrate the benefits of multi-modal analysis in social media.

S. Nikolopoulos (✉) · E. Giannakidou · I. Kompatsiaris
Informatics & Telematics Institute, Thermi, Thessaloniki, Greece
e-mail: nikolopo@iti.gr

E. Giannakidou
e-mail: igiannak@iti.gr

I. Kompatsiaris
e-mail: ikom@iti.gr

S. Nikolopoulos · I. Patras
School of Electronic Engineering and Computer Science, Queen Mary University of London,
E1 4NS, London, UK

I. Patras
e-mail: i.patras@eecs.qmul.ac.uk

E. Giannakidou · A. Vakali
Department of Computer Science, Aristotle University of Thessaloniki, Thessaloniki, Greece

A. Vakali
e-mail: avakali@csd.auth.gr

S.C.H. Hoi et al. (eds.), *Social Media Modeling and Computing*,
DOI 10.1007/978-0-85729-436-4_4, © Springer-Verlag London Limited 2011

1 Introduction

Content sharing through the Internet has become a common practice for the vast majority of web users. Due to the rapidly growing new communication technologies, a large number of people all over the planet can now share, tag, like or suggest a tremendous volume of multimedia content, which we generally refer to as social media. One of the most outstanding features for social media is their intrinsic multi-modal nature that opens-up new opportunities for content analysis and consumption. The goal of this chapter is to discuss the use of multi-modal approaches for social media analysis and demonstrate their effectiveness in certain application scenarios.

1.1 Social Media

The recent advances of Web technologies have effectively turned ordinary people into active members of the Web. Web users act as co-developers and their actions and collaborations with one another have added a new social dimension on Web data. Social media are commonly described by a high diversity of features. For instance, an image in Flickr is associated with the tags that have been assigned to it, the users that seem to like it and mark it as favorite, the visual features that describe the visual content of the image, and possibly spatial or temporal information that denote the spatial and temporal context of this particular image. Even though all these facets of information are not combined naturally with each other, still they carry knowledge about the resource, with each facet providing a representation of the particular resource in a different feature space.

This information provides added value to the shared content and enables the accomplishment of tasks that are not possible otherwise. Exploiting the information carried by social media can help tackle a variety of issues in different disciplines, such as content consumption (e.g., poor recall and precision), knowledge management (e.g., obsolescence, expertise), etc. However, the exploitation of such information is a big departure from traditional methods for multimedia analysis, since managing the diversity of features poses new requirements. For example, semantic analysis has to fuse information coming both from the content itself, the social context and the emergent social dynamics. Moreover, the unconstrained nature of content uploading and sharing has resulted in large amounts of spammy and noisy content and metadata, thus considerably compromising the quality of data to be analyzed. All these have motivated an increasing interest on investigating methods that will be able to exploit the intrinsic multi-modality of social media.

1.2 Multi-modal Analysis

Semantic multimedia indexing has been recognized as a particularly valuable task for various applications of content consumption. Current literature has made considerable progress in this direction especially for uni-modal scenarios. However, it is generally accepted that multi-modal analysis has the potential to further improve this process, provided that the obstacles arising from the heterogeneous nature of different modalities can be overcome. This is based on the fact that independently of whether these pieces of information act cumulatively or complementary, when combined; they encompass a higher amount of features that can be exploited to improve the efficiency of the performed task. Depending on the level of abstraction where the combination of different modalities takes place, we can distinguish between the result-level (or late fusion) and the feature-level (or early fusion) approaches. In the result-level approaches, features from each data source are initially extracted separately and, still separately, transformed into conceptual information to be utilized by the fusion process. In the feature-level approaches, features are extracted separately from each modality but they are integrated into a jointed, unique representation, before the employed approach transform them into conceptual information and deliver them to the fusion process. In this chapter we discuss methods that belong to the feature level of abstraction.

In feature-level approaches the need to obtain a jointed, unique representation for the multimedia object demands for techniques that will manage to handle the very different characteristics exhibited by the different types of data. This is true both in terms of the nature of raw features (e.g., sparse, high-dimensional word co-occurrence vectors extracted from text descriptions, compared to usually dense and low-dimensional descriptors extracted from visual content), as well as in terms of their semantic capacity (e.g., while abstract concepts like "freedom" are more easily described with text, concrete concepts like "sun" are more easily grounded using visual information). Based on the above one can pursue a solution to the multi-modal analysis problem by following two different approaches that, although similar in scope, differ in the way of handling the features. The first case, usually referred by the name "feature selection", aims at assigning appropriate weights to the features of the initial space. To do so, the correlations among objects in each individual feature space are examined. Although the dimensionality of the resulting feature space is identical with the dimensionality of the initial feature space, the process results in groups of related multimedia objects which lie in sub-variations of the initial feature space. The second case, which may be named a "feature combination", aims at defining a new feature space where the projection of the initial features will yield an improved and homogeneous representation of the multimedia object. In this case the dimensionality of the resulting feature space is typically smaller than the dimensionality of the initial space. In this respect we can claim that "feature selection" approaches primarily target at exploiting the different levels of semantic capacity exhibited by the different feature spaces, while the "feature combination" approaches aim at removing the problems arising from the heterogeneity of data and benefit from their efficient combination.

1.3 Examined Approaches & Applications

In this chapter we discuss methods falling under both feature handling approaches and present in detail one indicative method for every case. In the first case, we examine an ant-inspired algorithm for feature selection which is based on Ant Colony Optimization (ACO) metaheuristic. This algorithm is used to perform clustering on tagged images and its goal is to define appropriate weights so that each feature space weight sufficiently captures the local correlation of the resources along the specific dimension. This is done by simulating the way the ant colony finds the shortest path for solving a clustering problem in multi-feature spaces. The algorithm was applied on a dataset of Flickr images in which two feature spaces are taken into consideration: (i) tag features, and (ii) visual features. Our experimental study has shown that the ant-based clustering algorithm performs better than a typical clustering algorithm that relies on predefined feature spaces.

For the case of feature combination we examine an algorithm based on aspect models. These models assume that the content depicted in an image can be expressed as a mixture of multiple latent topics, defining a new, "semantically enhanced" feature space. Thus, the meaningful combination of visual and tag information is performed by projecting the initial features to the space of latent topics. In addition, in order to further exploit the cross-modal relations existing between the tag and visual content referring to the same abstract meaning, we examine the employment of a hierarchical version of the aspect model. Our experiments on using this algorithm to retrieval relevant images on a dataset of Flickr images, have demonstrated the effectiveness of the aspect models to provide an appropriate space for the combination of heterogeneous features.

Both clustering and retrieval scenarios that have been used to demonstrate the effectiveness of the examines approaches are particularly important in the context of social media. Indeed, the multi-faceted organization of content as well as the ability to retrieve relevant resources, act as the basis for various social network related applications. For instance, tag recommendation for images and friend recommendation for users are applications that both need to consider the available content from many different aspects. Multi-modal analysis is ideal for this task, since different types of information can be combined and exploited. Additionally, many of the functionalities provided by social networks are essentially built on top of the outcome of a clustering or a relevance ranking task.

The remaining of this chapter is organized as follows. Section 2 reviews the related literature on multi-modal analysis. Section 3 provides a formulation for the feature selection problem and presents how an ant-inspired algorithm can be used to solve the formulated optimization task. Section 4 discusses the use of aspect models for achieving optimal feature combination and shows how the employment of a topic hierarchy manages to outperform all other combination schemes. Conclusions and avenues for future research are presented in Sect. 5.

2 Related Work

In this section we review related works from the field of multi-modal analysis and social media. Initially we present some methods that can be considered as typical examples of multi-modal analysis. Subsequently, we review the related literature of multi-modal analysis methods that have been mainly proposed to facilitate the analysis of social media. Finally, we refer to a set of works that emphasize on the range of social media applications that can benefit from multi-modal analysis.

2.1 Methods for Multi-modal Analysis

Under the general objective of optimally combining heterogeneous types of information, current literature proposes methods that tackle the problem by exploiting the statistical properties of the data. Different types of transformations have been proposed for determining a space where features extracted from heterogeneous sources can be optimally combined. The work presented by Mogalhães and Rüger [29] is an indicative example of this category where information theory and a maximum entropy model are utilized to integrate heterogeneous data into a unique feature space. The authors use a minimum description length criterion to find the optimal feature space for text and visual data. Then, both feature spaces are merged in order to obtain a unique continuous feature space. Evaluation is performed on a document retrieval scenario based on only text, only visual and combined data. In [40] Wu et al. work on the same direction by introducing a method that initially finds statistical independent modalities from raw features and subsequently applies super-kernel fusion to determine their optimal combination. More specifically, an independent modality analysis scheme is initially presented, which applies Independent Component Analysis (ICA) on the raw set of features. Then, the modalities are fused by employing a scheme that finds the best feature combination through supervised learning. In [25] Li et al. present several cross-modal association approaches under the linear correlation model: the latent semantic indexing (LSI), canonical correlation analysis (CCA) and Cross-modal Factor Analysis (CFA). They claim that the proposed CFA approach manages to identify and exploit the intrinsic associations between different modalities by treating features from different modalities as two distinguished subsets and focusing only on the semantic patterns between these two subsets.

Another direction to facilitate mining of objects described in many modalities is to distinguish between important and less important features in the object's description. The techniques that detect clusters of objects in all possible variations of subspaces fall in the category of Subspace clustering [2]. Such techniques extract cluster structures that are hidden by noisy dimensions and aim at separating relevant and irrelevant dimensions locally (in each cluster). One of the first approaches to subspace clustering is CLIQUE (CLustering In QUEst) described in [1]. CLIQUE is a grid-based algorithm using an a priori-like method to recursively navigate through the set of possible subspaces in a bottom-up way. Then, a number of slight modifications of CLIQUE have been proposed like ENCLUS- ENtropy-based CLUStering, differing mostly at the criterion used for the subspace selection is the algorithm ([8]). A complete review of subspace clustering techniques for high-dimensional data can be found in [33].

2.2 Multi-modal Analysis of Social Media

The multi-modal aspect that is intrinsic in social media prompt many researchers to propose specialized methods for their multi-modal analysis. In this category of works we classify the ones relying on the use of aspect or topic models [19] and the definition of a latent semantic space. In [26] the authors use a model based on Probabilistic Latent Semantic Analysis (pLSA) [20] to support multi-modal image retrieval in Flickr, using both visual content and tags. They propose to extend the standard single-layer pLSA model to multiple layers by introducing not just a single layer of topics, but a hierarchy of topics. In this way they manage to effectively and efficiently combine the heterogeneous information carried by the different modalities of an image. In a similar fashion the authors of [38] propose an approach for multi-modal characterization of social media by combining text features (e.g., tags) with spatial knowledge (e.g., geotags). The proposed approach is based on multi-modal Bayesian models which allow to integrate spatial semantics of social media in well-formed, probabilistic manner. As in the previous case the authors aim to explain the observed properties of social media resources (i.e., tags and coordinates) by means of a Bayesian model with T latent topics. The approach is evaluated in the context of characteristic scenarios such as tag recommendation, content classification, and clustering.

Only recently, there has been an increasing interest in extending the aspect models to higher order through the use of Tensors [23]. Under this line of works we can mention the tag recommendation system presented in [39] that proposes a unified framework to model the three types of entities that exist in a social tagging system: users, items and tags. These data are represented by a 3-order tensor, on which latent semantic analysis and dimensionality reduction is performed using the Higher Order Singular Value Decomposition (HOSVD) technique [24]. Consequently, tags are recommended based on the proximity of the resources in the latent semantic space. A 3-order tensor is also used by the authors of [15] that propose an approach to capture the latent semantics of Web data by means of statistical methods. In order to do that the authors apply the PARAFAC decomposition [18] which can be considered as a multi-dimensional correspondent to a singular value decomposition of a matrix. In this case the extracted latent semantics are used for the task of relevance ranking and producing fine-grained and rich descriptions of Web data.

Furthermore, the problem of multi-modality has been given rise to applying subspace clustering techniques in the social media environments. Currently such approaches are rather few in this area. More specifically, in [4] the authors use *cluster ensemble* approaches [11] to get clusters of social media that are associated with events. They form a variety of representations of social media resources, using different context dimensions and combine these dimensions into a single clustering solution. Another novel subspace clustering technique that is based on ACO metaheuristic is presented in [34]. The method performs the subspace clustering on the visual features that describe an image and is tested in a Flickr dataset.

2.3 Social Media Applications with Multi-modal Analysis

The multi-modal analysis has been used as the core analysis component of various different applications in social media. First of all, the fact that most people are fond of uploading and sharing content in social media environments motivates research efforts toward better browsing and retrieval functionalities in such environments. Furthermore, the intrinsic limitations of these systems (e.g. tag ambiguities, erroneous metadata or lack of metadata, etc.) address the need for exploitation of features in multi-modalities, in order to provide users with as much as possible relevant content. To this end, in [3], the authors present a method for a social image database browsing and retrieval by exploiting both tag and visual features of the images in a supplementary way. Indeed, it is shown that the visual features can support the suggestion of new tags and contribute to the emergence of interesting (semantic) relationships between data sources. Through the use of a navigation map, these emergent relationships between users, tags and data may be explored. Another approach in this direction is met with in [16], where the authors present clustering algorithms that improve the retrieval in social media by exploiting features from multi-spaces. Specifically, a two-step clustering approach is proposed that uses tag features at the first step, in order to get resources clusters that refer to certain topics, and visual features at the second step, in order to further "clean" and improve the precision to the extracted clusters. The use of both visual and text features is also described in [32], where the authors deploy the visual annotations, also known as "notes" in Flickr, and it is shown that the retrieval of social media content improves significantly by combining tags and visual analysis techniques.

A number of works have addressed the problem of identifying photos from social media environments that depict a certain object, location or event [10, 22, 35]. In [22] they analyze location and temporal features from geotagged photos from Flickr, in order to track tags that have place semantics (i.e. they refer to an object in a restricted location) or event semantics (i.e. they are met in specified time periods). Then, they employ tag-based clustering on these specific tags, followed by clustering on their visual features, in order to capture distinct viewpoints of the object of interest. The same authors in [21] combine tags with content-based features and analysis techniques, in order to get groups of music events photos. Likewise, in [5, 10, 35] the authors use various modalities of photos (i.e. visual, textual, spatial, temporal proximity), in order to get photo collections in an unsupervised fashion. Apart from the obvious retrieval application, the outcome of the described methods that perform object or POI identification can be used for training of multimedia algorithms, whereas these methods that extract social media content associated with particular events can be exploited for faceted browsing of events and related activities in browsers.

Most of the aforementioned methodologies can be exploited for tag recommendations in the sense that they extract tags associated to a particular event, object, location or, in general, cluster of related resources. The problem of tag recommendation has been further studied in [27], where the authors suggest an approach for recommending tags by analyzing existent tags, visual context and user context in a multimedia social tagging system. Tag recommendation techniques were, also, proposed in [36], where the authors suggest four methods for ranking candidate tags and in addition, they present the semantics of tags in Flickr.

3 Combining Heterogeneous Information Using Ant Colony Optimization

In this section, we are going to tackle the problem of multi-modality in social media, using a feature selection technique. The method we present falls in the category of the so-called subspace clustering approaches that identify clusters of high-dimensional objects and their respective feature subspaces. Specifically, we aim at providing a clustering solution that assigns a feature weight to each dimension on each cluster, based on the correlation of the cluster's objects along the specific dimension. As we will show in 3.1, this is a combinatorial optimization problem and we approximate it using the Ant Colony Optimization (ACO) metaheuristic [12].

Ant colony optimization has been applied successfully to a large number of difficult discrete optimization problems including the traveling salesman problem, the quadratic assignment problem, scheduling, vehicle routing, etc., as well as to routing in telecommunication networks [6, 7, 13]. Although data clustering techniques for social media have been heavily researched, little research has been dedicated on the use of bio-inspired algorithms for extracting information from this type of content. In this section, we employ an ACO algorithm and demonstrate how it can be used to tackle the problem of combining multi-feature spaces in the clustering of social media problem. We tested the approach on a Flickr dataset and our preliminary experiments show promising results with respect to other baseline approaches.

3.1 Problem Formulation

Social media are commonly described by a high diversity of features. To benefit from all this available information, we assume, here, that each resource r is represented by D different feature vectors:

$$r = (F_1, F_2, \ldots, F_D),$$

where F_i, $1 \le i \le D$ is a feature vector from a corresponding feature space $\mathfrak{F}_i$. We can now define the distance between two resources by considering appropriate distance measures for each feature space. For instance, we calculate distances in the tag space, based on tag co-occurrence, whereas we use Euclidean distance to capture the difference in the geographical coordinates between two resources. Thus, given D valid distance measures between the corresponding D feature vectors of the resources r_1 and r_2, we can get their distance:

$$d^w(r_1, r_2) = \sum_{i=1}^{D} w_i d_i(F_{i_1}, F_{i_2}),$$

where d_i is the distance measure employed in feature space $\mathfrak{F}_i$, $1 \leq i \leq D$ and w_i is a feature weight that determines the influence of the resources' ith feature vector to the calculation of the overall distance. In other words, the use of feature weights allows to be given different degree of gravity along each dimension. It holds $\sum_{i=1}^{D} w_i = 1$ and $w_i > 0$.

An example scenario that shows the importance to detect clusters in different variations of feature space in social media follows. Assume that there are three groups of social content: Group A that contains photos depicting waves, Group B with photos depicting people waving, and Group C depicting various places from Paris. The tags that describe each group are *wave*, *wave*, *paris*, respectively.[1] If we try to detect clusters using only tag features, we will get a cluster that contains $A + B$ together and a separate cluster C. On the other hand, if we use only visual features, the cluster C will not be obtained. Using both modalities as equally important misses also Group C, and, in general, this approach fails to detect clusters that are associated with abstract concepts, as we will show in our Experimental Study in 3.3. We claim that managing to define appropriate feature weights for each feature space is a way to obtain in separate clusters the content that is contained in each of the groups A, B, and C.

In this section, the purpose is to perform clustering on social media resources by optimally combining multi-feature information. They key idea is not to combine all the features together, but to examine local correlations between resources across each dimension and, thus, detect resources' clusters in all feature subspaces. Such techniques are known as subspace clustering and the resulting clusters may refer to different feature subspaces. More formally, we aim at providing a solution to the following problem.

Problem 1 Given a set of N social media resources described by features from D different spaces, a set of D distance measures $d_1, d_2, \ldots, d_D$, one for each feature space, and an integer K, find a K-partitioning of resources $C_1, C_2, \ldots, C_K$, such that $\sum_{i=1}^{K} \sum_{r_1, r_2 \in C_i} d^w(r_1, r_2)$, where d^w a weighted distance in each cluster, is minimized.

In order to obtain the d^w, we should define appropriate values for feature weights w_i, $1 \leq i \leq D$, so that each feature weight sufficiently captures the local correlation of the resources along the specific dimension. To do so, we employ an ant-inspired algorithm, which is based on ACO metaheuristic. The method of ACO metaheuristic technique which was proposed by Dorigo is a model of the ant behavior, which is used for combinatorial problems [13]. In the next section, we present a modification of this algorithm which can be employed to solve the social media clustering in multiple feature spaces problem.

---

[1] As many users find the tagging process tedious, the scenario that most photos in each group have been assigned only one tag is not far from reality.

VF 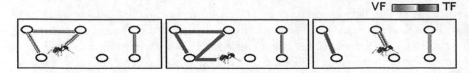 TF

Fig. 1 Combining multi-features in social media clustering using ACO

3.2 The Proposed Framework

Ant algorithms were inspired by the behavior of real ants when searching for food. When an ant finds food, it releases a chemical substance called pheromone along the path from the food to the nest. Pheromone provides an indirect communication among the ants, since ants typically follow pheromone trails. The amount of pheromone that exists in each path is proportional to the number of ants that have used this path. Pheromone evaporates in time, causing trails and paths that are no longer followed by ants to extinguish.

This pheromone-driven communication between ants have been modeled to solve a number of research problems, one of the most well-known being the Traveling Salesman Problem (TSP). The fact that pheromone evaporates in time causes pheromone trails in longer paths to weaken, as it takes more time for the ants to cross them. On the contrary, a short path is traversed faster, and, thus, the pheromone trail on this path becomes stronger, as it is laid on the path as fast as it can evaporate and many ants follow the trail and reinforce it. This behavior in ant colonies can be used to find shortest paths between nodes in a graph and, thus, providing good solutions to TSP in the following way: Agents are modeled as ants who cross the graph, as they search for food. Initially, the ants are moving randomly. If they meet pheromone trails, they follow them until they visit all the nodes in the graph, each ant constructing, in this way, an incremental solution to the problem. When an ant has visited all the nodes, it releases pheromone inversely proportionally to the length of the path. Thus, the shorter the path the bigger amount of pheromone is released, attracting other ants to follow the particular path. It is important to note that pheromone evaporation prevents sticking to local minima and allows a dynamic adaptation when the problem changes.

In this section, we present the way the ant colony behavior finding the shortest path can be simulated, in order to solve a clustering problem in multi-feature spaces. The idea is roughly depicted in Fig. 1, in which two feature spaces are taken into consideration: (i) tag features, and (ii) visual features of resources and the description follows: A large number of virtual ants are sent to explore many possible clustering solutions of social media resources. The resources are depicted as graph nodes and the ants join two nodes with an edge if they decide to assign them in the same cluster. The color of the edge shows the weight given by each ant to each feature space individually. The weight is based on the pheromone that there is in each edge. Initially, both feature spaces are given equal weight. Each ant probabilistically assigns each resource to a cluster, based on a measure combining the distance to the cluster center in each feature space individually and the amount of virtual pheromone deposited on the edge to the resource. The ants explore, depositing pheromone on each edge that they cross, until they have all completed their clustering. At this point, the pheromone to each clustering solution is updated (global pheromone updating), so that the edges that have been crossed by many ants become bolder, whereas the remaining ones (that haven't been selected by many ants) become thinner. The amount of pheromone deposited is proportional to the resources correlation along each feature space: the bigger the correlation in tag/visual space, the more pheromone is deposited. The color shows the correlation in each feature space, that is: a red color denotes more weight to tag features, whereas blue-colored paths signify clusters that contain objects with high visual similarity.

A pseudocode description of the approach is presented in Algorithm 1. At first, an initialization procedure takes place, during which: (i) each ant initializes K centroids randomly. Each centroid c_i is selected to be represented as $(c_{i1}, c_{i2}, \ldots, c_{iD})$, where c_{ij} is a vector from the feature space $\mathfrak{F}_j$, $1 \leq i \leq K$, and $1 \leq j \leq D$ (*lines 7–10*), (ii) the pheromone amount of all graph edges are set to 1 (*line 3*), (iii) the feature weights w_i are set to 0.5, which equals to $1/D$ (*lines 4–6*), (iv) the parameters ρ: pheromone evaporation factor, h: constant used to determine the influence of the distance measure against the pheromone value in the cluster assignment process, are initialized (*line 2*).

Then, the clustering process begins during which each ant will decide what edges to cross in the graph and what color to paint them. To do so, the following process is repeated for all resources: (i) each ant calculates the distance to each cluster centroid in each feature space individually (*lines 15–18*), (ii) considering the feature weights that are already calculated from the previous iteration of the algorithm, each ant estimates an overall distance from each resource to each cluster centroid (*line 19*), (iii) given the overall distance $d^w(r, c)$ calculated in the previous step, the pheromone amount that there is currently on graph edges and the constant h, each ant determines the probability that a resource r should be assigned in a cluster with centroid c, as follows:

$$p(r, c) = \frac{\tau(r, c) \cdot h / d^w(r, c)}{\sum_{i=1}^{K} \frac{\tau(r, c_i) \cdot h}{d^w(r, c_i)}}.$$

The ant assigns the resource to the cluster with the highest probability (*line 20*). This process is illustrated in the graph in Fig. 2, as an ant marking an edge between a resource and the other resources already in the cluster. The color of the edge depends on the values of the feature weights w_i.

Having performed the clustering process, new feature weights are calculated for each cluster with centroid c, based on the correlations that there are among the resources in each feature space in the cluster, as follows:

$$w(c, i) = \frac{\sum_{r \in c} d_i(r, c)}{\sum_{r \in c, l=1}^{D} d_l(r, c)}$$

for $1 \leq i \leq D$ and $d_i(r, c)$ is the distance from the resource r to the cluster centroid c in the feature space $\mathfrak{F}_i$ (*line 23–25*).

Algorithm 1: The ANT-BASED clustering algorithm combining features from multi-feature spaces

---

Input: N number of social media resources, S number of ants, K number of clusters, T number of iterations, D number of feature spaces $\mathfrak{F}_1, \mathfrak{F}_2, \ldots, \mathfrak{F}_\mathfrak{D}$

Output: A set $C = \{C_1, \ldots, C_K\}$ of K resources subsets and a feature weight vector $(w_{\mathfrak{F}_1}, w_{\mathfrak{F}_2}, \ldots, w_{\mathfrak{F}_\mathfrak{D}})$ that best describes each cluster.

  1: /*Initialization*/
  2: initialize the parameters h, ρ
  3: initialize the pheromone value τ to 1
  4: **for** $\mathfrak{F}_i$ in $[\mathfrak{F}_1, \ldots, \mathfrak{F}_\mathfrak{D}]$ **do**
  5:    $w_i \leftarrow 1/D$ /*Initialize feature weights*/
  6: **end for**
  7: **for** *ant* in $[1, S]$ **do**
  8:    **for** k in $[1, K]$ **do**
  9:       centroids $\leftarrow$ randomly $c = (c_1, c_2, \ldots, c_D)$, where $c_i \in \mathfrak{F}_i$ and $1 \leq i \leq D$
10:    **end for**
11: **end for**
12: /*Ant-based Clustering*/
13: **while** iter $<$ *NumberOfIterations* **do**
14:    **for** *ant* in $[1, S]$ and r in $[1, N]$ **do**
15:       **for** c in $[1, K]$ **do**
16:          **for** $\mathfrak{F}_i$ in $[\mathfrak{F}_1, \ldots, \mathfrak{F}_\mathfrak{D}]$ **do**
17:             $d_{\mathfrak{F}_i}(r, s) \leftarrow$ *CalculateDistance* in $\mathfrak{F}_i$
18:          **end for**
19:          $d^w(r, c) \leftarrow$ *CalculateOverallDistance*$(d_{\mathfrak{F}_i}, w_i)$
20:          $p(r, c) \leftarrow$ *CalculateProbability*(τ, d^w, h)
21:       **end for**
22:       **for** c in $[1, K]$ **do**
23:          **for** $\mathfrak{F}_i$ in $[\mathfrak{F}_1, \ldots, \mathfrak{F}_\mathfrak{D}]$ **do**
24:             $w_{(c, \mathfrak{F}_i)} \leftarrow$ *CalculateClusterCorrelation* in $\mathfrak{F}_i$
25:          **end for**
26:          centroids $\leftarrow$ *CalculateNewCentroids*
27:       **end for**
28:    **end for**
29:    /*Global pheromone update*/
30:    **for** r in $[1, N]$ and c in $[1, K]$ **do**
31:       $\tau(r, c)_{iter} = \rho \cdot \tau_{(iter-1)}(r, c) + \sum_{ant=1}^{S} \tau_{iter}(r, c)$
32:    **end for**
33: **end while**

Next, new centroids are calculated, based on the assignments in each cluster (*line 26*). After all ants have done their clustering, the pheromone amount to all solutions is recalculated (*lines 30–32*). To do so, the quality of each solution

(a) Cluster around the topic *rock*   (b) Cluster around the topic *Paris*
(Ambiguous tag)

Fig. 2 Indicative outcome of clustering using tag features

needs to be estimated, so that ants that provided good solutions generate more pheromone. The measure we use for ranking the solutions is derived from the definition of clustering, as given in [41] according to which the resources that belong in one cluster should be closely similar to each other, according to some metric of similarity, while the ones that belong to different clusters should be dissimilar. Thus, the most "efficient" ant generates a clustering where: (i) in each cluster with centroid c the intra-cluster distance is minimized, that is, $IntraDistance_{ant} = \min \sum_{r \in c} \sum_{i=1}^{D} w(c, i) \cdot d_{\mathfrak{F}_i}$, and (ii) the inter-cluster distance is maximized, that is, $InterDistance_{ant} = \max \sum_{r_1 \in c_1, r_2 \in c_2, c_1 \neq c_2} \sum_{i=1}^{D} d_{\mathfrak{F}_i}$. We assume that the quality of each solution is given by

$$q_{ant} = \frac{InterDistance_{ant}}{IntraDistance_{ant}}.$$

Calculating these measures for each solution, we update the current pheromone of each path by considering the total number of ants that have used that path and the quality of their solution. That is,

$$\Delta \tau(r, c) = \sum_{ant} q_{ant}, \quad \forall ant : (r, c) = 1,$$

where $1 \leq r \leq N, 1 \leq c \leq K$. Furthermore, during the global pheromone update, the current pheromone evaporates at a constant rate ρ at each iteration step. The presented ant-based clustering process (*lines 14–32*) is repeated for *NumberOfIteration* times until the Problem 1 is satisfied.

3.3 Experimental Study

In order to test the described algorithm, a dataset from Flickr online photo management and sharing application was crawled. As we were interested, initially, to check the functionality of the algorithm, we conducted experiments on a rather small dataset and examine how the ant-based clustering algorithm performs better than a typical clustering algorithm that relies on predefined feature spaces. Thus, the dataset was restricted to 3000 images (size 500×735) that depict cityscape, seaside, mountain, roadside, landscape and sport-side locations.[2]

At first, we applied typical clustering algorithms (K-Means, Hierarchical and Cobweb) for various values of K, based only on tag features. The distance measure used is a combination of tag co-occurrence and WordNet distance [16]. We examine the extracted clusters manually and observed that many clusters had poor accuracy, i.e. they contained resources not depicted related themes, although sharing related tags. Figure 2 shows some indicative snapshots of this type of clustering. Specifically, the limitation of algorithms relying solely on tag information to handle ambiguous terms is shown. A snapshot of a cluster containing social media resources about *Paris* is shown in (b).

To minimize the intrinsic shortcomings of tagging features, we embedded in the clustering process the visual features of the images. More specifically, we performed clustering using both tag and visual features in a sequential way: first we apply tag-based clustering and then clustering based on the visual features of the resources [16]. The visual feature extraction was based on the MPEG-7 standard [30] which defines appropriate descriptors together with their extraction techniques and similarity matching distances. More specifically, the MPEG-7 eXperimentation Model, XM provides a reference implementation which was utilized in our approach [31]. The descriptors used were the Color Structure Histogram (*CSH*) and Edge Histogram (*EH*) descriptors, chosen due to their effectiveness in similarity retrieval. Their extraction was performed according to the guidelines provided by the MPEG-7 XM and then, an image feature vector was produced, for every resource, by encompassing the extracted MPEG-7 descriptors in a single vector. Thus, typical clustering algorithms could be applied, using the distance functions that are defined in MPEG-7 XM [16]. A set of users checked the extracted clusters manually and assessed their quality. The results showed that in many cases the accuracy was improved. This was especially true for clusters that contained ambiguous terms (e.g. rock—stone, rock—music). Especially for cases that the two senses of the ambiguous tag differed a lot visually, the algorithm succeeded to distinguish the different senses of the ambiguous tag, by dividing the corresponding resources into different clusters (cf. Fig. 3). However, there were cases that the combination of tag and visual features worsen the clustering outcome. An example of such case is the *Paris*

---

[2]For Flickr resources and metadata download the Flickr API along with the utility wget were used.

(a) Cluster around the topic *rock*
(sense:stone)

(b) Cluster around the topic *rock*
(sense:music)

Fig. 3 Indicative outcome of clustering using tag features and visual features

cluster and, generally, clusters whose topic is not related to a particular visual representation (abstract concepts). Indeed, we saw that a cluster describing *Paris* was extracted based on tag features of resources. This cluster no longer exists, if we employ the visual features to the clustering. As shown in Fig. 3, this type of clustering succeeds in assigning resources with uniform visual appearance together. This way, though, it misses clusters of abstract resources that refer to the same topic but differ visually.

The aforementioned example shows that the equal consideration of diverse features describing a resource does not always yield the optimal results. Some cluster resources can be only extracted by using a specified combination of features. We apply the presented ACO-based method using two modalities of the images, i.e. textual and visual. For the representation of images in the tag space we used the approach described in [17] and for their representation in a visual space we used their Color Structure Histogram (*CSH*) and Edge Histogram (*EH*) descriptors, as described above. We conducted a number of experiments with different values of the parameters ρ and h. Figure 4 shows indicative clustering results of the ant-inspired algorithm. It can be seen that the algorithm sufficiently captures clusters in different feature subspaces and it managed to handle the *Paris* cluster well.

The presented experiments are preliminary and were performed to evaluate qualitatively the use of ACO methods in social media clustering. We reached the useful conclusion that we sum up as follows. It is apparent that the restriction in one feature space deprives information that can come out handy in the task of social media clustering. On the other hand, by considering all the feature spaces equally important we may miss clusters of related objects that have similarity using a specific combination of features. In this section we proposed applying subspace clustering for obtaining clusters of social media in various feature subspaces. An ant-inspired algorithm was presented to realize this task. Future work involves the testing of the algorithm on larger datasets.

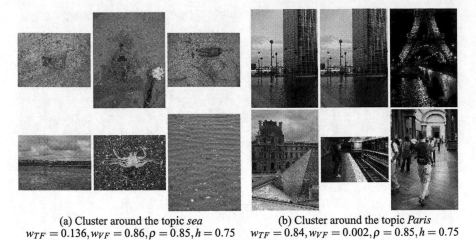

(a) Cluster around the topic *sea*   (b) Cluster around the topic *Paris*
$w_{TF} = 0.136, w_{VF} = 0.86, \rho = 0.85, h = 0.75$ $w_{TF} = 0.84, w_{VF} = 0.002, \rho = 0.85, h = 0.75$

Fig. 4 Indicative outcome of clustering using presented ACO algorithm

4 Combining Heterogeneous Information Using Aspect Models

As an alternative approach of feature selection, efficient multi-modal analysis can be also achieved by employing approaches for feature combination. In contrast to feature selection that handles multi-modal features by assigned them appropriate weights, feature combination aims at defining a new feature space suitable for projecting the multi-modal features. One very popular scenario for these approaches is the retrieval of relevant images using an example image. The multi-modal aspect of the image retrieval scenario has been primarily boosted by the rapid growth of social networks, which resulted in the abundant availability of tagged images on the Web. The existence of tags allow these images to be indexed based on both their visual and tag information, which is expected to better facilitate the retrieval of semantic relevant images. However, as will become apparent in the remaining of this section, the heterogeneous nature of visual content and tags makes their combination a challenging problem.

4.1 Motivation & Approach

Most existing content-based image retrieval systems are based either on the visual or textual information contained in the query image to retrieve relevant images. It is common consensus that combining the information carried by both modalities should lead to the improvement of retrieval results. However, the straightforward combination of both modalities that subsumes the words (i.e., type of features detailed in Sect. 4.2 that are extracted from visual or textual content and resemble the use of normal words in our every day language) extracted indiscriminately from both modalities to be parts of one common word set (usually called vocabulary), does not lead to the expected improvements. One possible reason is that by indiscriminately placing features extracted from heterogeneous information sources into a common feature space, the obtained image representations are likely to be dominated by one of the combined modalities or lose connection with their semantic meaning. Moreover, by simply considering the extracted words as independent elements of the same large vocabulary, we automatically assume that all these words are mutually independent. In this way we disregard the fact that in most cases, the words derived from the image visual and tag information are essentially two different expressions of the same abstract meaning. This implies a type of dependence that needs to be taken into consideration when designing the image representation scheme.

In order to facilitate the combination of heterogeneous modalities and avoid the aforementioned problems, we need to determine a feature space that will allow the extracted words to be expressed as a mixture of meanings. For this purpose the current literature proposes the use of Probabilistic Latent Semantic Analysis (pLSA)-based [20] aspect or topic models that allow to map a high-dimensional word distribution vector to a lower-dimensional topic vector (also called aspect vector). These models assume that the content depicted by every image can be expressed as a mixture of multiple topics and that the occurrences of words is a result of the topic mixture. Thus, the latent layer of topics that is introduced by pLSA between the image and the tag or visual words, acts as the feature space where both types of words can be combined meaningfully. However, even if these latent topics can be considered to satisfy the requirement of combining the words extracted from heterogeneous modalities without introducing any bias or rendering them meaningless, they still do not solve the problem that, being different expressions of the same abstract meaning, there is a certain amount of dependance between the tag and visual words that appear together very frequently. This additional requirement motivates the employment of methods that will allow the cross-words dependencies to influence the nature of the extracted latent topics. In this respect we examine the use of a second-level pLSA that treats the latent topics as the observed words. In this way we learn a new pLSA model that allows images to be represented as a vector of meta-topics.

In the following we describe the techniques used to represent an image based on a vocabulary of visual and tag words, respectively, we provide details on the application of the pLSA model on the extracted word-based image representations, and finally we present an experiment that verifies the efficiency of the presented model in combining heterogeneous types of information.

4.2 Representing Images Based on the Co-occurrence of Words

The employment of an efficient image representation scheme that will manage to extract all or most of the important information contained in an image, is a crucial pre-requisite for performing image indexing and retrieval. The scheme adopted in this chapter is based on defining a set of representative "words" that are able to span a sufficiently large portion of the information space that they are used to describe. Then, based on these words each image can be represented with respect to the existence of these words in its content. In the following we describe two techniques for applying the aforementioned general methodology to the spaces of visual content and tags.

4.2.1 Visual-Word Co-occurrence Image Representation

In order to represent the visual information carried by an image using a set of visual words, we need to build a bag-of-words representation for the visual content of the images. For the purposes of our work we have used the visual representation scheme adopted in [9] that consists of the following 3 steps: (a) the Difference of Gaussian filter is applied on the gray scale version of an image to detect a set of key-points and scales, respectively, (b) the Scale Invariant Feature Transformation (SIFT) [28] is computed over the local region defined by the key-point and scale, and (c) a Visual Word Vocabulary (Codebook) [37] is created by applying the k-means algorithm to cluster in 500 clusters, the total amount of SIFT descriptors that have been extracted from all images. Then, using this Visual Word Vocabulary we are able to vector quantize the SIFT descriptor of an interest point against the set of visual words. This is done by mapping the SIFT descriptor to its closest visual word (i.e., the cluster with minimum distance from its center among all 500 generated clusters) and increasing the corresponding word count. By doing this for all key-points found in an image, the resulting 500-dimensional representation is the visual-word co-occurrence vector of this image and holds the counts of the occurrences of visual words in its content.

4.2.2 Tag-Word Co-occurrence Image Representation

A similar approach has been adopted for representing the tag information that accompanies an image using a set of tag words. As in the previous case, we need to build a bag-of-words representation of the textual content of the image. However, since tags have clear semantics, in this case there is no need to employ clustering for determining which words should be included in the Tag Word Vocabulary (Codebook). Instead, from a large volume of utilized tags we need to select the ones with minimum level of noise and maximum usage by the users. For the purposes of our work we have used the Tag Word Vocabulary constructed by [9] using the following steps. 269,648 images were downloaded from Flickr along with their accompanying tags. Among the total set of 425,059 unique tags that have been used by the users to tag these images, there are 9,325 tags that appear more than 100 times. Many of these unique tags arise from spelling errors, while some of them are names etc., which are meaningless for general image annotation. Thus, all these 9,325 unique tags were checked against the WordNet Lexical Database [14] and after removing

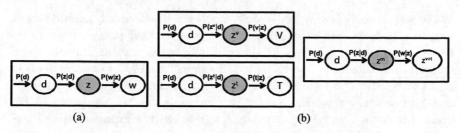

Fig. 5 Image representation using: (**a**) the standard pLSA model, (**b**) the second-level pLSA model

those tags that do not exist in WordNet, a list with 5,018 unique tags was determined. For the purposes of our work, out of the 5,018 unique tags the first 1,000 that were used most frequently were selected to form the Tag Word Vocabulary. Using this Tag Word Vocabulary we obtain for each image a 1000-dimensional tag-word co-occurrence vector that holds the counts of the occurrences of tag words in its associated set of tags.

4.3 Representing Images Using Aspect Models

As already mentioned the goal of pLSA is to introduce a latent (i.e., unobservable) topic layer between images and words. Let us denote $D = \{d_1, \ldots, d_N\}$ the set of images and $W = \{w_1, \ldots, w_M\}$ the set of words. The key idea is to map high-dimensional word count vectors, as the ones described in Sect. 4.2, to a lower-dimensional representation in a so-called latent semantic space [20]. pLSA is based on a statistical model which has been called the aspect model [19]. The aspect model is a latent variable model for co-occurrence data which associates an unobserved class variable $z \in Z = \{z_1, \ldots, z_K\}$ with each observation as shown in Fig. 5(a). A joint probability model over the set of images D and the set of words W is defined by the mixture:

$$P(d, w) = P(d)P(w|d), \quad P(w|d) = \sum_{z \in Z} P(w|z)P(z|d), \qquad (1)$$

where $P(d)$ denotes the probability of an image to be picked, $P(z|d)$ the probability of a topic given a current document, and $P(w|z)$ the probability of a word given a topic.

Once a topic mixture $P(z|d)$ is derived for an image d, we have a high-level representation of this image with less dimensions from the initial representation that was based on the co-occurrence of words. This is because we commonly choose the number of topics K to be much smaller than the number of words so as to act as bottleneck variables in predicting words. The resulting K-dimensional topic vectors can be used directly in a query-by-example image retrieval scenario, if we measure the similarity between two images by computing the distance (e.g., L_1, Euclidean, cosine) between their topic vectors.

For the purposes of our work the pLSA model was independently applied in both visual and tag information space in order to express the images as a mixture of visual and tag topics, respectively. More specifically, in the visual information space the visual-word co-occurrence vectors of all training images were used to train the pLSA model. Then, this model was applied to all testing images in the dataset to derive a new vector representation for each image. In this new representation the vector elements denote the degree to which an image can be expressed using a certain visual topic. Similarly in the tag information space, the tag-word co-occurrence vectors of all training images were used to train a pLSA model that was used to derive a new vector representation for all testing images. In this case the vector elements denote the degree to which an image can be expressed using a certain tag topic. 100 topics has been used in both cases resulting in two 100-dimensional vectors for each image.

Motivated by the fact that both topic vectors refer to the so-called latent semantic space and express probabilities (i.e., the degree to which a certain topic exists in the image), we assume that the topics obtained from both modalities are homogeneous and can be indiscriminately considered as the words of a common Topic Word Vocabulary. Based on this assumption an image representation that combines information from both modalities can be constructed by concatenating the two 100-dimensional topic vectors. Alternatively, and in order to exploit the cross-words relations between tags $T = \{t_1, \ldots, T_L\}$ and visual words $V = \{v_1, \ldots, v_Q\}$, we can treat the visual- and tag-topics as the observed words for learning a second-level pLSA model. This model allows an image to be represented as a vector of meta-topics as depicted in Fig. 5(b). For the purposes of our experiment we have selected the number of meta-topics to be 100, and for every testing image we obtained an 100-dimensional vector. The elements of this vector denote the degree to which an image can be expressed using a certain meta-topic.

4.4 Experimental Study

In the following we evaluate the efficiency of different feature spaces for performing image indexing and retrieval. Initially we create an index for testing all images using the corresponding feature space. Then, we use a small subset of the indexed images to perform queries on the index. Performance assessment is based on the relevance between the query and the retrieved images. In our experiment we compare the performance between five different feature spaces which are formulated by: (a) tag words, (b) visual words, (c) the straightforward concatenation of both types of words, (d) topics obtained by concatenating the output of the pLSA model applied on visual and tag words, and (e) meta-topics obtained by applying a second-level pLSA model on the previously extracted topics.

4.4.1 Test-bed

Our experiment has been conducted on the NUS-WIDE dataset[3] that was created by the NUS's Lab for Media Search [9]. The dataset contains 269,648 images that have been downloaded from Flickr together with their tags. For all images the authors released 500-dimensional co-occurrence vectors for visual words (as described in Sect. 4.2.1), as well as 1000-dimensional co-occurrence vectors for tag words (as described in Sect. 4.2.2). Moreover, the ground-truth for 81 concepts has been provided to facilitate evaluation. For the purposes of our evaluation we have used a subsample of 20,000 images for training (I^{train}) and 20,000 for testing (I^{test}). I^{train} has been used for training the pLSA models and I^{test} to create the index and perform image retrieval. Finally, 1,000 images from I^{test} were selected to act as queries I^{query}.

4.4.2 Evaluation Metric

Since we are considering an image retrieval scenario, the Average Precision (AP) metric was selected to assess the performance of the different feature spaces. AP favors the algorithms that are able not only to retrieve the correct images, but to retrieve them as earlier as possible in a ranked list of retrieved results. Thus, for two algorithms that retrieve the same amount of correct images, although achieving similar performance with respect to recall and precision, the one that retrieves the correct images earlier in the ranked list of results will exhibit highest score for AP. Average precision is expressed by the following equation:

$$AP = \frac{\sum_{r=1}^{N} Pr(r) \cdot rel(r)}{\# \text{ relevant images}}, \tag{2}$$

where r is the current rank, N is the number of retrieved images, $rel()$ is a binary function that determines the relevance of the image at the given rank with the query image. $rel()$ outputs 1 if the image in the given rank is annotated with at least one concept in common with the query image and 0 otherwise. $Pr(r)$ is the precision at the given rank and is calculated by

$$Pr(r) = \frac{\# \text{ relevant retrieved images of rank } r \text{ or less}}{r}. \tag{3}$$

AP measures the retrieval performance of the method using one image as query. In order to obtain one global performance score for all 1,000 images that we were used as queries, we employed the Mean Average Precision (MAP). MAP is the mean of AP scores over a set of queries. In our experiment the MAP was calculated over the 1,0000 query images included in I^{query}.

---

[3]http://lms.comp.nus.edu.sg/research/NUS-WIDE.htm.

Fig. 6 (a) Comparison diagram between five different feature spaces for image indexing and retrieval, (b) Indicative retrieval examples using tag words, visual words, and latent topics

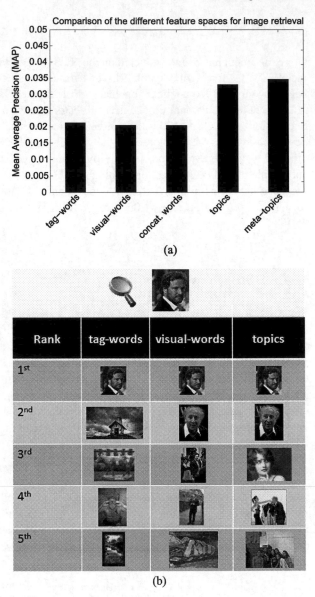

(a)

(b)

4.4.3 Results

Figure 6(a) depicts the MAP scores for all evaluated feature spaces. We notice that tag words and visual words exhibit almost similar performance, showing that both modalities carry equally important information for retrieving relevant images. As expected, the straightforward combination of both modalities by simply concatenating their word count vectors, fails to combine them efficiently and performs slightly worse than the uni-modal cases. This is not the case for the space of latent topics obtained using pLSA. We note a significant increase of the retrieval performance, which verifies the ability of the pLSA-generated space to efficiently combine information from heterogeneous sources. Finally, the space of meta-topics manages to further improve the retrieval performance by a small amount, showing that the exploitation of cross-word relations can only benefit the resulting feature space. Figure 6(b) shows indicative retrieval examples using tag words, visual words and topics.

In conclusion, we should stress the great potential of exploiting the information residing across different modalities, provided that we will manage to overcome the problems arising from the heterogeneous nature of sources. The use of aspect models has been proven to be an efficient method for combining the visual and tag information carried by the images on the Web. However, a similar methodology can be used to incorporate additional modalities such as geotagging or user-related information. In the end, we should also highlight the existence of dependencies between the information carried by different modalities, and the need to investigate methods that will manage to exploit these dependencies. By doing so, additional means can be discovered for boosting the efficiency of the combination of multi-modal data.

5 Conclusions

In this chapter we have discussed the importance of multi-modal analysis in social media. Given the widespread adoption of social networks and web 2.0, there is a major trend in the new digital landscape toward the interconnection of platforms, networks and most importantly data. Different types of information are associated with the same digital resource expressing different aspects of its meaning (e.g., textual and visual descriptions, spatio-temporal information, popularity, etc.). The existence of techniques that will manage to exploit all these aspects is crucial for successfully adopting to this new digital landscape. Initial works on multi-modal analysis have shown that the straightforward application of well-studied uni-modal methods are rarely beneficial in multi-modal settings. Problems arise from the heterogeneity of sources and the very different characteristics of the data. In this chapter we have presented two methods that alleviate the aforementioned problems in two scenarios involving tagged images.

The ant-inspired algorithm presented in Sect. 3 formulates the multi-modal analysis as a feature selection problem. Feature weights are used to favor the modality that best describes the analyzed image and image clustering is performed using the corresponding vectors of weighted features. Thus, depending on the calculated weights, the resulting clusters may refer to different feature subspaces, emphasizing on different aspects of the image content. The method presented in Sect. 4 emphasizes the need to discover techniques that will manage to exploit the relations existing across modalities, in cases where two or more of the modalities constitute different expressions of the same abstract meaning. Using the presented second-level pLSA model the extracted hierarchy of topics manages to exploit the cross-modal relations between the visual and tag features and improve the retrieval performance.

Both methods demonstrate their superiority against their uni-modal counterparts and underline the importance of efficient and effective methodologies for the optimal combination of multi-modal data.

As avenues for potential research we can refer to the need of investigating methods that will manage to efficiently combined a considerably higher number of modalities. Although many of the presented techniques claim that can be naturally scaled to support the combination of more than two modalities, only few of them have been evaluated with real world data. The need for such methods is particularly motivated by the constantly increasing level of information flow between different social networks, which leverages the multi-source aspect of social media. For instance an image in Flickr[4] can be bookmarked in delicious[5] or tagged using an event from last.fm,[6] allowing its association with information from multiple sources. This information flow can also be the motive for discovering new application scenarios that will be able to exploit the added value offered by performing a multi-modal analysis of the exchanged data.

Acknowledgements This work was sponsored by the European Commission as part of the Information Society Technologies (IST) programme under grant agreement n°215453—WeKnowIt and the contract FP7-248984 GLOCAL.

References

1. Agrawal, R., Gehrke, J., Gunopulos, D., Raghavan, P.: Automatic subspace clustering of high dimensional data for data mining applications. In: Proceedings of the ACM SIGMOD Int'l Conference on Management of Data, Seattle, Washington, pp. 94–105. ACM Press, New York (1998)
2. Agrawal, R., Gehrke, J., Gunopulos, D., Raghavan, P.: Automatic subspace clustering of high dimensional data. Data Min. Knowl. Discov. 11, 5–33 (2005)
3. Aurnhammer, M., Hanappe, P., Steels, L.: Augmenting navigation for collaborative tagging with emergent semantics. In: International Semantic Web Conference (2006)
4. Becker, H., Naaman, M., Gravano, L.: Event identification in social media. In: 12th International Workshop on the Web and Databases, WebDB (2009)
5. Becker, H., Naaman, M., Gravano, L.: Learning similarity metrics for event identification in social media. In: WSDM '10: Proceedings of the Third ACM International Conference on Web Search and Data Mining, pp. 291–300. ACM, New York (2010)
6. Blum, C.: Ant colony optimization: Introduction and recent trends. Phys. Life Rev. 2, 353–373 (2005)
7. Caro, G.D., Ducatelle, F., Gambardella, L.M.: Anthocnet: an adaptive nature-inspired algorithm for routing in mobile ad hoc networks. Eur. Trans. Telecommun. 16(5), 443–455 (2005)
8. Cheng, C.-H., Fu, A.W., Zhang, Y.: Entropy-based subspace clustering for mining numerical data. In: Proceedings of the Fifth ACM SIGKDD International Conference on Knowledge Discovery and Data Mining. KDD '99, pp. 84–93. ACM, New York (1999)

---

[4]http://www.flickr.com/.

[5]http://www.delicious.com/.

[6]http://www.last.fm.

9. Chua, T.-S., Tang, J., Hong, R., Li, H., Luo, Z., Zheng, Y.: Nus-wide: a real-world web image database from National University of Singapore. In: CIVR '09: Proceeding of the ACM International Conference on Image and Video Retrieval, pp. 1–9. ACM, New York (2009). http://doi.acm.org/10.1145/1646396.1646452

10. Crandall, D.J., Backstrom, L., Huttenlocher, D., Kleinberg, J.: Mapping the world's photos. In: Proceedings of the 18th International Conference on World Wide Web. WWW '09, pp. 761–770. ACM, New York (2009)

11. Domeniconi, C., Al-Razgan, M.: Weighted cluster ensembles: Methods and analysis. ACM Trans. Knowl. Discov. Data 2, 17–11740 (2009)

12. Dorigo, M.: Optimization, Learning and Natural Algorithms. Ph.D. thesis, Politecnico di Milano, Italy (1992)

13. Dorigo, M., Caro, G.D.: The ant colony optimization meta-heuristic (1999)

14. Fellbaum, C. (ed.): WordNet: An Electronic Lexical Database (Language, Speech, and Communication). MIT Press, Cambridge (1998)

15. Franz, T., Schultz, A., Sizov, S., Staab, S.: Triplerank: Ranking semantic web data by tensor decomposition. In: ISWC '09: Proceedings of the 8th International Semantic Web Conference, pp. 213–228. Springer, Berlin (2009)

16. Giannakidou, E., Kompatsiaris, I., Vakali, A.: Semsoc: Semantic, social and content-based clustering in multimedia collaborative tagging systems. In: ICSC, pp. 128–135 (2008)

17. Giannakidou, E., Koutsonikola, V.A., Vakali, A., Kompatsiaris, Y.: Co-clustering tags and social data sources. In: WAIM, pp. 317–324 (2008)

18. Harshman, R.A., Lundy, M.E.: Parafac: Parallel factor analysis. Comput. Stat. Data Anal. 18(1), 39–72 (1994)

19. Hofmann, T.: Unsupervised learning from dyadic data. In: NJPS, pp. 466–472. MIT Press, Cambridge (1998)

20. Hofmann, T.: Probabilistic latent semantic analysis. In: Proc. of Uncertainty in Artificial Intelligence, UAI'99, Stockholm (1999). URL citeseer.ist.psu.edu/hofmann99probabilistic.html

21. Kennedy, L., Naaman, M.: Less talk, more rock: automated organization of community-contributed collections of concert videos. In: Proceedings of the 18th International Conference on World Wide Web. WWW '09, pp. 311–320. ACM, New York (2009)

22. Kennedy, L.S., Naaman, M., Ahern, S., Nair, R., Rattenbury, T.: How flickr helps us make sense of the world: context and content in community-contributed media collections. In: ACM Multimedia, pp. 631–640 (2007)

23. Kolda, T.G., Bader, B.W.: Tensor decompositions and applications. SIAM Rev. 51(3), 455–500 (2009). doi:10.1137/07070111X

24. Lathauwer, L.D., Moor, B.D., Vandewalle, J.: A multilinear singular value decomposition. SIAM J. Matrix Anal. Appl. 21(4), 1253–1278 (2000)

25. Li, D., Dimitrova, N., Li, M., Sethi, I.K.: Multimedia content processing through cross-modal association. In: MULTIMEDIA '03, pp. 604–611. ACM, New York (2003)

26. Lienhart, R., Romberg, S., Hörster, E.: Multilayer plsa for multimodal image retrieval. In: CIVR '09: Proceeding of the ACM International Conference on Image and Video Retrieval, pp. 1–8. ACM, New York (2009). http://doi.acm.org/10.1145/1646396.1646408

27. Lindstaedt, S., Pammer, V., Mörzinger, R., Kern, R., Mülner, H., Wagner, C.: Recommending tags for pictures based on text, visual content and user context. In: Proceedings of the 2008 Third International Conference on Internet and Web Applications and Services, pp. 506–511. IEEE Computer Society, Washington (2008)

28. Lowe, D.G.: Distinctive image features from scale-invariant keypoints. Int. J. Comput. Vis. 60(2), 91–110 (2004)

29. Magalhaes, J., Rüger, S.: Information-theoretic semantic multimedia indexing. In: CIVR '07, pp. 619–626. ACM, New York (2007). http://doi.acm.org/10.1145/1282280.1282368

30. Manjunath, B.S., Ohm, J.R., Vinod, V.V., Yamada, A.: Colour and texture descriptors. IEEE Trans. Circuits Syst. Video Technol., Special Issue on MPEG-7 11(6), 703–715 (2001)

31. MPEG-7: Visual Experimentation Model (XM). Version 10.0, ISO/IEC/JTC1/SC29/WG11, Doc. N4062 (2001)

32. Olivares, X., Ciaramita, M., van Zwol, R.: Boosting image retrieval through aggregating search results based on visual annotations. In: Proceeding of the 16th ACM International Conference on Multimedia. MM '08, pp. 189–198. ACM, New York (2008)
33. Parsons, L., Haque, E., Liu, H.: Subspace clustering for high dimensional data: a review. SIGKDD Explor. Newsl. 6, 90–105 (2004)
34. Piatrik, T., Izquierdo, E.: Subspace clustering of images using ant colony optimisation. In: 16th IEEE International Conference on Image Processing (ICIP), pp. 229–232 (2009)
35. Quack, T., Leibe, B., Gool, L.J.V.: World-scale mining of objects and events from community photo collections. In: CIVR, pp. 47–56 (2008)
36. Sigurbjörnsson, B., van Zwol, R.: Flickr tag recommendation based on collective knowledge. In: Proceeding of the 17th International Conference on World Wide Web. WWW '08, pp. 327–336. ACM, New York (2008)
37. Sivic, J., Zisserman, A.: Video google: A text retrieval approach to object matching in videos. In: ICCV '03: Proceedings of the Ninth IEEE International Conference on Computer Vision, p. 1470. IEEE Computer Society, Washington (2003)
38. Sizov, S.: Geofolk: latent spatial semantics in web 2.0 social media. In: WSDM '10: Proceedings of the Third ACM International Conference on Web Search and Data Mining, pp. 281–290. ACM, New York (2010). http://doi.acm.org/10.1145/1718487.1718522
39. Symeonidis, P., Nanopoulos, A., Manolopoulos, Y.: Tag recommendations based on tensor dimensionality reduction. In: RecSys '08: Proceedings of the 2008 ACM Conference on Recommender Systems, pp. 43–50. ACM, New York (2008)
40. Wu, Y., Chang, E.Y., Chang, K.C.-C., Smith, J.R.: Optimal multimodal fusion for multimedia data analysis. In: MULTIMEDIA '04, pp. 572–579. ACM, New York (2004)
41. Xu, R., Wunsch, I.: Survey of clustering algorithms. IEEE Trans. Neural Netw. 16(3), 645–678 (2005)

Multi-label Image Annotation by Structural Grouping Sparsity

Yahong Han, Fei Wu, and Yueting Zhuang

Abstract We can obtain high-dimensional heterogeneous features from real-world images on photo-sharing website, for an example Flickr. Those features are implemented to describe their various aspects of visual characteristics, such as color, texture and shape etc. The heterogeneous features are often over-complete to describe certain semantic. Therefore, the selection of limited discriminative features for certain semantics is hence crucial to make the image understanding more interpretable. This chapter introduces one approach for multi-label image annotation with a regularized penalty. We call it Multi-label Image Boosting by the selection of heterogeneous features with structural Grouping Sparsity (MtBGS). MtBGS induces a (*structural*) sparse selection model to identify subgroups of homogeneous features for predicting a certain label. Moreover, the correlations among multiple tags are utilized in MtBGS to boost the performance of multi-label annotation. Extensive experiments on public image datasets show that the proposed approach has better multi-label image annotation performance and leads to a quite interpretable model for image understanding.

1 Introduction

Automatic annotating images with suitable multiple tags is a very active research field. From a machine learning point of view, the approaches of multi-label image annotation can be roughly classified into the generative model and the discriminative model. The generative model learns a joint distribution over image features and annotation tags. To annotate a new image, the learned generative model computes the conditional probability over tags given the visual features [1, 8]. On the other hand, the discriminative model trains a separate classifier from visual features for

Y. Han (✉) · F. Wu · Y. Zhuang
College of Computer Science, Zhejiang University, Hangzhou, China
e-mail: yahong@zju.edu.cn

F. Wu
e-mail: wufei@zju.edu.cn

Y. Zhuang
e-mail: yzhuang@zju.edu.cn

S.C.H. Hoi et al. (eds.), *Social Media Modeling and Computing*,
DOI 10.1007/978-0-85729-436-4_5, © Springer-Verlag London Limited 2011

(a) clouds sea structure (b) male people sea sky (c) bird clouds people (d) clouds sky structure
sunset   sunset   sea sky

Fig. 1 Sample images from Flickr (www.flickr.com) and corresponding labeled multiple tags

each tag. These classifiers are used to predict particular tags for test image samples [5, 13].

Since images are usually visually polysemous, for the real-world images on photo-sharing websites, users may label multiple tags for each image. Taking images in Fig. 1 for example, we can see that the tags for different images are usually overlap. Therefore, for the multi-label image annotation, correlations among multiple tags should be well explored to boost the annotation performance. Furthermore, we can extract high-dimensional heterogeneous features from one given image, such as global features (color, shape and texture) or local features (SBN [20], SIFT, Shape Context and GLOH (Gradient Location and Orientation Histogram)). Different subsets of heterogeneous features have different intrinsic discriminative power to characterize one image label. However, those heterogeneous features are often over-complete for the description of certain semantics. That is to say, only limited heterogeneous features distinguish their corresponding semantics from others. Therefore, the selected visual features to be used for the prediction of certain image semantics are usually sparse.

As a result, some *sparsity*-based multi-label learning approaches have been studied to impose structural penalty on feature and label spaces. For example, a multilabel sparse coding framework MLE [26] was proposed to utilize multi-label information for dimensionality reduction of visual features. Multi-task Sparse Discriminate Analysis (MtSDA) was implemented in [14] to avoid overfitting for highly correlated features and identify grouping effect in feature selection during multi-label annotation by ℓ_1-norm and penalized matrix. Moreover, Cao [4] proposed to learn different metric kernel functions for different features. They formulated the Heterogeneous Feature Machines (HFM) as a sparse logistic regression by the ℓ_1-norm at group level.

For above approaches, the ℓ_1-norm (namely *lasso*, least absolution shrinkage and selection operator) [25] was effectively implemented to make the learning model both sparse and interpretable. However, for group of features that the pairwise correlations among them are very high, lasso tends to select only one of the pairwise correlated features and does not induce the group effect. In the "large p, small n" problem, the "grouped features" situation is an important concern to facilitate a model's interpretability. In order to remedy the deficiency of lasso, group lasso [29] and elastic net [31] were proposed, respectively, in the past years. A feature selection approach by grouping structural sparsity is proposed in [28]. This approach in [28]

Fig. 2 Flowchart of the heterogeneous feature selection with structural grouping sparsity (MtBGS in [28]). Two representative images are illustrated with different labeled tags. Different colors of histograms indicate different kinds of heterogeneous features, such as colors, texture, and shape. Algorithm MtBGS [28] perform heterogeneous feature selection by two steps: group selection and within-group sparsity inducing. Coefficient vectors $\beta_j = 0$ indicates that the jth group of features are dropped out of the model, and $\beta_j = 1$ otherwise

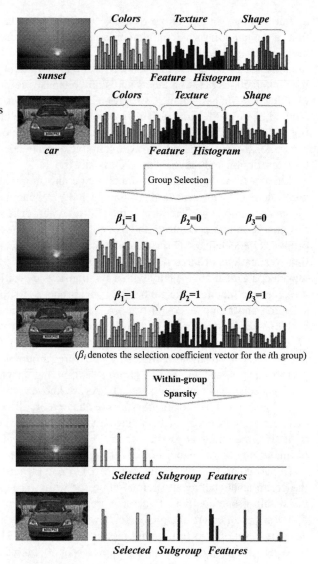

is called Multi-label Image Boosting by the selection of heterogeneous features with structural Grouping Sparsity (MtBGS). MtBGS is interested in seeking after an interpretable model for predicting particular tags for images. Basically speaking, MtBGS is to select finite groups of heterogeneous features and identify subgroup within homogeneous features. For example, as shown in Fig. 2, lots of heterogeneous features such as color, texture and shape can be extracted from images. Mt-BGS tend to discern those discriminative feature sets from each image and set their selection coefficients (β_i) as 1 and the selection coefficients of other insignificant feature sets as 0. MtBGS then identify the subgroup within each selected feature set as the representation of each image.

Furthermore, in the setting of images with multiple labels, the effective utilization of the latent information hidden in related labels can boost the performance of multi-label annotation. Kang [18] proposed a Correlated Label Propagation (CLP) model through an efficiently solved submodular function. The CLP method utilized interactions between labels and simultaneously co-propagated multiple labels to unlabeled images. Zhang [30] proposed a multi-label dimensionality reduction method, namely Multi-label Dimensionality reduction via Dependence Maximization (MDDM). The MDDM method tried to project the original data into a lower-dimensional feature space by maximizing the dependence between the original feature description and the associated class labels.

MtBGS formulates the multi-label image annotation as a multiple response regression model with structural grouping penalty. A benefit of performing multi-label image annotation via regression is the ability to introduce penalties. Many of penalties can be introduced into the regression model for better prediction. Hastie [15] proposed the Penalized Discriminant Analysis (PDA) to tackle problems of overfitting in situations of large numbers of highly correlated predictors (features). PDA introduced a quadratic penalty with a symmetric and positive definite matrix Ω into the objective function. Elastic net [31] was proposed to conduct automatic variable selection and group selection of correlated variables simultaneously by imposing both ℓ_1- and ℓ_2-norm penalties. Furthermore, motivated by elastic net, Clemmensen [7] extended PDA to sparse discriminant analysis (SDA).

The basic motivation of imposing structural grouping penalty in MtBGS is to perform heterogeneous feature group selection and subgroup identification within homogeneous features simultaneously. As we know, some subgroups of features in high-dimensional heterogeneous features have more discriminative power for predicting certain labels of a given image. Furthermore, the correlations between labels in MtBGS are utilized by a Curds and Whey procedure [3] to boost the performance of image annotation in multi-label setting.

In particular, for group selection, MtBGS employs a (not squared) ℓ_2-norm on the group-level coefficient vector. While for within-group sparsity, the ℓ_1-norm of the within-group coefficient vector is imposed. Both the group-level ℓ_2-norm and ℓ_1-norm penalties are integrated to form the structural grouping penalty. Similar as sparse group lasso (group and piecewise penalty) [11] and group pursuit (pairwise penalty) [23], the structural grouping sparsity in this paper not only selects the groups of heterogeneous features, but also discriminates the subgroups within homogeneous features, which is most responsible for outcomes of a label. As a whole, our primary objective is to achieve an interpretable and accurate model for multi-label prediction through a computationally efficient method.

Here we have to point out that the proposed sparsity-based feature selection is different from other approaches such as visual diversity modeling, in which mixture of image kernels were integrated to characterize the diverse visual similarity relationships between images [10].

The remainder of this chapter is organized as follows. We first briefly overview some sparse model for feature selection, then we introduce the details of MtBGS in [28]. The experimental analysis and conclusion are given in the end.

2 Sparse Model for Feature Selection

Heterogeneous visual features could be extracted from images. In social media annotation, it is important to select the most discriminative features for corresponding semantic tags by a trained model. From the *Principle of Parsimony*, we are told that entities must not be multiplied beyond necessity since the irrelevant or trivial factors possibly introduce noise. In the past years, many of approaches have been proposed in the statistics to seek after one interpretable model for feature selection such as lasso [25], subset selection [2], group lasso [29] and elastic net [31]

2.1 Notation

Assume that we have a training set of n labeled images with J labels (tags): $\{(\mathbf{x}_i, \mathbf{y}_i) \in \mathbb{R}^p \times \{0, 1\}^J : i = 1, 2, \dots, n\}$, where $\mathbf{x}_i = (x_{i1}, \dots, x_{ip})^T \in \mathbb{R}^p$ represents the predictors (features) vector for the ith image, p represents the dimensionality of features. And $\mathbf{y}_i = (y_{i1}, \dots, y_{iJ})^T \in \{0, 1\}^J$ is the corresponding label vector, $y_{ij} = 1$ if the ith image has the jth label and $y_{ij} = 0$ otherwise. Unlike the traditional multi-class problem where each sample only belongs to a single category: $\sum_{j=1}^{J} y_{ij} = 1$, in multi-label setting, we relax the constraint to $\sum_{j=1}^{J} y_{ij} \geq 0$. Let $\mathbf{X} = (\mathbf{x}_1, \dots, \mathbf{x}_n)^T$ be the $n \times p$ training data matrix, and $\mathbf{Y} = (\mathbf{y}_1, \dots, \mathbf{y}_n)^T$ the corresponding $n \times J$ label indicator matrix.

Suppose we can extract p high-dimensional heterogeneous features from images, and these p features are divided into L disjoint groups of homogeneous features, with p_l the number of features in the lth group, i.e., $\sum_l^L p_l = p$. For ease of notation, we use a matrix $\mathbf{X}_l \in \mathbb{R}^{n \times p_l}$ to represent the features of training data corresponding to the lth group, with corresponding coefficient vector $\beta_{jl} \in \mathbb{R}^{p_l} (l = 1, 2, \dots, L)$ for the jth label. Let $\boldsymbol{\beta}_j = (\beta_{j1}^T, \dots, \beta_{jL}^T)^T$ be the entire coefficient vector for the jth label; we have

$$\mathbf{X}\boldsymbol{\beta}_j = \sum_{l=1}^{L} \mathbf{X}_l \beta_{jl}. \tag{1}$$

In the following, we assume that the label indicator matrix $\mathbf{Y}$ is centered and the feature matrix $\mathbf{X}$ is centered and standardized, namely $\sum_{i=1}^{n} y_{ij} = 0$, $\sum_{i=1}^{n} x_{id} = 0$, and $\sum_{i=1}^{n} x_{id}^2 = 1$, for $j = 1, 2, \dots, J$ and $d = 1, 2, \dots, p$. Our algorithm can be generalized naturally to the unstandardized case. Moreover, we let $\|\beta_{jl}\|_2^2$ and $\|\beta_{jl}\|_1$ denote the ℓ_2-norm and the ℓ_1-norm of vector β_{jl}.

2.2 Lasso

In statistical community, lasso (least absolute shrinkage and selection operator) [25] is a shrinkage and variable selection method for linear regression, which is a penalized least square method imposing an ℓ_1-norm penalty on the regression co-efficients. Due to the nature of the ℓ_1-norm penalty, lasso continuously shrinks the coefficients toward zero, and achieves its prediction accuracy via the bias-variance trade-off. In signal processing, lasso always produces sparse representation that selects the subset compactly expressing the input signal. By this way, lasso can encode more discriminative information. In computer vision, the lasso-based sparse representation methods have been successfully used to solve problems such as face recognition [27], image classification [22], image annotation [26], image retrieval [21], and so on.

In order to select the most discriminative features for annotation of images by the jth tag, lasso is defined to train a model $\boldsymbol{\beta}_j$ on the training set of images $\mathbf{X}$ by a ℓ_1-norm penalized least square regression:

$$\min_{\boldsymbol{\beta}_j} \left(\| \mathbf{Y}_{(:,j)} - \mathbf{X}\boldsymbol{\beta}_j \|_2^2 + \lambda \| \boldsymbol{\beta}_j \|_1 \right), \tag{2}$$

where $\lambda > 0$ is the regularized parameter. Due to the nature of the ℓ_1-norm penalty, by solving (2), most coefficients in $\boldsymbol{\beta}_j$ will be shrinked to zero, which could be used to select the discriminative features. It is clear that formula (2) is an unconstrained convex optimization problem. Many algorithms have been proposed to solve problem (2), like the Quadratic Programming methods [25], Least Angle Regression [9], Gauss–Seidel [24] etc.

However, the sparsity induced by lasso is yielded by treating each variable individually, regardless of its correlations and position in the input feature vector, so that existing relationships and structures between the variables are merely disregarded. Therefore, lasso could not benefit from the prior knowledge, e.g., correlated features, grouping structure, spatial, hierarchical or related to the physics of the problem at hand, which could lead to less interpretability and worse prediction performance.

2.3 Elastic Net

Although lasso has shown success in many real-world applications, as pointed out by Zou and Hastie [31], it has some limitations.

1. First, of all the p features for n data samples, lasso selects at most n features in the $p > n$ case;
2. Second, if there are high correlations between input features, the prediction performance of the lasso may not be optimal.

Elastic net [31] generalizes the lasso to overcome these drawbacks. For any non-negative λ_1 and λ_2, elastic net is defined as an optimization problem:

$$\min_{\boldsymbol{\beta}_j} \left(\| \mathbf{Y}_{(:,j)} - \mathbf{X}\boldsymbol{\beta}_j \|_2^2 + \lambda \| \boldsymbol{\beta}_j \|_2^2 + \lambda \| \boldsymbol{\beta}_j \|_1 \right). \tag{3}$$

Let $\alpha = \lambda_2/(\lambda_1 + \lambda_2)$, then we can reformulate (3) as a constrained convex optimization problem [31]:

$$\min_{\boldsymbol{\beta}_j} \|\mathbf{Y}_{(:,j)} - \mathbf{X}\boldsymbol{\beta}_j\|_2^2$$

$$\text{s.t.} \quad \alpha\|\boldsymbol{\beta}_j\|_2^2 + (1-\alpha)\lambda\|\boldsymbol{\beta}_j\|_1 \leq t \quad \text{for some } t, \tag{4}$$

where $\alpha\|\boldsymbol{\beta}_j\|_2^2 + (1-\alpha)\lambda\|\boldsymbol{\beta}_j\|_1$ is called the *elastic-net penalty* [31], which is a convex combination of the ℓ_1-norm and ℓ_2-norm penalty. The elastic-net criterion (4) can be written as

$$\min_{\boldsymbol{\beta}_j^*}\left(\|\mathbf{Y}_{(:,j)}^* - \mathbf{X}^*\boldsymbol{\beta}_j^*\|_2^2 + \gamma\|\boldsymbol{\beta}_j^*\|_1\right), \tag{5}$$

where $\gamma = \lambda_1/\sqrt{1+\lambda_2}$, $\boldsymbol{\beta}_j^* = \sqrt{1+\lambda_2}\boldsymbol{\beta}_j$, $\mathbf{Y}_{(:,j)}^* = [\mathbf{Y}_{(:,j)}^T, 0]^T \in \mathbb{R}^{n+p}$, $\mathbf{X}^* \in \mathbb{R}^{(n+p)\times p}$, and $\mathbf{X}^* = (1+\lambda_2)^{-1/2}[\mathbf{X}^T, \sqrt{\lambda_2}\mathbf{I}]^T$. Therefore, formula (5) can be solved by lasso algorithms. Furthermore, elastic net can potentially select all p input features even in the $p > n$ case.

Obviously, lasso is a special case of the elastic net when $\lambda_2 = 0$. Given a fixed λ_2, the elastic net can be efficiently solved by the LARSEN algorithm [31]. Experimental studies in [31] showed that elastic net performs better in prediction while enjoying a similar sparsity of features selection.

2.4 Group Lasso

Yuan and Lin [29] proposed the group lasso which solves the convex optimization problem:

$$\min_{\boldsymbol{\beta}_j} \sum_{j=1}^{J}\left(\left\|\mathbf{Y}_{(:,j)} - \sum_{l=1}^{L}\mathbf{X}_l\beta_{jl}\right\|_2^2 + \lambda\sum_{l=1}^{L}\sqrt{p_l}\|\beta_{jl}\|_2\right), \tag{6}$$

where p dimension features are divided into L groups, with p_l the number in group l. Note that $\|\cdot\|_2$ is the *not squared* Euclidean norm. This procedure acts like the lasso at the group level: depending on λ, an entire group of features may be dropped out of the model. In fact if the group sizes are all one, it reduces to the lasso.

Clearly, it is straightforward to employ group lasso to undertake the heterogeneous features selection for images. Taking L kinds of heterogeneous features, like colors, shapes, or textures, extracted from the images as a group, respectively, we can use $\mathbf{X}_l$ to represent the input samples for the corresponding lth feature group. Therefore, by group lasso, we can perform feature selection at group level.

However, the group lasso does not yield sparsity within a group. That is, if a group of features is non-zero, they will all be non-zero. For social image annotation, we intend to perform heterogeneous feature selection both at the groups level and within the groups, so as to select the most discriminative features for predicting tags for test images more effectively.

3 Multi-label Boosting by Structural Grouping Sparsity

3.1 Problem Formulation and Solution

In this section, we describe the framework of the proposed Multi-label Boosting by selecting heterogeneous features with structural Grouping Sparsity (MtBGS).

For the jth label, we tend to train a regression model with a penalty term as follows to select discriminative features:

$$\min_{\boldsymbol{\beta}_j}\left(\left\|\mathbf{Y}_{(:,j)} - \sum_{l=1}^{L}\mathbf{X}_l\beta_{jl}\right\|_2^2 + \lambda P(\boldsymbol{\beta}_j)\right), \tag{7}$$

where $\mathbf{Y}_{(:,j)} \in (0, 1)^{(n \times 1)}$ is the jth column of indicator matrix $\mathbf{Y}$ and encodes the label information for the jth label, $P(\boldsymbol{\beta}_j)$ is the regularizer which can impose certain structural priors of input data. For example, the ridge regression uses the ℓ_2-norm to avoid overfitting and lasso produces sparsity on $\boldsymbol{\beta}_j$ by the ℓ_1-norm.

Basically, MtBGS comprises two steps, namely regression with structural grouping penalty and multi-label boosting by curds and whey.

3.1.1 Step 1: Regression with Structural Grouping Penalty

Since there are high-dimensional heterogeneous features in images, it is very *natural* to perform feature selection at group level (inter heterogeneous feature sets) first and then identify subgroup within a homogeneous feature set. The motivation of structural grouping penalty in MtBGS is to set most of coefficients in vectors β_{jl} to zero and only keep in the model limited number of coefficients, whose corresponding groups of features are discriminative to the jth label. That is to say, only discriminative subgroups of homogeneous features are selected out.

For each label j and its corresponding indicator vector, the regression model of MtBGS is defined as follows:

$$\min_{\boldsymbol{\beta}_j}\sum_{j=1}^{J}\left(\left\|\mathbf{Y}_{(:,j)} - \sum_{l=1}^{L}\mathbf{X}_l\beta_{jl}\right\|_2^2 + \lambda_1\sum_{l=1}^{L}\|\beta_{jl}\|_2 + \lambda_2\|\boldsymbol{\beta}_j\|_1\right), \tag{8}$$

where $\lambda_1\sum_{l=1}^{L}\|\beta_{jl}\|_2 + \lambda_2\|\boldsymbol{\beta}_j\|_1$ is the regularizer $P(\boldsymbol{\beta}_j)$ in (7) and is called the *structural grouping penalty*.

Let $\hat{\boldsymbol{\beta}}_j$ be the solution of formula (8), we can predict the probability $\hat{\mathbf{y}}_u$ that unlabeled images $\mathbf{X}^u$ belong to the jth label as follows:

$$\hat{\mathbf{y}}_u = \mathbf{X}^u\hat{\boldsymbol{\beta}}_j. \tag{9}$$

3.1.2 Step 2: Multi-label Boosting by Curds and Whey

The usual procedure of performing individual regression of each label on the common set of features ignores the correlations between labels. We propose to take advantage of correlations between labels to improve predictive accuracy. We call this method the multi-label boosting by Curds and Whey (C&W) [3].

Curds and Whey sets up the connection between multiple response regression and canonical correlation analysis. Therefore, the C&W method can be used to boost the performance of multi-label prediction given the prediction results from the individual regression of each label, and hence it can be easily integrated into our MtBGS framework.

3.2 Regularized Regression with Structural Grouping Penalty

Unlike group lasso, our structural grouping penalty in (8) not only selects the groups of heterogeneous features, but also identifies the subgroup of homogeneous features within each selected group.

Note that when $\lambda_1 = 0$, the formula (8) reduces to the traditional lasso under the multi-label learning setting, and $\lambda_2 = 0$ for the group lasso [29].

Therefore the framework of MtBGS puts forth a more flexible mechanism to the selection of heterogeneous features for the image understanding with multiple labels.

3.2.1 Group Selection

For each label j, we discuss how to obtain the coefficient vector $\boldsymbol{\beta}_j$ in the consequent sections. If $\beta_{jl} \neq \{0\}^{p_l}$, it means that the lth group of homogeneous features is selected for the jth label.

According to [11], the subgradient equations of first two terms in (8) are

$$-\mathbf{X}_l^T \left(\mathbf{Y}_{(:,j)} - \sum_l \mathbf{X}_l \beta_{jl} \right) + \lambda_1 s_{jl} = 0; \quad l = 1, \ldots, L; j = 1, \ldots, J, \quad (10)$$

where $s_{jl} = \beta_{jl}/\|\beta_{jl}\|_2$ if $\beta_{jl} \neq \{0\}^{p_l}$ and s_{jl} is a vector with $\|s_{jl}\|_2 \leq 1$ otherwise. We now focus on the solution for one group and hold other coefficients fixed.

Let the solutions of (10) to be $\hat{\beta}_{j1}, \hat{\beta}_{j2}, \ldots, \hat{\beta}_{jL}$. If

$$\left\| \mathbf{X}_l^T \left(\mathbf{Y}_{(:,j)} - \sum_{k \neq l} \mathbf{X}_k \hat{\beta}_{jk} \right) \right\| < \lambda_1 \quad (11)$$

then $\hat{\beta}_{jl}$ is set to zero; otherwise it satisfies

$$\hat{\beta}_{jl} = \left(\mathbf{X}_l^T \mathbf{X}_l + \lambda_1/\|\hat{\beta}_{jl}\|_2 \right)^{-1} \mathbf{X}_l^T \left(\mathbf{Y}_{(:,j)} - \sum_{k \neq l} \mathbf{X}_k \hat{\beta}_{jk} \right). \quad (12)$$

This leads to an algorithm that cycles through the groups, which is a blockwise coordinate descent procedure [11, 29]. The criterion (8) is convex and separable so that the blockwise coordinate descent at group level and piecewise coordinate descent within group for individual features can be used for optimization.

We first focus on just one group l of label j, and denote the corresponding p_l-dimensional homogeneous features of jth label by $\mathbf{X}_l = (X_1^l, X_2^l, \ldots, X_{p_l}^l)$. Since our structural grouping penalty attends to identify the subgroup within each selected group, we assume the lth group is selected and the coefficients $\beta_{jl} = \boldsymbol{\theta}_{jl} = (\theta_1, \theta_2, \ldots, \theta_{p_l})$. We let $\mathbf{r}_{jl} = \mathbf{Y}_{(:,j)} - \sum_{k \neq l} \mathbf{X}_k \beta_{jk}$ denote the partial residual when the lth group is removed.

The subgradient equations of (8) with respect to θ_m are

$$-X_m^{l\,T} \left(\mathbf{r}_{jl} - \sum_{m=1}^{p_l} X_m^l \theta_m \right) + \lambda_1 s_m + \lambda_2 t_m = 0, \quad m = 1, \ldots, p_l, \qquad (13)$$

where $s_m = \theta_m / \|\boldsymbol{\theta}_{jl}\|_2$ if $\theta_m \neq 0$ and s_m is a vector satisfying $\|s_m\|_2 \leq 1$ otherwise, and $t_m \in \mathrm{sign}(\theta_m)$, that is, $t_m = \mathrm{sign}(\theta_m)$ if $\theta_m \neq 0$ and $t_m \in [-1, 1]$ if $\theta_m = 0$.

Letting $\mathbf{a} = \mathbf{X}_l^T \mathbf{r}_{jl}$, then a necessary and sufficient condition for $\boldsymbol{\theta}_{jl}$ to be zero, which means the lth group is dropped out of the model, is that the system of equations

$$\mathbf{a}_m = \lambda_1 s_m + \lambda_2 t_m \qquad (14)$$

has a solution with $\|s_m\|_2 \leq 1$ and $t_m \in [-1, 1]$. We can determine this by minimizing

$$J(t) = \frac{1}{\lambda_1^2} \sum_{m=1}^{p_l} (\mathbf{a}_m - \lambda_2 t_m)^2 = \sum_{m=1}^{p_l} s_m^2 \qquad (15)$$

with respect to $t_m \in [-1, 1]$ and then check if $J(\hat{t}) \leq 1$, which means $\boldsymbol{\theta}_{jl} = 0$ and therefore the lth group is dropped out of the model.

Now if $J(\hat{t}) > 1$, which means the lth group is selected, then we must minimize the following criterion to identify the subgroup of homogeneous feature sets after the lth group is selected:

$$\left\| \mathbf{r}_{jl} - \sum_{m=1}^{p_l} X_m^l \theta_m \right\|_2^2 + \lambda_1 \|\boldsymbol{\theta}_{jl}\|_2 + \lambda_2 \sum_{m=1}^{p_l} \|\theta_m\|_1. \qquad (16)$$

Formula (16) is the sum of a convex differentiable function (first two terms) and a separable penalty. In next section we develop the Gauss–Seidel Coordinate Descent (GSCD) algorithm [24] to minimize (16) by a one-dimensional search over θ_m.

We summarize the algorithm for solving the regularized regression with structural grouping penalty in Algorithm 1.

Algorithm 1: Regularized Regression with Structural Grouping Penalty for Group Selection

---

1: **iterate** over groups $l = 1, 2, \ldots, L$
2:   **if** $J(\hat{t}) \leq 1$ **then**
3:     $\hat{\beta}_{jl} \leftarrow 0$
4:   **else**
5:     **iterate** over $m = 1, 2, \ldots, p_l, 1, \ldots,$
6:       minimize (16) by the GSCD method
7:     **until** convergence
8:   **end if**
9: **until** convergence
output the estimated coefficient vector $\hat{\boldsymbol{\beta}}_j$.

3.2.2 Subgroup Identification by GSCD

We now derive the algorithm for solving the step 6 in Algorithm 1 to identify subgroup. We know that formula (16) is a convex function, therefore a global optimized result can be calculated.

The subgradient equation of (16) is

$$g_m = -X_m^{l\,T} \left(\mathbf{r}_{jl} - \sum_{m=1}^{p_l} X_m^l \theta_m \right) + \lambda_1 \theta_m / \| \boldsymbol{\theta}_{jl} \|_2 + \lambda_2 t_m = 0. \tag{17}$$

Let us define

$$viol_m = \begin{cases} |\lambda_2 - G_m|, & \theta_m > 0, \\ |\lambda_2 + G_m|, & \theta_m < 0, \\ \max(G_m - \lambda_2, -\lambda_2 - G_m, 0), & \theta_m = 0, \end{cases} \tag{18}$$

where

$$G_m = X_m^{l\,T} \left(-\mathbf{r}_{jl} + \sum_{m=1}^{p_l} X_m^l \theta_m \right) - \lambda_1 \theta_m / \| \boldsymbol{\theta}_{jl} \|_2, \tag{19}$$

according to the Karush–Kuhn–Tucker (KKT) conditions, the first order optimality conditions for (16) can be written as

$$voil_m \leq \tau, \quad \forall m \in \{1, 2, \ldots, p_l\}, \tag{20}$$

where $\tau > 0$ is the error tolerance. In fact, we refer to (20) as optimality with tolerance τ.

In solving (16) by the Gauss–Seidel method, one variable θ_m with the maximum $viol_m$ that violates the optimality conditions (20) is chosen and the optimization subproblem is solved with respect to this variable θ_m alone, keeping the other θs

---

Algorithm 2: Subgroup Identification by GSCD

1: Initialize $I_z = \{1, 2, \ldots, p_l\}$ and $I_{nz} = \emptyset$
2: **while** optimality violator exists in I_z
3:    find the maximum violator $viol_m (m \in I_z)$
4:    add m to I_{nz}
5:    **repeat**
6:    **while** $voil_m > \tau$
7:        update θ_m by (21)
8:        **if** $\theta_m^{new} \leq L$ **or** $\theta_m^{new} \geq H$
9:            $\theta_m^{new} = (L + H)/2$
10:           compute g_m
11:       **if** $g_m > \tau$
12:           $H = \theta_m$
13:       **else if** $g_m < -\tau$
14:           $L = \theta_m$
15:   **end while**
16:       find the maximum violator $viol_m (m \in I_{nz})$
17:   **until** no violator exists in I_{nz}
18: **end while**
output the estimated coefficient vector $\hat{\beta}_{jl}$.

---

fixed. This procedure is repeated as long as there exists a variable which violates conditions (20).

Let us define the following two sets $I_z = \{m : \theta_m = 0\}$ and $I_{nz} = \{m : \theta_m \neq 0\}$. The key to efficiently solve (16) by Gauss–Seidel methods is the selection of the variable θ_m in each iteration with respect to which the objective function is optimized. A combination of the bisection method and Newton method [24] is used to optimize (16). In this method, two points L and H for which the derivative of the objective function in (16) has opposite signs are chosen, which ensures the root always lies in an interval $[L, H]$.

The minimizer computation through a Newton update is

$$\theta_m^{new} = \theta_m - g_m/H_{mm}, \tag{21}$$

where H_{mm} is the diagonal elements of the Hessian $H = {X_m^l}^T X_m^l$ for (16) with respect to θ_m. This procedure can be best explained using Algorithm 2.

It is important to note that the objective function in (16) has different right-hand and left-hand derivatives with respect to θ_m at $\theta_m = 0$. Therefore, in case when the current value of θ_m is 0, we have to try both directions and compute g_m in the step 10 of Algorithm 2 according to the method in [12].

3.3 Multi-label Boosting by Curds and Whey

In order to take advantage of correlations between the labels to boost multi-label annotation, we propose to utilize the curds and whey (C&W) [3] method and integrate it into our MtBGS framework.

Let $\hat{\boldsymbol{\beta}}_j$ be the estimated coefficient vector for the jth label output by Algorithm 1, and $\hat{\mathbf{y}}_j$ denote corresponding estimated indicator vector of the jth label, we have

$$\hat{\mathbf{y}}_j = \mathbf{X}\hat{\boldsymbol{\beta}}_j. \tag{22}$$

According to [3], if the labels are correlated we may be able to obtain a more accurate prediction $\tilde{\mathbf{y}}_j$ by a linear combination $\tilde{\mathbf{y}}_j = \mathbf{B}\hat{\mathbf{y}}_j$. The matrix $\mathbf{B} \in \mathbb{R}^{J \times J}$ takes the form

$$\mathbf{B} = \mathbf{C}^{-1}\mathbf{W}\mathbf{C}, \tag{23}$$

where $\mathbf{C}$ is the $J \times J$ matrix whose rows are the label ($\mathbf{y}$) canonical coordinates output by canonical correlation analysis (CCA) [16] and $\mathbf{W} = \mathrm{diag}(w_1, w_2, \ldots, w_J)$ is a diagonal matrix. In this way, the C&W procedure is a form of multivariate shrinking of $\hat{\mathbf{y}}_j$. It transforms (by $\mathbf{C}$), shrinks (multiplies by $\mathbf{W}$) and then transforms back (by $\mathbf{C}^{-1}$). In an idealized setting that the i.i.d. predicting errors are independent of the labels, the optimal shrinkage matrix $\mathbf{B}^*$ can be derived by CCA. CCA computes two canonical coordinates vectors, $v_{x_j} \in \mathbb{R}^p$ and $v_{y_j} \in \mathbb{R}^J$, such that the correlation coefficient

$$\rho_j = \frac{v_{x_j}^T \mathbf{X}^T \mathbf{Y} v_{y_j}}{\sqrt{(v_{x_j}^T \mathbf{X}^T \mathbf{X} v_{x_j})(v_{y_j}^T \mathbf{Y}^T \mathbf{Y} v_{y_j})}} \tag{24}$$

is maximized, where $j = 1, 2, \ldots, J$ (we suppose $J < p$ here). Breiman and Friedman [3] derived that the rows of the matrix $\mathbf{C}$ in (23) are the label ($\mathbf{y}$) canonical coordinates $v_{y_j}^T$, and w_j ($j = 1, 2, \ldots, J$) in matrix $\mathbf{W}$ are

$$w_j = \frac{\rho_j^2}{\rho_j^2 + \gamma(1 - \rho_j^2)}, \tag{25}$$

where $\gamma = p/n$. We summarize the multi-label boosting by Curds and Whey method in Algorithm 3.

4 Experiments

In this section, we systematically evaluate the effectiveness of our proposed MtBGS framework in automatic multi-tag image annotation.

Algorithm 3: Multi-label Boosting by C&W

1: Perform CCA on selected features $\mathbf{X}$ and labels $\mathbf{Y}$
2: Output v_{y_j} and ρ_j $(j = 1, 2, \ldots, J)$
3: Compute w_j by (25)
4: Form matrix $\mathbf{W} = \text{diag}(w_1, w_2, \ldots, w_J)$
5: Form matrix $\mathbf{C} = (v_{y_1}, \ldots, v_{y_J})'$
6: Compute matrix $\mathbf{B}$ by (23)
7: **for** $j = 1, 2, \ldots, J$ **do**
8:      Compute $\tilde{\mathbf{y}}_j = \mathbf{B}\hat{\mathbf{y}}_j = \mathbf{C}^{-1}\mathbf{W}\mathbf{C}\mathbf{X}\hat{\boldsymbol{\beta}}_j$
9: **end for**
output the estimated indicators $\tilde{\mathbf{y}}_j$ $(j = 1, 2, \ldots, J)$.

4.1 Experimental Configuration

4.1.1 Dataset

Three benchmark image datasets are used in our experiments: *Microsoft Research Cambridge* (MSRC), MIML [32], and NUS-WIDE [6]. Twenty-three and five class labels (tags) are, respectively, associated with images in MSRC and MIML, which are multi-tagged and can be used as annotation ground truth. We randomly sampled 10, 000 images from NUS-WIDE in our experiments. For the ground truth of NUS-WIDE we chose two indicator matrices from the selected data samples to form two datasets—NUS-6 and NUS-16. In these two datasets, the top 6 and 16 tags which label the maximum numbers of positive instances were selected, respectively.

Multiple heterogeneous features were extracted and concatenated as a visual feature vector for each image. Taking each type of homogeneous features as a group, we sequentially numbered the feature groups in the following sections. Details of features, dimensionality, and also the sequence numbers for each of the three datasets are listed as follows:

MSRC and MIML 638-D features are sequentially divided into seven groups. 1: 256-D color histogram; 2: 6-D color moments; 3: 128-D color coherence; 4: 15-D textures; 5: 10-D tamura-texture coarseness; 6: 8-D tamura-texture directionality; 7: 80-D edge orientation histogram; 8 (only for MIML): 135-D SBN colors [20]. Note that the eighth group of features is only used in MIML dataset. Therefore, the dimensionality of visual feature vector for images in MSRC is 503-D.

NUS 634-D features are sequentially divided into five groups. 1: 64-D color histogram; 2: 144-D color correlogram; 3: 73-D edge direction histogram; 4: 128-D wavelet texture; 5: 225-D blockwise color moments.

4.1.2 Evaluation Metrics

The area under the ROC curve (AUC) and F1 score are used to measure the performance of image annotation. Since there are multiple labels (tags) in our experiments, to measure both the global performance across multiple tags and the average performance of all tags, according to [17, 19] we use both the *microaveraging* and *macroaveraging* methods. Therefore, the evaluation metrics we used are micro-AUC, macro-AUC, micro-F1, and macro-F1.

In particular, for the training data, we randomly sampled 300, 500, and 1000 samples from MSRC, MIML, and NUS datasets, respectively. The remaining data were used as the corresponding test data. For each dataset, this process was repeated ten times to generate ten random training/test partitions. The average performance in terms of AUC and F1 score and standard deviation are evaluated.

4.2 Parameter Tuning

The parameters λ_1 and λ_2 in (8) need to be tuned. At the first training/test partition we choose those parameters by a 5-fold cross validation on the training dataset. These chosen parameters were then fixed to train the MtBGS model for all the ten partitions. Note that different features play different roles in our MtBGS framework for different labels. Therefore, the parameter tuning process is performing separately for each tag. We depict four examples of parameter tuning by the 5-fold cross validation with respect to micro-AUC in Fig. 3. We can observe that the highest performance on three concepts is achieved at some intermediate values of λ_1 and λ_2.

4.3 Heterogeneous Feature Selection

We explored the differences of heterogeneous feature selection between group lasso, lasso, and MtBGS on MSRC and MIML dataset for each label, respectively. Sample images for 2 instance labels from MSRC and MIML are listed in Fig. 4 and Fig. 5, respectively. As can be seen, images with different labels (semantics) have different heterogeneous low-level features, such as color and texture etc. Therefore, training a model for heterogeneous feature selection is crucial for understanding the semantic content in these images.

In order to uncover the different mechanism of heterogeneous feature selection for group lasso, lasso and MtBGS, we output the coefficient vectors $\boldsymbol{\beta}_j$, respectively, from the three algorithms after 10-round repetition, and investigate the results of group selection for each round. The results of heterogeneous feature selection for label "tree" in Fig. 4 are depicted in Fig. 6. We observe that though group lasso and MtBGS can both select groups of features, the coefficient values of $\boldsymbol{\beta}_j$ within groups are obviously different. MtBGS successfully induces sparsity of coefficient values, i.e., shrink to zeros, within groups, which is like lasso. On the contrary, group lasso intends to include all the coefficients into the model. Comparing the group selection results between group lasso and MtBGS, MtBGS produces more consistent group selection with respect to the 10-round repetition training process.

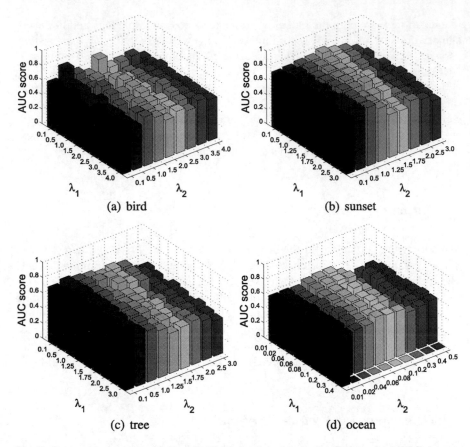

(a) bird

(b) sunset

(c) tree

(d) ocean

Fig. 3 Parameters tuning examples of MtBGS for three labels: "bird" from the MSRC dataset, "sunset" and "tree" from the MIML dataset, and "ocean" from the NUS dataset. The respective ranges of λ_1 and λ_2 for MSRC, MIML, and NUS are: {0.1, 0.5, 1.0, 1.5, 2.0, 2.5, 3.0, 3.5, 4.0}, {0.1, 0.5, 1.0, 1.25, 1.5, 1.75, 2.0, 2.5, 3.0}, and {0.01, 0.02, 0.04, 0.06, 0.08, 0.1, 0.2, 0.3, 0.4, 0.5}

Fig. 4 Sample images for labels "tree" and "bird" from the MSRC dataset

Fig. 5 Sample images for labels "mountain" and "sunset" from the MIML dataset

Furthermore, we explore the results of heterogeneous feature selection by Mt-BGS for different sizes of training data. Let us consider Fig. 7, where we depict the results by MtBGS for images of the label "mountain" in the MIML dataset with different sizes of training data. Note that the coefficient values are plotted from one round, and the group selection are plotted from 10-round repetition. As can be seen, the heterogeneous feature selection is more consistent and interpretable when the size of training data is increasing. For example, the most discriminative features for label "mountain" (see sample images in Fig. 5) are color and shape. The corresponding extracted feature groups in our experiments are 1: 256-D color histogram, 2: 6-D color moments, 3: 128-D color coherence, 8: 135-D SBN, and 7: 80-D edge orientation histogram. Comparing the results in Fig. 7, noisy feature groups, i.e., the texture feature groups, are almost excluded from the models when the number of training data reaches 900. In particular, the coefficient vector output from the 900 training samples is more sparse.

4.4 Performance of Multi-label Learning and Annotation

We first investigate the learning performance of MtBGS before C&W. MtBGS for each label is trained separately on the training data with different sizes, i.e., {500, 600, 700, 800, 900, 1,000} and {1,000, 1,2000, 1,400, 1,600, 1,800, 2,000} for MIML and NUS-6, respectively. This process is repeated for 10-round by randomly sampling ten times for each size of training data. From Fig. 8 we can observe that the MtBGS produces better learning performance with more training samples. Moreover, the performance improving ratio of MIML is higher, since the number of test samples in NUS-6 is far more than that of MIML.

To show the whole performance of multi-label annotation by MtBGS framework, we compare MtBGS (C&W(test)) algorithm with four other algorithms: CCA-ridge, CCA-SVM, SVM, and MTL-LS [17]. Note that algorithm MTL-LS is a multi-label shared subspace algorithm, and the other three algorithms perform binary classification for each label separately. For details of CCA-ridge, CCA-SVM, and SVM

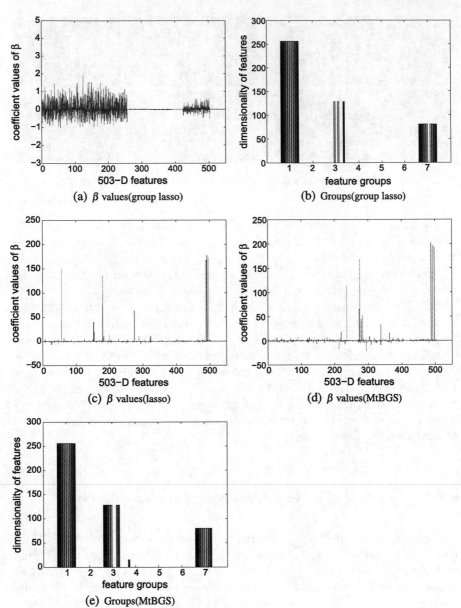

Fig. 6 Heterogeneous feature selection results from group lasso, lasso, and MtBGS for 10-round repetition of label "tree" in the MSRC dataset. Different colors indicate different rounds

please refer to [17]. The average performance and standard deviations from 10-round of repetition for each algorithm are reported in Table 1 and Table 2. We can see that the MtBGS framework outputs the best image annotation results in terms of AUC and F1 score. Furthermore, the performance of multi-label annotation by

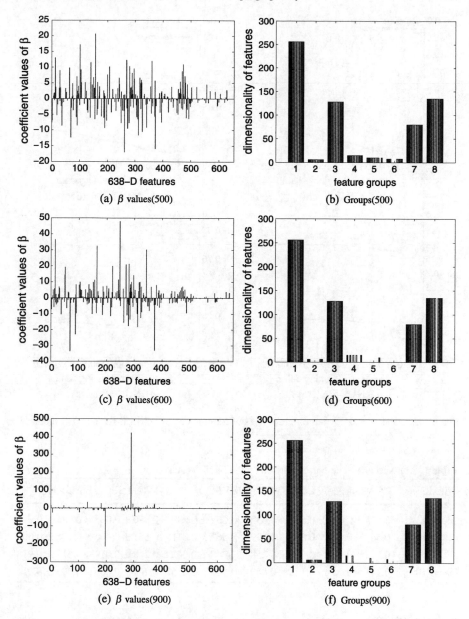

Fig. 7 Heterogeneous feature selection results from MtBGS for different sizes of training data, i.e., 500, 600, and 900, respectively, of concept "mountain" in the MIML dataset

MtBGS from NUS-6 is better than from NUS-16, since the correlations between tags in NUS-6 are relative more dense than those in NUS-16.

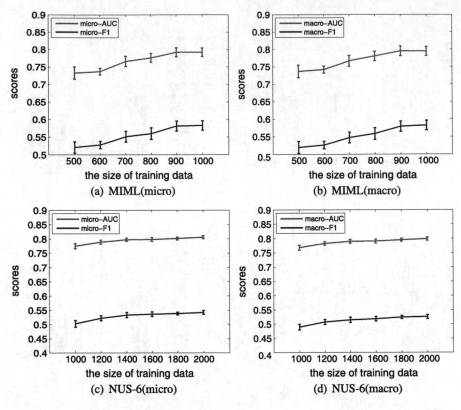

Fig. 8 AUC and F1 score versus different sizes of training data for the MIML and NUS-6 dataset by MtBGS

Table 1 Multi-label annotation comparison on the NUS-6 dataset

Criterion	CCA-ridge	CCA-SVM	SVM	MTL-LS	MtBGS
micro-AUC	0.615 ± 0.037	0.602 ± 0.032	0.607 ± 0.039	0.586 ± 0.031	0.784 ± 0.009
macro-AUC	0.561 ± 0.005	0.560 ± 0.009	0.563 ± 0.011	0.561 ± 0.006	0.776 ± 0.008
micro-F1	0.218 ± 0.036	0.265 ± 0.058	0.248 ± 0.042	0.228 ± 0.019	0.513 ± 0.013
macro-F1	0.141 ± 0.021	0.123 ± 0.029	0.109 ± 0.035	0.206 ± 0.006	0.498 ± 0.011

5 Conclusion

This paper proposes a framework of multi-label learning for image annotation, called the MtBGS. The MtBGS method is attractive due to its subgroup feature identification by structural grouping penalty in heterogeneous feature settings along with its multi-label boosting capability. Experiments show that the MtBGS not only is more interpretable for image annotation, but also achieves better results than the CCA-ridge, CCA-SVM, SVM, and MTL-LS methods.

Table 2 Multi-label annotation comparison on the NUS-16 dataset

Criterion	CCA-ridge	CCA-SVM	SVM	MTL-LS	MtBGS
micro-AUC	0.660 ± 0.111	0.661 ± 0.093	0.672 ± 0.101	0.688 ± 0.125	0.766 ± 0.009
macro-AUC	0.706 ± 0.063	0.706 ± 0.067	0.711 ± 0.078	0.731 ± 0.087	0.734 ± 0.009
micro-F1	0.201 ± 0.100	0.3235 ± 0.082	0.336 ± 0.098	0.222 ± 0.111	0.388 ± 0.016
macro-F1	0.180 ± 0.073	0.172 ± 0.077	0.174 ± 0.094	0.208 ± 0.089	0.292 ± 0.010

Acknowledgements This work is supported by NSFC (90920303, 61070068), 863 Program (2006 AA010107) and Program for Changjiang Scholars and Innovative Research Team in University (IRT0652, PCSIRT).

References

1. Barnard, K., Duygulu, P., Forsyth, D., De Freitas, N., Blei, D.M., Jordan, M.I.: Matching words and pictures. J. Mach. Learn. Res. **3**, 1107–1135 (2003)
2. Breiman, L.: Heuristics of instability and stabilization in model selection. Ann. Stat. **24**(6), 2350–2383 (1996)
3. Breiman, L., Friedman, J.: Predicting multivariate responses in multiple linear regression. J. R. Stat. Soc. B **59**(1), 3–54 (1997)
4. Cao, L., Luo, J., Liang, F., Huang, T.: Heterogeneous feature machines for visual recognition. In: Proceedings of the IEEE International Conference on Computer Vision (ICCV) (2009)
5. Chen, Y., Wang, J.Z., Geman, D.: Image categorization by learning and reasoning with regions. J. Mach. Learn. Res. **5**, 913–939 (2004)
6. Chua, T.S., Tang, J., Hong, R., Li, H., Luo, Z., Zheng, Y.: Nus-wide: A real-world web image database from National University of Singapore. In: Proceedings of the ACM International Conference on Image and Video Retrieval, pp. 1–9. ACM, New York (2009)
7. Clemmensen, L., Hastie, T., Ersbøll, B.: Sparse discriminant analysis. http://www-stat.stanford.edu/~hastie/Papers/ (2008)
8. Duygulu, P., Barnard, K., De Freitas, J., Forsyth, D.: Object recognition as machine translation: Learning a lexicon for a fixed image vocabulary. In: Computer Vision, ECCV 2002, pp. 349–354 (2002)
9. Efron, B., Hastie, T., Johnstone, I., Tibshirani, R.: Least angle regression. Ann. Stat. **32**(2), 407–451 (2004)
10. Fan, J., Gao, Y., Luo, H.: Integrating concept ontology and multitask learning to achieve more effective classifier training for multilevel image annotation. IEEE Trans. Image Process. **17**(3), 407 (2008)
11. Friedman, J., Hastie, T., Tibshirani, R.: A note on the group lasso and a sparse group lasso. http://www-stat.stanford.edu/~tibs/research.html (2010)
12. Genkin, A., Lewis, D.D., Madigan, D.: Large-scale Bayesian logistic regression for text categorization. Technometrics **49**(3), 291–304 (2007)
13. Grangier, D., Bengio, S.: A discriminative kernel-based approach to rank images from text queries. IEEE Trans. Pattern Anal. Mach. Intell. **30**(8), 1371–1384 (2008)
14. Han, Y., Wu, F., Jia, J., Zhuang, Y., Yu, B.: Multi-task sparse discriminant analysis (MtSDA) with overlapping categories. In: Proceedings of the Twenty-Fourth AAAI Conference on Artificial Intelligence (AAAI-10), pp. 469–474 (2010)
15. Hastie, T., Buja, A., Tibshirani, R.: Penalized discriminant analysis. Ann. Stat. **23**(1), 73–102 (1995)
16. Hotelling, H.: Relations between two sets of variates. Biometrika **28**(3), 321–377 (1936)

17. Ji, S., Tang, L., Yu, S., Ye, J.: Extracting shared subspace for multi-label classification. In: Proceedings of the ACM SIGKDD International Conference on Knowledge Discovery and Data Mining (KDD), pp. 381–389. ACM, New York (2008)
18. Kang, F., Jin, R., Sukthankar, R.: Correlated label propagation with application to multi-label learning. In: Proceedings of the IEEE Computer Society Conference on Computer Vision and Pattern Recognition (CVPR), pp. 1719–1726 (2006)
19. Lewis, D.D.: Evaluating text categorization. In: Proceedings of Speech and Natural Language Workshop, pp. 312–318 (1991)
20. Maron, O., Ratan, A.L.: Multiple-instance learning for natural scene classification. In: Proceedings of the International Conference on Machine Learning (ICML), pp. 341–349 (1998)
21. Praks, P., Kucera, R., Izquierdo, E.: The sparse image representation for automated image retrieval. In: Image Processing, 2008. ICIP 2008. 15th IEEE International Conference on, pp. 25–28. IEEE, New York (2008)
22. Quattoni, A., Collins, M., Darrell, T.: Transfer learning for image classification with sparse prototype representations. In: Computer Vision and Pattern Recognition, 2008. CVPR 2008. IEEE Conference on, pp. 1–8. IEEE, New York (2008)
23. Shen, X., Huang, H.: Grouping pursuit through a regularization solution surface. J. Am. Stat. Assoc. **105**(490), 727–739 (2010)
24. Shevade, S., Keerthi, S.: A simple and efficient algorithm for gene selection using sparse logistic regression. Bioinformatics **19**(17), 2246–2253 (2003)
25. Tibshirani, R.: Regression shrinkage and selection via the lasso. J. R. Stat. Soc., Ser. B, Stat. Methodol. **58**(1), 267–288 (1996)
26. Wang, C., Yan, S., Zhang, L., Zhang, H.: Multi-label sparse coding for automatic image annotation. In: Proceedings of the IEEE Computer Society Conference on Computer Vision and Pattern Recognition (CVPR), pp. 1643–1650 (2009)
27. Wright, J., Yang, A.Y., Ganesh, A., Sastry, S.S., Ma, Y.: Robust face recognition via sparse representation. IEEE Trans. Pattern Anal. Mach. Intell. **31**(2), 210–227 (2008)
28. Wu, F., Han, Y.H., Tian, Q., Zhuang, Y.T.: Multi-label boosting for image annotation by structural grouping sparsity. In: Proceedings of the 2010 ACM International Conference on Multimedia (ACM Multimedia), pp. 15–24. ACM, New York (2010)
29. Yuan, M., Lin, Y.: Model selection and estimation in regression with grouped variables. J. R. Stat. Soc. B **68**(1), 49–67 (2006)
30. Zhang, Y., Zhou, Z.: Multi-label dimensionality reduction via dependence maximization. In: Proceedings of AAAI Conference on Artificial Intelligence (AAAI), pp. 1503–1505 (2008)
31. Zou, H., Hastie, T.: Regularization and variable selection via the elastic net. J. R. Stat. Soc. Ser. B., Stat. Methodol. **67**(2), 301–320 (2005)
32. Zhou, Z.H., Zhang, M.L.: Multi-instance multi-label learning with application to scene classification. In: Proceedings of Neural Information Processing Systems (NIPS) (2007)

Part II
Social Media System Design and Analysis

Mechanism Design for Incentivizing Social Media Contributions

Vivek K. Singh, Ramesh Jain, and Mohan Kankanhalli

Abstract Despite recent advancements in user-driven social media platforms, tools for studying user behavior patterns and motivations remain primitive. We highlight the voluntary nature of user contributions and that users can choose when (and when not) to contribute to the common media pool. A Game theoretic framework is proposed to study the dynamics of social media networks where contribution costs are individual but gains are common. We model users as rational selfish agents, and consider domain attributes like voluntary participation, virtual reward structure, network effect, and public-sharing to model the dynamics of this interaction. The created model describes the most appropriate contribution strategy from each user's perspective and also highlights issues like 'free-rider' problem and individual rationality leading to irrational (i.e. sub-optimal) group behavior. We also consider the perspective of the system designer who is interested in finding the best incentive mechanisms to influence the selfish end-users so that the overall system utility is maximized. We propose and compare multiple mechanisms (based on optimal bonus payment, social incentive leveraging, and second price auction) to study how a system designer can exploit the selfishness of its users, to design incentive mechanisms which improve the overall task-completion probability and system performance, while possibly still benefiting the individual users.

1 Introduction

With the emergence of Web 2.0 and multiple related social media applications (e.g. Flickr, Youtube, Facebook, Wikipedia) research interest has grown in multiple as-

V.K. Singh (✉) · R. Jain
University of California, Irvine, Irvine, USA
e-mail: singhv@uci.edu

R. Jain
e-mail: jain@ics.uci.edu

M. Kankanhalli
National University of Singapore, Singapore, Singapore
e-mail: mohan@comp.nus.edu.sg

S.C.H. Hoi et al. (eds.), *Social Media Modeling and Computing*,
DOI 10.1007/978-0-85729-436-4_6, © Springer-Verlag London Limited 2011

pects of social media including data sharing, image tagging, media processing, ontologies, retrieval etc. While these contributions have significantly advanced the state of the art from the technology perspective, not much research attention has been given till now to the *end-user* or *social aspect* of social media research. Despite significant interest in concepts like crowd-sourcing [6], collective intelligence [9], human-computation [25] etc., the tools to undertake *user behavior analysis in social media networks* are still in their infancy and no theoretical frameworks are available to mathematically analyze why and how often do users contribute to such social media?

That notwithstanding, social media networks are becoming increasingly relevant each day. Citizen-journalists are already providing interesting event information and images for common benefit to various news agencies [12]. Similarly, multiple users are already using tools like Google Image Labeler [4] to tag images and contributing content to Wikipedia [26], thus creating a rich collective information mechanism which can provide common benefits to a larger society.

An important point to consider in all these applications is that the user contribution is *totally voluntary*. Further the decision making is completely distributed and there are no means for central coordination or explicit communication between the various participating users. This brings us to the important issue of user *motivation* and that the individual users will contribute to such social media networks only based on their personal utility decisions.

Such a setup, though compelling, leads to multiple conflicting goals. While, the task-completion costs are incurred by the individuals, the benefits are common. Thus while the owners of systems such as New York Times, Google Labeler, or Wikipedia are interested in maximizing the tasks accomplished, individual agents may be interested in maximizing their personal utility gain in such a sensing/content-provision mechanism. A key question which arises in such a scenario is how can an individual user optimally decide his/her contribution strategy i.e. *when (and when not) should he/she undertake the social media task*. A system administrator on the other hands is interested in *finding the optimal incentive mechanisms to influence these selfish end-users so that the overall system utility is maximized*.

Clearly, there are no currently available tools which can answer such questions. The analysis and answer to such questions requires explicit modeling of user behavior as well as considering the specific characteristics of the domain being considered. Hence we propose the use of a game-theoretic framework, which models users as rational (selfish) agents and incorporates the dynamics of social media (e.g. voluntary participation, *virtual* reward structure, social benefits, and public-sharing) to gain some insights/explanations for user behavior patterns and also obtain certain prescriptive guidelines for system designers to motivate their users.

We demonstrate how game-theoretic modeling can be used to answer the above-mentioned questions. We study the user-user interaction and show how a user can find her optimal contribution level. Further, we demonstrate how a system designer can draw insights from such behavior patterns and exploit the selfishness of its users, to design multiple incentive mechanisms which help in improving the overall system performance, while possibly still benefiting the individual users.

2 Related Work and Domains

2.1 Why Are Social Media Networks Different?

Similar problems have been studied in multiple contexts in the past. From an economics perspective, the problem of 'public goods' [14] and optimal taxation [2] is well studied. However, emerging web-based 'societies' are fundamentally different as participation in them is voluntary and as such no taxation can be enforced. Only incentives, (if appropriate) can be given. Further, the reward on these social media sites etc. is typically a 'virtual currency' which has very different dynamics than real money. Such virtual currency (e.g. reputation points, extra bandwidth, virtual weaponry, gadgets etc.) is like 'fairy gold-dust' and typically costs the system designers exponentially less than their *perceived* value from user perspective. While some of this virtual currency is starting to be traded by users for real-world money [23], the marginal cost for system designers to grant such currency remains very low.

The issue of selfishness and contributions to a society also differ from scientists, and open-source software developers, as their 'contributions' are typically in-sync with their full time vocation. Hence they have direct and indirect professional benefits (grants, citations, downloads, jobs) from demonstrating their skill level. While a small percentage of contributors in media networks (e.g. directors on Youtube, or photographers on Flickr) might generate some career benefits from their contributions, these benefits remain atypical. More frequently the contributions to social media sites like Google Image Labeler, Photo-synth [11], Wikipedia do not involve rights and recognition as is common in open-source or scientific communities.

Social media network paradigms also differ from P2P [3, 17] or network routing disciplines as you cannot really calculate or regulate the usage characteristics. The produced content is truly a *public good* [14] for everybody like 'sunshine'.

Similarly, typical social media networks are also different from Mechanical Turk because the Turk users are not working to create any 'public good'. They are carrying out well defined tasks for an 'employer' who will 'privately' consume the generated media. Social media networks like Google Image Labeler, GalaxyZoo, Photo-synth, Wikipedia, Ushahidi on the other hand focus on creating 'public goods' for an open community.

Thus social media contributions deal with a unique set of parameters involving, voluntary participation, no taxation, real cost, virtual incentives, rare career benefits, and no regulations on usage characteristics. In this work we consider these differences in modeling and studying the media networks. Table 1 provides a summary of the comparison between different related scenarios and how social media contributions differs from each of them.

2.2 Related Work in Social Media

There have been attempts at enhancing user experience, and using that to get social media related tasks undertaken. *Human-computing* work by Von Ahn [25] is an

Table 1 Distinct characteristics of different type of contribution mechanisms

Case	Participation	Taxation	Reward currency	Career benefits	Usage pattern
Social media	*Voluntary*	*Not enforceable*	*Virtual*	*Rare*	*public good*
Physical societies	Mandatory	Enforceable	Real	–	–
Open-source software & scientific contributions	Voluntary	–	–	Yes	Partially regulated
P2P/ networking	Voluntary	–	Virtual	–	Monitored & regulated
Mechanical Turk	Voluntary	–	Real	Rare	Private

excellent example of this. Similarly 'Cognitive Surplus' [20] work has been arguing a case for providing mechanisms for users to contribute for common good.

Works like [10], study user behavior patterns in terms of the way they interact with social media sites (Youtube). They classify the users into different categories based on their access patterns, comment frequency, subscriptions etc. These are very important studies from the perspective of understanding general user behavior patterns. We maintain our focus in this paper though on user behavior from a *motivation* perspective and on *incentivizing* user contributions for better system performance.

Other works study the motivation of contributors on MovieLens, Wikipedia etc. from a sociological or psychological perspective [5, 19, 22]. Schroer et al. [19] discuss the intrinsic and extrinsic motivations for German Wikipedia contributors. Works like [5, 22] have highlighted how different forms of motivation (e.g. locked-out tools/ features in Slash-dot, extra weapons in World-of-Warcraft forum and comparative reputation/status within community etc.) can be used to motivate users. Similarly, Nov et al. [13] study how factors like 'user tenure', 'structural embeddedness', and 'motivation of self-development' affect user contributions on Flickr. However, all these studies are 'qualitative' and aimed at identifying what *type* of motivations work well in on-line communities. We, however, aim to provide 'quantitative' mechanisms to find out *how many* such extra features, weapons, or *how much* (e.g. extra bandwidth, reputation points etc.) are most suitable for different scenarios.

This book chapter builds upon a workshop paper [21], and reflects the advancements in our thinking process. Specifically, this chapter discusses multiple (instead of one 'paying the bonus' option discussed earlier) mechanism design options (e.g. social incentives, second price auction) available to designers. Further, this version relaxes the constraint of 'individually rational' contributions, and discusses how system designers can handle the cases wherein it is individually irrational for each user to contribute.

Mechanism design (i.e. defining rules of a game to achieve certain outcomes) is an area of growing importance (including recent Nobel prizes) in economics. It is also slowly making inroads into on-line communities (e.g. for creating optimal reputation feedback mechanisms in eBay like auction scenarios [1]).

3 Background: Game Theory

Game theory is a branch of applied mathematics that is used in the social sciences (most notably economics), biology, engineering, political science, international relations and is becoming increasingly relevant in computer science. It is used to mathematically capture behavior in strategic situations, in which an individual's utility from choices undertaken *depends on the choices made by others*. Thus it is often used for studying optimality and stable points in multi-agent problems, as opposed to conventional operation research or calculus based approaches which are well-suited for single agent optimization.

Here, we provide a quick refresher for some of the game-theoretic terms and concepts as relevant to this work.

1. *Game:* A game refers to any situation wherein multiple (2 or more) agents are making strategy decisions, and the chosen strategy effects the utility obtained by that agent *as well as* the other agents involved. Games can be *zero-sum*, wherein one agent's loss is considered other agent's gain e.g. war-like situations, or *non-zero-sum*, where one agent's loss does not necessarily means others gain. In our formalism the users (among themselves in Sect. 4) and the users and system designers (in Sect. 5) are both playing non-zero-sum games.
2. *Nash equilibrium:* Nash equilibrium is a solution concept in game theory which defines a point where each agent knows other agent's strategy options, and from which no agent has anything to gain by changing only her own strategy *unilaterally*. It is useful in giving guaranteed utility bounds to users, as once they choose their strategy based on the Nash equilibrium, it is in other agent's benefit to respond with their Nash equilibrium response. Any other response can only decrease their utility. Please note that multiple Nash equilibria may exist in the same game and agents can move or converge bilaterally to another Nash equilibrium (especially in repeated games).
3. *Mixed Strategy Nash equilibrium (MSNE):* A mixed strategy Nash equilibrium is a probabilistic variant of Nash equilibrium wherein the agents do not fix themselves to a single strategy but rather decide on the appropriate *mixture of strategies* which guarantees that no agent can gain anything by unilaterally diverting from it. Pure Nash equilibriums can be considered to be boundary cases of mixed strategy Nash equilibria.
4. *Mechanism design:* Mechanism design is the process of defining the rules of the game so as to lead it to a certain desired outcomes.

4 A Game-Theoretic Framework: The User Viewpoint

In this section we model user-user interaction patterns, and describe how rational (selfish) users may make optimal contribution decisions.

4.1 Problem Motivation

To motivate and ground the problem to a real life scenario from start, let us consider a citizen-journalism task (T) where a 'suspicious bag' left unattended at a train station can be reported by any of the N persons (agents) walking past. The gain (G) is common but the cost incurred (c_i) is individual. The problem from an agent(i)'s perspective is to find the percentage of times which he/she should report the bag himself/herself.

4.2 Problem Formulation

Let there be N social agents which can undertake a common task T. Let the cost for an agent i to undertake task T be c_i. While the costs are individual, the gains incurred (G) are taken to be common i.e. everybody gains equally. Each user can incur gain G, from a task if either it completes the task, or it does not, but somebody else completes it. Hence, the net utility of each agent EU_i is a function of its cost, gain, its chosen strategy in terms of how often to undertake the task (P_i), as well as the probability of task being undertaken by (at least one of the) *other* agents ($P_{\text{Do}}^{\text{All}-\{i\}}$). Hence, the problem from each agent's perspective is to find its best response strategy, (i.e. probability of doing task) which maximizes its net utility.

$$\underset{P_i \in [0,1]}{\text{argmax}}\, EU_i = f\left(c_i, G, P_i, P_{\text{Do}}^{\text{All}-\{i\}}\right). \tag{1}$$

The provided formulation incorporates two important characteristics of social media networks. Voluntary participation characteristic is innately represented in the problem statement, and the property of common gain once the task is completed is also made explicit.

In the formulation presented here, we assume that the users are selfish agents, that there is no collusion or agreement between them, and that the cost incurred is positive and less than gain $0 < c \leq G$ (we relax this constrain later). Also, in this formulation we use the term 'social media task', generically to include all relevant scenarios like those involving photo/video sharing, image tagging, commenting, content provision, linking, or content flagging. Lastly, we use 'agent' as a neutral term to represent any contributor who can undertake the relevant task.

4.3 Approach

We employ a game-theoretic framework to solve Eq. (1). To solve this problem, we start with a simple two person non-zero-sum game to study the interaction between two homogeneous agents and then iteratively add more complexities.

Table 2 Game between two users: matrix showing net utility for each user, under different strategies adopted by each player

Agent1 ⟍ Other agent	Do	Don't
Do	$G-c, G-c$	$G-c, G$
Don't	$G, G-c$	$0, 0$

Table 3 Game between user (agent$_i$) and others: matrix showing net utility for agent$_i$, under different strategies adopted

Agent$_i$ ⟍ Other agents	Do	Don't
Do	$G-c_i$	$G-c_i$
Don't	G	0

4.3.1 Two Agents, One Social Media Task

As shown in Table 2, for agent 1 there are two possible strategy options. He/she can either 'do' the task or 'don't' do it. If he/she chooses to do the task and the other agent also undertakes the task, then both will get the gain G but also incur the cost c. Agent 1's best case scenario is when he/she does not undertake the task but the other agent does it. Hence agent 1 will receive gain G without any cost while other agent will incur it. However, if both agents choose the 'don't' strategy, then there will be no gain achieved as the task is not undertaken.

The solution concept used in such settings where other agent's decisions affect your utilities is Nash equilibrium. The Nash equilibrium occurs when none of the agents can *unilaterally move to a better rewarding state* [16]. In this particular scenario, both the agents have a choice to either use the strategy 'Do' or 'Don't' and there exist three Nash equilibria. Two pure Nash equilibria exist at states [Do, Don't] and [Don't, Do] for agents 1 and 2, respectively. However, they favor one agent or the other and are unlikely to be maintained in long term. Hence, a mixed strategy solution seems a stable long term solution. The mixed strategy Nash equilibrium guarantees that:

$$P_i^* \in [0, 1], P_i \neq P_i^*: \quad EU_i\left(P_i^*, P_{\text{Do}}^{\text{All}-\{i\}^*}\right) \geq EU_i\left(P_i, P_{\text{Do}}^{\text{All}-\{i\}^*}\right), \quad (2)$$

where P_i^* is the optimal strategy for agent i, and $P_{\text{Do}}^{\text{All}-\{i\}^*}$ represents the cumulative effect of best possible strategy choices made by other agent(s).

A mixed strategy Nash equilibrium (MSNE) can be computed based on the condition of *choice indifference* i.e. when the agents do not gain (or lose) by changing their strategies [16]. This makes for a good equilibrium point because if the agents prefer one choice, obviously they shall go for the better choice. Thus the equilibrium needs to take place at a point where both agents do not stand to gain (or lose) any value by strategy selection.

In the given scenario (Table 2), if we equate the two options for (say) player 1. We get

$$p \cdot (G - c) + (1 - p) \cdot (G - c) = p \cdot (G) + (1 - p) \cdot 0, \quad (3)$$

where p is the probability of agent 2 choosing strategy 1 i.e. Do. This gives the value of p:

$$p = \frac{G - c}{G}. \tag{4}$$

For heterogeneous agents the formulation changes to

$$p_2 \cdot (G - c_1) + (1 - p_2) \cdot (G - c_1) = p_2 \cdot (G) + (1 - p_2) \cdot 0, \tag{5}$$

where p_2 is the probability of agent 2 choosing strategy 1 i.e. Do. This gives the value of p_2 as:

$$p_2 = \frac{G - c_1}{G} \tag{6}$$

and similarly p_1 is

$$p_1 = \frac{G - c_2}{G}. \tag{7}$$

If each agent chooses to undertake the task with just p_1 (resp. p_2) probability, s/he will get the same net utility as doing the task *always* by him/her self.

4.3.2 N Agents, One Social Media Task

For the *heterogeneous*, N agent case let us look again at Table 2. For a Nash Equilibrium to exist the two strategy options for agent i must provide same net utility. Thus:

$$(G - c_i) \cdot \left(P_{\text{Do}}^{\text{All}-\{i\}}\right) + (G - c_i) \cdot (1 - P_{\text{Don't}}^{\text{All}-\{i\}}) = P_{\text{Do}}^{\text{All}-\{i\}} \cdot G + 0, \tag{8}$$

where $P_{\text{Do}}^{\text{All}-\{i\}}$ is the probability of the task being 'done' by at least one of the $N-1$ agents left after removing the ith agent from the set of 'all' agents.

Using the above equation, the equilibrium probability of the task being 'not done' by any of the other agents can be calculated as

$$P_{\text{Don't}}^{\text{All}-\{i\}} = \frac{c_i}{G}. \tag{9}$$

Similar equations can be formulated for all values of i.

$$P_{\text{Don't}}^{\text{All}-\{1\}} = \frac{c_1}{G},$$

$$P_{\text{Don't}}^{\text{All}-\{2\}} = \frac{c_2}{G},$$

$$\vdots$$

$$P_{\text{Don't}}^{\text{All}-\{N\}} = \frac{c_N}{G}. \tag{10}$$

Combining (multiplying) all of these equations gives

$$\{\overline{P_1} \cdot \overline{P_2} \cdots \overline{P_N}\}^{N-1} = \prod_{i=1}^{N} \frac{c_i}{G}, \tag{11}$$

where $\overline{P_i}$ is the probability of the task not being done by agent i.
Thus,

$$P_{\text{Don't}}^{\text{All}} = \sqrt[N-1]{\prod_{i=1}^{N} \frac{c_i}{G}} \tag{12}$$

or:

$$P_{\text{Do}}^{\text{All}} = 1 - \sqrt[N-1]{\prod_{i=1}^{N} \frac{c_i}{G}}, \tag{13}$$

$$P_{\text{Don't}}^{\text{All}} = P_{\text{Don't}}^{\text{All}-\{i\}} \cdot \overline{P_i} \tag{14}$$

and solving for $\overline{P_i}$ using values from Eq. (9) and Eq. (12) gives us the optimal contribution strategy, i.e. equilibrium probability for the agent i to 'not' undertake the task, as follows:

$$\overline{P_i} = \sqrt[N-1]{\prod_{i=1}^{N} \frac{c_i}{G}} \times \frac{G}{c_i}. \tag{15}$$

Note that the feasibility condition of a solution in which agent i must participate in the task is the condition that

$$\frac{c_i}{G} \geq \sqrt[N-1]{\prod_{i=1}^{N} \frac{c_i}{G}} \tag{16}$$

and that for homogeneous case (if applicable) the above equation reduces to

$$\overline{P_i} = \left(\frac{c}{G}\right)^{\frac{1}{N-1}}. \tag{17}$$

4.4 First Insights

To illustrate the basic concepts let us consider how the model and the derived solution works for a simple scenario of the unattended bag reporting where we have three agents each with a cost of 50, 60 and 70, respectively, while the common gain from reporting is 100. Thus using the parameter values ($c_1 = 50$, $c_2 = 60$, $c_3 = 70$,

Fig. 1 Effect of different task-completion strategies upon agent 1's utility

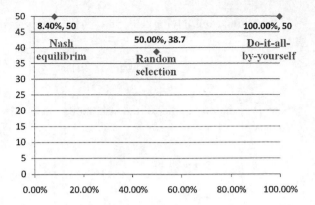

$G = 100$) in Eq. (15), we get the equilibrium probabilities for each agent to undertake the task to be 0.084, 0.346 and 0.445, respectively. The utility for each agent was found to decrease if it moved away from the equilibrium point. It was also interesting to note that in spite of doing the task much lesser times, the agents obtained the same utility (values 50, 40, 30 resp.) as they would have achieved by doing the task *always* by themselves. This is shown in Fig. 1, for agent 1, who at MSNE, made a net gain of 50, by contributing just 8.4% times. Not changing the other agents response, this utility is the same as that obtainable by a naive 'do-it-all-by-yourself' approach which involves 100% contribution rate, and is more than that obtainable by random selection which involves 50% contribution rate.

We next proceeded to model the dynamics of a game scenario wherein a large number of selfish users are considering a common task ($c = 50$, $G = 100$, $N \in [1, 100]$). Upon varying the gain and costs we found the expected results of each user's utility increasing if the gain was high and decreasing if the cost was high. Since each user was selfishly guarding his/her incentives the utility of each agent was unaffected by the change in N.

However, the change in N had a dramatic impact on the percentage of times the common task was completed. As can be seen from Fig. 2, the task-completion probability decreases (from 1.0 to 0.5) as N increases. This was an interesting observation as intuitively one thinks that the probability of task getting done should increase with N, because if we multiply individual probabilities for everyone not doing the task, the overall probability of all not doing the task should be extremely low.

However, as the game-theoretic model makes explicit, the knowledge about large N, makes each agent adjust its task-completion probabilities in such a way which guards its individual utilities but can bring down the overall task completion. It reminds us of the apathy which can exist in large groups of selfish individuals undertaking common tasks. In hind-sight it also resonates well with how the 'free-rider' [8] problem is non-existent in single person teams. In n-person teams (especially non-coordinated teams), there is always a finite possibility of everybody deciding to free-ride on a particular task.

Fig. 2 Effect of large number of users on task-completion probability

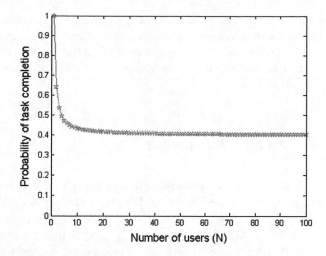

4.5 Individual vs. Group Rationality

Our discussion so far has focused on the scenario where it was *rational* for an individual agent to undertake the task. This translated into a constraint that $c_i < G$ i.e. each agent should have some utility incentive for undertaking the task. We now relax this constraint i.e. also consider scenarios where an individual agent acting on its own would have *no incentive* for completing the task. This effect can be seen from Table 3, where $c_i > G$ setting means that *Do* strategy can only yield a negative utility. The *Don't* strategy on the other guarantees a zero or higher utility. Hence, in game-theoretic terms, the *Don't* strategy strictly dominates the *Do* strategy. This means that in a society of N agents, it is individually rational for each agent to not undertake the task. Unfortunately this also implies that the task will *never* get done in a such a setting.

Obviously though, from the perspective of the entire society, everybody will benefit if one person does indeed undertake the task. That one person would incur a loss but, $N - 1$ people will gain from it. *Hence what is rational to an individual is not the same as what is rational for the society.* The onus thus lies on the society and the system designer to device ways to encourage that one person to undertake the task.

To summarize, the model studied in Sects. 4.1 through 4.5, makes explicit two problems in a large setup of rational contributors. One, the probability of task completion decreases with larger N, and two, the tasks which are rational at group level, might never get done if they are irrational from individual agent perspective.

Both of these are alarming issues requiring corrective actions from the system designer.

5 The Designer's Viewpoint

While the issues mentioned in the previous section are alarming, the system designer has the advantage that it can actually define the 'rules of the game', which will benefit the system performance. In fact, it can use the knowledge of how a rational user would behave in such systems, to devise effective mechanisms which will steer the system response in the desired direction. In this section, we study different mechanisms available for the system designer to do this, and their relative advantages and disadvantages.

5.1 Problem Formulation

Let us consider a case where the system designer has an interest in maximizing the probability of task completion. Let her benefit from each task completed be G_s. Hence, without any mechanism design the net utility obtained by the system designer is $(P_{\text{NoBonus}}^{\text{All}} \cdot G_s)$, where $P_{\text{NoBonus}}^{\text{All}}$ is as found in previous section (Eq. (13)). However, using mechanism design, the system designer can enhance this performance.

Let us assume that the system designer is open to granting an extra benefit b to each user completing the task, so as to influence the users' (selfish) decision process of choosing how often to undertake the task. Clearly, providing the extra bonus b does entail some additional cost on the system.

Thus the overall utility problem for system designer is

$$\underbrace{\operatorname{argmax}}_{C_b \in [0,\infty]} EU_s = \left(P_{\text{Bonus}}^{\text{All}} \right) \cdot G_s - \sum_{i=1}^{N} P_{i,\text{Bonus}} \cdot C_b, \tag{18}$$

where $P_{\text{Bonus}}^{\text{All}}$ is the overall probability of the task being undertaken by any of the agents after the bonus. P_{Bonus}^{i} is the probability of the task being undertaken by the ith agent after the bonus. C_b is the cost incurred by the system designer in granting the bonus.

Thus the system designer's problem is to design the best mechanism for granting the bonus b with system cost of C_b, such that overall system utility EU_s is maximized. EU_s will be maximized when a large increase is observed in probability of task completion due to the extra bonus, but the bonus cost is still low. Such a maxima will clearly involve trade-offs in terms of the bonus b's *amount* as well as *how it is granted*. We study three different mechanisms to support this.

5.2 Mechanism 1: Paying the Extra Benefit

The first option that the system designer can consider is paying the extra benefit b herself, if it provides overall system benefit. Note, however, that as per the dynamics of social media systems, such benefits are quite likely to be 'virtual' (e.g.

granting 'additional bandwidth', 'enhanced weaponry', 'titles/badges' or 'memora-
bilia'), and cost the system designer exponentially less than their *perceived* benefit
by the user.[1]

For the current discussion, let us consider system cost for providing this addi-
tional bonus to be $C_b = \alpha \cdot b^{\frac{1}{\beta}}$, where α, β can be chosen based on the domain.

To quantify these parameters let us make simplifying assumptions of homogeneous costs and $C_b = b^{\frac{1}{2}}$ (i.e. $\alpha = 1$ and $\beta = 2$).

Based on extensions of the ideas already discussed under user-user interaction in
Sect. 4.3, the various parameters involved in Eq. (18) can be computed as follows.

Extension of Eq. (15) defines the probability of task completion (with bonus) for
agent i.

$$\overline{P_{i,\text{bonus}}} = \sqrt[N-1]{\prod_{i=1}^{N} \frac{c_i - b}{G}} \times \frac{G}{c_i - b} \tag{19}$$

which for the homogeneous case translates to

$$P_{i,\text{Bonus}} = 1 - \left(\frac{c-b}{G}\right)^{\frac{1}{N-1}}. \tag{20}$$

Similarly, extension of Eq. (13) can be used to compute the probability of overall
task completion after bonus incentive.

$$P_{\text{Bonus}}^{\text{All}} = 1 - \left(\frac{c-b}{G}\right)^{\frac{N}{N-1}}. \tag{21}$$

Note that now we have the values for all the parametric components of Eq. (18),
and the value of optimal bonus which maximizes EU_s can be computed using the
standard calculus maximization methods or by choosing maxima as obtained by
numerical methods.

5.3 Mechanism 2: Social Incentives

The second option which the system designer can consider is exploiting the 'social' aspect of social media networks, and realize that the friendships, contacts and
mutual role-play is an important incentive to the users. To study this aspect, let us
consider the common gain being discussed so far to be G_1. Let the social gain (G_2)
for each user be dependent on the size of her social network:

$$G_{2,i} = k_1 \cdot S_i. \tag{22}$$

---

[1]The use of perceived changes in games to try and influence agent interaction is well studied under
hyper-game theory [24].

Table 4 Game between user (agent$_i$) and others in case of social incentives: matrix showing net utility for agent$_i$, under different strategies adopted

Agent$_i$ / Other agents	Do	Don't
Do	$G_1 + G_{2,i} - c_i$	$G_1 + G_{2,i} - c_i$
Don't	G_1	0

Over large user set, lets define the size of user's social network to be dependent on the size of the network as follows: $S_i = k_2 \cdot N^{\frac{1}{\beta}}$, where α, β can be chosen based on the domain. For the ease of presentation, let us assume that $S_i = k_2 \cdot \sqrt{N}$. Hence we can rewrite Eq. (22) as follows:

$$G_{2,i} = k_1 \cdot k_2 \cdot \sqrt{N}. \tag{23}$$

As shown in Table 4, and by extension of Eq. (9), we get

$$P_{\text{Don't,social}}^{\text{All}-\{i\}} = \frac{c_i - G_{2,i}}{G_1} \tag{24}$$

or if we define $\phi = c_i - G_{2,i}$:

$$P_{\text{Don't,social}}^{\text{All}-\{i\}} = \frac{\phi_i}{G_1} \tag{25}$$

which gives

$$P_{\text{Social}}^{\text{All}} = 1 - \left(\frac{\phi}{G_1}\right)^{\frac{N}{N-1}} \tag{26}$$

and

$$P_{i,\text{social}} = 1 - \left(\frac{\phi_i}{G}\right)^{\frac{1}{N-1}}. \tag{27}$$

This additional social benefit G_2 can be compared to the bonus (b) granted by the administrator in previous section. In fact, using Eq. (23), we can compute the size of network N at which the socially derived incentive will become equal to the system administrator granted bonus (b):

$$N = \left(\frac{b}{k_1 \cdot k_2}\right)^2. \tag{28}$$

The *'tipping point'* i.e. the size of the network beyond which, network will generate enough benefit to effect the task-completion probability and consequently enhance user/system utilities occurs at a specific point when $b = G - c$ i.e.

$$N_1 = \left(\frac{G - c}{k_1 \cdot k_2}\right)^2. \tag{29}$$

Table 5 Game between user
(agent$_i$) and others: matrix
showing net utility for agent$_i$,
under different strategies
adopted

Agent$_i$ / Other agents	Do	Don't
Do	$G - c_i + b^*$	$G - c_i + b^*$
Don't	G	0

There also exists a second threshold N_2 beyond which the bonus exceeds the cost ($b > c$) incurred and all the tasks get completed and system designer's utility reaches its maximum possible value.

$$N_2 = \left(\frac{c}{k_1 \cdot k_2} \right)^2. \tag{30}$$

In handling such large networks, the system designer's responsibility is limited to supporting the infra-structure for larger network of users, which is typically much smaller than the benefits accrued. Thus this option might perform better than that of explicitly providing benefits (as in Sect. 5.2) for networks with large user base.

5.4 Mechanism 3: Second Price Auction Based Mechanism

The 'second price auction' inspired mechanism involves the system designer announcing a bonus value which is 'slightly less' than the second lowest cost user ($b^* = c_2 - \epsilon$). As shown in Table 5, this would ensure that the 'Do' strategy dominates for exactly one user (the one with the lowest cost). This mechanism works on the assumption that the users realize (or are made aware with a one-time broadcast e.g. at networking joining) that there will be always one user whose cost will be lower than the bonus offered. Thus at 'run-time', the agents do not need any additional information, collaboration, or collusion, and are practically assured of task completion by some other agent *if* their cost is greater than the incentive offered.

If their cost is indeed lesser than the bonus then the user *knows* that she should actually undertake the task, both for everybody's benefit (group rationality) as well as individual rationality ('Do' strategy dominates). In a way this strategy works on the basis on (implicitly) assigning the responsibility to one agent (rather than distributing it between everybody), and rewarding her appropriately.

This mechanism (where applicable) ensures task completion with a (theoretical) probability of 1. The overall system performance would touch theoretical bounds, as it is (almost) as efficient as best possible. Further it incentivizes the lowest cost user, by guaranteeing it more than its fair share i.e. the 'Shapley value' of cooperating with such a coalition.

5.4.1 Shapley Value

The Shapley value in Game theory, captures the 'fair' estimate of an individual agent i's contribution to the overall coalition. It is computed as a function of marginal utility delivered by agent i, averaging over all the different sequences according to which the most profitable set S could be built up from the empty set. Mathematically, it is defined as

$$\phi(i) = \sum_{S \subseteq N - \{i\}} \frac{|S|!(N - |S| - 1)!}{N!} \left(v(S \cup \{i\}) - v(S)\right), \tag{31}$$

where S is the set of agents deciding to join the 'coalition', N is the size of the overall network, $v(S)$ is the value attainable by the set S.

For the formulation being considered here, $v(S \cup \{i\})$ i.e. the value of the Set including the lowest cost agent i is

$$v(S \cup \{i\}) = G_s - c_1. \tag{32}$$

The value of the set without the lowest cost agent is the case where the second lowest cost agent undertakes the task i.e.

$$v(S) = G_s - c_2. \tag{33}$$

All the other agents present do not affect this computation, rather they simply gain from whichever agent completes the task. Hence, the critical point is the case with size $n = S - 1$, with the lowest cost agent deciding to join (or not to join) the set. Using Eq. (31), thus the Shapley value of the agent with lowest cost is $c_2 - c_1$, which will be greater than zero. Hence, if the system designer pays the lowest cost agent its cost, plus the additional value which it brings to the coalition, it should have no utilitarian reasons to defect. This in turn assures the system designer of a (near[2]) optimum system performance.

5.5 Case Study

To study the impact of the proposed mechanisms we undertook experimental case studies. We considered a scenario with system gains as $G = 100$ and $G_s = 50$ and varied the N and costs to study different scenarios. The observed effects of each of the three mechanisms designed, on the performance of the system gave interesting insights.

---

[2]Strictly speaking, system designer needs to provide the lowest cost agent with a bonus that is just a fraction above its cost (i.e. $b = c_1 + \epsilon$). This will make the 'Do' strategy dominate for the user. However, in a cooperative setting, it is often considered better to grant a 'fair share' of the additional benefit the agent brings to the system by participating. Further still, the extra bonus serves as an implicit signaling mechanism to ensure overall system gains.

Fig. 3 Mechanism 1: System utility vs. bonus incentive

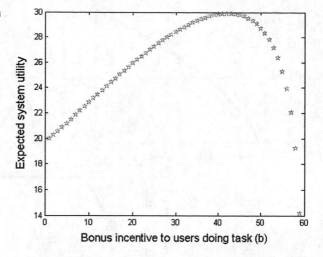

Fig. 4 (Color online) Mechanism 1: Effect of bonus on task-completion probability

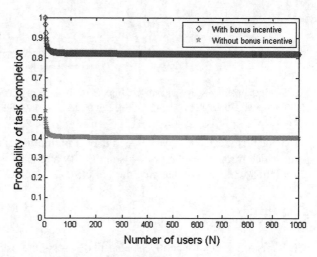

5.5.1 Mechanism 1: Paying the Extra Benefit

We varied the bonus provided to the users in the range $b \in [0, 50]$ (see Fig. 3), and found the system's utility is maximized at $b = 33$. Needless to say, similar values can be obtained for other scenarios too by simple parameter changes.

The net system utility for this task was found to be 31.32, which is higher than the value of 25, as obtained without mechanism design.

As can be seen from Fig. 4, the probability of the task being undertaken by at least one of the N users, increases to around 0.83 (red colored plot) with the use of this additional incentive value. This is as opposed to the 0.50 probability without the incentive mechanism (green plot, also see Fig. 2). The value of the net utility for the homogeneous players was also found to increase to 83 (from 50.0 without bonus).

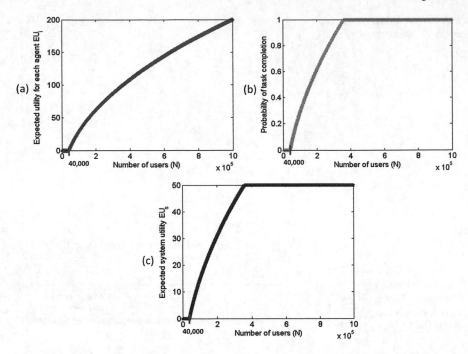

Fig. 5 Mechanism 2: social incentives. Impact of the size of network on the (**a**) profit for each additional user, (**b**) system designer's utility, and (**c**) overall probability of task completion

Hence this mechanism was indeed useful in finding an optimal level of incentive level which maximizes the system's net utility and increases the probability of task completion while also enhancing the net utility of each user.

5.5.2 Mechanism 2: Social Incentives

Mechanism 2 'Social incentives' also had a very interesting impact on the system and user performance. For example, under individually irrational (i.e. $c_i > G$) settings the task was completed 0% of times without any mechanism design. However, the social incentives created by the large size of network was indeed found to be effective in providing the social incentive for users to undertake the task. The *tipping point* value of the network size for the settings of $c = 150$, $G = 100$, $N \in [2, 1Million]$ was found to be at $N_1 = 40,000$. This clearly corroborates Eq. (29) which estimates this value.

As shown in Fig. 5(a), each additional agent joining the network beyond this point obtained more returns. we consider this '*tipping point*' to be important because each new user now has increasing benefits to join the network. This can explain the snow-ball effect noticed in social media networks, where the size of the network grows exponentially beyond a certain critical point. This also corroborates well with the notion of 'tipping point' as postulated and observed in both offline [18] and online [15] networks.

Fig. 6 System utility for
Mechanism 3: Second price
auction based mechanism at
different network sizes

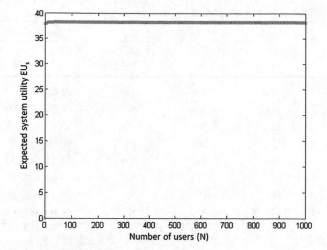

The increased number of users, and utility, in turn benefits the system utility and probability of task completion too. As shown in Fig. 5(b), the utility for the system designed also tipped at the value of $N_1 = 40,000$ and continued until $N_2 = 360,000$, causing it to jump to its maximum value of 50. Similarly, the probability of task completion also kept increasing beyond N_1 and reached its maximum possible value of 1.0 at N_2.

5.5.3 Mechanism 3: Second Price Auction Based Mechanism

The second price auction mechanism also showed some interesting effects. For example, under a large heterogeneous user base where it is individually irrational for users to contribute ($c_i \in [150 \pm 10]$, $G = 100$, $N \in [2, 1000]$), the base case scenario resulted in 0% task completion and zero system utility. However, paying the lowest cost user a perceived bonus of 140.07, resulted in task-completion probability of 1.0, and system utility of 38.17. This is shown in Fig. 6 where we also notice that system utility (and task-completion probability) were independent of the number of users on the network. This is quite different from the reduced probability of task completion for larger network sizes, as was earlier seen in Fig. 2.

5.6 Comparison of Different Approaches

To understand the impact of different mechanisms on the system designer's utility, we undertook a computational experiment. We studied the best utility attainable by the system designer under different situations of the application domain. The variables used for different situations were as follows:

$G_s = 50$ (System designer's gain from task completion)
$G = 100$ (Each user's gain from task completion)

Table 6 Effect of different mechanisms on system performance

S. no	Settings			Mechanism used			
	Homogeneous agents	Very Large N	Individually Rational	Base case	Paying the extra benefit	Social incentives	2nd price auction
1	Yes	Yes	Yes	25.00	31.32	50.00	−15.10
2	Yes	Yes	No	00.00	22.00	50.00	−62.80
3	Yes	No	Yes	25.02	31.33	50.00	−14.89
4	Yes	No	No	00.00	22.01	00.00	−62.40
5	No	Yes	Yes	25.17	−22.53	50.00	43.68
6	No	Yes	No	00.00	−22.53	23.79	38.17
7	No	No	Yes	25.12	−22.80	37.10	43.67
8	No	No	No	00.00	−22.53	00.00	38.17

The cost for each agent (c_i) was 50 for the individually rational situation (i.e. $G > c_i$, hence each agent can have some reasons to undertake the task) and 150 for the individually irrational situation (i.e. $G < c_i$, thus each agent individually has no motivation to undertake the task).

Homogeneous agents all had exactly the above-mentioned costs, while the *Heterogeneous* agent's cost varied randomly in the range ±10 from the mean value.

The *very large N* setting was studied on the agent population of 1,000,000 (1 million) while *non very large N* was studied on a population of 1,000.

As shown in Table 6, there is no *one-fits-all* mechanism available to enhance the system designer performance. However, it is interesting to note that in each situation, one or more mechanisms designed outperform the base case scenario (of not using any mechanism to influence the system performance). Broadly speaking, the base case scenario is unable to generate any system utility under the cases where it is individually irrational for agents to undertake the task. Mechanism 1 (i.e. paying the extra benefit) outperforms the base case in homogeneous settings but does not work well under heterogeneous user setting. The second price auction (Mechanism 3) typically outperforms all other mechanisms in the heterogeneous agent setting. The only exception is the *very large N* scenario, where Mechanism 2 (social incentives) works well. The second price auction mechanism is not suited for homogeneous agents case, and leveraging the social benefits is often a good choice there. In fact, the social incentive mechanism works well irrespective of the homogeneous or heterogeneous nature of agents, if the network size is very large.

While summarizing the mechanisms, this table clearly demonstrates that one or more mechanisms always outperform the base case scenario. It also provides prescriptive guidelines for the system designer to choose the most appropriate mechanism design based on the settings at hand. For example, a system designer may choose to Mechanism 1 and pay the bonus herself initially, but switch to Mechanism 2 i.e. social incentives beyond the 'tipping point'. In fact a modeling approach like ours allows the system designer to estimate (and cater for) this value much before when the tipping point actually occurs in the network.

Note also that the discussed formulation and mechanisms, consider the distinct characteristics of social media systems as we consider voluntary participation, common gain amongst all users, virtual reward currency which typically costs exponentially less to the system, and social benefits which members bring to each other.

6 Discussion and Future Work

We realize that the framework discussed works on a strong rationality or selfishness assumption. In near future, we plan to extend the work to consider a 'bounded rationality' [7] model for humans. Also, our current model considers only explicitly quantifiable incentives. We realize that other than very few scenarios (e.g. second-life monetization [23]), explicit quantification of gains and costs is still difficult. As what happens with all nascent fields, no numerical data are readily available on costs and gains for social media contributions (e.g. Wiki content provision, or Youtube video sharing). While we had to study the current framework using numerical case studies, we want to undertake more work to better quantify such costs and gains.

Our current model considers tasks that only need contribution from one user and other contributions are redundant. We are working on extending the approach to consider cases which require k different contributions or viewpoints (e.g. minimum two images required for stereoscopy or minimum five spam flags for post removal etc.). We are also considering a graded utility model wherein the value of each successive contribution gets lower but is still finite. Lastly, it would also be relevant to consider scenarios involving j tasks, each needing k contributions amongst the N users.

We also intend to broaden the motivation factors to considered to include intrinsic motivation factors and concepts like Maslow's hierarchy and using them appropriately in the future models. Lastly, the enhancements obtained due to mechanism design were gained (amongst other reasons like optimality based incentive levels), because of the setting that benefits granted were 'virtual', while the costs and gains were 'real-world'. However, we feel this is indeed true in many social media environments like citizen-journalism, image-labeling, Wiki-contributions etc.

While we admit, that our modeling is by no means perfect, this is meant to be a first step in drawing research interest toward this area. The value of this paper lies in providing food-for-thought to social media designers and developers charged with creating crowd-sourcing, media applications that require individual contributions to enhance the overall value of the application and its content.

7 Conclusions

In this work we have proposed a game-theoretic framework for studying user behavior and motivation patterns in social media networks. We have modeled users

as rational selfish agents, and considered domain attributes like voluntary participation, *virtual* reward structure, social incentives, and public-sharing to model the
dynamics of this interaction. We first studied the aspects of user-user interaction
and used that to find the most appropriate contribution strategy from each user's
perspective. The model created showed how the probability of task completion may
decrease with large N and made explicit the concepts like free-rider problem. It also
explained how individually irrational tasks may never get done in a collective network. We next studied the dynamics of system-user interaction, and showed how a
system designer can design different incentive mechanisms which can help in improving the overall system performance under different settings, while possibly still
benefiting the individual users.

References

1. Dellarocas, C.: Reputation mechanism design in online trading environments with pure moral
   hazard. Inf. Syst. Res. **16**(2), 209–230 (2005)
2. Diamond, P.A., Mirrlees, J.A.: Optimal taxation and public production II: Tax rules. Am.
   Econ. Rev. **61**(3), 261–278 (1971)
3. Friedman, E., Halpern, J., Kash, I.: Efficiency and Nash equilibria in a scrip system for p2p
   networks. In: Proceedings of the 7th ACM Conference on Electronic Commerce. ACM, New
   York (2006)
4. Google Image Labeler: http://images.google.com/imagelabeler/, Last accessed: 07/06/2009
5. Harper, F.M., Li, S.X., Chen, Y., Konstan, J.A.: Social comparisons to motivate contributions
   to an online community. Persuasive Technology, 4744/2007, 2007
6. Howe, J.: The rise of crowdsourcing. Wired Mag. **14**(6), 1–4 (2006)
7. Kahneman, D.: Maps of bounded rationality: Psychology for behavioral economics. Am.
   Econ. Rev. **93**(5), 1449–1475 (2003)
8. Kim, O., Walker, M.: The free rider problem: Experimental evidence. Public Choice **43**(1),
   3–24 (1984)
9. Lévy, P.: Collective Intelligence: Mankind's Emerging World in Cyberspace. Perseus Books,
   Cambridge (1997)
10. Maia, M., Almeida, J., Almeida, V.: Identifying user behavior in online social networks. In:
    SocialNets '08: Proceedings of the 1st Workshop on Social Network Systems, pp. 1–6 (2008)
11. Microsoft photo-synth project: http://photosynth.net/, Last accessed: 07/06/2009
12. New York Times launches 'citizen journalism' sites: http://washingtonsquarepark.wordpress.
    com/2009/03/03/new-york-times-launches-citizen-journalism-sites/, Last accessed: 07/06/
    2009
13. Nov, O., Naaman, M., Ye, C.: Motivational, structural, and tenure factors that impact online
    community photo sharing. In: Proceedings of the Third International AAAI Conference on
    Weblogs and Social Media (ICWSM 2009). Retrieved November, vol. 13, p. 2009 (2009)
14. Olson, M.: The Logic of Collective Action: Public Goods and the Theory of Groups. Harvard
    Univ. Press, Cambridge (1971)
15. Onnela, J.-P., Reed-Tsochas, F.: Spontaneous emergence of social influence in online systems.
    Proc. Natl. Acad. Sci. (2010)
16. Osborne, M.J.: An Introduction to Game Theory. Oxford University Press, Oxford (2003)
17. Park, J., van der Schaar, M.: A game theoretic analysis of incentives in content production and
    sharing over peer-to-peer networks. In: IEEE Thematic Meetings on Signal Processing: Signal
    and Information Processing for Social Networks, 2009
18. Schelling, T.C.: Micromotives and Macrobehavior. Norton, New York (1978)

19. Schroer, J., Hertel, G.: Voluntary engagement in an open web-based encyclopedia: Wikipedians and why they do it. Media Psychol. **12**(1), 96–120 (2009)
20. Shirky, C.: Cognitive Surplus: Creativity and Generosity in a Connected Age. Penguin, Baltimore (2010)
21. Singh, V., Jain, R., Kankanhalli, M.: Motivating contributors in social media networks. In: Proceedings of the first SIGMM Workshop on Social Media, pp. 11–18. ACM, New York (2009)
22. Sun, L., Vassileva, J.: Social visualization encouraging participation in online communities. In: Groupware: Design, Implementation, and Use, 2006
23. Terdiman, D.: The Entrepreneur's Guide to Second Life: Making Money in the Metaverse. Sybex, Berkeley (2007)
24. Vane, R.: Advances in hypergame theory. In: Workshop on Game Theoretic and Decision Theoretic Agents—Conference on Autonomous Agents and Multi-Agent Systems, 2006
25. von Ahn, L.: Games with a purpose. Computer **39**(6), 92–94 (2006)
26. Wikipedia: http://www.wikipedia.org

Efficient Access Control in Multimedia Social Networks

Amit Sachan and Sabu Emmanuel

Abstract Multimedia social networks (MMSNs) have provided a convenient way to share multimedia contents such as images, videos, blogs, etc. Contents shared by a person can be easily accessed by anybody else over the Internet. However, due to various privacy, security, and legal concerns people often want to selectively share the contents only with their friends, family, colleagues, etc. Access control mechanisms play an important role in this situation. With access control mechanisms one can decide the persons who can access a shared content and who cannot. But continuously growing content uploads and accesses, fine grained access control requirements (e.g. different access control parameters for different parts in a picture), and specific access control requirements for multimedia contents can make the time complexity of access control to be very large. So, it is important to study an efficient access control mechanism suitable for MMSNs. In this chapter we present an efficient bit-vector transform based access control mechanism for MMSNs. The proposed approach is also compatible with other requirements of MMSNs, such as access rights modification, content deletion, etc. Mathematical analysis and experimental results show the effectiveness and efficiency of our proposed approach.

1 Introduction

Over the past few years with the advent of web 2.0 technologies, social media such as blogs, images, videos, etc. have become much popular due to their wide reach and easy accessibility. Social media depending on the type of media is generally shared over various types of social networks. In particular, the multimedia social networks (MMSNs) such as YouTube [30], Facebook [8], Flickr [9] etc. which allow sharing of multimedia contents, such as images, videos, audios, etc. have become much popular. MMSNs allow easy sharing and spread of multimedia contents. People can

A. Sachan (✉) · S. Emmanuel
School of Computer Engineering, Nanyang Technological University, Singapore, Singapore
e-mail: amit0009@ntu.edu.sg

S. Emmanuel
e-mail: asemmanuel@ntu.edu.sg

S.C.H. Hoi et al. (eds.), *Social Media Modeling and Computing*,
DOI 10.1007/978-0-85729-436-4_7, © Springer-Verlag London Limited 2011

easily share any multimedia contents from anywhere in the world and the shared contents can be accessed conveniently anywhere.

Although people can easily share their multimedia contents over MMSNs, there are often various privacy, security, and legal concerns [17, 18, 25, 28] due to online sharing of personal multimedia contents. Privacy and security concerns are about unwillingness to disclose contents to a particular group of people, unintentional disclosure of identity and sensitive information, and threat of content modification for unethical purposes. For example, a cancer patient may wish to share the pictures related to his disease only with his doctors and family members [28]. Or due to the threat of content modification, a person may wish to share his pictures only with trustworthy friends. Legal concerns are about unsuitability of content to a group of persons and restrictions associated with copyrighted contents. For example, due to legal restrictions a person may wish to share a video containing violent scenes with the persons above some specific age only. Or due to copyright issues, some contents may not be shared to the users in some countries. All privacy, security and legal issues may socially and economically harm a person. Therefore, people usually want to selectively share their multimedia contents.

Access control mechanisms [5, 6, 14] provide one way to selectively share the contents in MMSNs. By access control mechanisms a person can define the credentials [4] required by anybody else to access the contents shared by the person. Credentials are in the form of social relationship parameters such as friendship level, trust level, age, allowed countries, etc. [5, 12, 16]. Similarly, each individual has credentials associated with his profile. Access control mechanisms work by verifying the credentials of an individual accessing a content with the credentials required to access the content. If an individual has sufficient credentials to access a content, then only he is allowed to access the content.

Access control mechanisms are simple and only require comparison of the credentials. But large number of contents upload and accesses make the access control difficult in MMSNs. For instance, according to the statistics provided by Youtube [30] currently every minute about 24 hours of video is uploaded on Youtube and 2 billion videos are watched everyday on Youtube. Furthermore, large number of users (according to Facebook [8] there are more than 500 million active users are on Facebook), and rapid growth rate of users over MMSNs (according to Nielsen online [19], Facebook recorded a growth rate of 228% over the period of February, 2008 to February, 2009) makes the task of access control more difficult.

Also, as suggested in [3, 11, 26], users may require fine grained access control for their shared contents. For example, a user may wish to protect some words in his blog, or specific parts in a picture from specific persons. Another specific requirement for multimedia contents may be to allow the users to specify several discrete access control parameters instead of only binary access parameters (in which someone either can or cannot access a content). For example, an access value of 0.5 may refer to access to a low resolution version of the original picture. To satisfy these multimedia specific requirements, we need to treat each specific part of a content (or contents with different access parameters) as an independent content.

Thus, due to the large growth rate, large number of content uploads and accesses, fine grained access control requirements, and multimedia specific access control requirements, the access control time may grow several times in MMSNs. This necessitates an efficient access control mechanism suitable for MMSNs. However, most of the existing works on access control in social networks focus on new social network models [14], policy description [4, 16], and privacy and security issues [3, 18] in social networks. Authors in reference [27] discussed the issue of complexity of access control in social networks and requirements of an efficient access control solution, and proposed an efficient access control scheme. However, as we discuss in Sect. 2, the proposed efficient control solutions is user based (no access rights are associated with the contents so if a person is allowed to access then the person can access all the contents) not the content based, which may not be suitable for access control in present day MMSNs. To the best of our knowledge there is no existing work that discusses efficient content based efficient access control mechanism (a preliminary version of this work appeared in [23]).

In this chapter, we focus on designing an efficient access control mechanism suitable for access control in present day MMSNs. For this purpose, we propose a bit-vector transform [21] based access control method. In the proposed approach we model the contents, content access rights and users in MMSNs for efficient access control. In addition, we also propose an improvement to make the proposed method more suitable when multiple contents share the identical access rights. The proposed approach is also able to provide the functionalities required in MMSNs such as multimedia content deletion and access rights modification using data in the bit-vector transform domain. The proposed access control mechanism is efficient due to efficient representation of data in the bit-vector transform domain and efficient operations on data after the bit-vector transform. Mathematical performance analysis and experimental results show effectiveness and efficiency of our proposed mechanism for MMSNs.

The rest of this chapter is organized as follows. Section 2 discusses the related works. In Sect. 3, we present the access control model. In Sect. 4 our proposed access rights organization based access control mechanism is discussed. In Sect. 5 we propose a technique to make the access control more efficient when multiple contents share the same access rights. Performance analysis is in Sect. 6. Finally, the chapter is concluded in Sect. 7.

2 Related Works

In this section we discuss about various access control mechanisms in social networks, and requirement of efficient access control in social networks.

2.1 Access Control in Social Networks

In literature, a variety of access control mechanisms have been proposed for the social networks to address various aspects, such as new models of access control

[4–6, 14], security and privacy [3, 18, 24], and policy description [16], etc. have been proposed in the literature.

Carminati et al. in [5, 6] described the access control policies using friend of a friend (FOAF) [4] scripting language. FOAF provides vocabulary to manage the access control based on the relationship between the individuals. Each relationship can be defined on a scale from 0 to a maximum value, called the domain of relationship (D) [14]. For example, the level of friendship can be defined using the values between 0 and 100. The authors in [5] defined access rule for an object with ID oid using the tuple (oid, $cset$), where $cset$ is a set of conditions $\{cond_1, cond_2, \ldots, cond_m\}$ that must be fulfilled by an individual to access the object oid. All the conditions must be fulfilled by an individual who wants to access oid. There can be more than one rule defined for an object. In this case all the rules need to be verified one by one until a valid proof, if any, is obtained. The conditions in the access rules can be trust level, friendship level, country, name of persons, etc. [5, 12, 16].

In [14] authors proposed a digital rights management (DRM) [10, 15, 22] based solution of doing the access control in social networks. In the proposed mechanism digital contents are considered as physical good. The authors proposed solutions similar to that exist in physical world. For example, in physical world a book can be rendered to only one person at a time so allow access of an e-book only to one person at a time. The proposed method is suitable for copyrighted contents. However, it may limit the distribution capability of Internet.

Ianella in [16] emphasized the need of inter-operability between the contents shared between different social networks so that users need not to share their contents multiple times. But it requires same access control parameters for different social networks so that the same policy may be applied. It may be difficult as presently different existing social networks have different access policies. Furthermore, due to privacy and business related reasons social network providers may not agree for inter-operable framework.

Various authors have discussed about different types of privacy concerns in social networks and access control mechanisms to deal with the privacy concerns. Beato et al. in [3] discussed about privacy threats from the social network providers. The authors proposed an access control model that is not regulated by the social network provider, but it is under the control of users. But in order to use the proposed system users must know technical details of access control mechanism and cryptographic protocols, which may be very difficult practically. Loukides and Gkoulalas-Divanis in [18] discussed privacy concerns of a user resulting from other users in the social network and social network provider. The main privacy concerns due to other users in social networks according to the authors are identity disclosure, and content disclosure. Access control mechanisms mainly deal with the privacy concerns due to content disclosure.

Authors in [7] and [29] argued the use of decentralized approach to online social networking to handle privacy and inter-operability issues in present day social networks. Using decentralized system users can privately share their own data by maintaining their data on their own trusted servers. The data of other users can be accessed using FOAF vocabulary [4]. But enforcement of decentralized access control policies may be difficult and inefficient in present day social networks due to relationship based access control in present day social networks [7]. Furthermore, although decentralized approach may be more effective in terms of privacy but it will lack a good user interface and interaction (e.g. in the form of status updates) between users as provided by present day social networks. Good user interface and interaction are some of the main reasons of the popularity of present day social networks over other mediums of sharing the contents such as email. To tackle these problems, Baden et al. in [2] presented a social network model called Persona using public key cryptography and attribute based encryption. Persona uses a decentralized approach yet it is able to provide the interface and interaction as provided by present day social networks. For this purpose, it uses a group based content sharing, where users in a group can access any content shared by a user in the group for the group. However, the proposed mechanism may involve a large overheads due to cryptographic operations during formation of group, or removal of any member from the group. Furthermore, using a decentralized approach users have to pay for storage and computations involved as opposed to free storage and computation power provided in present day social networks, which make them very popular.

Shehab et al. in [24] discussed the privacy infringement due to third party applications on the social networks. These application require user data but users often do not know how much data is being disclosed to the third party applications. So, authors proposed a finite state machine based approach for providing data access to the third party applications.

Although various access control mechanisms exist for different privacy requirements, in this work we mainly focus on access control mechanisms for content disclosure to other users in the social networks.

From the access control models studied in this section, we found that the access control model proposed by Carminati et al. in [5, 6] is more suitable for current social networks. So, we use an extension of social network model proposed by Carminati et al. as the basis, which we discuss in Sect. 3.

2.2 Efficient Access Control

Various authors recently have discussed the need of finer and efficient access control requirements [7, 11, 26, 27] in various scenarios. In [26], Tootoonchian et al. proposed an inter-operability framework for different social networks. The motivation behind that is that users are generally on different social networks and moving a content from one social network to another social network is difficult. In such cases, due to the different policies in different social networks, finer and higher numbers of access control parameters may be needed. Gates in [11] has stated four key requirements while designing an access control system for social networks. One of the requirements according to Gates is the fine grained access control i.e. access control mechanisms should also be able to manage the access control for fine grained details inside the object. For example, a user may wish to protect some words in his blog, or specific parts in a picture from specific persons.

Authors in [27] discussed the effect of fine grained access control on rising access control time complexity. In [27] authors proposed a trusted distance classifier based scheme to efficient access control. In the scheme, for each user profile, other users are classified into three categories viz. acceptance, attestation, and rejection. Users in the acceptance zone are accepted immediately and the users in the rejection zone are rejected immediately. Requests in attestation zone require additional authorization, which is done by attesters designated by the user. The proposed scheme in [27] can reduce the access control time as it eliminates the need of comparison of attributes associated with users accessing the contents with the attributes associated with the contents. But the scheme may not be suitable for access control in present day social networks because of the following two reasons. First, the proposed access control mechanism does the access control on the basis of users not the contents but practically users may have different access control requirements for different contents. Second, for the users in attestation zone manual attestation by designated attesters is required, which may cause significant delay and inconvenience to users. The bit-vector transform based method presented in this chapter does efficient access control and it is also suitable for present day social networks.

3 Model of Access Control

In this work, we model the system by modifying the access control model proposed by Carminati et al. in [5, 6]. In the access control model in [5, 6], an access rights vector is associated with each content. Let the access rights vector (R^c for content c) be given by $R^c = \{r_1, r_2, \ldots, r_M\}$, where $r_1, r_2, \ldots,$ and r_M are M access rights. Each access right is in the form of an interval and has a domain of all possible allowed values. If the domain of the jth access right is given by D_j then $r_j \in D_j$. Let the attribute vector of an individual accessing the content be defined as $A = \{A_1, A_2, \ldots, A_M\}$, where $A_1, A_2, \ldots,$ and A_M are M attribute values. Each attribute in the attribute vector corresponds to the respective access right in the access right vector (R^c). Note that some attributes such as trust level, friendship level, etc. in the attribute vector of an individual are not fixed and dependent upon the profile individual is visiting. Such attributes need to be obtained first during the access control process

The individual can access the content c if $A_j \in r_j, \forall j \leq M$. When the profile of an individual I_1 is visited by another individual I_2 then all the contents to which I_2 is authorized to view are identified and displayed, as shown in Example 1.

Example 1 Let an individual I_1 has three contents, c_1, c_2 and c_3 in his profile with access rights vector R^{c_1}, R^{c_2} and R^{c_3} given as (with access rights as friendship level (F), trust level (T) and age (AG), each having domain 0 to 100):

$$R^{c_1} = \{F = (40, 100], T = (30, 80], AG = (0, 100]\},$$
$$R^{c_2} = \{F = (24, 60], T = (63, 100], AG = (18, 100]\},$$
$$R^{c_3} = \{F = (40, 80], T = (70, 100], AG = (16, 100]\}.$$

Access right vector R^{c_1} states that the content c_1 can be accessed by a person having friendship level between 40 and 100, trust level between 30 and 80, and age between 0 and 100. Similarly, R^{c_2} and R^{c_3} can be interpreted. Let an individual I_2 with the attribute vector $A = \{50, 40, 25\}$ visits the profile of I_1. Now, the attributes 50, 40, and 25 are within the ranges (40, 100], (30, 80], and (0, 100], respectively. Therefore I_2 can access c_1. But for c_2 and c_3, trust level $= 40$ of the individual I_2 is not within the access rights ranges (63, 100] and (70, 100], respectively. So, I_2 cannot access the contents c_2 and c_3 and only c_1 will be displayed.

The model presented above uses only a single range for each access right but access rights in present day social networks may be discrete and may consist of multiple discrete ranges. For example, a user may allow access of a content in few different regions, which may not be represented with a single range. So, to reflect the existing social networks, instead of directly using the same model in [5, 6], we use a social network model in which access rights can have multiple discrete ranges. However, in the rest of this chapter, for the sake of simplicity, we first present the case of all access rights with a single range and then provide the extensions required to accommodate the multiple access rights ranges.

4 Proposed Efficient Access Control Mechanism

In this section, we first present our proposed bit-vector transform based access rights organization and an access control mechanism using the data after the organization. Then we also propose the mechanisms (in the bit-vector transform domain) for deletion of contents from the profile and modification of access rights associated with a content.

4.1 Access Rights Organization

Let each content has M access rights associated with it. We organize the access rights associated with the contents into an M dimensional space. As shown in Fig. 1, each dimension corresponds to a particular access right and divided into several elementary ranges. Each elementary range has a bit-vector associated with it. The bit-vectors are string of bits '0' or '1'. Number of bits in the bit-vectors is equal to the number of contents in the profile of the user. Each bit in a bit-vector corresponds to a particular content. Thus, if a user has N content items in his profile then the length of bit-vectors will be N bits; and the nth bit in the bit-vector will correspond to the nth content. For example, Fig. 3(e) represents the dimension for friendship level (F) in Example 1. There are five elementary ranges viz. 0 to 24, 24 to 40, 40 to 60, 60 to 80, and 80 to 100. Since there are three contents in Example 1 so in Fig. 3(e) each elementary range has a three bits length bit-vector (shown in rectangular box) associated with it.

Fig. 1 Illustration of elementary ranges and bit-vectors

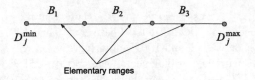

Initially, each access right's dimension is assumed to contain only one elementary range in the entire domain $D_j = (D_j^{min}, D_j^{max}]$ of the jth access right. D_j^{min} and D_j^{max} are the minimum and maximum values, respectively, in the jth access right's domain. No bit-vector is assumed to be present for the initial elementary range (the first bit in a bit-vector is inserted when the first content is inserted). Two steps viz. access right's range insertion and modification of bit-vectors, are required for access rights' organization. In the first step, the range of access rights in the contents is inserted along the respective access right's dimension. In the second step, existing bit-vectors are modified by appending a new bit to them.

(1) *Access Right's Range Insertion:* Let the range of the jth access right for the nth content be $[a_j^n, b_j^n]$. We call *AR_Insert*(a_j^n) and *AR_Insert*(b_j^n) for the insertion of $(a_j^n, b_j^n]$. The process *AR_Insert*(x_j) is as defined in Algorithm 1. During the insertion process the point x_j is inserted in the numerical order if it was not already present along the jth access right's dimension. If x_j is inserted then the same bit-vector as the elementary range in which it is inserted is assigned to both the elementary ranges formed after insertion. The same process is used for all M dimensions.

Figure 2(a) shows the initial range of friendship dimension in Example 1. To insert the access right's range (which is (40, 100]) in the first content initially Algorithm 1 is called with the parameter $x_j = 40$. Since $x_j = 40$ was not present along the access right's range in Fig. 2(a) so $x_j = 40$ inserted in the numerical order between 0 and 100 as shown in Fig. 2(b). Since there was no bit-vector present for initial elementary range (0, 100] so no bit-vector is assigned to newly formed elementary ranges viz. (0, 40] and (40, 100]. Next Algorithm 1 is called with the parameter $x_j = 100$. Since 100 is already present along the access right's dimension in Fig. 2(b) so we need not to insert it again. The access right's dimension remains same as in Figs. 2(b) and (c) after calling the algorithm with $x_j = 100$.

(2) *Modification of Bit-vectors:* Each bit in a bit-vector corresponds to a particular content. Thus, if $n - 1$ contents are present then bit-vectors will be of length $n - 1$ bits, which needs to be changed to n bits while inserting a new content. Bit-vectors of all the elementary ranges are modified by appending a bit equal to 0 or 1 to them. We call the Algorithm 2, *BV_Modify*(j, a_j^n, b_j^n), to modify the bit-vectors. The algorithm appends a bit equal to 1 in the bit-vectors corresponding to all the elementary ranges between a_j^n and b_j^n and 0 to rest of the bit-vectors. Thus, in the bit-vector transform domain if the nth bit for a content is 1 in an elementary range then the elementary range will be within the respective access right's range in the nth content. This is used as a basis in access control mechanism in Sect. 4.2.

Algorithm 1: $AR\_Insert(j, x_j)$

Input: j: A numerical value between 1 and M do determine the access right dimension.

x_j: A numerical value to be inserted along the jth access right's dimension.

Output: Modified jth access right's dimension.

Procedure:

Search x_j along the jth dimension.

if x_j *is already present along the* j*th access right's dimension* **then**

| Exit.

else

| 1. Insert x_j in numerical order along the jth access right's dimension.
| 2. Assign the same bit-vector as previous elementary range to both the
| newly generated elementary ranges formed due to the insertion of x_j
| (as in Figs. 3(b) after insertion of points x_j=24 and x_j=60 in Fig. 3(a)).
| 3. Return the modified jth access right's dimension.

end

Fig. 2 (**a**) Initial friendship (F) access right dimension. (**b**) Access right dimension after insertion of the end point 40 in the first content. (**c**) Access right dimension after insertion of the end point 100 in the first content

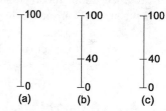

(a)   (b)   (c)

Algorithm 2: $BV\_Modify(j, a_j^n, b_j^n)$

Input: a_j^n, b_j^n: End points of the jth access right's range in the nth content.

Output: Modified jth access rights dimension.

Procedure:

1. Append a bit equal to 0 to the LHS of all the bit-vectors present between $D_j^{\min}$ and a_j^n along the jth access right's dimension.
2. Append a bit equal to 1 to the LHS of all the bit-vectors present between a_j^n and b_j^n along the jth access right's dimension.
3. Append a bit equal to 0 to the LHS of all the bit-vectors present between b_j^n and $D_j^{\max}$ along the jth access right's dimension.
4. Return the modified jth access right's dimension.

Figure 3(a) shows the friendship access right's dimension after insertion of initial bit-vectors in Fig. 2(b). Figures 3(b) and 3(d) show access right's range insertion steps for the second and third content, respectively. Figures 3(c) and 3(e)

Fig. 3 Illustration of the content insertion process

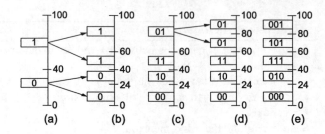

show bit-vector modification step after the insertion of second and third content, respectively.

If multiple discrete ranges are present for an access right associated with a content then insertion process is modified slightly. Let d number of discrete ranges viz. $(a^n_{j_1}, b^n_{j_1}], (a^n_{j_2}, b^n_{j_2}], \ldots, (a^n_{j_d}, b^n_{j_d}]$ are present for the jth access right. In the first step, all the end points of all the ranges are inserted along the jth dimension using Algorithm 1. For the bit-vector modification step, initially Algorithm 2, $BV\_Modify(a^n_{j_1}, b^n_{j_1})$ is called (for the first range). For doing bit-vector modification using all other ranges, the bit-vector modification step is slightly modified. In the modified algorithm for the ith $(1 < i \le d)$ range, we do not insert a new bit but change the nth bit to 1 in all the bit-vectors present between $a^n_{j_i}$ and $b^n_{j_i}$. This ensures that the size of the bit-vectors remain n bits if n contents are inserted, irrespective of the number of ranges.

4.2 Access Control Mechanism

Let the attribute vector of an individual accessing the contents be given by $A = \{A_1, A_2, \ldots, A_M\}$. Initially, for each value of j, a search is made for A_j along the jth dimension. Let the elementary range which contains A_j be given by E_j and respective bit-vector be given by B_j. The contents for which the jth access right's range contains E_j, their corresponding bit will be equal to 1 in B_j (see Sect. 4.1). Thus, the jth access right's range will also contain A_j as $A_j \in E_j$.

A content (say the nth) can be accessed by an individual if he satisfies all M access rights conditions to access the content. Thus, the nth bit must be equal to 1 in all M bit-vectors searched over all access right's dimensions. This information can be obtained by taking an AND operation between the bit-vectors obtained for all access right dimensions (if a particular bit is 1 in all bit-vectors then that bit will also be equal to 1 in the bit-vector obtained after AND operation). As shown in Eq. (1), final bit-vector B is obtained by performing AND operation between all the bit-vectors.

$$B = B_1 \wedge B_2 \wedge \cdots \wedge B_M. \tag{1}$$

Finally, we scan the final bit-vector B to identify the contents bits corresponding to which is 1. To identify the nth $(1 \le n \le N)$ bit, we perform an AND operation of B

Fig. 4 (a) Friendship
dimension (F), (b) trust
dimension (T), and (c) age
dimension (AG) after
insertion of contents in
Example 1

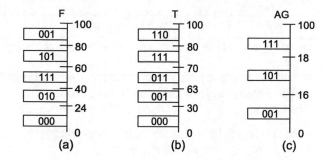

with a bit vector containing nth bit 1 and other bits 0. If the result is 1 then the nth content can be accessed.

Example 2 Consider the individual I_2 in Example 1 accesses the contents shared by I_1. The attribute vector of I_2 is $A = \{50, 40, 25\}$. Figure 4 shows friendship (F), trust (T) and age dimensions after the insertion of all three contents in Example 1. The first attribute (having value 50), belongs to the elementary range 40 to 60 in Fig. 4(a). Hence, $B_1 = 111$ in this case. Similarly, for other two access rights bit-vectors can be calculated (using Figs. 4(b) and 4(c)) and are given by $B_2 = 001$ and $B_3 = 111$. In this case, $B = 111 \wedge 001 \wedge 111 = 001$. Since, only the bit corresponding to c_1 is 1 therefore I_2 can only access the content c_1, which is in accordance with Example 1.

The access control mechanism is also valid if multiple ranges are possible for an access right as the bit corresponding to a content is 1 in the bit-vectors corresponding to all the ranges present for the content.

4.3 Modification of Access Rights

The access rights associated with the contents can be modified by the content owners. These changes must be reflected in the bit-vector transformed domain. Let the user change a range in the jth access right associated with the nth content from $[a_j, b_j]$ to $[a'_j, b'_j]$. Then Algorithm 3, $AR\_Modification(n, j, a_j, b_j, a'_j, b'_j)$, is used to reflect the change in bit-vector transform domain. In the algorithm, we first change the nth bit in every bit-vector between a_j and b_j to 0. After that the algorithm calls $AR\_Insert(a'_j)$ and $AR\_Insert(b'_j)$ (Algorithm 1) to insert the points a'_j, and b'_j if they are not already present. Then it sets the nth bit in all the bit-vectors between a'_j, and b'_j to 1. Finally, the algorithm removes a_j and/or b_j if no other content shares the end points a_j and/or b_j using Algorithm 4. This is to reduce the search time and storage space by removing any redundant point along the access right's dimension.

Algorithm $delete\_point(j, x_j)$ first obtains the bit-vectors for the elementary ranges just before and after x_j along the jth access right's dimension. If both are

---

Algorithm 3: $AR\_Modification(n, j, a_j, b_j, a'_j, b'_j)$

Input: a_j and b_j: Original end points of the jth access right's range for the nth content.
a'_j and b'_j: New end points of the jth access right's range for the nth content.
Output: Modified jth access right's dimension.
Procedure:

1. Make the nth bit to 0 in all the bit-vectors between a_j and b_j.
2. Call $AR\_Insert(a'_j)$ and $AR\_Insert(b'_j)$.
3. Set the nth bit to 1 in all the bit-vectors between a'_j and b'_j.
4. Call $delete\_point(j, a_j)$.
5. Call $delete\_point(j, b_j)$.
6. Return jth access right's dimension.

Algorithm 4: $delete\_point(j, x_j)$

Input: x_j: The point to be deleted from the jth access right's range.
Output: Modified jth access right's dimension.
Procedure:
if $x_j = D_j^{min}$ or $x_j = D_j^{max}$ **then**
| Exit.
else
| Let the bit-vectors for the elementary ranges just before and after x_j be
| given by B_{low} and B_{high}, respectively.
end
if $B_{low} = B_{high}$ **then**
| Delete x_j from the jth access right's range.
end
Return jth access right's dimension.

---

equal this implies that no content has x_j as an end point for the jth access right. Thus, the point x_j can be deleted.

4.4 Deletion of a Content

In social networks, a user can delete a content from his profile. The Algorithm 5, $delete\_content(n)$, is used to delete the nth content from the user's profile. Two steps are required. In the first step, the nth bit in all the bit-vectors is made 0. Next, if no other content shares the end points a_j and/or b_j then remove a_j and/or b_j from the jth dimension. Algorithm 4 is used to remove a_j and/or b_j.

Algorithm 5: *delete_content(n)*

Input: n: ID of the content to be deleted.
Output: Modified version of all M access rights' dimensions.
Procedure:
for $j = 1$ to M **do**

> 1. Make the nth bit in each bit-vector equal to 0.
> 2. Let the range of jth access right in the nth content be given by $[a_j, b_j]$.
> 3. Call *delete_point(j, a_j)*.
> 4. Call *delete_point(j, b_j)*.

end

4.5 Efficient Data Representation

In the bit-vector transform domain, end points of elementary ranges along each access right dimension are present in the increasing order of magnitude. This suggests use of efficient data structures such as binary search trees (BST), AVL trees, red black trees [1] etc. to represent each access right dimension. As AVL trees are more search efficient [1, 20] so we use an AVL tree to represent each access right's dimension. A separate AVL tree is designed for each access right's dimension. In this section, we briefly describe the procedure for insertion and searching of data in AVL trees.

There are two types of nodes in each AVL tree: internal nodes and leaf nodes. As shown in Fig. 5, the internal nodes (in circles) in each AVL tree stores the points along the access right's dimension. Whereas leaf nodes (in rectangles) store the bit-vector corresponding to an elementary range determined by the values stored in internal nodes. For example, in Fig. 5(b) the bit-vectors 00, 10, 11, and 01 (from left to right) corresponds to elementary ranges 0 to 24, 24 to 40, 40 to 60, and 60 to 100, respectively.

Two steps (corresponding to access rights insertion and bit-vector modification steps in Sect. 4.1) are required for the insertion of access rights in an AVL tree. The first step is access right's range insertion and the second step is bit-vector modification. During the access right's range insertion process, the end points of the access right's ranges are inserted one by one using the normal insertion process in AVL trees [1]. During the bit-vector modification step, an in-order traversal (recursive processing of the tree in the order: the left sub-tree, root, and right sub-tree) in the AVL tree is performed. If the range of the jth access right is given by $[a_j, b_j]$ then all the bit-vectors in between a_j and b_j are appended with a bit equal to 1 and rest of the bit-vectors are appended with a bit equal to 0. Figure 5(a), 5(b), and 5(c) illustrates an AVL tree designed for the access right dimension shown in Fig. 3(a), 3(c), and 3(e), respectively.

For the access control mechanism discussed in Sect. 4.2, a search along each access right's dimension is required. Following algorithm (Algorithm 6) is used to search along the bit-vector along the jth dimension (let the jth attribute in the attribute vector of a person accessing the content be given by A_j).

Algorithm 6: *Search*(j, A_j)

Input: j: Dimension to search.

A_j: A numerical value to be searched along jth dimension.

Output: Bit-vector corresponding to A_j.

Procedure:

1. Set the root node as current node.
2. Compare the value A_j with the value stored in the current node. If A_j is greater than the value stored in the current node then assign the right child of the current node as current node. Else assign the left child of the current node as current node.
3. If current node is a leaf node then bit-vector stored in the node is the bit-vector required. Else go to step 2.

Fig. 5 Insertion process in AVL tree

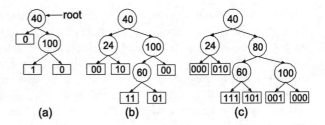

5 Grouping of Contents with Same Access Rights

Practically in present social networks, a number of contents shared by a user may have the identical access rights vector. This fact may be used to do the access control more efficiently (as compared to bit-vector transform proposed in Sect. 4). In this section, we present an algorithm to do the access control more efficiently by identifying the contents with identical access rights vector. The algorithm works efficiently by deriving the smaller length bit-vectors after identification of contents with the identical access rights vectors. The proposed algorithm consists of two steps. First the grouping of contents with similar access rights vector and smaller length bit-vector derivation, and second efficient access control using the smaller length bit-vectors derived. Next, we discuss both these steps in detail.

5.1 Grouping of Contents

Let a user has previously $n - 1$ ($n > 1$) number of contents in his profile and these contents are divided into p ($p \leq n - 1$) different groups such that contents in each group have identical access rights vector (i.e. all M access rights ranges have identical end point values for all the contents in a group). To do the access control more efficiently in such cases, instead of using $n - 1$ length bit-vectors we use p length

group ID	Access rights vector	content IDs
1	$R_1 = \{r_{11}, r_{12}, \ldots, r_{1M}\}$	1, 3, 8, 10, 11, 15
2	$R_2 = \{r_{21}, r_{22}, \ldots, r_{2M}\}$	2, 12, 16
3	$R_3 = \{r_{31}, r_{32}, \ldots, r_{3M}\}$	4, 7, 14
4	$R_4 = \{r_{41}, r_{42}, \ldots, r_{4M}\}$	5, 6, 9, 13, 17

Table 1 Mapping of group ID with access rights vector and content IDs

bit-vectors. The ith bit in a bit-vector represents the ith group of contents. To identify the access rights vector and contents in each group we maintain a table of the form Table 1 mapping the group IDs with the rights vectors and content IDs. The following process is used when nth content is added to the profile.

Let the jth access right's range in the nth content be given by $[a_j^n, b_j^n]$. Initially we obtain the bit-vector at the points a_j^n and b_j^n. The ith bit's value (0 or 1) in these bit-vectors give information on whether a_j^n and/or b_j^n are present in the jth access right's range in the ith group of contents. In order to find all such groups (with bits $= 1$), we take an AND operation between these two bit-vectors obtained at a_j^n and b_j^n. Let B be the resultant bit-vector obtained after taking the AND operation. If the ith bit of B is equal to 1 then both a_j^n and b_j^n will be within (not necessarily exactly identical) the access rights' ranges in all the contents in the ith group of contents. Note that there can be multiple bits $= 1$ in B, each position of a bit $= 1$ implies that all the access rights' ranges in the nth content are within the access rights' ranges of the group at the bit position. Finally, we need to find the group whose access rights' ranges exactly match the access rights' ranges of the nth content. For this purpose, we compare the access rights ranges in the nth content with the access rights ranges of all group for which bit is 1 in B. If any such group is found then the content is added to that group and no further comparisons are required (as access rights associated with each group are different and at most one group's access rights can exactly match the access rights associated with the content). In this case no change is required in the p length bit-vectors associated with the elementary ranges. Else if no such group is found then a new group containing only the nth content is created. And new elementary ranges are inserted and a new $(p + 1)$th bit is added to each bit-vector according to Algorithms 1 and 2. The same process is applied every time a new content is added to the profile.

5.2 Access Control After Grouping of Contents

Let the attribute vector of an individual accessing the contents be given by $A = \{A_1, A_2, \ldots, A_M\}$. Initially, we follow the same process as discussed in Sect. 4.2 to obtain the resultant bit-vector B. Let there be total p groups of contents then the resultant bit-vector obtained will consist of p bits, each bit corresponds to a particular group of contents. The value of the bit for a group of contents is 1 if all the contents in the group can be accessed by the individual. So, we scan the bits in B. Then in the mapping table between group IDs and content IDs, go to the groups respective to bits = 1 in B and then present all the content in the groups to the individual accessing the contents.

The method presented is efficient as the bit-vectors, after identification of contents with identical access rights vector, consist of less number of bits. Hence the number of comparisons during AND operation and scanning of bit-vectors will be low.

6 Performance Analysis

In this section, we analyze both mathematical as well as experimental performance of our proposed method in terms of time required to access the contents, storage space, and insertion time. For experimental performance analysis, we use relational database (RDB) model as reference for storing the access rights. This is because most of the literature [5, 6] and existing social networks [13] use relational database for storing the access rights. In the RDB model, access rights are stored in tabular format in a relational database (DB). Each row in the table corresponds to a particular content and each column corresponds to a particular access right. In this section, we first present the reason for efficient access control and then we present the mathematical and experimental analysis.

The proposed method of access rights organization using bit-vector transform outperforms the RDB model of access control because of following reasons. Firstly, the maximum possible elementary ranges along each access right's dimension cannot be more than maximum possible values in the domain of that access right. Thus, in our proposed arrangement the search space is limited to the number of values in the domain of the access right. Secondly, the search time along each access rights dimension is further reduced as each dimension can be represented using AVL tree structure. For example, If there are 1000 contents with a person. To verify the credential of an individual accessing the content (assuming a single access right), 2000 comparisons are needed (assuming only single range with each access right) if we use RDB based access control model. If the domain of that particular access contain 100 values then our method requires 100 comparisons if we do not represent access rights with an AVL tree. Only 8 to 10 comparisons are needed for the same purpose when we represent the dimension using an AVL tree. In case of multiple access rights associated with each content, our method requires $M - 1$ more AND operation between the bit-vectors obtained for each access right's dimension, where M is the number of access rights associated with each content. But still our method remains much more efficient. As discussed in mathematical and experimental analysis, the relative gain becomes even more for the case of multiple ranges per access right.

6.1 Mathematical Performance Analysis

To analyze the mathematical performance, we assume that there are N number of content present and each content is defined with M access rights. For ease of understanding, we derive the expressions for access rights with single range only. We discuss the effect of multiple discrete ranges on performance in Sect. 6.2.

(1) *Access Time Required:* Let after insertion of N contents, jth access right's dimension is divided into n_j number of elementary ranges. The complexity for the searching step will be $O(\log_2(n_j))$ for the jth access right's dimension. If there are N contents then each bit-vector will be N bits long. It can be represented using $\lceil N/k \rceil$ integers in computer, where k is the number of bits in the data format (e.g. integer or long) using which bit-vectors represented in computers (N bit long bit-vectors are implemented using a linked list containing $\lceil N/k \rceil$ elements). Further, $M-1$ AND operations will be required to get the final bit-vector. Thus, the time required for the second step will of $O((M-1) \times \lceil N/k \rceil)$. Finally, the bit-vector obtained is scanned to find the bits which are equal to 1 for finding the contents which a person can access. This step requires N number of AND operations. Thus, the total time required can be given as $k_1 \times \sum_{j=1}^{M} (\log_2(n_j)) + k_2 \times ((M-1) \times \lceil N/k \rceil + N)$. Here, k_1 and k_2 are arbitrary system dependent constants.

(2) *Space Complexity:* The space complexity is given by the space required to store the bit-vectors and end points of elementary ranges. Each bit-vector consists of N bits and there n_j number of bit-vectors along the jth access rights dimension. Thus, the space required to store the bit-vectors will be $\sum_{j=1}^{M} n_j * N$ bits or if bits are represented in integer format then the space required will be $\sum_{j=1}^{M} n_j \times \lceil N/k \rceil \times k$. To store the end points of elementary ranges, we require to store n_j integers along the jth access right's dimension. Thus, the space required to store elementary ranges will be $\sum_{j=1}^{M} n_j \times k$. In addition, $2 \times N \times M \times k$ bits of space is required to provide an interface for the access rights. Thus, the total space required will be $\sum_{j=1}^{M} n_j \times (\lceil N/k \rceil \times k + k) + 2 \times N \times M \times k$ bits.

(3) *Insertion Time Complexity:* The first step of the insertion process is to insert the both end points of all access rights. The time required for this step is $k_1 \times 2 \times \log(n_j)$ for the jth access right's dimension. The second step is the bit-vector modification. Let the range of jth access right be given by $[a_j, b_j]$. Let the number of elementary ranges between a_j and b_j be given by n'_j. Then the time required for the second step would be $k_2 \times \sum_{j=1}^{M} n'_j$. Thus, the overall time complexity would be $2 \times k_1 \times \sum_{j=1}^{M} \log(n_j) + k_2 \times \sum_{j=1}^{M} n'_j$.

6.2 Experimental Performance Analysis

All the experiments were performed on Intel(R) core(2) 2.40 GHz 32-bit CPU with 2 GB RAM. We perform the experiments for access time required for the number of

Fig. 6 Access control time

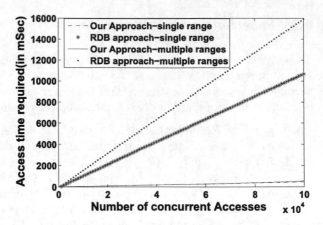

concurrent profile accesses in the system, assuming that on an average 1000 contents are present in each user's profile. For storage space and insertion time complexity, we perform experiments for up to 10000 contents (N) in the user's profile. For the experiments purpose, we assume that the number of access rights associated with the contents are between 7 and 15. The number of values in the domain of access rights is randomly chosen in between 10 and 100. The value of k is 32 in our case as we represent bit-vectors using integer format. We compare the performance after considering both single-ranged and multiple-ranged access rights. For multi-ranged access rights we assume that thee access rights out of all access rights can have multiple discrete ranges. To show the effect of multi-ranged access rights, we do the experiments by assuming up to four ranges for these access rights.

(1) *Access Time Required:* Figure 6 shows the comparison os access time performance of our approach with RDB based approach for the case of single range and multi-ranged access rights. As shown in Fig. 6, our approach outperforms the RDB based approach for all the values of concurrent content accesses. It can also be observed that, in contrast to RDB approach, our approach takes almost same time in both single-ranged and multi-ranged access rights cases. This is because in our method number of *AND* operations required are same for both the cases. The only difference is searching along the access right dimensions. The search time along each access right's dimension also becomes almost same as the number of elementary ranges (n_j) reaches to maximum possible elementary ranges in access rights' domain. Thus, the proposed mechanism is more suitable for present social networks, which may have access rights in the form of multiple discrete ranges.

(2) *Space Complexity:* The storage space is given by the space required to store the bit-vectors, end points of elementary ranges and access rights in the original RDB form (required for providing an interface to users). Figure 7 compares the performance in terms of storage space required to store N contents in a profile. Although the storage of access rights in bit-vector transform takes lesser time but additional space is required to store the access rights in the original RDB form along with the contents. The overall overhead for the case of single-ranged

Fig. 7 Storage space required

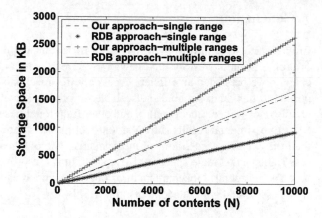

Fig. 8 Insertion time complexity

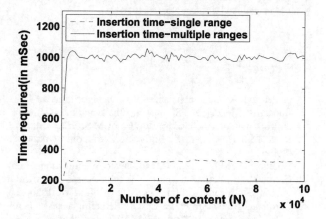

access rights is about 60–70%. The overhead is relatively small for the case of multi-ranged access rights due to finite possible access rights' ranges.

(3) *Insertion Time Complexity:* Figure 8 shows the insertion time complexity for insertion of Nth content when $N - 1$ contents are already present. As derived in Sect. 6.1, the insertion time depends on n_j and n'_j, it does not depend on N. So, the curve initially rises until maximum elementary ranges are reached then it becomes almost constant. The overhead due to the insertion is very less. For most of the values of N, it is much less than the time required to do the access control with RDB approach. In particular, we observe that it is about three times to 30 times less for $N = 1000$ to $N = 10000$ (see Figs. 6 and 8). In case of multi-ranged access rights, the insertion time is proportional to the number of ranges. However, we need to insert the contents only once. And in general, every content in MMSNs is accessed several times so the overall effect of insertion complexity on the system performance would be small.

7 Conclusion

Efficient access control in MMSNs is an important requirement with the fast rate of proliferation of MMSNs and new innovative access control requirements. In this chapter, we presented an efficient access control mechanism for MMSNs. The proposed mechanism is suitable and scalable for present social networks as it can easily handle fine grained access control and other functionalities required in existing MM-SNs. Experimental results show that our technique is about 30 times more efficient than the existing access control mechanisms. The overhead due to insertion of access rights and storage space is also small. Thus, our proposed bit-vector transform based access control mechanism turns out to be a good choice for storing the access rights associated with the contents in MMSNs.

Acknowledgement   Thanks to the Agency for Science, Technology and Research (A-STAR), Singapore for supporting this work under the project "Digital Rights Violation Detection for Digital Asset Management" (Project No: 0721010022).

References

1. Andersson, A.: General balanced trees. J. Algorithms **30**(1), 1–18 (1999)
2. Baden, R., Bender, A., Spring, N., Bhattacharjee, B., Starin, D.: Persona: an online social network with user-defined privacy. In: ACM SIGCOMM, pp. 135–146 (2009)
3. Beato, M.K.F., Wouters, K.: Enforcing access control in social networks. In: HotPets, pp. 1–10 (2009)
4. Brickley, D., Miller, L.: FOAF vocabulary specification (2005)
5. Carminati, B., Ferrari, E., Perego, A.: Rule-based access control for social networks. In: On the Move to Meaningful Internet Systems: OTM Workshops, pp. 1734–1744 (2006)
6. Carminati, B., Ferrari, E., Perego, A.: Enforcing access control in web-based social networks. ACM Trans. Inf. Syst. Secur. **13**(1), 191–233 (2009)
7. Carminati, B., Ferrari, E., Perego, A.: Privacy-aware access control in social networks: Issues and solutions. In: Privacy and Anonymity in Information Management Systems, pp. 181–195 (2010)
8. Facebook statistics. Available at: http://www.facebook.com/press/info.php?statistics
9. Flickr. www.flickr.com/
10. Diehl, E.: A four-layer model for security of digital rights management. In: 8th ACM Workshop on Digital Rights Management, pp. 19–28 (2008)
11. Gates, C.: Access control requirements for web 2.0 security and privacy. In: IEEE Web 2.0 Privacy and Security Workshop (2007)
12. Governatori, G., Iannella, R.: Modelling and reasoning languages for social networks policies. In: 13th IEEE International Conference on Enterprise Distributed Object Computing (2009)
13. Graham, W.: Reaching users through facebook: A guide to implementing facebook athenaeum. Code4Lib J. (5) (2008)
14. Grzonkowski, S., Ensor, B., Kruk, S.R., Gzella, A., Decker, S., McDaniel, B.: A DRM solution based on social networks and enabling the idea of fair use. In: Proceedings of Media in Transition (2007)
15. Iannella, R.: Digital rights management (DRM) architectures. D-Lib Mag. **7**(6) (2001)
16. Iannella, R.: A framework for the policy-oriented web in social networks. In: 7th International Workshop for Technical, Economic and Legal Aspects of Business Models for Virtual Goods (2009)

17. Kolovski, V., Katz, Y., Hendler, J., Weitzner, D., Berners-Lee, T.: Towards a policy-aware web. In: Semantic Web and Policy Workshop at the 4th International Semantic Web Conference (2005)
18. Loukides, G., Gkoulalas-Divanis, A.: Privacy challenges and solutions in the social web. ACM Crossroads **16**(2), 14–18 (2009)
19. Neilsen online technical report 2009. Available at: http://en-us.nielsen.com/
20. Pfaff, B.: Performance analysis of BSTs in system software. ACM SIGMETRICS Perform. Eval. Rev. **32**(1), 410–411 (2004)
21. Sachan, A., Emmanuel, S., Kankanhalli, M.S.: Efficient license validation in MPML DRM architecture. In: 9th ACM Workshop on Digital Rights Management, pp. 73–82 (2009)
22. Sachan, A., Emmanuel, S., Kankanhalli, M.S.: Efficient aggregate licenses validation in DRM. In: 15th Database Systems for Advanced Application (DASFAA), pp. 313–319 (2010)
23. Sachan, A., Emmanuel, S., Kankanhalli, M.S.: An efficient access control method for multimedia social networks. In: 2nd ACM Multimedia Workshop on Social Media (WSM) (2010)
24. Shehab, M., Squicciarini, A., Ahn, G.J.: Beyond user-to-user access control for online social networks. In: Information and Communications Security, pp. 174–189 (2008)
25. Squicciarini, A.C., Shehab, M., Paci, F.: Collective privacy management in social networks. In: 18th International Conference on World Wide Web, pp. 521–530 (2009)
26. Tootoonchian, A., Gollu, K.K., Saroiu, S., Ganjali, Y., Wolman, A.: Lockr: social access control for web 2.0. In: First ACM Workshop on Online Social Networks, pp. 43–48 (2008)
27. Wilfred, V., Bader, A., Muthucumaru, M.: An access control scheme for protecting personal data. In: Sixth Annual Conference on Privacy, Security and Trust (2008)
28. Williams, J.: Social networking applications in health care: threats to the privacy and security of health information. In: ICSE Workshop on Software Engineering in Health Care (2010)
29. Yeung, C.A., Liccardi, I., Lu, K., Seneviratne, K., Berners-Lee, T.: Decentralization: The future of online social networking. In: W3C Workshop on the Future of Social Networking (2009)
30. YouTube fact sheet. Available at: http://www.youtube.com/t/fact_sheet

Call Me Guru: User Categories and Large-Scale Behavior in YouTube

Joan-Isaac Biel and Daniel Gatica-Perez

Abstract While existing studies on YouTube's massive user-generated video content have mostly focused on the analysis of *videos*, their characteristics, and network properties, little attention has been paid to the analysis of *users' long-term behavior* as it relates to the roles they self-define and (explicitly or not) play in the site. In this chapter, we present a statistical analysis of aggregated user behavior in YouTube from the perspective of user categories, a feature that allows people to ascribe to popular roles and to potentially reach certain communities. Using a sample of 270,000 users, we found that a high level of interaction and participation is concentrated on a relatively small, yet significant, group of users, following recognizable patterns of personal and social involvement. Based on our analysis, we also show that by using simple behavioral features from user profiles, people can be automatically classified according to their category with accuracy rates of up to 73%.

1 Introduction

Social media sites have become mainstream publishing and communication tools that have globally changed media production and consumption patterns. Among them, YouTube is one of the best examples of this explosion of online user-generated content receiving 24 h of new videos every minute (the equivalent of 140,000 Hollywood movies per week) [22], and surpassing 2 billion views per day [21]. While the first key achievement of YouTube was the creation of an easy-to-use integrated platform aimed to upload, share, and watch online videos, thus removing barriers to the online video scene, it further promoted participation allowing users to comment, rate, explore, and post related videos. As a result, YouTube has become a site for people and communities to join and interact, from aspiring rockstars to top politicians.

J.-I. Biel (✉) · D. Gatica-Perez
Idiap Research Institute, Ecole Polytechnique Fédérale de Lausanne (EPFL), Lausanne, Switzerland
e-mail: jibiel@idiap.ch

D. Gatica-Perez
e-mail: gatica@idiap.ch

S.C.H. Hoi et al. (eds.), *Social Media Modeling and Computing*,
DOI 10.1007/978-0-85729-436-4_8, © Springer-Verlag London Limited 2011

Recently, research on YouTube has analyzed the statistics and social network of uploaded videos, revealing properties of the nature of video-sharing systems that may be key for the future of such services [4, 5, 16]. However, few works have focused on characterizing long-term user behavior Existing works have provided a brief statistical analysis on the use of YouTube social-oriented features [9], studied the properties of the social network of friends and subscriptions [16], and a similar characterization based on user video interactions [1]. Understanding how users typically behave and interact, and how they perceive YouTube as both a system and a social outlet is fundamental to improve its performance. Despite this realization, existing work has mainly treated YouTube users as a single homogeneous group, ignoring potential differences between groups of users. We believe that this is an essential point when analyzing users in large social networks, due to the likely wide variety of behavioral patterns.

This chapter presents one of the first attempts to analyze large-scale aggregated behavior of YouTube users under the lens of *user categories*, i.e., self-assigned roles that people can choose among *Director*, *Comedian*, *Guru*, *Musician*, or *Reporter*. We hypothesize that users' choices and the implicit or explicit ways in which people respond to these roles give rise to different collective behavior, which can be measured quantitatively. Our work has two contributions. First, on a large user dataset, we present a statistical analysis of YouTube users and categories based on easy-to-extract, long-term user behavioral features, which do not require any video or metadata processing. Our analysis reveals clear trends regarding people's category choices, and differences on user behavior (both individual and social) across categories and gender, which suggest that the emerging communities do have differences that could lead the way to automatic modeling of groups of users. Second, we use such behavioral cues in various classification tasks, in order to explore whether, alone or together, they can be used to infer user categories, obtaining promising performance. Overall, our work aims at complementing the emerging (and much needed) work in sociology and ethnography on the understanding of users' motivations to select roles and to create and maintain self and group identities in social media outlets like YouTube, and enquires about some fundamental needs for personalized applications.

This chapter is organized as follows. Section 2 reviews some of the recent literature on YouTube, with focus on user behavior research. Section 3 provides a basic overview on YouTube channels user categories. Section 4 describes the set of behavioral features extracted from the use channels. Section 5 presents a statistical analysis of the feature distributions to study the differences between different user categories. Section 6 focuses on the use of behavioral features for user category classification. Finally, Sect. 7 summarizes the chapter and discusses future work.

2 Research in YouTube

Today, research in social media has mainly studied YouTube as a video repository system and as a user-generated content site, focusing on the analysis of the network of videos and the typical characteristics of video content itself. Using analytical methods from social networks to investigate the macroscopic characteristics of the network of videos, works have studied the impact of user-generated content in underlying video-on-demand architectures [4, 5], and in local networks [7, 23]. By concentrating specifically on videos, research has also studied the daily cycles of video reception (based on the number of views), in an attempt to automatically predict their popularity [20]. In relation to video content, several studies have manually coded samples of videos to categorize the types and properties of YouTube content to gain understanding about user-generated media production [3, 10, 11]. Furthermore, other works have attempted to automatically model the topic and ideological perspective of content [14].

Compared to the aforementioned approaches, research on YouTube user behavior, rather scarce specially with respect to automatic analysis, includes a variety of research questions, data sample sizes, and methods. From sociology to communication, some works have focused on studying the practices of small groups of people (typically less than 100) to understand why and how people participate in online video-sharing sites like YouTube. Some works have done so by observing both the computer-mediated and offline behavior of people to understand the purposes of using YouTube in everyday life [13] and the influence of feedback, criticism and hate behaviors [12]. Others have analyzed videos and their related text content to study how users present themselves from the perspective of creating an online identity [8]. A third set of works have used manual coding and questionnaires to analyze the processes of creation and reception of online video [17, 19]. Overall, due to their nature, the analysis methods used in all these works are not extensible to study larger samples, which limits the statistical significance of their findings. In addition, findings obtained from the study of small groups and specific communities (e.g., school students or elders) are likely to generalize poorly to the large population of YouTube users. In contrast, very few works in computer science have been devoted to the study of user behavior on large-scale data samples gathered using YouTube's API or web crawlers. Using statistical methodologies, they have focused on analyzing the structure and topology of the social networks that emerge from user interaction, to reveal network characteristics that are relevant for information and communications services [16], and to detect anti-social and spam behaviors [1]. Despite the relevance of their findings, these works do not provide any understanding on the nature of users' behaviors and their motivations to participate and to create and maintain self and group identities.

Few works have focused on studying user behavior as in our work, using the metadata attributes available on YouTube to characterize common user and group patterns that arise from long-term behavior. Halvey and Keane [9] provided a first statistical analysis on the use of some features such as the number of videos watched, uploads, friends, subscriptions, groups, and comments. Their study evidenced that a big part of users participate in YouTube as consumers rather than as contributors of content, and that few users participate actively, both contributing with content and interacting socially with other users, as is shown by the power-law behavior of some of these feature distributions. Furthermore, Maia et al. [15] identified different groups of users based on a similar set of social features. Using an unsupervised clustering algorithm, and estimating the number of clusters automatically, they found five different groups of users which were, respectively, characterized as (1) not active, (2) producers, (3) consumers, (4) producers and consumers, and (5) others. Compared to Halvey and Keane [9], who treated YouTube users as a whole, our analysis emphasizes the potential differences between groups of users. We believe that this is an essential point when analyzing users in large social networks, due to the likely wide variety of behavioral patterns. In addition, compared to Maia et al. [15], our work differs in our focus on predetermined, self-assigned user categories, investigating the significant differences among their behaviors. A preliminary version of our work appeared in [2].

3 YouTube Channels and User Categories

Most of the people watching videos in YouTube are familiar with the default YouTube *video page* (see Fig. 1, left), which allows users not only to watch a video, but to leave comments usually referred to the video, browse related videos suggested by YouTube, or navigate to video answers left by other users. In addition, YouTube provides a *user channel* to registered users (see Fig. 1, right), which is equivalent to a user profile in other social networks.

The user channel is a dedicated user page that gathers all the videos uploaded by the user, and thus facilitates interested people to browse videos of a specific user, uploaded at anytime. Furthermore, it includes user information such as the name, location, age, personal description, and interests, together with user participation statistics such as the number of videos uploaded or watched, and links to the user

Fig. 1 The YouTube video page (*left*) is designed to watch a video, leave comments, and navigate to related videos, which are not necessarily from the same user. In contrast, the user channel (*right*) is a user-dedicated page that gathers all the user's videos, in addition to personal information, usage statistics and comments addressed to the user

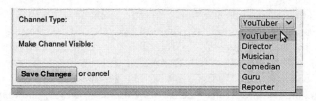

Fig. 2 YouTube users can choose to belong to a specific category by changing the default settings of their user channels. Standard, Director, Musician, Comedian, Guru, and Reporter are open to everybody, whereas Politician and Non-profit are granted under special request

subscriptions, subscribers, and friends. The user is allowed to control the information made public on the channel, as well as, to some extent, customize the look of the channel. In addition, users visiting a channel can leave comments which contrary to the comments in the video page, do no typically relate to any video in particular, but address the user in a more general way.

As with user channels, YouTube is continuously introducing new features to its platform, aiming to enhance the user experience responding to their demands as the community grows and diversifies. Special user categories are another example of features gradually introduced by YouTube and originally serving different purposes.

In April 2006, YouTube introduced the *Director* program in response to a video duration limitation earlier installed to prevent copyright infringement, most likely to be brought about by long videos. A user proving to be a legitimate creator of his/her uploaded content could apply for a *Director* account that allowed one to upload videos longer than 10 minutes (eventually, with the creation of other user account types, new *Director* accounts were limited to 10 minutes as well). In a span of five months, YouTube created special accounts for other users willing to promote their work. Users with a *Musician* or a *Comedian* accounts had the possibility to customize their user profiles by publishing performer information and a schedule of show dates. By June 2008, four more account categories had been introduced. *Guru* and *Reporter* accounts were, respectively, addressed to people devoted to create "how to" videos (i.e., videos that teach certain skills or explain how to do something) and to people dedicated to inform others about news and events occurring around them. While these accounts allowed anyone to sign up, two other ones, *Non-profit* and *Politician*, were only to be held by real non-profit organizations and politicians. The first one aimed to support advocacy campaigns and fund-raising efforts. The second one was created for candidates of the 2008 United States presidential election and some other elections.

Today, a new user signing up for a YouTube account receives by default a *Standard* or *YouTuber* account, with the basic YouTube features such as uploading, commenting, etc. (we use the term *Standard* to avoid confusing *YouTubers* with all YouTube users). This status remains unchanged unless users *intentionally* modify their channel type to one and only one of the special categories (see Fig. 2). In doing so, they are allowed a certain level of customization on their channel, which also exhibits a label with the name of the user category.

Why would users be interested in becoming special users? And why would they choose one category or another? A potential benefit for special users is that only them qualify for the *channels page* in YouTube, where the most subscribed and the most viewed channels are featured. Compared to browsing and searching, video and channel promotion in YouTube are advantageous ways of attracting viewers, and so that results in an obvious incentive for users. However, one may argue that this only benefits a small set of users, which then accumulate a high number of sub-scriptions and views. Moreover, though the different user categories are described in the YouTube help section, users are free to assign a user category to themselves independently of how well they fit with the respective category description, possibly augmenting the overlap among categories in terms of typical behaviors. For some users, like *Musicians*, the answer may be on the goodness of fit under a specific description. For others, we hypothesize that the process of self-assigning a specific user category conveys a sense of belonging to a particular community of users. If this is true, users might tend to acquire the same user category than the users he follows or interacts with, somehow reassuring his presence in that community. A way to verify this could be to use networked data to compare the user category labels of users in a same social network, as well as to study the behavioral patterns of different communities of users. Alternatively, in our work, we directly focus on user categories, and hypothesize that users belonging to the same user category, do in fact behave in similar ways.

4 Extracting User Behavioral Features from YouTube

We gathered a dataset from YouTube user channels. Using YouTube's API, we followed a two-step data collection procedure that consisted on first obtaining the last uploaded videos from the site and extracting the username of the uploader, and then retrieving the channel information for every user. Since video search feeds are constantly updated with a short period of time, we repeated this procedure every 5 minutes, from March 5th to March 9th, 2009. We used video-category specific queries to overcome a 999 entries per feed limitation existing in the API feeds, thus augmenting our capacity to obtain the last uploaded videos.

We collected a dataset of 273,000 distinct users, for whom we obtained a set of descriptive behavioral features. We explicitly limited the set of features to all the attributes that can be easily extracted from the users' channel, being aware that there might be other features that are richer descriptors of behavior at higher computational cost. We divided the behavioral features in two different groups, capturing the individual participation and the social-oriented behavior of users, respectively. In addition, we extracted the user category information from the user channels.

The *individual participation features* are direct indicators of individual user activity in YouTube, both in terms of production and consumption.

- *Number of Uploads.* The number of videos uploaded by the user is a measure of how much the user contributes to YouTube with content. It is an interesting measure from the point of view of user-generated content production and online video broadcasting.

- *Number of Videos watched.* The number of videos watched is a measure of how much a user participates in the site consuming video content. Watching videos is the simplest, most passive form of participation in YouTube, and it does not require users to be logged-in. Therefore, whereas this feature may be a reliable estimate for some users (those who log-in to interact in the site while watching videos), for others it may vary largely from the actual number of videos watched. Whatever the case, we argue that the feature may tell something about the way users consume video in YouTube.
- *Number of Favorites.* Marking a video as a "favorite" (a.k.a. "fave"-or) is a useful practice for users that helps to maintain a list of videos preferred videos, which then can be later disseminated in blogs or other websites, or can simply be used to replay and share videos with other people at anytime. It is therefore a descriptor of a specific way of engaging with videos online.

The *social-oriented features* are measures of an interaction between users. We differentiate between incoming or outgoing features, depending on the role of the users in the interaction. Incoming features describe how a user is perceived by others, and they are a measure of the social attention achieved by the user.

- *Number of Views.* The accumulated number of views, as it appears in the user channel, is an aggregate of the views over all the videos from the user. The number of views has been typically used as a measure of popularity of videos, as it resembles the way audiences are measures in traditional mainstream media [3]. Here, we use it as a measure of the level of reception of a user's content from other people, which includes registered users as well as not registered. Note, however, that the number of views does not account for the distribution of views among videos. For example, for some users it could be biased to few highly viewed videos.
- *Number of subscribers.* Subscriptions are a common form of syndication to users and content in social media. In YouTube, users subscribe to other users' channels in order to be notified whenever the users they are subscribed upload new videos to the site. Since it accounts only for registered users, the total number of subscribers of a user is different measure of popularity that complements the number of views.

Alternatively, the outgoing features reveal the level of disposition of a user to proactively interact with other users:

- *Number of subscriptions.* The total number of subscriptions is a measure of the interest of a user to follow other users' content, which clearly denotes social behavior, that goes beyond simply uploading content, being watched, or being followed.
- *Number of friends.* Friendship is an alternative way of connecting with other users in YouTube which does not imply following other users' content. In fact, whereas subscriptions are directed links between users, and therefore do not ensure reciprocity, friendship creates a reciprocal (non-directed) link between two users. As

compared to other social media sites, the specific use of friendship connections has not been investigated in YouTube. We hypothesize that for some users it might refer to "true" offline friendships, as opposed to subscription-based connections.

5 Behavioral Data Analysis

There is a large number of research questions related to the ways in which users participate and interact in YouTube. Here, we focus on issues related to the long-term behavior of users that can be addressed by inspecting the features available from the user channels, which result from the aggregation of the users behavior over their online lifespan. Other questions would likely require more detailed, time-sampled data, and cannot be explored here.

5.1 How Do Features Correlate?

We first investigate the interdependence between behavioral features, by computing Pearson's correlation for all the pair-wise combinations, shown in Table 1. Among participative features, the number of uploads and videos watched showed only moderate correlation ($r = 0.36$). This evidences that uploading and watching videos are two different ways of participation, and that whereas some users contribute to YouTube with content, other users prefer watching videos. Instead, the number of videos watched and times favorited show a larger correlation ($r = 0.55$), which probably relates to the fact that favoriting a video generally implies having watching it. Overall, we observe larger correlations between social features, as for example, between the number of subscribers and views ($r = 0.84$), which agrees with the idea that as users have larger pools of subscribers their content is accessed more. In addition, there is a significant correlation across the two groups of features, as for example, between the uploads and the number of views ($r = 0.67$) and between uploads and subscriptions ($r = 0.53$). This indicates a certain correlation between the level of attention of users and their content contribution to the site.

Despite what may be suggested by the above results, we hypothesized that the behavioral patterns of users may vary a lot depending on how active users are. For example, we were interested on exploring whether the same correlation levels hold whenever users "specialize" (i.e. they are more active) in one of the features. With this in mind, we recomputed the pair-wise correlations for users contributing to the top ten percentiles of each feature distribution and show them in Table 2. Note that in this case, the correlation matrix is not symmetric and should be read row-wise. Interestingly, we observe a general decrease of the strength of the interdependence, which is significant for some of the pairs. As an example, top uploaders (first row) show lower correlation between uploads and views ($r = 0.21$) and between uploads and subscribers ($r = 0.29$) than the ones showed in Table 1 ($r = 0.36$ and $r = 0.53$, respectively). This suggests that, compared to the rest of users, top uploaders may

Table 1 Correlation between all pairs of features. Feature values were log-scaled. All values are significant with $p < 0.0001$

	1	2	3	4	5	6	7
1. uploads		0.36	0.28	0.67	0.53	0.32	0.42
2. watched	0.36		0.55	0.55	0.38	0.49	0.47
3. favorites	0.28	0.55		0.43	0.27	0.53	0.47
4. views	0.67	0.55	0.43		0.84	0.49	0.68
5. subscribers	0.53	0.38	0.27	0.84		0.44	0.68
6. subscriptions	0.32	0.49	0.53	0.49	0.44		0.63
7. friends	0.42	0.47	0.47	0.68	0.68	0.63	

Table 2 Correlation between all pairs of features for the most active users in each feature. The correlation coefficient r_{xy} between feature x (in rows) and y (in columns) is computed after selecting the users contributing to the top ten percentiles of feature x's distribution

	1	2	3	4	5	6	7
1. uploads		0.21***	0.17*	0.41***	0.29***	0.23***	0.24***
2. watched	0.12***		0.36***	0.14***	0.15***	0.32***	0.26***
3. favorites	0.01	0.21*		0.02*	0.01	0.28	0.17
4. views	0.47***	0.32***	0.25		0.78***	0.38***	0.55***
5. subscribers	0.38***	0.28***	0.19*	0.78***		0.40***	0.58***
6. subscriptions	0.03*	0.27***	0.31***	0.05***	0.03***		0.32***
7. friends	0.17***	0.29***	0.27	0.32***	0.33***	0.49***	

*$p < 0.01$

**$p < 0.001$

***$p < 0.0001$

have other motifs to contribute to YouTube rather than only social attention. Similarly, the number of favorites and the number of videos watched ($r = 0.21$) show low correlation for those who favorited the most (third row), compared to the whole sample ($r = 0.55$). Finally, those who have a lot of subscriptions (fifth row), show low correlation between the number of subscriptions and videos watched ($r = 0.27$ compared to $r = 0.49$), and no correlation between subscriptions and number of subscribers ($r = 0.03$ compared to $r = 0.44$). The later emphasizes the anti-reciprocity of the subscription links, indicating that active subscribers do not necessarily receive subscriptions from other users, which rather depends on how much they contribute in terms of content. Furthermore, we observe the strength of other relationships, such as the one between views and subscribers ($r = 0.78$), which continues to hold (and is symmetric) for both the top users receiving views and the top users on the number of subscribers.

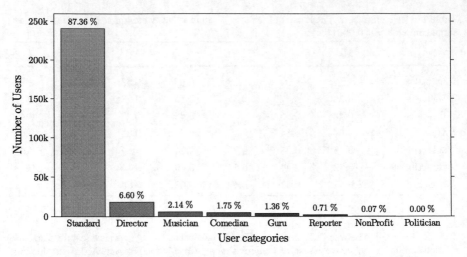

Fig. 3 Distribution of user categories in our dataset. 12.6% of the users self-assigned themselves a special user category (*Director*, *Musician*, *Comedian*, *Guru*, *Reporter*, *Non-profit*, and *Politician*)

This analysis emphasizes that (1) the relationships between pairs of behavioral features are more complex than the linear relation, and (2) these relationships vary between different subsamples of users, depending on their behavior (i.e., how active they are).

5.2 Are You Special?

We were interested in exploring the level of popularity that user categories have among the YouTube community. The distribution of user categories is shown in Fig. 3. This distribution reveals that 12.6% of the users choose to label themselves with a category different than *Standard*. The relatively moderate level of popularity of special categories could be explained by the poor advertising of such feature in the site. We hypothesize that users are more likely to find about categories by "word of mouth", after seeing other users with labels such as *Director* or *Comedian*. Among special user categories, Directors (52.4%), Musicians (16.8%), Comedians (13.8%), and Gurus (10.8%) are the most popular, followed by Reporters (5.6%), Non-Profit organizations (0.5%) and Politicians (0.0001%). This distribution seems to be biased by the chronological order in which categories were introduced, which could suggest, in fact, that the process of choosing a category is influenced by a "rich-get-richer" effect, in which new users would tend to choose the most numerous category. Unfortunately, our data do not allow one to check this hypothesis. Alternatively, it could also be that *Directors* is perceived as a more broad category than *Musicians* or *Comedians*, and thus users self-associate to it more easily. Whatever the case, this may indicate that the *Director* category is bringing together a larger variety of different users and behaviors, compared to *Comedians*, *Musicians*, or *Gurus*.

Table 3 Mean, median and coefficient of variation (cov) values of participatory feature distributions for each user category. First row ("All") groups the totality of users in the dataset, indistinctly of their user category

Category	uploads			watched			favorites		
	mean	median	cov	mean	median	cov	mean	median	cov
All	31.10	7.00	6.35	2493.42	841.00	2.02	35.99	2.00	2.67
Standard	23.77	6.00	5.13	2054.12	699.00	1.96	28.21	1.00	2.92
Special	81.75	21.00	5.51	5403.49	2803.50	1.62	89.80	22.00	1.68
Director	95.03	25.00	4.33	5975.35	3301.00	1.61	101.72	28.00	1.58
Musician	41.84	14.00	3.05	4123.72	2054.50	1.73	68.49	15.00	1.84
Comedian	40.60	15.00	3.82	5114.65	2580.50	1.56	91.57	23.00	1.68
Guru	94.85	23.00	8.70	5746.53	3163.00	1.42	85.38	22.00	1.70
Non-Profit	64.67	26.00	2.47	1447.12	507.00	2.09	15.73	3.00	3.17
Reporter	127.69	30.00	3.89	4048.75	1415.00	1.77	58.17	8.00	2.10
Politician	33.57	23.00	1.39	1087.57	591.00	1.42	62.57	6.00	2.43

5.3 How Participative Are You?

Based on our sample, users in YouTube uploaded a median of seven videos, watched 841 videos, and favorited two videos. Despite their variance, these figures indicate a relatively low level of individual participation in YouTube compared to other social media sites, as was exposed in earlier work [9]. However, our category-based analysis reveals that this result is biased by the very low participation of *Standard* users, compared to special users. As shown in Table 3, which gathers some basic statistics of the participatory features for the different user categories, *Standard* users uploaded a median of six videos, watched 699 videos, and "favorited" only one video, versus the 21 uploads, 2803 videos watched and 22 favorites of special users. In addition, we note that some differences between these statistics for the different user categories.

We propose a methodology to further investigate the differences among user categories at different degrees of activity, going from the most passive to the most active users for each of the features. For this analysis, we first consider a scale of ten different activity levels $l(i)$, $i = 1 \ldots 10$, which are determined for each behavioral feature based on the complete feature distribution deciles, independent from the user categories. Secondly, we define the discrete distribution $p(u, i)$ as the relative frequency of the user category u on the activity level i, which we computed for each of the user categories in the dataset. In the third place, we build a null model by shuffling the user categories among all the feature values, i.e., we destroy the relational links between features and user categories, keeping the feature values and the proportion of categories. The goal of this null model is to determine the distribution $q(u, i)$ of expected relative frequencies of the user category u given a uniform dis-

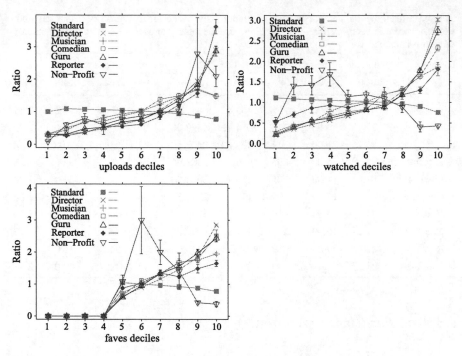

Fig. 4 Mean $\hat{r}(u, i)$ values and confidence intervals of $r(u, i)$ ratio for participative features (confidence values equal to one standard deviation). For each feature, the ten activity levels $l(i)$, $i = 1 \ldots 10$ are fixed by the distribution deciles (i.e. the 1st and 10th deciles correspond to the bottom ten and top ten feature distribution values, respectively)

tribution of the users from this category across the range of feature values. Finally, we can compute the ratio $r(u, i)$ between both distributions:

$$r(u, i) = \frac{p(u, i)}{q(u, i)}, \tag{1}$$

which measures to what extent the feature distribution of a given user category departs from a uniform distribution among all the activity levels. Note that $r(u, i)$ is not a distribution itself, but a measure that indicates how much the category u is underrepresented ($r(u, i) < 1$) or overrepresented ($r(u, i) > 1$) in the ith bin, as compared to what would result from a uniform distribution. Note also that the accuracy of $r(u, i)$ may vary when used to analyze different user categories, given the differences between sample sizes for the user categories in our dataset. Thus, by repeating the sample procedure several times, which implies a different assignment of user categories to the levels of activity, we are able to build confidence intervals around a mean ratio on $\hat{r}(u, i)$. These confidence intervals help to assess whether differences between ratios computed for samples of different sizes are significant.

Figure 4 shows the $\hat{r}(u, i)$ values and confidence intervals (equal to one standard deviation) for the three participative features and different user categories. Note that the confidence intervals are larger for categories such as *Non-Profit*, due to the scarcity of data (we do not show *Politicians* for this specific reason). We shall remark two main observations form simple inspection of the figures. First, the feature distributions show clear differences among several user categories. These differences are accentuated when we look at more active levels (see ninth and tenth deciles). Second, we observe a clear difference between *Standard* users and *Special* users behavior. Whereas *Standards* are distributed uniformly along the ranking, *Special* users' behavior is inclined towards higher participation, or in other words, active users (who clearly find valuable their participation in YouTube) also choose to belong to a specific user category. This trend is emphasized as we get closer to the top of the rankings.

We now discuss specific differences for each behavioral feature.

5.3.1 Directors and Gurus Consistently Upload More Videos

In terms of uploads, we observe that very few special users appear among the low participation users. In particular, for the first decile we obtain $\hat{r}(Directors, 1) = 0.20$, $\hat{r}(Gurus, 1) = 0.30$, and $\hat{r}(Musicians, 1) = 0.31$, and $\hat{r}(Comedians, 1) = 0.30$, compared to $\hat{r}(Standards, 1) = 1.00$. Special users show ratios larger than one starting from the seventh decile, which clearly indicates that they tend to upload more videos than *Standards*. Focusing on the top percentile we find $\hat{r}(Reporters, 10) = 3.59$, $\hat{r}(Directors, 10) = 2.97$, $\hat{r}(Gurus, 10) = 2.96$, and $\hat{r}(Musicians, 10) = 1.54$, and $\hat{r}(Comedians, 10) = 1.47$. In contrast, $\hat{r}(Standards, 10) = 0.77$. We observe that taken in pairs, *Director* and *Guru*, and *Comedian* and *Musician* are similarly distributed not only on the tenth decile, but across all active levels. We conducted two-sample Kolmogorov–Smirnov (KS) tests[1] for the pair-wise combinations of the original user categories' distributions to assess whether these similarities are indeed significant. Tests reported *p*-values larger than 0.1 for these two pairs of user categories, indicating no significant difference on the distributions of uploads, and reported values smaller than 0.001 for the rest of pairs. In addition, right-sided KS tests reported the number of uploads for *Directors* and *Gurus* to be significantly larger than the rest. We argue that the patterns of uploading of different categories are influenced by the time required to create their videos, which in turn may unveil that their videos serve different purposes.

5.3.2 Comedians, Musicians, and Reporters Significantly Watch Less Videos

In terms of videos watched, the ratios of special categories for lower active levels do not differ much from those of uploads. In particular, for the first decile,

---

[1] The two-sample KS test is a non-parametric method which is sensitive to differences in both location and shape of the empirical cumulative distribution functions (CDFs) of two samples, and makes no assumption about the distribution of data. The null hypothesis of this statistic is that the samples are drawn from the same distribution. Thus, a KS test that yields a *p*-value less than a specified α, leads to the rejection of the null hypothesis, and favors the hypothesis that distributions are different [6].

the ratio $\hat{r}(Directors, 1) = 0.20$, $\hat{r}(Gurus, 1) = 0.22$, and $\hat{r}(Musicians, 1) = 0.31$, $\hat{r}(Comedians, 1) = 0.22$, compared to the ratio of Standards $\hat{r}(Standards, 1) = 1.11$. Focusing on the most active levels, Directors and Gurus again show larger ratios than other categories with $\hat{r}(Directors, 10) = 3.02$ and $\hat{r}(Gurus, 10) = 2.94$, which denote a higher interest of these users for consuming content on YouTube. As with uploads, the no significant difference was found between these two categories across all levels of activity, as reported by KS tests p-values being larger than 0.1. Comedians ($\hat{r}(Comedians, 10) = 2.5$), Musicians ($\hat{r}(Musicians, 10) = 1.9$) and Reporters ($\hat{r}(Comedians, 10) = 1.7$), in this order, are the next on the ranking of videos watched, whereas Standards ($\hat{r}(Standards, 10) = 0.75$) remain the last. We argue that compared to Directors and Gurus, the other special users may be interested in releasing their work or spreading their messages, rather than on exploring other YouTube content.

5.3.3 Directors, Comedians, and Gurus Favorite the Most

The distribution of the number of videos favorited per user, with up to 45% of the users with zero favorites, imposes a null $p(u, i)$ value for the first four deciles which results in empty bins for the computation of $\hat{r}(u, i)$, $i = 1 \ldots 4$ (see Fig. 4), and all these users are concentrated in the fifth decile. For the fifth decile, we find $\hat{r}(Directors, 5) = 0.61$, $\hat{r}(Gurus, 5) = 0.58$, $\hat{r}(Musicians, 5) = 0.74$, and $\hat{r}(Comedians, 5) = 0.65$, which indicate a closer trend to the uniform distribution, compared to uploads and videos watched. Among the most active users in terms of videos favorited, we find Directors ($\hat{r}(Directors, 10) = 2.80$), Comedians ($\hat{r}(Comedian, 10) = 2.49$), and Gurus ($\hat{r}(Guru, 10) = 2.41$). Contrary to what may be suggested from their $\hat{r}(u, 10)$ values, no significant differences were found between Comedian and Gurus across all levels of activity, with two-sided KS tests p-value being larger than 0.1. In addition, one-sided KS tests suggests that the number of favorites is larger for Directors than for the rest of categories.

Summing up, we find that Directors and Gurus are among the most participative in all the aspects, followed by Comedians and Musicians. Instead, Non-profit, and Reporters follow a different pattern of participation. Whereas they are also very active uploaders, they typically display lower numbers of videos watched and "favorited", which may indicate that they are more interested in releasing their work or spreading their messages, rather than exploring the site's content.

5.4 How Social Are You?

Social-oriented features follow a similar pattern than participative features regarding the differences between Standard users and special users. As shown in Table 4 (right), Standards accumulated, in median values, 89 views and four subscribers, versus the 958 views and 19 subscribers of special users. Standards have also no

Table 4 Mean, median and coefficient of variation (cov) values of social feature distributions for each user category. First row ("All") groups the totality of users in the dataset, indistinctly of their user category

Category	views			subscribers			subscriptions			friends		
	mean	median	cov	mean	median	cov	mean	median	cov	mean	median	cov
All	3114.52	121.00	24.30	89.84	5.00	21.40	14.30	0.00	7.62	21.55	0.00	14.74
Standard	1390.23	89.00	21.59	31.69	4.00	9.49	8.30	0.00	7.18	9.27	0.00	17.71
Special	14158.82	958.00	13.50	300.27	19.00	13.61	55.83	11.00	4.65	106.46	13.00	7.30
Director	17929.58	1212.00	14.00	320.36	22.00	15.70	59.43	13.00	4.79	104.52	16.00	7.20
Musician	4179.42	489.00	7.01	114.39	9.00	8.40	33.12	5.00	3.93	88.71	8.00	10.67
Comedian	9568.23	506.50	11.50	260.06	10.00	14.20	52.32	12.00	5.16	109.52	11.00	8.23
Guru	17085.11	1250.50	6.86	459.91	33.00	6.58	72.78	18.00	3.66	128.78	18.00	4.40
Non-Profit	10614.01	1639.50	3.75	397.34	30.00	4.67	29.36	1.00	3.91	81.37	4.00	4.02
Reporter	11102.75	1016.50	5.43	284.35	22.00	6.13	58.50	6.00	4.82	120.08	8.00	5.39
Politician	3737.14	2241.00	1.30	52.14	16.00	1.63	44.86	12.00	1.62	16.43	6.00	1.55

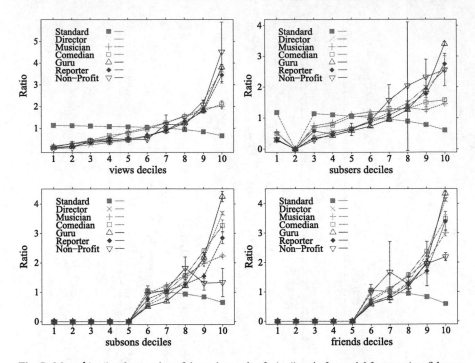

Fig. 5 Mean $\hat{r}(u, i)$ values and confidence intervals of $r(u, i)$ ratio for social features (confidence values equal to one standard deviation). For each feature, the ten activity levels $l(i)$, $i = 1, \ldots, 10$ are fixed by the distribution deciles (i.e. the first and tenth deciles correspond to the bottom ten and top ten feature distribution values, respectively)

subscriptions or friends in median value. This likely has to do with the motivation behind YouTube users. *Standard* users, in general, might be more interested in sharing few casual videos with their relatives or friends, which would potentially generate a small number of views. Instead, special users seem to be more interested in interacting with the YouTube community at large through videos that are of wider interest among other users, thus receiving more views and subscriptions.

5.4.1 Incoming Social Features

Figure 5 (top) shows the ratio values for different activity levels of incoming social features. Compared to participatory features, the ratios of special users appearing among the lower activity levels in terms of views are lower, which emphasizes the differences between special users and *Standard* users. We find $\hat{r}(Directors, 1) = 0.09$, $\hat{r}(Gurus, 1) = 0.13$, and $\hat{r}(Musicians, 1) = 0.19$, and $\hat{r}(Comedians, 1) = 0.15$, compared to the $\hat{r}(Standard, 1) = 1.13$. Clearly, *Gurus*, *Directors*, and *Reporters*, are the ones who get more attention from the community in terms of accumulated views, with $\hat{r}(Gurus, 10) = 3.79$, $\hat{r}(Directors, 10) = 3.63$, and $\hat{r}(Reporter, 10) =$

3.46, respectively. Compared to them, the ratio for the most active *Comedians* and *Musicians* is roughly cut in half, with $\hat{r}(Comedians, 10) = 2.06$ and $\hat{r}(Musicians, 10) = 1.97$. We performed KS tests for pair-wise combinations of these distributions. Two-sided KS tests reported no significant differences between Comedians and Musicians across all the levels of activity. In addition, one-sided KS tests indicate that the differences between the Comedians and Musicians and the rest of the special users are consistent, and that they are significantly receiving less views.

In terms of subscriptions, we find similar patterns on the differences between user categories. Gurus, Reporters, and Directors are the ones concentrating more subscribers, with $\hat{r}(Gurus, 10) = 3.42$, $\hat{r}(Reporters, 10) = 2.71$, and $\hat{r}(Directors, 10) = 2.55$, respectively; followed by Comedians and Musicians, with $\hat{r}(Comedians, 10) = 1.65$ and $\hat{r}(Musicians, 10) = 1.41$. This time, two-sided KS tests reported no significant differences between Directors and Reporters. In addition, one-sided KS tests suggest that differences between Gurus, Reporters, and Directors are significant.

5.4.2 Outgoing Social Features

Figure 5 (bottom) shows the ratio values for different activity levels of outgoing social features. The distributions for subscriptions and friends show that a large percentage of users, both Standard and Special, do not actually use these features, as is shown by the number of empty deciles. However, among those that use them, there are clear differences between *Special* and *Standard* uses. For the most active level, for example, we find *Gurus*, *Directors*, and *Comedians* as the top categories with $\hat{r}(Gurus, 10) = 4.25$, $\hat{r}(Directors, 10) = 3.64$, $\hat{r}(Comedians, 10) = 3.19$. Compared to them, Reporters and Musicians seem to be less prominent in terms of subscriptions, with $\hat{r}(Reporters, 10) = 2.86$, $\hat{r}(Musicians, 10) = 2.26$. This is accentuated for Standards $\hat{r}(Standards, 10) = 0.65$. Interestingly, the same ordering holds among the users having more friends, which suggests that YouTube-specific contacts and "real life" contacts might have a similar presence in their online interaction.

5.5 Male or Female?

Gender analysis, and in particular, gender distribution, uncovers interesting aspects of large-scale behavior in YouTube. Based on our data, YouTube concentrates a higher participation number of men (73% of the users) than women (27%). Moreover, we find that male users are more likely to enroll in special user categories, with a proportion of 13% compared to the 9% of females. A two-proportion z-test[2] indicate that this difference is significant with $p < 10^{-3}$.

---

[2]The two-proportion z-test is used to compare proportions of two independent binomial samples. The null hypothesis of this statistic is that the two proportions are equal. Thus, a two-proportion

Table 5 Mean, median and coefficient of variation (cov) values of participatory feature distributions for each gender

Category	uploads			watched			favorites		
	mean	median	cov	mean	median	cov	mean	median	cov
Males	29.56	7.00	6.30	2582.60	884.00	2.03	32.78	1.00	2.78
Females	24.98	7.00	5.43	2115.06	684.00	2.00	43.16	2.00	2.45

Table 6 Mean, median and coefficient of variation (cov) values of social feature distributions for each gender

Category	views			subscribers			subscriptions			friends		
	mean	median	cov	mean	median	cov	mean	median	cov	mean	median	cov
Males	2394.78	117.00	22.37	70.60	5.00	19.64	13.76	0.00	8.54	18.57	0.00	14.97
Females	2413.76	105.00	20.41	64.74	4.00	11.82	14.43	1.00	5.05	22.49	1.00	6.09

Gender differences in the distribution of special categories are very small. However, the distribution of both participative and social-oriented features show very different patterns of behavior between men and women. As shown by their median values in Table 5, whereas men and women upload the same number of videos (a median of seven videos), men tend to watch more videos than women (884 and 684 videos watched, respectively). Instead, special female users "favorited" a median of two videos, compared to the one favorite of men, which suggests a different pattern on the way women watch and engage with video content. One-sided KS-tests among the corresponding features distributions indicate that all these differences are significant with $p < 10^{-3}$.

Regarding social features as shown in Table 6, we find men to receive more attention than women. Men accumulated 117 views and five subscribers compared to the 105 views and four subscribers of women. These differences are significant as reported by one-sided KS-tests ($p < 10^{-3}$). However, women accumulate more subscriptions, and more friends (a median of one subscription compared to zero of men), which suggests that women, overall, they have a more social-driven behavior in YouTube than men. These differences were also significant, as reported by one-sided KS-tests ($p < 10^{-3}$).

Some of these findings are not completely new but are backed up by substantially more data. In a manual analysis of a small random sample of 100 YouTube vlogs, Molyneaux et al. [17] found a higher presence of male users. They also found that women were most likely to interact with the YouTube community through their videos, and that they receive a higher number of views than men. These results we present here use three orders of magnitude more data.

---

z-test giving a p-value less than a specific α (typically 0.05), leads to the rejection of the null hypothesis, and indicates that the proportions are different [18].

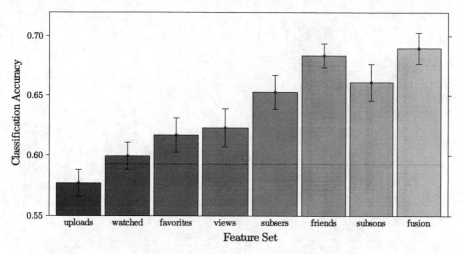

Fig. 6 *Standard* vs. non-*Standard* CAR using behavioral features alone and in combination. Best CARs are obtained for the fusion of features, as well as for "friends" alone

6 Classifying YouTube Users

The analysis of the previous section suggests that the basic features the YouTube users' channel could be used to characterize user categories. In order to explore the goodness of this characterization, we defined a series of classification tasks where a YouTube user is classified between two given user categories using different combinations of features. We use the results not only to evaluate the discriminative power of the features, but to measure the similarity between the behavior of different types of users.

For each task we performed a 10-fold cross-validation using a Support Vector Machine (SVM) classifier with a Gaussian Kernel. In each case, we optimized the Kernel parameters (σ and C) using 5-fold cross-validation on the training data.

Our first binary classification task was between *Standard* and non-*Standard* users (as one unique category) on a balanced subset of 10,000 users (5,000 per category) randomly selected from our dataset. For special users, we only considered the most popular special categories: *Directors*, *Musicians*, *Comedians* and *Gurus*, which were also balanced among the 5,000 corresponding samples. Results in Fig. 6 show an average classification accuracy rate (CAR) of 68.9% ± 1.2 for the fusion of features, which performs better than the 50% CAR corresponding to a random decision. However, we found that using the number of friends as a single feature one could achieve a classification rate of 68.3% ± 1.4. This indicates that differences in user behavior between *Standard* users and special users are to be found mainly in the level and pattern of interaction with other users, that is, in how social they are. This observation would also explain why subscriptions and subscribers are the next best single features.

The rest of the binary tasks were defined between pairs of single user categories (see Fig. 7), using up to 5,000 users per category. Data used on tasks involving

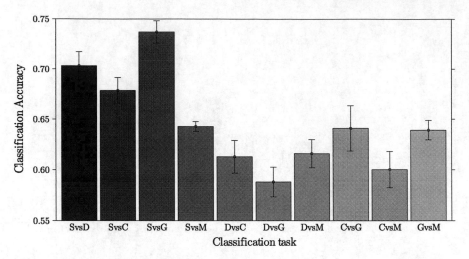

Fig. 7 Best CARs on binary tasks. *Capital letters in horizontal axis* correspond to the initials of the categories' names (i.e. *S = Standard*, *D = Director*, *M = Musician*, *C = Comedian*, and *G = Guru*). Except for those tasks involving Standard users, CARs were obtained with a fusion of at least three social features

categories with less than 5,000 users (e.g. *Gurus*) were balanced to the minimum among the number of users of such categories. Except for those tasks involving *Standards*, the best CARs were obtained with several combinations (of at least three) social-oriented features, which indicates that higher similarity of special categories requires more complex descriptors of behavior. The use of single features results in a drop of the best CAR to 53%. For tasks involving *Directors* and *Gurus*, the number of views appeared in almost all winning combinations, whereas for *Comedians* and *Musicians* different combinations led to similar results. In some cases, replacing only one of the social features for a participative feature would not cause a drop in performance, suggesting that the latter features still contain information useful to discriminate between special categories.

As suggested in previous sections, Directors and Gurus, and Comedians and Musicians are similar categories on what concerns to several behavioral aspects, which results in the lowest CARs, with $58.8\% \pm 1.4$ and $60.0\% \pm 1.7$, respectively. In contrast, Comedians and Musicians, and Gurus and Musicians are the pair-wise combinations with best CARs among special users, with $64.1\% \pm 2.2$ and $63.3\% \pm 0.9$, respectively.

7 Conclusions

In this paper, we have presented an analysis of YouTube users' long-term behavior using easy-to-extract features from the users' channels and large-scale data. We have shown that the group of special YouTube users is an undeniably active social community, as opposed to *Standard* users, and we have revealed different patterns of participation and interaction and highlighted some of the possible motivations behind them. Furthermore, we have backed up earlier findings on gender behavioral division using (by three orders of magnitude) more data. A series of binary classification tasks between YouTube users categories has shown social-oriented features to be key when describing differences between user groups' behaviors.

Whereas the features obtained from the user channels are capturing broad statistics on different aspects of long-term user behavior, finer aspects could be obtained by extracting other features in a more computationally expensive manner, which could hopefully lead to a better characterization of users. As an example, new participative features could include the frequency of the uploads, the number of comments posted, or user-specific videos features, including metadata and audiovisual features. Social-oriented features such as friends, subscriptions, or subscribers could be further divided in inter-category and intra-category relations. In addition, considering the antiquity of YouTube users (i.e. the age of their channels) could help to clarify the similarities between users of the same behavioral group. Furthermore, users could be also categorized based on the content they upload in YouTube. Video content is probably one of the most reliable indicators of the interest of users, which drive the way they use and behave in social video-sharing sites. The use of more computationally expensive features to capture finer aspects of the users' behavior will be the subject of our future work.

Acknowledgements   We thank for the support provided by the Swiss National Science Foundation (SNSF) through the Swiss National Center of Competence in Research (NCCR) on Interactive Multimodal Information Management (IM)2.

References

1. Benevenuto, F., Duarte, F., Rodrigues, T., Almeida, V.A.F., Almeida, J.M., Ross, K.W.: Understanding video interactions in YouTube. In: MM '08: Proceeding of the 16th ACM International Conference on Multimedia, pp. 761–764. ACM, New York (2008)
2. Biel, J.-I., Gatica-Perez, D.: Wearing a YouTube hat: directors, comedians, gurus, and user aggregated behavior. In: MM '09: Proceedings of the Seventeen ACM International Conference on Multimedia, pp. 833–836 (2009)
3. Burgess, J., Green, J.: YouTube: Online Video and Participatory Culture. Polity, Cambridge (2009)
4. Cha, M., Kwak, H., Rodriguez, P., Ahn, Y.-Y., Moon, S.: I tube, you tube, everybody tubes: analyzing the world's largest user generated content video system. In: IMC '07: Proceedings of the 7th ACM SIGCOMM Conference on Internet Measurement, pp. 1–14. ACM, New York (2007)
5. Cheng, X., Dale, C., Liu, J.: Statistics and social network of YouTube videos. In: Quality of Service, 2008. IWQoS 2008. 16th International Workshop on, pp. 229–238 (2008)
6. Conover, W.J.: Practical Nonparametric Statistics. Wiley, New York (1971)
7. Gill, P., Arlitt, M., Li, Z., Mahanti, A.: YouTube traffic characterization: a view from the edge. In: Proceedings of the 7th ACM SIGCOMM Conference on Internet Measurement, pp. 15–28 (2007)
8. Griffith, M.: Looking for you: An analysis of video blogs. In: Annual Meeting of the Association for Education in Journalism and Mass Communication (2007)

9. Halvey, M., Keane, M.T.: Exploring social dynamics in online media sharing. In: Proc. of the 16th International Conference on World Wide Web, pp. 1273–1274 (2007)
10. Kruitbosch, G., Nack, F.: Broadcast yourself on YouTube—really? In: Proceedings of the 3rd ACM International Workshop on Human-Centered Computing, pp. 7–10 (2008)
11. Landry, B.M., Guzdial, M.: Art or circus? characterizing user-created video on YouTube. Technical report, Georgia Institute of Technology (2008)
12. Lange, P.G.: Commenting on comments: investigating responses to antagonism on YouTube. In: Conference on Society for Applied Anthropology (2007)
13. Lange, P.G.: Publicly private and privately public: social networking on YouTube. J. Comput. Mediat. Commun. 1(13) (2007)
14. Lin, W.-H., Hauptmann, A.: Identifying ideological perspectives of web videos using folksonomies. In: AAAI Fall Symposium on Multimedia Information Extraction (2008)
15. Maia, M., Almeida, J., Almeida, V.: Identifying user behavior in online social networks. In: SocialNets '08: Proceedings of the 1st Workshop on Social Network Systems, pp. 1–6. ACM, New York (2008)
16. Mislove, A., Marcon, M., Gummadi, K.P., Druschel, P., Bhattacharjee, B.: Measurement and analysis of online social networks. In: Proceedings of the 7th ACM SIGCOMM Conference on Internet Measurement, pp. 29–42 (2007)
17. Molyneaux, H., O'Donnell, S., Gibson, K., Singer, J.: Exploring the gender divide on YouTube: An analysis of the creation and reception of vlogs. Am. Commun. J. 10(2) (2008)
18. Newcombe, R.G.: Two-sided confidence intervals for the single proportion: comparison of seven methods. Stat. Med. 8(17), 857–872 (1998)
19. O'Donnell, S., Gibson, K., Milliken, M., Singer, J.: Reacting to YouTube videos: Exploring differences among user groups. In: Proceedings of the International Communication Association Annual Conference, pp. 22–26 (2008)
20. Szabo, G., Huberman, B.A.: Predicting the popularity of online content. Commun. ACM 53(8), 80–88 (2010)
21. Website Monitoring Blog. YouTube Facts & Figures (history & Statistics). http://www.website-monitoring.com/blog/2010/05/17/youtube-facts-and-figures-history-statistics/
22. YouTube Fact Sheet. http://www.youtube.com/t/fact_sheet. Accessed November 2010
23. Zink, M., Suh, K., Gu, Y., Kurose, J.: Watch global, cache local: YouTube network traffic at a campus network—Measurements and implications. In: MMCN '08: Proceedings of SPIE/ACM Conference on Multimedia Computing and Networking (2008)

Social Media Visual Analytics for Events

Nicholas Diakopoulos, Mor Naaman, Tayebeh Yazdani,
and Funda Kivran-Swaine

Abstract For large-scale multimedia events such as televised debates and speeches,
the amount of content on social media channels such as Facebook or Twitter can
easily become overwhelming, yet still contain information that may aid and aug-
ment understanding of the multimedia content via individual social media items, or
aggregate information from the crowd's response. In this work we discuss this opportunity in the context of a social media visual analytic tool, Vox Civitas, designed
to help journalists, media professionals, or other researchers make sense of large-
scale aggregations of social media content around multimedia broadcast events. We
discuss the design of the tool, present and evaluate the text analysis techniques used
to enable the presentation, and detail the visual and interaction design. We provide
an exploratory evaluation based on a user study in which journalists interacted with
the system to analyze and report on a dataset of over one 100 000 Twitter messages
collected during the broadcast of the U.S. State of the Union presidential address
in 2010.

1 Introduction

Social media systems have proven to be valuable sources for information and communication about media events, in particular during large-scale televised events.
Events such as the annual Academy Awards (Oscar's) ceremony in Hollywood, the
Superbowl (the American National Football League's championship game), the last
episode of a TV series, or other events such as televised speeches or emergency
events increasingly draw massive amounts of audience attention and commentary
via social media. This rush of information from millions of new "human sensors"
contributing information about events and other news stories suggests new opportunities for reasoning both about the content of the event as well as about the crowd's
response to it. However, the sheer scale of the contribution leads to the challenge of
making sense of the response, both at an individual and aggregate level of analysis.

N. Diakopoulos (✉) · M. Naaman · T. Yazdani · F. Kivran-Swaine
School of Communication and Information, Rutgers University, 4 Huntington St.,
New Brunswick, NJ 08901, USA
e-mail: nicholas.diakopoulos@gmail.com

S.C.H. Hoi et al. (eds.), *Social Media Modeling and Computing*,
DOI 10.1007/978-0-85729-436-4_9, © Springer-Verlag London Limited 2011

Social media content such as Twitter or Facebook posts offers real-time commentary about many multimedia events that can be used to reason about the event content. The stream of social media messages parallels and reflects on the multimedia content as it's being broadcast. This new stream—a crowd-sourced, interpretive "close-captioning" analogue—presents new opportunities for reasoning about the presented content using these text-based comments, which essentially serve as indirect annotations. The main assumption in this work is that most of the social media content posted in response to a broadcast event provides some reflection on a *specific segment* of the event, and that the segment's time is close to the time of the posting of the message.

In this work, we focus on how social media content contributed around large-scale broadcast news events can inform visual analytic investigation and produce insight regarding the response to the event. Here we define visual analytics as the use of a visual interface to amplify analytic reasoning, including both deriving insights from data as well as producing and communicating judgments based on that analysis [27]. Our use case and design process is motivated by the context of journalistic investigation. Journalists are increasingly turning to social media sources like Twitter, Facebook, and other online sources of user content in an effort to track the importance of stories and to find sources of expertise to drive new stories [17]. Here we detail the design and evaluation of a visual analytics system, Vox Civitas, whose goal is to make the social media (e.g., Twitter) response to broadcast more amenable to journalistic investigation and sense making. Furthermore, we report on our evaluations of the various text analysis components that enable the Vox Civitas interface, such as relevance, novelty, and sentiment detection algorithms.

2 Related Work

Our work is most inspired by the work of Shamma et al. [23, 24] who have looked at revealing (and to a more limited extent visualizing) the structure and dynamics of twitter content around broadcast media events such as the Presidential Debates. In their work, the authors identify usage cues (magnitude of response) and content cues (salient keyword extraction) as indicators of interesting occurrences in the event such as topic shifts. Our work builds on these ideas in several important ways by integrating such usage and content cues with powerful filtering and interaction mechanisms, derivative data facets such as sentiment, and visual methods for schematizing analyses for analytic purposes.

Other related work has examined social media content as an information source for non-broadcast events, in the context of emergency response and crisis scenarios such as earthquakes [22], fires [5] and floods [26]. Indeed, Starbird et al.'s [26] study of the Twitter response to the Red River flooding in early 2009 showed that Twitter users are participating in useful information generation and synthesis activities but are part of a larger ecosystem involving information from traditional media outlets. It is the generative and synthetic activity of social media users that we hope to harness in the context of visual analytics for journalism.

The analysis of text corpora over time has been addressed by a variety of systems including ThemeRiver [11], which looks at the evolution of topics over time; Narratives [8], which allows users to track, analyze, and correlate the blog response to news stories over time; and MemeTracker [14], which visualizes the patterns of phrases that appear in news and social media content over time. Recent research has also looked at assessing thematic story visualization in the context of dynamically evolving information *streams* [21]. Our approach differs insofar as thematic change in social media is not the analytic end goal but rather an input in a matrix of analytic enablers including sentiment analysis and journalistically motivated data filters.

The analysis of text corpora derived from social media communication in order to better reason about multimedia content has been proposed in a number of prior studies. Most directly related to our work here, Diakopoulos and Shamma [6] presented temporal visuals which depict sentiment patterns (e.g. periodicity, strength or weakness of actors) in the context of the real-time social media response to the televised U.S. presidential debates. Shamma et al. [25] use chat activity in instant messaging to reason about the content of shared online videos; De Choudhury et al. [4] analyze comments on YouTube videos to derive interestingness and topics; and Mertens et al. use community activity for social navigation of web lectures [16]. Here, we go beyond these prior systems to connect text patterns with topicality and the magnitude of the response in a visual and interactive exploratory analytics application.

3 Computational Enablers

Previous work on the evaluation of visual analytics systems has highlighted the importance of directing attention and providing appropriate starting points for analysis [12]. In this section we begin by describing each of the content analysis components of Vox Civitas that enable different aspects of filtering and attention shaping in the resulting interface. We leverage four types of automatic content analysis to do this: *relevance*, *novelty*, *sentiment*, and *keyword extraction*. These automatic analyses provide capabilities both for searching and filtering raw information in analytically meaningful ways, as well as providing aggregate or derivative values (e.g. of sentiment) that can inform analyses.

Where appropriate we validate and characterize our computational techniques and parameters through comparisons with ground truth human ratings. For these evaluations as well as for the interface evaluation (presented in a later section) we gathered a collection of Twitter messages from the State of the Union address given by U.S. President Barack Obama in early 2010. This broadcast event is traditionally heavily covered by mainstream media, and generates high news interest. We anticipated the event would result in a large social media response on Twitter and other forums. Indeed, immediately after the event we collected 101,285 English language Twitter messages containing the terms "SOTU" (for "State of the Union"), "Obama", or "State of the Union" using the Twitter API. Note that this keyword-based sampling method does not ensure collection of *all* relevant messages for the event: relevant messages not containing these terms will not be retrieved.

3.1 Relevance

Assessing the relevance of social media messages is important for helping to reduce the amount of noise and focus on information more germane to the event. We define relevance of social media messages with respect to the underlying audio channel of event content: specifically, the topics expressed in the transcript of the spoken word audio channel of the event. For many large-scale televised events, such as the State of the Union, transcripts are readily available from news services such as C-SPAN. Our definition of relevance also incorporates a temporal component by assessing relevance for a message at a *particular* point in time. We acknowledge that different definitions of relevance can lead to different types of analytic capabilities and we explore this idea further in our evaluation below.

We compute relevance by calculating term-vector similarity of messages to the moment in the event during which the messages were posted. In order to compute relevance at a finer level of granularity than the entire event, we further structured the raw transcript by breaking it into one-minute segments, and consider the text from each segment as the basis for relevance. We chose a segmentation interval of one minute because (1) it is a meaningful unit of analysis for events on the scale that we are currently concerned with (e.g. a 70 minute speech), and (2) one minute of transcript provided enough text to create meaningful term vectors.

For each message, relevance was computed as the cosine distance [15] of the term-vector space representations of the message and of the transcript for the minute when the message occurred (the transcript and messages were first filtered through a standard stop word list). To control for possible lag in the social media response, we used a running window (with weighting) over the previous two minutes. This method is designed to account for some delayed reaction to the speech, and compute a temporally sensitive relevance score, rather than assess the relevance of messages with a potentially unlimited lag. This enables filtering for the *real-time* conversation happening on social media, and serves to dampen conversational echoes and shadows [23]. To calculate the relevance of a social media message at time m (S_m) to the transcript at time m (T_m) we take the time-interval weighted sum of the cosine similarity of the associated term vectors (see Fig. 1),

$$rel(S_m, m) = 2 \times \frac{\vec{V}(S_m) \bullet \vec{V}(T_m)}{|\vec{V}(S_m)||\vec{V}(T_m)|} + \frac{\vec{V}(S_m) \bullet \vec{V}(T_{m-1})}{|\vec{V}(S_m)||\vec{V}(T_{m-1})|}$$

In order to characterize and optimize how this operationalization of relevance affects the performance of the filter in Vox Civitas we undertook an evaluation to compare the automatically computed relevance scores to a manually coded ground truth. The ground truth was developed by first randomly sampling 2,000 messages from our State of the Union dataset. For each of these messages, one of the researchers then manually applied our definition of relevancy to classify each of the 2,000 messages as either relevant or not relevant (i.e. a binary classification). The definition of relevance used for the manual coding was that the message had to have some topical relevance to the transcript of the speech during that minute or the previous minute. For example, *"Hope Obama will show leadership on climate"* which

Fig. 1 Relevance is computed for a social media message at time m by comparing to the text in the transcript at times m and $m - 1$

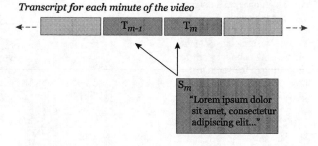

Fig. 2 A plot of precision, recall, and F-measure for varying relevance score thresholds. A message with a relevance score below the threshold was classified as not relevant

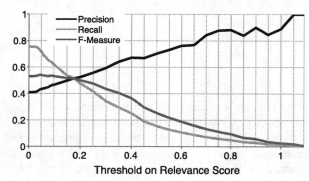

was sent during the part of the speech where Obama was addressing climate change was tagged as relevant. In keeping with the temporal emphasis of our definition, general opinions (e.g. "Obama Rocks!") or status updates (e.g. "watching the state of the union") which were not germane to the content of the speech during that time period were classified as not relevant.

Applying our definition of relevance, we found that of the 2,000 ground truth messages, 29.6% of them were deemed relevant. Fifty-seven messages were relevant to the current minute without being relevant to the previous minute and 351 messages were relevant to the previous minute without being relevant to the current minute, with 185 messages being relevant to both minutes. These descriptive numbers indicate that there is some (expected, perhaps) lag in the relevancy of the messages with respect to the multimedia content (i.e. a majority of people need a bit of time to think, type, and respond appropriately).

The accuracy of the relevancy computation with respect to the ground truth necessarily depends on the threshold chosen to make the binary distinction between relevant or not relevant. We computed standard information retrieval measures such as precision, recall, and F-measure to better characterize the performance of the algorithm and show the tradeoffs associated with choosing a threshold (see Fig. 2).

Based on our analysis, a threshold of 0.175 represents a good tradeoff between precision and recall, resulting in 29.7% of messages being categorized as relevant and an accuracy of 71.2% with respect to the ground truth. But we also need to think about how this threshold will affect the interface and the ability to effectively use the system: it may be more meaningful to minimize either false positives *or* false negatives, and depending on how strict a threshold is applied this will impact the

Fig. 3 A conceptual diagram
showing the relationship
between message novelty and
utility. Those messages in the
middle gray band may be
interesting in the sense that
they are unusual but still
relevant to the discussion3

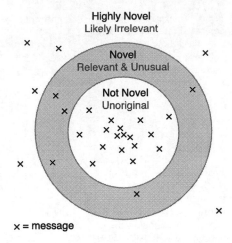

amount of information visible. For instance, a user doing an exhaustive search may
be more interested in reducing false negatives (high recall), whereas a user doing
a more exploratory search may be more interested in reducing false positives (high
precision). In general practice the threshold should be tuned for the context and
demands of the situation, but since a threshold of 0.175 results in a relevance set of
almost exactly the same size as that found in the ground truth (29%) we use this as
the default value in our system.

One might note that our definition of relevance misses messages which are topically related to the speech but which occur after more than a delay of one minute.
Indeed, in our development of the ground truth we did find many messages that were
germane to a speech topic but were posted at later minutes. We contend that integrating a temporal aspect into our definition of relevance can help an analyst tune
into the *immediate* response to an event, but that relaxing the temporal aspect (e.g.
having a longer time window) could be useful for other tasks such as exploring the
ongoing conversation around a particular topic.

3.2 Novelty

In the context of social media, "unusual" may manifest itself as more unique or
novel messages when compared to other social media messages provided that the
messages are still relevant to the content of the event (see Fig. 3). Definitions of
"newsworthiness" and "news values" in journalism, our use scenario for the Vox
system, often espouse the importance of the *unusual* or *unexpected* in the selection
criteria for what becomes "news" [9, 10]. We incorporate this concept into our system by developing a message novelty metric, which can be used to direct attention
toward what may be more unusual contributions.

Here we define the novelty of a message in relation to the other messages sent
during the same time interval. In this sense novelty can also be thought of as a measure of the *conversational relevance* (i.e. how (dis)similar is a message to all of the

other messages being shared at a particular point in time). According to our definition, novelty is then a measure of how different a message is from what everyone else is talking about. We compute novelty as the difference between the term-vector space representation of the message to the centroid term-vector representation of all of the messages for that particular aggregation interval of the event (again one minute). As above, messages were filtered through a standard stop word list. The centroid vector for each minute is constructed from the top 200 most frequent terms for that minute. For a social media message at time m (S_m) and the centroid for aggregate minute m (C_m) we calculated novelty using the cosine similarity of term vectors as

$$novelty(S_m) = 1 - \frac{\vec{V}(S_m) \bullet \vec{V}(C_m)}{|\vec{V}(S_m)||\vec{V}(C_m)|}.$$

A message that uses words unusual for that minute will not share many words with the centroid and will thus have a low cosine similarity score. We then define the "interesting" range of novelty for the filter presented in the interface by thresholding novelty values between a minimum and maximum value as suggested in Fig. 3.

We evaluated our method for computing message novelty in order to assess whether the novelty score corresponds to human judgments of novelty. We also wanted to characterize what would be effective upper and lower thresholds for determining the "interesting" range of novel messages. This range defines unusual contributions that are not completely irrelevant.

We sampled the State of the Union dataset for one "anchor" message per minute (70 messages total) and 30 "comparison" messages from each of those same minutes (2100 messages total). Both the anchor and comparison messages were selected randomly for each minute. The anchor message in each minute was manually compared to each of the comparison messages and a binary similarity evaluation was recorded for that pair (i.e. the pair of messages was judged as similar or not similar). Thus, for each anchor there were 30 similarity ratings (1 or 0), which in turn were averaged and subtracted from one to compute a novelty score for the anchor message in relation to the other messages sent during that same time interval.

The manual comparison was based on a *semantic* similarity between the messages rather than looking at a lexical similarity. In instances where the anchor message consisted of several clauses, if any of the clauses was similar to a comparison message the pair was evaluated as similar. Messages that contained the same topic (e.g. health care reform) but were different in their meaning were not considered similar. For instance, for the anchor message, *"He's getting defensive. Not backing down on defending the stimulus. Good, but that'll turn away indeps"* a message rated as similar was *"Obama says 2 million jobs created via recovery act. Hmmm."* because of the reference to the stimulus, and a message rated as not similar was *"I love how animated VP Biden is."* because there is no semantic similarity to the anchor.

We computed the Pearson correlation coefficient between the automatically computed novelty scores and the manually computed average novelty scores for the anchor messages. We found there to be a correlation ($r = 0.279$, $p < 0.05$) indicating that there is a statistically significant correlation between how a human judge rates novelty based on semantic similarity and how our algorithm rates novelty based on lexical similarity. This indicates that even a relatively simple method based on keyword term vectors produces results that are consistent with how a human rater judges novelty.

To determine practical workable values for upper and lower novelty thresholds we assume a reasonable reduction in the amount of messages in the interface for the novelty filter would be about 10%. We thus chose the upper and lower thresholds to be 0.99 and 0.95, which results in 11.6% of messages being labeled "novel". Similarly to the relevance thresholding, for the current application we felt that this proportion of messages in the filter was appropriate, however, we could have also included facilities in the interface to tweak the proportion of messages filtered based on thresholds allowing an analyst more leeway in self-defining what was the "interesting" range of novelty scores.

3.3 Sentiment

Sentiment analysis can be broadly construed as facilitating the understanding of opinion, emotion, and subjectivity in text [18]. Here we focus more specifically on sentiment analysis to inform an understanding of the *polarity* (i.e. positive versus negative) of the social media reaction to the event content. Prior work has shown that sentiment analysis of social media text polarity can inform analyses of the aggregate reactivity of the audience to an event topic, issue, or actor [6].

Classifying social media messages from sources such as Twitter poses a significant challenge. Despite considerable progress in the maturation and accuracy of sentiment polarity classification algorithms, these algorithms are still far from perfect [18]. Exacerbating the problem is the fact that social media content, often due to constraints on message length, is riddled with irregular language such as inconsistent abbreviations, internet-speak and other slang, and acronyms.

Attempting to handle these issues, we applied a supervised learning algorithm (language model) trained with 1900 manually tagged messages randomly sampled from the State of the Union dataset. In this case each message was tagged by a single human coder. The coding schema that we used was based on three categories: *objective* (e.g. factual and free from personal feelings or interpretations), *positive* (e.g. a positive evaluation, opinion, emotion, or speculation), or *negative* (e.g. a negative evaluation, opinion, emotion, or speculation). In order to simplify the schema we elected not to have additional categories for messages that contained both positive and negative sentiment, or for neutral messages—which, while making the scheme easier to apply for coders, resulted in the loss of some precision in coding these other types of messages. We found the best performance using a language model including all n-grams of length less than or equal to four. The classifier resulted in a 10-fold cross validated accuracy of 63.5%.

In an attempt to improve the accuracy further by using more reliable training data we undertook to have multiple raters per message and to also assess the inter-rater reliability of the training data. In this case, we randomly selected a different set of 750 messages from the State of the Union dataset. The same coding scheme was used as before. Each of three coders independently applied the sentiment schema to each message. The majority vote category was taken as the final rating for each message. Coders were fluent in English and lived in the U.S. or Canada for at least eight years; they were familiar with the cultural context of the dataset. We computed the Fleiss κ for this ground truth as 0.706, indicating a fair level of reliability and agreement among the coders [1]. At the same time, this value of kappa indicates that this is a difficult task for even highly motivated and careful human coders, and that the inherent ambiguity in the training data is a challenge to training an accurate classifier. Similar to above we then developed a language model based on this new training set. We found the best performance using a language model including all n-grams of length less than or equal to four. The classifier resulted in a 10-fold cross validated accuracy of 63.4%, essentially equivalent to the results we found for the larger but less reliable 1900 message training set. In looking at the contingency tables for misclassification errors we found that most of the error is concentrated in negative messages misclassified as positive, and positive messages misclassified as negative. Thus while sufficient for giving an overall impression of sentiment, the classifier still fails on difficult cases such as those involving sarcasm or slang. For example, *"whats goodietwiggaz..im watchin Obama talk about how he gna clear my student loans..i kno there was a reason i voted for him lol!"* was classified as negative by the algorithm but is arguably positive. These results generally indicate that having more highly reliable training data is not the limiting factor in improving the classification accuracy for sentiment polarity.

3.4 Keyword Extraction

In keeping with the design goal of jump-starting analysis, we aimed to identify keywords used in the social media stream that could be useful and interesting for users exploring the content and response to the event. To this end, we extracted descriptive keywords for each minute of the aggregate message content. For each minute we extract the top 10 keywords ranked by their tf-idf score [15], comparing the keyword's frequency at that minute to its frequency in the rest of the dataset. We found tf-idf performed adequately for identifying salient keywords, although other methods for extracting salient key phrases [21] or words [3] could be implemented and integrated into our data processing pipeline.

To compute the document frequency portion of the tf-idf scores we define pseudo-documents temporally as the aggregate of the words of all messages for each minute. Words are first stemmed using the Porter stemming algorithm and after computing tf-idf scores on word stems we apply reverse stemming to the most common full keyword mapping so that complete words are visible in the interface [3].

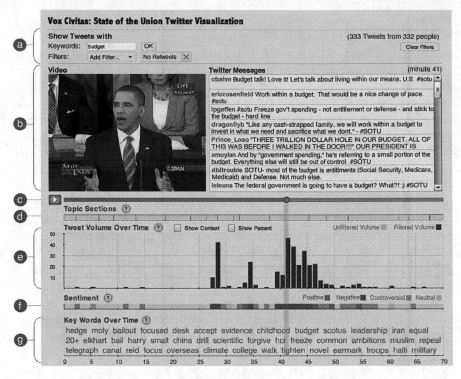

Fig. 4 Vox Civitas User Interface. ((**a**) Keyword Search & Filtering, (**b**) Video & Twitter Messages, (**c**) Video Timeline, (**d**) Topic Sections, (**e**) Message Volume Graph, (**f**) Trends in overall Tweet Sentiment, (**g**) Salient Key Words Over Time)

4 Visual Representations and Interactions

The Vox Civitas interface integrates video from an event with the ability to visually assess the textual social media response to that event at both (1) individual, and (2) aggregate levels of analysis. The unifying schema for organizing information in Vox Civitas is temporal, which facilitates looking at responses and trends over time in the social media stream, in relationship to the underlying event video. Figure 2 shows an overview of the interface.

Filtering messages is done via the module shown in Fig. 4a. Browsing and analysis of individual responses is facilitated by a view of the actual Twitter messages posted about the event (next to the video content, in Fig. 4b). Aggregate response analysis is enabled by three views: volume graph (4e), sentiment timeline (4f); and the keywords component (4g). These views are all aligned to the video timeline (4c) and the topic timeline (4d) and are connected visually to the timeline via a light gray vertical bar which tracks the navigation thumb of the video timeline. In the rest of this section, we explain the main interactive elements of our interface. For each element, we explain the interaction and, where appropriate, how the interaction builds on the computational foundations laid out above.

4.1 Content Component

The content component (Fig. 4b) displays the "raw" content from the event and its social media response. On the left, the video feed from the event is shown. The video is controlled by the timeline (Fig. 4c) that allows for start, pause and nonlinear navigation of the video steam. On the right side of Fig. 4b, the interface shows the set of messages about the event that were posted during the minute currently selected by the user via the various timeline interactions, mirroring the currently-viewed portion of the video. The messages displayed can be filtered using the filtering module as we explain next.

4.2 Filtering Module

The filtering module, shown in Fig. 4a, allows Vox Civitas users to filter the social media responses to the event according to a number of criteria or search terms. The filtering has a number of outcomes: it determines which messages are displayed in the main content pane (4b), as well as the aggregate statistics in the message volume graph (4e) and sentiment timeline (4f). All these components update interactively with the filter. In our current implementation, filtering does not change the keyword pane (4g).

The filtering module options build on some of the computational aspects described above. Users can apply the following filters to the messages, individually or in conjunctive combination: (1) messages with specific keywords or authors, (2) messages with quotes (i.e., quotation marks), (3) messages that are retweets (messages that are repeated or forwarded from other users and usually marked "RT" at the beginning), (4) messages that include links, (5) messages classified as being topically relevant, (6) messages classified as novel, and (7) messages with positive or negative sentiment. The system also allows for filtering out quotes, retweets or links. In Fig. 4, for example, the active filters are the keyword "budget" and "no retweets".

4.3 Topic Timeline

We included a topic segmentation timeline (Fig. 4d) that facilitates building connections between topicality, time, and the social media response. The topic timeline shows the temporal extent of topic sections of the speech and is aligned with the video timeline (Fig. 4c). Hovering over a topic section shows the section's label and clicking navigates the content component (video and messages) to the beginning of that section. Note that the topics appearing on the timeline and their time range could be automatically detected from the message or the event content, or provided by a human editor. For the purposes of the evaluation we present later, we opted to produce the topic segmentation manually so as to provide the highest quality experience to the users.

4.4 Message Volume Graph

The message volume graph (Fig. 4e) shows the message volume over time as a histogram, where each bar represents one minute. The heights of the bars represent the aggregate volume of messages according to the currently applied filter. By default, the overall volume of messages is shown. Changes to the filters initiate an animated transition on the graph so that differences can be tracked visually. Check boxes allow the user to compare the current filtered set to the total volume, as well as change the vertical scale from absolute to percent in order to assess the proportional filtered response over time. Hovering over the graph shows a popup of the exact count or percent of messages at that minute as well as the number of unique users contributing to those messages. The message volume graph also acts as an interactive timeline: clicking the graph navigates the video and messages of the content component to that minute.

4.5 Sentiment Timeline

The sentiment timeline (Fig. 4f) shows an aggregate of the sentiment response for each minute of the event, as derived by the sentiment analysis procedure detailed previously. The timeline is color-coded according to one of four categories: positive (green), negative (red), controversial (yellow), or neutral (gray). A minute is categorized as controversial if the ratio of positive to negative messages for that minute is between 0.45 and 0.55. If there are no positive or negative messages then that minute is categorized as neutral. If either positive or negative messages dominate the dataset for that minute (the ratio is above 0.55) then that minute is categorized as positive or negative respectively. The coloring for positive or negative minutes has five grades of intensity depending on the ratio of how much one sentiment dominates the other. Hovering over the sentiment graph will show the number of positive and negative messages for that minute. The sentiment timeline changes to reflect the currently applied filter, and is interactive: clicking navigates the video and messages of the content component to that minute.

The sentiment representation is explicitly designed to give only an *impression* of aggregate sentiment due to concerns over the accuracy of the sentiment classifier. We do not represent the automatic sentiment classification of individual messages in the message list (Fig. 4b) since we assume users can quickly surmise sentiment as they are skimming the short text messages. Also, we do not represent absolute magnitude of the aggregate sentiment response (or show the distribution of positive and negative magnitudes). During the design process we spoke to prospective journalist users who believed that until the accuracy of the classifier was ~70–80% or higher, visual representations could easily mislead the analyst if they showed absolute magnitudes. Our visual representation helps cope with the depiction of uncertainty in the accuracy of the sentiment classifier by not giving undue weight to the comparative magnitude of positive versus negative messages. Moreover, if we assume that the error in the classifier is uniformly distributed in time, temporal sentiment trends are still meaningful.

4.6 Keywords Component

The keywords component (Fig. 4g) depicts the salient keywords extracted over time. It is similar to a tag cloud that has been laid out so that word positions are correlated with the time span when the chosen word was most salient in the event. We chose to keep the visual depiction simple by not visually encoding any additional facets of information (e.g. degree of salience into color intensity or font size) beyond just the keyword and its approximate time span. Clicking on a word in the keyword component filters the dataset using that keyword, which in turn affects the other components as described above.

The component is laid out from left to right and top to bottom using a greedy algorithm. For each minute, we have a list of salient keywords ranked by their tf-idf scores. For a given layout position we compute the layout score of a proposed keyword as the sum of the word's tf-idf scores for all minute intervals that the keyword would span when laid out. So for example, if a word when added to the component would span five minutes worth of space, that word's score is the sum of its tf-idf scores for all of those five minutes. This way, we give preference to words that are potentially relevant for more than a single minute in time. For each time position, we select the keyword with the highest layout score, add it to the layout, and advance to the next position (after the current word plus a padding offset). Once a word has been added to the component it is removed from the ranked lists of keywords for the minute intervals it spans. This prevents duplicate words from being added to the component adjacent to each other, but also allows for duplicate words if they are relevant at different sections of the event. The depth of the layout can be expanded to include as many rows of words as desired.

5 Exploratory Study

We designed and executed an exploratory evaluation of Vox Civitas to assess its effectiveness in a journalistically motivated sense making scenario. Journalism is just one use case for Vox Civitas though we believe there is much to be learned from studying specific contexts and user populations (i.e. journalists and media professionals). The goals of the evaluation were to develop an understanding of how journalists use the tool, and how Vox Civitas matches the journalists' requirements and work process. We addressed the following research questions:

- How useful and effective was the tool for journalists in generating story ideas and reporting on the broadcast event?
- What kind of insights and analysis does Vox Civitas support?

- What are the shortcomings of Vox Civitas for journalists analyzing social media streams?
- How do journalists interact with the system and which parts of the interaction are most salient?

To answer these questions, we deployed Vox Civitas using a popular broadcast event as a content source, recruited participants with a background in journalism, and deployed the system while collecting questionnaire feedback and analyzing interaction logs. We analyzed the open-ended questionnaire items using a grounded-theory inspired methodology. This methodology involves iterative coding of concepts and their relationships apparent in the text in order to form typologies of use and patterns of interaction grounded in the participants' textual response data.

5.1 Procedure

Vox Civitas is a Web-based system[1] and the evaluation was conducted online. We chose an online evaluation rather than a lab study to enhance the ecological and external validity of the study. The experiment was deployed using "natural" settings in terms of work environment, time constraints and so forth. The online nature of the deployment also enhanced the ability to include a larger number of journalism professionals from around the U.S. We logged participants' actions with the interface and recorded open-ended survey responses. We identified interactions or survey responses too short to be meaningful and excluded one response from our analysis as a result.

To solicit participation, a convenience sample of journalists and journalism students was emailed with a request to participate in our study, for which they were entered into a drawing to win a $50 gift card. The call for participation was also published in other venues that we thought likely to bring participants (e.g., Twitter and mailing lists). Participants were directed to a website, where, upon consent to become a research participant, they were presented with the Vox Civitas system. An overview description of the tool and its functionality was displayed next to the tool itself, briefly explaining to the users the interface's main features.

The instructions and scenario for the experiment were persistently displayed next to the tool. The instructions to participants specifically read, "Imagine that the State of The Union just occurred are you're using this tool to find stories to pitch to a national news editor. Come up with at least two story angles which, with some more reporting, you think will make good news stories". We intentionally left the task somewhat open-ended in order to allow participants leeway in how they chose to employ the tool. Interactions with the interface (mouse hovers, clicks, time spent using the tool) were logged to give an indication of feature usage.

When ready with their story angles, participants were asked to fill out an online questionnaire. The bulk of the questionnaire was composed of open-ended questions

---

[1] http://sm.rutgers.edu/vox.

including the story angles the participants developed, the ways in which the tool enabled them to develop the story angles, how they would use such a tool to inform their reporting on a broadcast media event, and what they liked or disliked about the user interface. The questionnaire also included demographic data, as well as questions about the participant's training in journalism and the frequency of their usage of social media services.

5.2 Participants

Eighteen participants were recruited, 15 of which had formal or on the job training in journalism according to their responses: seven participants identified themselves as professional journalists, five as journalism students, and one as a citizen journalist; two additional participants did not identify as journalists but specified that they had an undergraduate degree or "on the job" experience in journalism. Six respondents were male, and 12 were female. The ages of the participants ranged from 21 to 55 ($\mu = 34$). Eleven of the participants indicated that they use social media services such as Twitter all the time, while five indicated they use them "often", and only two indicated that they use them "sometimes".

5.3 Results

We first report on our findings based on the grounded analysis of open-ended questionnaire items. We then briefly report on the usage of the application and its various features as captured by the interaction log.

6 Perceived Utility

In the questionnaire, participants answered the open-ended question *"If you were to use this or a similar application to inform your reporting on a broadcast media event, how would you use it?"* We used a grounded approach to categorize and code the open-ended responses to this question. We identified two primary use cases for Vox Civitas: (1) as a mechanism for finding sources to interview and (2) as an ideation tool for driving follow-up journalistic activity.

Finding and interviewing credible primary sources is an important aspect of journalistic storytelling [13]. Indeed, prior studies assessing tools for journalists have shown the primacy of sourcing in appealing to the journalistic mindset [7]. As such, it is perhaps unsurprising that several users of Vox Civitas suggested it would be a valuable tool for helping to identify sources. As one participant put it, *"I might use it to track sources reacting to an event that I could quickly turn to for an interview"* (P11).

Beyond sourcing, several participants noted that Vox Civitas would be useful for helping to find unusual story angles and statements that resonated with the audience: "*I would use it for drilling down to the outlier sentiments in response to the State of the Union*" (P16) and "*Using the quotes and retweet filters, I can also easily figure out what statement resonated the most with the public*" (P8). These responses reaffirm the newsworthiness values which Vox Civitas was designed to support, such as helping to identify novel contributions, or "decisive moments" which draw heavy audience response [2, 10]. Other participants identified related uses for driving journalistic activities such as helping to *measure interest* for particular follow-up stories or as an input to a discussion panel after the event.

It is important to note that, while predominantly positive in their outlook for Vox Civitas, several responses indicated healthy suspicions about relying solely on the tool for reporting. Concerns revolved around the recognition that Twitter does not represent an accurate population sample for measuring global sentiment, and that tools like Vox Civitas are useful "*as long as they are used as a compliment to stories that include more sound data*" (P4) or "*as a jumping off point for stories, as long as it is clear that the tweets aren't representative for the whole country*" (P9).

7 Story Angles

In order to assess more specifically what kinds of story ideas and types of insight might be generated with Vox Civitas we asked participants to consider the scenario of using the tool to come up with two story angles they might pitch to a news editor of a national publication. Of course, this scenario serves only as a (reasonable) proxy for real journalistic practice, since real story angles would depend on the context of publication and audience.

Again, we used a grounded approach to categorize and iteratively code participants' open-ended responses. We address the types of story angles, as well as the Vox Civitas features that drove and enabled the development of stories.

Two main foci of story angles emerged from our analysis: stories that focus and reference the *event content* and stories that reference *audience responses* to the event. Event content story angles focused on topics, issues, or personalities in the event such as words spoken, or the body language or appearance of people in the video. Most often, these story angles referred to topics or issues that were referenced in the speech. One story pitch reads

Obama's plan to increase Pell grants: What kind of students, majors and schools would give the government the best return on their investment to get the kinds of workers the country needs? (P1)

Notice that these stories emerged from examining Vox Civitas, but the participants did not *directly* reference the social media response in their story angle.

On the other hand, story angles referencing *audience responses* focused on the reactions of the audience to the event, including both reactions captured in individual messages, as well as the magnitude or sentiment of the aggregate audience response to various aspects of the event and the issues being discussed therein. One participant wrote:

The two topics that did create a 'controversial' exchange were 'People's Struggles' and 'Stimulus: Tax cuts and Employment.' This could compliment other data about job losses and the economy and ... could make for an interesting angle on what topics in public sentiment are most polarized. (P4)

A more minor focus (two story angles in our survey) was *audience meta discussion*. These stories focused on the characteristics of the audience in the social media channel (e.g., its demographic), rather than the audience response to the event.

How exactly did Vox Civitas support the creation of these story ideas? Some participants reported that their story angles were informed through the use of keyword searches and further filtering (e.g. sentiment) to help them identify individual or aggregate responses. One participant started an inquiry in response to an individual tweet she saw referencing low college loan payments. The story angle read: *"Further investigation into statistics on college loan debt. How much are students carrying? And how long does it take to pay off?"* (P16). Other participants, like P4 above, looked to aggregate cues such as the magnitude or sentiment of a response to a keyword or topic to drive ideation:

I liked using the keywords to elicit the popularity of a certain topic. For example, 'college' was probably by far the most powerful statement, showing 500 tweets immediately after Obama's 'no one should go broke' statement... (P8).
I chose the keyword 'overseas'. This gave me more of mixed emotions for the audience due to the slash in tax breaks being given to companies who ship their jobs overseas (P18).

Indeed, many of the story angles that were reported mentioned aspects of the visuals and interface that were used to enable those thoughts. We turn briefly in the following section to aspects of the log analysis that further support these findings.

8 Usage of Interface Features

We see the results of the log analysis as illustrative and use them to support our findings on the utility of features for journalists, although we did not have enough participants to be able to derive statistically meaningful patterns from the log data. Participants spent an average of 21.6 minutes interacting with the application, with 89% of users spending more than five minutes.

The utility and popularity of searching for keywords and combining those searches with further filters was evident in the logs. All 18 participants performed some keyword searching and filtering activity. Users searched for an average of 9.67 unique words each ($\sigma = 10.2$). Half of the participants also used compound filters, meaning they combined a keyword search with a filter modifier. Among these, two people filtered for relevancy, three for novelty, six for negative sentiment, two for positive sentiment, two for retweets, four for no retweets, three for quotes, and one each for no quotes and links. Judging from these counts, filters for sentiment and retweets were used most in conjunction with the keyword filters, with other filters used to a lesser extent.

An average of 4.67 keyword searches per user were initiated from the keywords over time component, meaning that 48% of all keyword queries came from users interacting with that interface feature (the remaining keyword queries were initiated by users typing words into the search box). However, we note that only eight of the 18 participants clicked to filter by a keyword via the keyword component, with five users making heavy use of the component to drive the filtering. When we looked at the use of the keyword component by professional journalists versus all others (students, citizen journalists, and non-journalists) there was a clear trend of the professionals using the keyword component *less*: only one journalist used it.

The topic timeline, volume graph, and sentiment timeline all saw robust usage in terms of users gleaning data details from hovering over these representations. Sixteen out of 18 users hovered over the topic timeline (mean of 34 operations per user) and when normalized for interaction duration, seven users averaged more than one hover operation per minute of use. A total of 17 users hovered over the volume graph ($\mu = 392$) with 15 users averaging more than one hover operation per minute. Similarly, 15 users hovered over the sentiment timeline for details ($\mu = 54$) and 13 users averaged more than one sentiment hover operation per minute. Combined with the prevalence for searching and filtering for keywords, these numbers tend to indicate that users informed their analyses by employing the volume graph most, followed by the sentiment timeline, and topic timeline.

9 Discussion

Our results suggest that Vox Civitas' utility is in divergent modes of sense making, where the tool is used to (1) drive analysts to gather information from identified sources, and (2) to otherwise inform journalists in more "creative" follow-up activities such as finding unusual story angles, or as a *starting point* for further inquiry on a topic or sentiment reaction. The goal in this use case is not so much to provide rigorous assessment and decision support about hypotheses (i.e. deductive reasoning), but rather to spur the divergent and creative generation of hypotheses, insights, and questions for follow-up activities (i.e. abductive reasoning) [19].

Let us consider a sense making model such as that of Pirolli and Card [20], which consists of *information foraging* (collecting from external data sources, shoeboxing, building an evidence file) and *sense making loops* (scheme generation, hypothesis generation, and final presentation). Vox Civitas seems to best support aspects of hypothesis generation in the sense making loop, as well as rapid transition back to the foraging loop in terms of facilitating connecting to external data sources. This support was assisted by a design that provided for a sense making schema, thus organizing the information visually according to cues expected to be of interest (topic, magnitude, sentiment, novelty) to the user.

Vox Civitas obviates the initial phases of the sense making process (data collection and schema generation) and allows analysts to focus on divergent thinking and hypothesis generation around the data. This divergent thinking can then connect back to the foraging loop to collect data from external sources to support a follow-up story. We believe that designers of similar visual analytics systems may be able to extend this notion to other domains of expert analysts by tailoring filtering and initial visual scheme presentation in order to jump start the sense making process at a high level of thinking.

The keywords component drove a substantial portion of the keyword searching and filtering activity, albeit the utility of this component for professional journalists may be less than for citizen journalists or student journalists. Nonetheless, the component raises the idea of driving different people to different parts of the information space so as to jumpstart analysis along different dimensions. For instance, we could imagine producing a keyword timeline that varies depending on the news genre that someone is interested in reporting on. Keywords for business, sports, technology, or fashion would tend to drive analysts to think about those term-sets in relation to the event.

Our evaluation of relevance, novelty, and sentiment revealed several nuances that could help the design of future visual analytics applications. For example, our definition of relevance, though useful for defining a temporal notion of importance, may not be appropriate to all situations. Other visual representations (e.g. stream graphs) could be incorporated to better depict overlapping and ongoing "relevant" conversations. Our assessment of sentiment classification found that more reliable training data did not increase overall classification accuracy. Future avenues to explore for improving accuracy could involve collecting *more* training data since we only had 750 messages, or in linking to and incorporating dictionaries of slang such as the Urban Dictionary.

Figure 4 depicts the State of the Union event filtered for the keyword "budget"— looking at the volume graph one can see three distinct peaks of activity. The third peak corresponds to what one might expect, people are commenting on the budget because Obama just mentioned it; however, the first two peaks are different in nature. Looking carefully at the messages there one can see that oftentimes the *same* message was sent out by different accounts—indeed these different accounts are all linked implicitly in that they are related to the military (i.e. the accounts correspond to Air Force or other military bases). It would then appear that the U.S. military was using Twitter to "spam" the State of the Union by sending out the same message from multiple accounts simultaneously. This vignette draws attention to the need for integrating network analysis into the tool. Ideally such network analysis would help show the relationship of Twitter accounts not only to each other, but also to similar content, and to time.

In our evaluation of both the computational enablers and the interface we focused on a single event, the State of the Union address, in a distinctly journalistic context. There is, however, a huge range of events, and analytic contexts, where an adapted version of Vox Civitas could still be met with substantial utility. For example, one can imagine a use case of Vox Civitas (or the analytic methods we propose) where the goal is to reason directly about the event content, rather than focus on the response to it.

In addition, different types of events, and maybe even those that do not even have a video channel may also be interesting to examine. For instance, social media related to the FDA (Food and Drug Administration) recalls, alerts, or outbreaks, could be investigated by analysts to help determine how individuals are connected, or how an outbreak is evolving over time. Such investigation does not need to be limited to formal "events", but rather can be applied to longer term evolving issues that could benefit from temporally driven investigation.

10 Conclusion

Increasingly, broadcast and other media events can be associated with a set of postings from various social media channels (e.g., Facebook and Twitter) about the event. Posted in real time, the social media content is roughly aligned with the multimedia content of the event, as we have shown above. This new channel of meta-content about the event offers, at the same time, an opportunity to reason about the media content, and about the nature of the response to the content by social media users.

In this context, we presented a tool to support media professionals interested in the social media response to a broadcast event by collecting, analyzing, aggregating and visualizing content from one major broadcast event, the U.S. State of the Union address of 2010. We have shown that journalists (and others) effectively use the tool to generate insight about the social media response to the event, and about the event itself. We intend to pursue an in-depth case-study approach to understanding the tool's efficacy and how it can be iterated upon to be more useful in a wide variety of contexts.

An interesting question for future work would be how to support signal-level analysis of the multimedia content for the event using the social media data, and how to integrate the video and textual content analysis in one analytic framework. The "social media signal" for any broadcast event greatly enhances the availability of textual descriptors for the event content. While it is not yet clear how the temporally aligned social media content relates to the video content for different types of events (sports, speeches, TV dramas), it is clear that it can provide significant cues that are often hard to reliably extract from the video—like, for example, when a goal was scored in a football match.

References

1. Artstein, R., Poesio, M.: Inter-coder agreement for computational linguistics. Comput. Linguist. **34**(4), 555–596 (2008)
2. Clayman, S.: Defining moments, presidential debates, and the dynamics of quotability. J. Commun. **45**(3), 118–146 (1995)
3. Collins, C., Viégas, F., Wattenberg, M.: Parallel tag coulds to explore and analyze faceted text corpora. In: IEEE Symposium on Visual Analytics Science and Technology (VAST) (2009)
4. De Choudhury, M., Sundaram, H., John, A., Seligmann, D.D.: What makes conversations interesting?: Themes, participants and consequences of conversations in online social media. In: Proc. WWW (2009)

5. De Longueville, B., Smith, R., Luraschi, G.: "OMG, from here, I can see the flames!": A use case of mining location based social networks to acquire spatio-temporal data on forest fires. In: Workshop on Location Based Social Networks (LBSN) (2009)

6. Diakopoulos, N., Shamma, D.A.: Characterizing debate performance via aggregated twitter sentiment. In: Proc. CHI (2010)

7. Diakopoulos, N., Goldenberg, S., Essa, I.: Videolyzer: Quality analysis of online informational video for bloggers and journalists. In: Proceedings of CHI (2009)

8. Fisher, D., Hoff, A., Robertson, G., Hurst, M.: Narratives: A visualization to track narrative events as they develop. In: IEEE Symposium on Visual Analytics Science and Technology (VAST) (2008)

9. Franklin, B., Hamer, M., Hanna, M., Kinsey, M., Richardson, J.E.: Key Concepts in Journalism Studies. Sage, Thousand Oaks (2005)

10. Harcup, T., O'Neill, D.: What is news? Galtung and ruge revisited. Journal. Stud. 2(2), 261–280 (2001)

11. Havre, S., Hetzler, E., Whitney, P., Nowell, L.: ThemeRiver: Visualizing thematic changes in large document collections. IEEE Trans. Vis. Comput. Graph. 8(1), 9–20 (2002)

12. Kang, Y.-a., Görg, C., Stasko, J.: Evaluating visual analytics systems for investigative analysis: Deriving design principles from a case study. In: IEEE Symposium on Visual Analytics Science and Technology (2009)

13. Kovach, B., Rosenstiel, T.: The Elements of Journalism: What Newspeople Should Know and the Public Should Expect. Three Rivers Press, New York (2007)

14. Leskovec, J., Backstrom, L., Kleinberg, J.: Meme-tracking and the dynamics of the news cycle. In: Conference on Knowledge Discovery and Data Mining (KDD) (2009)

15. Manning, C., Raghavan, P., Schütze, H.: Introduction to Information Retrieval. Cambridge University Press, Cambridge (2008)

16. Mertens, R., Farzan, R., Brusilovsky, P.: Social navigation in web lectures. In: Proc. Hypertext and Hypermedia (2006)

17. Nagar, N.a.: The loud public: Users' comments and the online news media. In: Online Journalism Symposium (2009)

18. Pang, B., Lee, L.: Opinion Mining and Sentiment Analysis (2008)

19. Pike, W., Stasko, J., Chang, R., O'Connell, T.: The science of interaction. Inf. Vis. 8(4), 263–274 (2009)

20. Pirolli, P., Card, S.: The sensemaking process and leverage points for analyst technology as identified through cognitive task analysis. In: International Conference on Intelligence Analysis (2005)

21. Rose, S., Butner, S., Cowley, W., Gregory, M., Walker, J.: Describing story evolution from dynamic information streams. In: IEEE Symposium on Visual Analytics Science and Technology (VAST) (2009)

22. Sakaki, T., Okazako, M., Matsuo, Y.: Earthquake shakes twitter users: Real-time event detection by social sensors. In: Proc. WWW (2010)

23. Shamma, D., Kennedy, L., Churchill, E.: Conversational shadows: Describing live media events using short messages. In: Proceedings of ICWSM (2010)

24. Shamma, D.A., Kennedy, L., Churchill, E.: Tweet the debates. In: ACM Multimedia Workshop on Social Media (WSM) (2009)

25. Shamma, D.A., Shaw, R., Shafton, P.L., Liu, Y.: Watch what I watch: Using community activity to understand content. In: Proc. MIR: Workshop on Multimedia Information Retrieval (2007)

26. Starbird, K., Palen, L., Hughes, A., Vieweg, S.: Chatter on the red: What hazards threat reveals about the social life of microblogged information. In: Proceedings of CSCW (2010)

27. Thomas, J., Cook, K. (eds.): Illuminating the Path. IEEE, New York (2005)

Part III
Social Media Applications

Using Rich Social Media Information for Music Recommendation via Hypergraph Model

Shulong Tan, Jiajun Bu, Chun Chen, and Xiaofei He

Abstract There are various kinds of social media information, including different types of objects and relations among these objects, in music social communities such as Last.fm and Pandora. This information is valuable for music recommendation. However, there are two main challenges to exploit this rich social media information: (a) There are many different types of objects and relations in music social communities, which makes it difficult to develop a unified framework taking into account all objects and relations. (b) In these communities, some relations are much more sophisticated than pairwise relation, and thus cannot be simply modeled by a graph. We propose a novel music recommendation algorithm by using both multiple kinds of social media information and music acoustic-based content. Instead of graph, we use hypergraph to model the various objects and relations, and consider music recommendation as a ranking problem on this hypergraph. While an edge of an ordinary graph connects only two objects, a hyperedge represents a set of objects. In this way, hypergraph can be naturally used to model high-order relations.

S. Tan (✉) · J. Bu · C. Chen
Zhejiang Key Laboratory of Service Robot, College of Computer Science, Zhejiang University, Hangzhou 310027, China
e-mail: shulongtan@zju.edu.cn

J. Bu
e-mail: bjj@zju.edu.cn

C. Chen
e-mail: chenc@zju.edu.cn

X. He
State Key Laboratory of CAD&CG, College of Computer Science, Zhejiang University, Hangzhou 310027, China
e-mail: xiaofeihe@cad.zju.edu.cn

S.C.H. Hoi et al. (eds.), *Social Media Modeling and Computing*,
DOI 10.1007/978-0-85729-436-4_10, © Springer-Verlag London Limited 2011

1 Introduction

With the recent advances in social media communities (e.g., Last.fm[1] Flickr[2] and YouTube[3]), there is an emerging presence of social media information, e.g., user collective actions, implicit social networking structure and relations among media objects. This information not only facilitates users in communication and organizing online resources, but is also valuable in some research tasks such as social networks analysis and information retrieval. In particular, these kinds of social media information are important sources of information for recommender systems [21, 23].

Among these kinds of social media information, explicit feedback (e.g., in terms of ratings or use frequencies) from users is the most important for recommendation. Traditional recommender systems use techniques such as Collaborative Filtering (CF) [18, 24, 32], which only apply user-item explicit feedback matrix. As a kind of user collective action, explicit feedback presents collective information among users. Based on explicit feedback, recommendation can be done among similar users or items. Another type of collective action is social tagging, e.g., Last.fm allows users to tag artists, albums or music tracks and Del.icio.us[4] allows users to tag webpages. Social tags carry useful information not only about the tagged items, but also about the preference of users who tag. Several algorithms have been proposed for exploiting social tagging information in recommender systems [14, 17, 43].

In social media communities, users can make friends with other users or join some interest groups. These actions build a implicit social networking structure. This social networking structure is useful for predicting users' preferences, because the users' interests may be affected by their friends or neighbors in interest groups. There have been some papers already in utilizing friendship relations for recommendation [21, 28]. But no previous works exploit membership information about interest groups in recommendation.

Moreover, relations among media objects (e.g., inclusion relations among music tracks, albums and artists in Last.fm, inclusion relations between collections and photos in Flickr) not only can be used to organize resource items, but are also valuable in recommendation. We found that this information greatly improves the recommendation performance (see Sect. 6.5). But to the best of our knowledge, no emphasis has been placed on recommendation based on this kind of information.

Figure 1 shows an example of social media information in online music social community Last.fm. This information includes friendships, memberships, listening histories, tagging relations, inclusion relations among resources and similarities between music tracks which can be computed based on music content.

---

[1]http://www.last.fm.

[2]http://www.flickr.com.

[3]http://www.youtube.com.

[4]http://delicious.com.

Fig. 1 Various types of objects and relations in the music social community Last.fm. The relations include friendship relations, membership relations, listening relations, tagging relations, inclusion relations among resources (e.g., tracks and albums) and similarity relations between music tracks

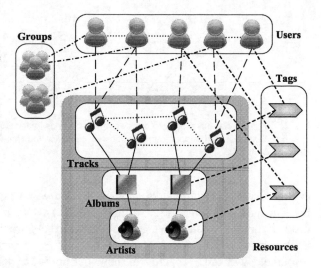

1.1 Motivation

We focus on music recommendation here. For the tasks of music recommendation, the most common approach is to directly analyze the audio signal. These methods are called acoustic-based music recommendation [9, 10, 25, 33]. Due to the semantic gap between low level acoustic features and high level music concepts [11], the results of acoustic-based music recommendation are not satisfactory. It is necessary to consider more information in music recommendation [12]. Some researchers try to utilize the user rating information by applying collaborative filtering methods [22, 42, 44, 45]. There is also work which exploits the information in the meta data (e.g., genre) associated with music tracks [4, 30, 31]. However, all these approaches only utilize limited kinds of information, without considering rich social media information.

The various social media information mentioned above is very useful for music recommendation. However, there are several challenges to exploit all this information. First, it is difficult to take in account all types of media objects and relations in a unified framework simultaneously. It is difficult for traditional methods such as k-nearest neighbor (kNN) Collaborative Filtering and matrix or tensor factorization (MF/TF) to expand and utilize more kinds of social information. Second, in social media communities, some relations are beyond pairwise and are high-order relations. For example, multiple items belong to the same sets, or a user use a tag to bookmark a resource. Traditional methods that deal with pairwise relations cannot properly model these high-order relations. Third, because most social media communities do not allow for free access to all user profiles, such as friend lists or interest group lists, there is not a concrete dataset yet that includes all social media information mentioned above.

Recently, there has been considerable interest in making use of social media information to enhance the recommendation performance [21, 28, 36, 40, 43, 46]. For

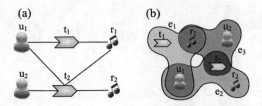

Fig. 2 Tagging relations represented in two models: (**a**) ordinary graph model, and (**b**) our unified hypergraph model. This hypergraph contains six vertices and three hyperedges, i.e., (u_1, t_1, r_1), (u_1, t_2, r_2), and (u_2, t_2, r_1)

example, some previous works employed ordinary graphs to model tagging data for recommendation problems [21, 46]. Figure 2(a) shows a simple example of using ordinary graph to model the tagging relations. There are three tagging relations: u_1 bookmarks resources r_1 and r_2 with tags t_1 and t_2, respectively, and u_2 bookmarks resource r_1 with tag t_2. Figure 2(b) shows our unified hypergraph approach for modeling the tagging relations. In our unified hypergraph model, the high-order relations among the three types of objects can be naturally represented as triples: (u_1, t_1, r_1), (u_1, t_2, r_2), and (u_2, t_2, r_1). Clearly, the ordinary graph model fails to capture the tagging relations precisely. For example, from Fig. 2(a), it is unclear whether u_2 bookmarks r_1, r_2, or both.

1.2 Contributions

We use unified hypergraphs to model multi-type objects and relations in music social communities. Similarities between music tracks based on acoustic signals are treated as one kind of relations. In this way, we combine acoustic-based and collaborative filtering recommendation in a unified framework. A hypergraph is a generalization of the ordinary graph in which the edges, called *hyperedges*, are arbitrary non-empty subsets of the vertex set [3]. Each vertex of the hypergraph corresponds to an object of any type. The hyperedges are used to model high-order relations, as shown in Fig. 2(b). By using the unified hypergraph model, we can accurately capture the high-order relations among various types of objects without loss of any information. We further consider music recommendation as a ranking problem on this hypergraph to find the music tracks that each user desires.

The points below highlight the contributions of this work:

1. **Multi-source information fusion.** We integrate multi-source media information, including multiple kinds of social media information and music acoustic signals, in music recommendation to improve the performance.
2. We propose to model high-order relations in social media information by hypergraphs instead of traditional graphs. In this way, there is no information loss in representing various types of relations.

3. We empirically explore the contributions of different types of social media information to recommendation performance. Our results are helpful for practical music recommender systems.

This work is an extended and improved follow-up to our earlier paper [7]. In comparison, we add a substantially theoretical analysis and computational complexity analysis about our algorithm. We also extend the experiments here.

2 Related Work

Our method combines acoustic-based and collaborative filtering music recommendation methods to exploit rich social media information and acoustic-based content information using hypergraph-based learning techniques. Our work is related to hybrid music recommendation, recommendation using social media information and graph/hypergraph-based learning. In this section we provide a brief review of these works.

2.1 Hybrid Music Recommendation

There are several hybrid approaches combining acoustic-based and collaborative filtering music recommendation to improve the overall accuracy of predictions [15, 22, 42, 44, 45]. Yoshii et al. [44, 45] integrate both rating and music content information by using probabilistic models. Unobservable user preferences are directly represented by introducing latent variables. Li et al. [22] propose an item-based probabilistic model utilizing audio features to capture accurate similarities among items (i.e., music). Tiemann et al. [42] investigate ensemble learning methods for hybrid music recommendation. They apply ensemble learning methods to combine outputs of item-based collaborative filtering and acoustic-based recommendation. Donaldson [15] exploits music co-occurring information in playlists and acoustic signals for a hybrid music recommender system by unifying spectral graph and acoustic feature vectors. All the above works use conventional collaborative filtering methods and only utilize limited kinds of information, without considering more sophisticated social media information.

2.2 Recommendation Using Social Media Information

It has been shown that social media information, such as tagging relations and friendship relations, is valuable for recommendation. Tso-Sutter et al. [43] reduce three types of objects in tagging relations (users, resources and tags) to two types by treating tags as either users or resources, and then apply traditional item-based or user-based collaborative filtering algorithms [1], respectively. Diederich et al. [14] introduce TF-IDF tag profiles for the users and use these profile vectors to measure user–user similarities in the user-based CF algorithm. Zhang et al. [46] propose a recommendation algorithm by integrating diffusion on user-tag-item tripartite graphs. Ma et al. [28] propose a probabilistic factor analysis framework which naturally fuses the users' preferences and their trusted friends' favors together. To utilize both friendship and tagging relations, Konstas et al. [21] create a collaborative recommender system which constructs a social graph over users, tags and resources. Sen et al. [36] address resource recommendation by inferring users' tag preferences firstly and then compute resource item preferences based on tag preferences. They propose some heuristic methods to make use of various social media information, such as clickthrough and search information, in the step of tag preferences generation. Knees et al. [20] utilize web-based musical artist similarity information to reduce the number of necessary acoustic-based music similarity calculations and then use music similarity in the task of music playlist generation.

Although the above approaches have achieved great success in resource recommendation applications, they fail to make full use of the high-order relations in the social media communities. We propose to use hypergraph, rather than the ordinary graph, to precisely capture the high-order relations and hence enhance the recommendation performance.

2.3 Graph-Based Ranking and Hypergraph

Our work is also related to graph-based ranking and hypergraph learning [2, 3, 8, 13, 38, 48, 49].

Zhou et al. propose a manifold ranking algorithm which ranks data objects with respect to the intrinsic geometrical structure in the data [49]. They first construct a weighted graph and set the query point, then let all data points spread their ranking scores to their nearby neighbors via the weighted graph. The spread process is repeated until a global stable state is achieved. Agarwal [2] proposes to model the data objects as a weighted graph, and incorporate this graph structure into the ranking function as a regularizer. In this way, the obtained ranking function varies smoothly over the graph. To generate personalized tag recommendation, Guan et al. propose a graph-based ranking algorithm for interrelated multi-type objects [16].

Recently, there has been a lot of interest in learning with hypergraph [3, 8, 13, 38, 48]. Bulò et al. introduce a hypergraph clustering algorithm to extract maximally coherent groups from a set of objects using high-order (rather than pairwise) similarities [8]. Zhou et al. develop a general framework which is applicable to classification, clustering and embedding on hypergraph data [48]. These studies only focus on classification, clustering and embedding on hypergraphs. However, by modeling the multiple types of social media objects and their relations as a unified hypergraph, we consider music recommendation as a ranking problem on unified hypergraph.

3 Background of Ranking on Graph Data

Let $G(V, E, w)$ denote a ordinary graph where $V = \{v_1, \ldots, v_{|V|}\}$ is the set of vertices, E is the set of the pairwise edges, and w is a weight function defined as $w : E \rightarrow \mathbb{R}$. The *weighted adjacency matrix* of the ordinary graph is the matrix $\mathbf{W} = (w_{ij})_{i,j=1,\ldots,|V|}$. The degree of a vertex $v_i \in V$ is defined as

$$d_i = \sum_{j=1}^{|V|} w_{ij}. \tag{1}$$

The *vertex degree matrix* $\mathbf{D}$ of the ordinary graph is defined as the diagonal matrix with the degrees $d_1, \ldots, d_n$ on the diagonal.

The problem of ranking on graph data is addressed in a "query and ranking" manner as follows. Given some query vertices from V, rank the other vertices on the graph according to their relevance to the queries. Let $\mathbf{y} = [y_1, y_2, \ldots, y_{|V|}]^T$ denote the query vector and y_i denotes the initial score of the ith vertex. Similarly, let $\mathbf{f} = [f_1, f_2, \ldots, f_{|V|}]^T$ denote the ranking scores.

3.1 Regularization Framework for Ranking on Graph

The cost function of the regularization framework for ranking on graph data is [16, 49]

$$Q(\mathbf{f}) = \frac{1}{2} \sum_{i,j=1}^{|V|} W_{ij} \left\| \frac{f_i}{\sqrt{D_{ii}}} - \frac{f_j}{\sqrt{D_{jj}}} \right\|^2$$

$$+ \mu \sum_{i=1}^{|V|} \| f_i - y_i \|^2, \tag{2}$$

where $\mu > 0$ is the regularization parameter. The optimal ranking result $\mathbf{f}^*$ is achieved when $Q(\mathbf{f})$ is minimized:

$$\mathbf{f}^* = \arg \min_{\mathbf{f}} Q(\mathbf{f}). \tag{3}$$

The first term of the right-hand side in Eq. (2) is the smoothness constraint, which means that vertices should have similar ranking scores if they are near. The second term measures the difference between the obtained ranking scores and the pre-given labels which needs to be minimized. The parameter μ controls the relative importance of these two terms.

We define a matrix

$$\mathbf{S} = \mathbf{D}^{-1/2} \mathbf{W} \mathbf{D}^{-1/2}. \tag{4}$$

Then we can rewrite the cost function (2) in the matrix-vector form:

$$Q(\mathbf{f}) = \mathbf{f}^T(\mathbf{I} - \mathbf{S})\mathbf{f} + \mu(\mathbf{f} - \mathbf{y})^T(\mathbf{f} - \mathbf{y}).$$

Requiring that the gradient of $Q(\mathbf{f})$ vanish gives the following equation:

$$\frac{\partial Q}{\partial \mathbf{f}}\bigg|_{\mathbf{f}=\mathbf{f}^*} = (\mathbf{I} - \mathbf{S})\mathbf{f}^* + \mu(\mathbf{f}^* - \mathbf{y}) = 0.$$

Following some simple algebraic steps, we have

$$\mathbf{f}^* = \frac{\mu}{1+\mu}\left(\mathbf{I} - \frac{1}{1+\mu}\mathbf{S}\right)^{-1}\mathbf{y}. \tag{5}$$

We define $\alpha = 1/(1+\mu)$. Noticing that $\mu/(1+\mu)$ is a constant and does not change the ranking results, we can rewrite $\mathbf{f}^*$ as follows:

$$\mathbf{f}^* = (\mathbf{I} - \alpha\mathbf{S})^{-1}\mathbf{y}. \tag{6}$$

3.2 Random Walks with Restarts Model

In the view of random walks with restarts theory [21, 27], we can model ranking on graph as follows. Starting from a particular vertex in the starting vertex set V^*, the model is performed by following a edge to another vertex or restarting from one vertex in V^* at each step. In every step there is a probability α to walk to neighbors of the current vertex and a probability $1 - \alpha$ to restart from the starting vertex set V^*. If the current vertex is v_i and the model walks to the neighbors, there is a probability $p_{ij} = w_{ij}/D_{ii}$ to the vertex v_j. Let $\mathbf{p}^{(t)}$ be a column vector where $p_i^{(t)}$ denotes the probability that the random walk at step t is at node v_i. $\mathbf{q}$ is a column vector of zeros with 1s corresponding to vertices in the starting vertex set (i.e., $q_i = 1$, if $v_i \in V^*$). The transition probability matrix of the graph is $\mathbf{T} = \mathbf{D}^{-1}\mathbf{W}$. The stationary probabilities for each vertex can be obtained by recursively applying Eq. (7) until convergence,

$$\mathbf{p}^{(t+1)} = \alpha\mathbf{T}\mathbf{p}^{(t)} + (1 - \alpha)\mathbf{q}. \tag{7}$$

The stationary probabilities present the long term visit rate of each vertex given a bias toward the starting vertex set V^*. Therefore each stationary probability corresponding to a vertex v_i can be considered as a measure of relatedness between v_i and the starting vertex set.

To find $\mathbf{p}^c$, where c is the state after convergence, we set $\mathbf{p}^{(t+1)} = \mathbf{p}^{(t)} = \mathbf{p}^c$. Then we can get this equation:

$$\mathbf{p}^c = (1 - \alpha)(\mathbf{I} - \alpha\mathbf{T})^{-1}\mathbf{q}. \tag{8}$$

Since $1 - \alpha$ does not change the ranking results, we can rewrite $\mathbf{p}^c$ as follows:

$$\mathbf{p}^c = (\mathbf{I} - \alpha \mathbf{T})^{-1} \mathbf{q}. \tag{9}$$

We find that this expression is similar to the ranking result deduced by the regularization framework.

4 Ranking on Unified Hypergraph

In this section we discuss how to model various types of objects and their relations in a unified hypergraph model and how to perform ranking on unified hypergraph. We begin with the description of the problem and the notations.

4.1 Notation and Problem Definition

Let $G(V, E_h, w)$ denote a hypergraph where E^h is the set of hyperedges. Different from ordinary graphs, each hyperedge $e \in E_h$ is a subset of V. The degree of a hyperedge e is defined by $\delta(e) = |e|$, that is, the cardinality of e. If every hyperedge has a degree of 2, the hypergraph reduces to an ordinary graph. The degree $d(v)$ of a vertex v is $d(v) = \sum_{e \in E_h | v \in e} w(e)$. We say that there is a *hyperpath* between vertices v_1 and v_k if there is an alternative sequence of distinct vertices and hyperedges $v_1, e_1, v_2, e_2, \ldots, e_{k-1}, v_k$, such that $\{v_i, v_{i+1}\} \subseteq e_i$ for $1 \leq i \leq k - 1$. A hypergraph is *connected* if there is a hyperpath for every pair of vertices [48]. We define a vertex–hyperedge incidence matrix $\mathbf{H} \in \mathbb{R}^{|V| \times |E_h|}$ whose entry $h(v, e)$ is 1 if $v \in e$ and 0 otherwise. Then we have

$$d(v) = \sum_{e \in E_h} w(e) h(v, e), \tag{10}$$

$$\delta(e) = \sum_{v \in V} h(v, e). \tag{11}$$

Let $\mathbf{D}_e$ and $\mathbf{D}_v$ be two diagonal matrices consisting of hyperedge and vertex degrees, respectively. Let $\mathbf{W}_h$ be a $|E_h| \times |E_h|$ diagonal matrix containing hyperedge weights.

In the following, we define *unified hypergraph* which will be used to model the high-order relations among different types of objects. A unified hypergraph is a hypergraph that has multi-type vertices and hyperedges. Suppose a unified hypergraph has m types of vertices and n types of hyperedges. The vertex set of the ith type is denoted by $V^{(i)}$ and the hyperedge set of the jth type is denoted by $E_h^{(j)}$. We define $V = \bigcup_{i=1}^{m} V^{(i)}$ and $E_h = \bigcup_{j=1}^{n} E_h^{(j)}$. In social music communities, different kinds of objects, such as users, tags, resources and groups, can be viewed as different types of vertices in a unified hypergraph, and different types of relations among objects can be viewed as different types of hyperedges. A hyperedge in unified hypergraph can be a set of vertices with either the same type or different types. The former kind of hyperedge captures the relations among the same type of objects, while the latter one captures the relations across different types of objects.

The problem of ranking on unified hypergraphs is similar to ranking on ordinary graphs. Given some query vertices from V, rank the other vertices on the unified hypergraph according to their relevance to the queries. Let $\mathbf{y} = [y_1, y_2, \ldots, y_{|V|}]^T$ denote the query vector and y_i, $i = 1, \ldots, |V|$, denote the initial score of the ith vertex. We will discuss how to set the query vector in detail in Sect. 5.4. Similarly, let $\mathbf{f} = [f_1, f_2, \ldots, f_{|V|}]^T$ be the vector of ranking scores.

4.2 Regularization Framework for Ranking on Unified Hypergraph

There are many existing algorithms for learning on hypergraph [3, 8, 13, 38, 48]. However, most of them focus on classification, clustering, and Euclidean embedding. In this subsection, we discuss how to perform ranking on unified hypergraph by using similar idea of [48].

The cost function of $\mathbf{f}$ is defined by

$$Q(\mathbf{f}) = \frac{1}{2} \sum_{i,j=1}^{|V|} \sum_{e \in E_h} \frac{w(e)h(v_i,e)h(v_j,e)}{\delta(e)} \left\| \frac{f_i}{\sqrt{d(v_i)}} - \frac{f_j}{\sqrt{d(v_j)}} \right\|^2$$
$$+ \mu \sum_{i=1}^{|V|} \| f_i - y_i \|^2, \tag{12}$$

where $\mu > 0$ is the regularization parameter. This function is similar to Eq. (2). The optimal ranking result is achieved when $Q(\mathbf{f})$ is minimized:

$$\mathbf{f}^* = \arg\min_{\mathbf{f}} Q(\mathbf{f}). \tag{13}$$

The first term of the right-hand side in Eq. (12) is a smoothness constraint too. Minimizing it means that vertices should have similar ranking scores if they are contained in many common hyperedges. For instance, if two music tracks are listened by many common users, they will probably have similar ranking scores. Another example is the ranking of the users. If two users join in many common interest groups (or if they listen to many common music tracks, etc.), they will probably have similar ranking scores. Note that each hyperedge is normalized by its degree $\delta(e)$, that is, the number of vertices contained in this hyperedge. In this way, the hyperedges with different sizes will be equally treated. The second term and the parameter μ play the same roles as in Eq. (2).

The first term of the right-hand side in the cost function (12) can be rewritten as follows:

$$\frac{1}{2} \sum_{i,j=1}^{|V|} \sum_{e \in E_h} \frac{w(e)h(v_i,e)h(v_j,e)}{\delta(e)} \left\| \frac{f_i}{\sqrt{d(v_i)}} - \frac{f_j}{\sqrt{d(v_j)}} \right\|^2$$

$$= \sum_{i,j=1}^{|V|} \sum_{e \in E_h} \frac{w(e)h(v_i,e)h(v_j,e)}{\delta(e)} \left(\frac{f_i^2}{d(v_i)} - \frac{f_i f_j}{\sqrt{d(v_i)d(v_j)}} \right)$$

$$= \sum_{i=1}^{|V|} f_i^2 \sum_{e \in E_h} \frac{w(e)h(v_i,e)}{d(v_i)} \sum_{j=1}^{|V|} \frac{h(v_j,e)}{\delta(e)}$$

$$- \sum_{i,j=1}^{|V|} \sum_{e \in E_h} \frac{f_i w(e)h(v_i,e)h(v_j,e)f_j}{\sqrt{d(v_i)d(v_j)}\delta(e)}$$

$$= \sum_{i=1}^{|V|} f_i^2 - \sum_{i,j=1}^{|V|} \sum_{e \in E_h} \frac{f_i w(e)h(v_i,e)h(v_j,e)f_j}{\sqrt{d(v_i)d(v_j)}\delta(e)}$$

$$= \mathbf{f}^T \mathbf{f} - \mathbf{f}^T \mathbf{D}_v^{-1/2} \mathbf{H} \mathbf{W}_h \mathbf{D}_e^{-1} \mathbf{H}^T \mathbf{D}_v^{-1/2} \mathbf{f}. \tag{14}$$

We define a matrix

$$\mathbf{A} = \mathbf{D}_v^{-1/2} \mathbf{H} \mathbf{W}_h \mathbf{D}_e^{-1} \mathbf{H}^T \mathbf{D}_v^{-1/2}. \tag{15}$$

Then we can rewrite the cost function (12) in the matrix-vector form:

$$Q(\mathbf{f}) = \mathbf{f}^T (\mathbf{I} - \mathbf{A}) \mathbf{f} + \mu (\mathbf{f} - \mathbf{y})^T (\mathbf{f} - \mathbf{y}).$$

The following formal deductions are the same as the ways in Sect. 3.1 and we can get the ranking result

$$\mathbf{f}^* = (\mathbf{I} - \alpha \mathbf{A})^{-1} \mathbf{y}. \tag{16}$$

There is a variant of the results: $\mathbf{f}^* = (\mathbf{I} - \alpha \mathbf{A})^{-1} \mathbf{y}$ and $\mathbf{A} = \mathbf{D}_v^{-1} \mathbf{H} \mathbf{W}_h \mathbf{D}_e^{-1} \mathbf{H}^T$, which is corresponding to a Random Walks with Restart model. We will compare this variant with our results in experiments.

5 Music Recommendation via Hypergraph

In this section, we introduce our approach for Music Recommendation via Hypergraph (MRH).

Table 1 Objects in our data set

Objects	Notations	Count
Users	U	2596
Groups	G	1124
Tags	Ta	3255
Tracks	Tr	16055
Albums	Al	4694
Artists	Ar	371

5.1 Data Collection

To evaluate our algorithm, we have collected data from Last.fm in December 2009. Firstly, we collected the top 340 most popular artists, as well as the users who are interested in those artists. Adding all these users' friends, we obtained the candidate set of the users. Then we reduced the candidate set of users by restricting that each user has at least one friend within the set. The final user set is denoted by U. We collected other objects and relations based on this user set. We downloaded all the groups in which these users join, and reduced the set of groups by ensuring that each group has at least five members in the final user set. The final group set is denoted by G. For resource objects and relations, we crawled each user's top 500 frequently played music tracks to form the candidate set of tracks. In order to get the inclusion relations among resources, we downloaded all corresponding artists and albums of all tracks in the candidate track set, and removed those albums that contain less than five tracks in the candidate track set. After that, we obtained the final sets of resources, i.e., track set, album set and artist set, denoted by Tr, Al, and Ar, respectively. We collected the tagging relations which are essentially triples, i.e., (user, tag, music track), (user, tag, music album) or (user, tag, artist). For each user, we downloaded all his/her tagging relations. We only kept those relations in which the resource is in Tr, Al or Ar obtained previously. The final set of tags is denoted by Ta. Finally, we downloaded the music files (in mp3 or wma formats) from the Web. The objects and relations used in our experiments are summarized in Table 1 and Table 2, respectively. Similarities between music tracks are computed based on music content.

5.2 Acoustic-Based Music Similarity

Acoustic measures of music similarity have been extensively studied in recent years [5, 26, 29, 41]. These algorithms mainly focus on several central problems: (1) what representative features to extract; (2) how to model the feature distributions of music; (3) how to measure the similarity between distribution models.

To compactly represent the music content, we derive features from Mel-frequency cepstral coefficients (MFCCs) [5]. MFCCs are prevalent in audio classification. A given music track is segmented into short frames and the MFCC is

Table 2 Relations in our data set

Relations	Notations	Count
Friendship relations	R_1	4503
Membership relations	R_2	1124
Listening relations	R_3	304860
Tagging relations on tracks	R_4	10936
Tagging relations on albums	R_5	730
Tagging relations on artists	R_6	36812
Track-album inclusion relations	R_7	4694
Album-artist inclusion relations	R_8	371
Similarities between tracks	R_9	–

computed for each frame. Similar to [26], we use K-means to group all the frames of each track into several clusters. For all the clusters, the means, covariances, and weights are computed as the signature of the music track. To compare the signatures for two different tracks, we employ the Earth-Mover's Distance (EMD) [34].

5.3 Unified Hypergraph Construction

We take into account six types of objects and nine types of relations in the data set mentioned above. The objects include users, groups, tags and three types of resources (i.e., tracks, albums and artists). The relations are divided into four categories, social relations, actions on resources, inclusion relations among resources, and acoustic-based music similarity relations. Social relations include friendship relations and membership relations (e.g., an interest group), denoted by R_1 and R_2, respectively. Actions on resources involve four types of relations, i.e., listening relations (R_3), and tagging relations on tracks, albums and artists (R_4, R_5 and R_6). Inclusion relations among resources are the inclusion relations between tracks and albums, albums and artists (R_7 and R_8). Acoustic-based music similarity relations are denoted by R_9.

The six types of objects form the vertex set of the unified hypergraph. So $V = U \cup G \cup Ta \cup Tr \cup Al \cup Ar$. And there are nine types of hyperedges in the unified hypergraph, each corresponding to a certain type of relations, as listed in Table 2. We denote the hyperedge sets as $E_h^{(i)}$ corresponding to R_i, $i = 1, \ldots, 9$. The construction of the nine types of hyperedges is listed as follows:

- $E_h^{(1)}$: We build a hyperedge corresponding to each pairwise friendship and set the hyperedge weight to be 1.
- $E_h^{(2)}$: For each group, we build a hyperedge which contains vertices corresponding to all the users in this group, as well as the group itself. Note that a group itself is also an object. We set the hyperedge weight to be 1.

- $E_h^{(3)}$: For each user-track listening relation, we build a hyperedge containing the user and the music track. The weight $w(e_{ij}^{(3)})$ ($e_{ij}^{(3)} \in E_h^{(3)}$) is set to be the frequency that the user u_i listens to the track tr_j

$$w(e_{ij}^{(3)}) = |\{(u_i, tr_j)|u_i \in U \text{ and } tr_j \in Tr\}|,$$

where $|Q|$ denotes the number of elements contained in set Q. To eliminate the bias, we normalize the weight as

$$w(e_{ij}^{(3)})' = \frac{w(e_{ij}^{(3)})}{\sqrt{\sum_{k=1}^{|Tr|} w(e_{ik}^{(3)})}\sqrt{\sum_{l=1}^{|U|} w(e_{lj}^{(3)})}}. \tag{17}$$

Moreover, in order to treat different types of relations (except similarity relations between tracks) equally, the weight is further normalized as follows:

$$w(e_{ij}^{(3)})^* = \frac{w(e_{ij}^{(3)})'}{ave(w(e_{i.}^{(3)})')}, \tag{18}$$

where $ave(w(e_{i.}^{(3)})')$ is the average of normalized weights for user u_i.

- $E_h^{(4)}/E_h^{(5)}/E_h^{(6)}$: We build hyperedges for tagging relations on three types of resources as illustrated in Fig. 2(b). Each hyperedge contains three vertices (corresponding to a user, a tag and a resource) and the weight is set to be 1.
- $E_h^{(7)}/E_h^{(8)}$: We build a hyperedge for each album which contains all the tracks in this album and the album itself. Similarly, the hyperedge for an artist contains all the albums belonging to the artist and the artist oneself. The weights of the hyperedges corresponding to albums and artists are set to be 1.
- $E_h^{(9)}$: We build a k nearest neighbor (knn) graph based on acoustic-based music similarities and build hyperedges for our unified hypergraph corresponding to the edges of the knn graph. The weight $w(e_{ij}^{(9)})$ is the similarity of tracks tr_i and tr_j computed in Sect. 4.2. To eliminate the bias, we normalize the weight as

$$w(e_{ij}^{(9)})' = \frac{w(e_{ij}^{(9)})}{\max(w(e^{(9)}))}, \tag{19}$$

where $\max(w(e^{(9)}))$ is the maximum of all music similarities. We introduce a parameter c to control the relative importance between acoustic content of music tracks and other social media information. Finally, the weight is

$$w(e_{ij}^{(9)})^* = c \times w(e_{ij}^{(9)})'. \tag{20}$$

Finally, we get the vertex–hyperedge incidence matrix $\mathbf{H}$, as shown in Table 3, and the weight matrix $\mathbf{W}_h$.

Table 3 The incidence matrix **H** of the unified hypergraph and the sub-matrices

	$E_h^{(1)}$	$E_h^{(2)}$	$E_h^{(3)}$	$E_h^{(4)}$	$E_h^{(5)}$	$E_h^{(6)}$	$E_h^{(7)}$	$E_h^{(8)}$	$E_h^{(9)}$
U	$UE_h^{(1)}$	$UE_h^{(2)}$	$UE_h^{(3)}$	$UE_h^{(4)}$	$UE_h^{(5)}$	$UE_h^{(6)}$	0	0	0
G	0	$GE_h^{(2)}$	0	0	0	0	0	0	0
Ta	0	0	0	$TaE_h^{(4)}$	$TaE_h^{(5)}$	$TaE_h^{(6)}$	0	0	0
Tr	0	0	$TrE_h^{(3)}$	$TrE_h^{(4)}$	0	0	$TrE_h^{(7)}$	0	$TrE_h^{(9)}$
Al	0	0	0	0	$AlE_h^{(5)}$	0	$AlE_h^{(7)}$	$AlE_h^{(8)}$	0
Ar	0	0	0	0	0	$ArE_h^{(6)}$	0	$ArE_h^{(8)}$	0

5.4 Methodology

Our music recommendation algorithm MRH contains two phases, offline training and online recommendation. In the offline training phase, we first construct the unified hypergraph as described above and get the vertex–hyperedge incidence matrix **H** and the weight matrix $\mathbf{W}_h$. Then the vertex degree matrix $\mathbf{D}_v$ and the hyperedge degree matrix $\mathbf{D}_e$ are computed based on **H** and $\mathbf{W}_h$. Finally, we calculate $(\mathbf{I} - \alpha \mathbf{D}_v^{-1/2} \mathbf{H} \mathbf{W}_h \mathbf{D}_e^{-1} \mathbf{H}^T \mathbf{D}_v^{-1/2})^{-1}$, denoted as $(\mathbf{I} - \alpha \mathbf{A})^{-1}$, with α properly set. In the online recommendation phase, we need to build the query vector **y** first. Then the ranking results $\mathbf{f}^*$ can be computed.

Our approach can also be applied to other applications by choosing different vertices as queries and considering the ranking results of different vertex types. For example, if we choose a user as the query, the ranking results of music tracks can be used for music track recommendation (i.e., the primary focus of this work), the ranking results of the users can be used for friend recommendation, and the ranking results of groups can be used for interest group recommendation. For the tag recommendation problem [16, 37], we should set the target user and the target resource as queries and consider the ranking results of tags.

There are three methods to set the query vector **y** for music track recommendation: (1) Set the entry of **y** corresponding to the target user u to be 1 and all others to be 0. (2) Set the entries of **y** corresponding to the target user u, as well as all the other objects connected to u by some hyperedge, to be 1. (3) Set the entry of **y** corresponding to the target user u to be 1. Also, if u is connected to an object v, then set the entry of **y** corresponding to v to be $A_{u,v}$. Note that $A_{u,v}$ is a measure of the relatedness between u and v. The first method fails to consider the closely related objects which may also reflect the user's interest. The second method may not be a good choice, since intuitively different objects reflect the user's interest with different degrees. Therefore, in our experiments we adopt the third method. After setting the query vector, the ranking results $\mathbf{f}^*$ can be computed. For the music track recommendation problem, we only consider the ranking results of music tracks as mentioned above. Finally, we can recommend to the user the top ranked tracks which he/she has not listened to before.

5.5 Computational Complexity Analysis

Now let us analyze the computational cost of MRH. Let m denote the number of vertices and n denote the number of hyperedges in the unified hypergraph. Let p be the density of the matrix $\mathbf{H}$, i.e., the probability of non-zero entries. To calculate matrix $\mathbf{A}$, it requires $O(p^2nm^2)$ operations and $(1 - (1 - p^2)^n)m^2$ memory, where $1 - (1 - p^2)^n$ is the density of matrix $\mathbf{A}$. If p is very small (e.g., p is 7.3×10^{-5} in our data), $\mathbf{A}$ and $\mathbf{I} - \alpha\mathbf{A}$ are highly sparse. Computing the inverse of matrix $\mathbf{I} - \alpha\mathbf{A}$ requires $O(n^3)$ operations and m^2 memory. Since $\mathbf{I} - \alpha\mathbf{A}$ is sparse, the computation of matrix inversion will be efficient [39].

In real-world social media communities, the size of matrix $(\mathbf{I} - \alpha\mathbf{A})$, despite its sparsity, may be potentially huge. By analyzing the RUH recommendation method, we can find the most time is consumed when computing the inverse of matrix $\mathbf{I} - \alpha\mathbf{A}$. If the size of this matrix is very large, it is time consuming. However, this computation can be performed offline in advance.

6 Experiments

6.1 Compared Algorithms

We compare our MRH algorithm with other four recommendation algorithms. The first one is an user-based Collaborative Filtering (CF) method [21, 32] which only uses listening relations. We choose user-based CF algorithm because that our data set has much more music tracks than users. Given a target user u_i, let r_{u_i,tr_p} be a predicted ranking score of user u_i for music track tr_p, which is given by [21]

$$r_{u_i,tr_p} = \overline{w}\big(e_{i.}^{(3)}\big)^* + \frac{\sum_{j=1}^{k}(w(e_{jp}^{(3)})^* - \overline{w}(e_{j.}^{(3)})^*)s_{u_i,u_j}}{\sum_{j=1}^{k}s_{u_i,u_j}}, \qquad (21)$$

where

$$\overline{w}\big(e_{i.}^{(3)}\big)^* = \frac{\sum_{p=1}^{|Tr|}w(e_{ip}^{(3)})^*}{|\{tr_p|tr_p \in Tr \text{ and } w(e_{ip}^{(3)})^* \neq 0\}|} \qquad (22)$$

and s_{u_i,u_j} is the similarity weight between users u_i and u_j. k is the number of nearest neighbors of user u_i. We employ the cosine-based approach [6, 35] to compute the similarities between users:

$$s_{u_i,u_j} = \frac{\sum_{p=1}^{|Tr|}w(e_{ip}^{(3)})^* w(e_{jp}^{(3)})^*}{\sqrt{\sum_{p=1}^{|Tr|}(w(e_{ip}^{(3)})^*)^2}\sqrt{\sum_{p=1}^{|Tr|}(w(e_{jp}^{(3)})^*)^2}}. \qquad (23)$$

Based on the obtained similarities, we use the significance weighting method proposed in [19] to improve the recommendation performance. Specifically, if the number of co-listened music tracks between two users, denoted by n, is less than a

Fig. 3 Inclusion relations represented in two models: (a) our unified hypergraph model, and (b) ordinary graph model

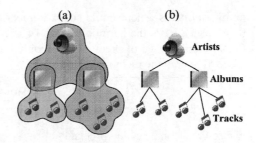

threshold number N, then we multiply their similarity by n/N. In our experiment, we empirically set the value of N to be 20, and the number of nearest neighbors k to be 5, to achieve the best performance.

The second compared algorithm is a acoustic-based music recommendation method [42] which uses listening relations and music similarity relations. It is denoted by *AB*.

The third compared algorithm uses all the information in our downloaded data set. Unlike MRH, we use the ordinary graph to model social media information. Specifically, we model the tagging relations by graph structure as shown in Fig. 2(a), and model the membership and inclusion relations by tree structure as shown in Fig. 3. The graph ranking algorithm described in [49] is applied to compute the optimal ranking scores. We call this algorithm *Recommendation on Unified Graph* (*RUG*).

The fourth compared algorithm is the variant of our proposed MRH method mentioned in Sect. 4.2, which is named as *MRH-variant*.

We also compare the performances of our proposed method on different subsets of information. The first one is our MRH method but only using listening relations and music similarity relations (i.e., R_3 and R_9). This method is denoted by *MRH-hybrid*. The second one is our MRH method but not using music similarity relations. It uses all the other eight types of relations. This method is denoted by *MRH-social*.

6.2 Evaluation

To evaluate the performance of our MRH algorithm and the other compared algorithms, for each user, we randomly select 20% listening relations as test data for evaluation purpose. If the user has access to a certain track *tr* in the test set, we require that he/she has no access to *tr* in the training set. To achieve this, we remove all the corresponding tagging relations, leaving us with the final training set.

For evaluation metrics, we use Precision, Recall, F1, Mean Average Precision (MAP) and Normalized Discount Cumulative Gain (NDCG) to measure the performance of different recommendation algorithms. Precision is defined as the number of correctly recommended items divided by the total number of recommended items. Recall is defined as the number of correctly recommended items divided by the total number of items which should be recommended (i.e., those actually listened by the target user). F1 is the harmonic mean of Precision and Recall. Average Precision (AP) is the average of precisions computed at the point of each correctly recommended item in the recommendation list:

$$AP = \frac{\sum_i^N \text{Precision}@i \times \text{corr}_i}{\text{Number of correctly recommended items}}, \tag{24}$$

where Precision@i is the precision at ranking position i, N is the number of recommended items, and corr$_i = 1$ if the item at position i is correctly recommended, otherwise corr$_i = 0$. MAP is the mean of average precision scores over all users. NDCG at position n is defined by

$$NDCG@n = \frac{1}{\text{IDCG}} \times \sum_{i=1}^{n} \frac{2^{r_i} - 1}{\log_2(i + 1)}, \tag{25}$$

where r_i is the relevance rating of item at rank i. In our case, r_i is 1 if the user has listened to this recommended music and 0 otherwise. IDCG is chosen so that the perfect ranking has a NDCG value of 1.

6.3 Performance Comparison

We use all evaluation metrics mentioned in Sect. 6.2 to measure the performance of each recommendation algorithm. Figure 4 shows the recall-precision curves for all the methods. We report the performance of all algorithms in terms of MAP, F1 and NDCG in Table 4 (MAP and F1) and Table 5 (NDCG). It is evident that our proposed algorithm significantly outperforms other recommendation algorithms in most cases, especially at lower ranks. Note that our proposed MRH algorithm models the high-order relations by hyperedges, whereas RUG uses the ordinary graph to approximate these high-order relations. The superiority of MRH over RUG indicates that the hypergraph is indeed a better choice for modeling complex relations in social media communities. Acoustic-based (AB) method works the worst. This is because acoustic-based method incurs the semantic gap and similarities based on acoustic content are not always consistent with human knowledge [11]. CF algorithm does not work well either. This is probably because the user-track matrix in our data set is highly sparse, with only about 0.6% non-zero entries. MRH-hybrid only uses similarity relations among music tracks and listening relations, but it works much better than AB and CF.

Comparing to MRH-social, MRH uses similarity relations among music tracks additionally. We find that using this acoustic-based information can improve the recommendation result, especially when recall is small. This is because acoustic-based information can alleviate some well-known problems associated with data sparseness in collaborative recommender systems, e.g., user bias, non-association and cold-start problems [22].

Fig. 4 Recall–Precision
curves for all the methods

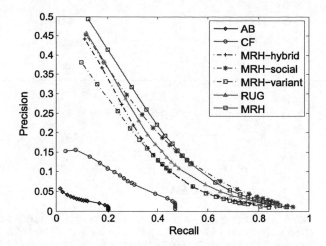

Table 4 Comparison of recommendation algorithms in terms of MAP and F1

	MAP	F1@5	F1@10	F1@20	F1@30	F1@50	F1@70	F1@100	F1@200
CF	0.1632	0.0557	0.0929	0.1243	0.1329	0.1294	0.1197	0.1064	0.0765
AB	0.0762	0.0226	0.0303	0.0377	0.0403	0.0421	0.0415	0.0401	0.0334
RUG	0.2626	0.1729	0.2323	0.2587	0.2516	0.2237	0.1988	0.1701	0.1169
MRH-variant	0.2380	0.1442	0.1973	0.2285	0.2275	0.2079	0.1864	0.1599	0.1093
MRH-hybrid	0.2470	0.1653	0.2224	0.2451	0.2377	0.2099	0.1855	0.1581	0.1076
MRH-social	0.2755	0.1705	0.2311	0.2654	0.2660	0.2440	0.2202	**0.1906**	**0.1318***
MRH	**0.2948***	**0.1855***	**0.2510***	**0.2839***	**0.2799***	**0.2509***	**0.2227**	0.1892	0.1270

Bold typeset indicates the best performance

*indicates statistical significance at $p < 0.001$ compared to the second best

Table 5 Comparison of recommendation algorithms in terms of NDCG

	NDCG@5	NDCG@10	NDCG@30	NDCG@50	NDCG@100	NDCG@200
CF	0.1522	0.1713	0.2519	0.2987	0.3579	0.4120
AB	0.0733	0.0820	0.1241	0.1532	0.2027	0.2556
RUG	0.4849	0.4318	0.3826	0.4109	0.4587	0.5037
MRH-variant	0.3970	0.3626	0.3482	0.3820	0.4297	0.4715
MRH-hybrid	0.4587	0.4091	0.3640	0.3911	0.4346	0.4753
MRH-social	0.4759	0.4268	0.3866	0.4197	0.4763	0.5264
MRH	**0.5192***	**0.4650***	**0.4174***	**0.4484***	**0.4987***	**0.5419***

Bold typeset indicates the best performance

*indicates statistical significance at $p < 0.001$ compared to the second best

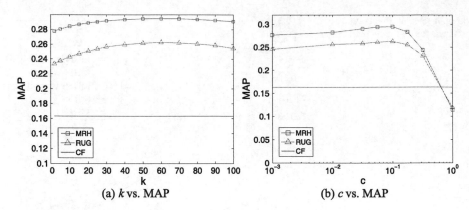

(a) k vs. MAP   (b) c vs. MAP

Fig. 5 The parameter settings of k and c for music similarity relations. Firstly, we fix c at 0.1 empirically and let k vary. (**a**) The performance measured by MAP. Then we fix k at 60 and let c vary. (**b**) The performance measured by MAP

The superiority of MRH over MRH-variant indicates the normalized form of MRH is better which is consistent with previous findings [47].

6.4 Exploring Parameter Settings

There are three parameters in our algorithm, i.e., the number of nearest neighbors k mentioned in Sect. 5.3, c in Eq. (20) and α in Eq. (16).

To explore the influence of the parameters k and c, we use MAP as the evaluation metric and fix α to be 0.98. Figure 5 shows the results. Firstly, we fix c at 0.1 empirically and let k vary. Figure 5(a) shows the performance measured as a function of k. The best result is obtained when k is around 60. Then we fix k at 60 and let c vary. Figure 5(b) shows the performance measured as a function of c. The best result is obtained when $c = 0.1$. As can be seen, our algorithm consistently outperforms the other two compared algorithms in a wide range of parameter variation. In our experiments, we set k to be 60 and c to be 0.1 for MRH, MRH-hybrid and RUG. α is a common parameter shared by our MRH algorithm and RUG [49]. In our performance comparison experiments, we just set α to be 0.98 for MRH, MRH-hybrid, MRH-social, MRH-variant and RUG empirically. We explore the optimal value of α here. Figure 6 shows the results by MAP. The MRH algorithm obtains the best performance when α is close to 0.97 and RUG obtains best performance when α is close to 0.96. It also can be seen, MRH outperforms RUG and CF algorithms in a wide range of parameter variation. When $\alpha > 0.98$, the performance drop dramatically. And when $\alpha = 0.999$ (i.e. the restart probability is close to 0), the performance becomes very bad. This is because the larger the value of α, the smaller the effect of the query. Restart probability 0 means that there is no relationship between the ranking results and the query.

Fig. 6 Exploring the influence of the parameter α setting for MRH and RUG algorithms. We use MAP evaluation metric here

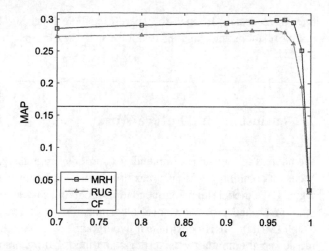

Table 6 Comparison of MRH on different subsets of social information in terms of MAP and F1

	MAP	F1@5	F1@10	F1@30	F1@40	F1@70	F1@100	F1@200
MRH on R_3	0.2303	0.1430	0.1996	0.2332	0.2143	0.1772	0.1695	0.1184
MRH on R_1, R_2, R_3	**0.2308**	**0.1444**	**0.1998**	**0.2337**	**0.2146**	0.1772	0.1695	0.1181
MRH on R_3, R_4	0.2303	**0.1432**	**0.1997**	0.2332	0.2143	**0.1773**	0.1695	0.1184
MRH on R_3, R_7, R_8	**0.2757**[*]	**0.1748**[*]	**0.2339**[*]	**0.2642**[*]	**0.2413**[*]	**0.1970**[*]	**0.1878**[*]	**0.1299**[*]

Bold typeset indicates that the performance is better than that of using the listening relations (R_3) alone

[*]indicates statistical significance at $p < 0.001$ compared to the algorithm by using listening relations alone

6.5 Social Information Contribution

To explore the contributions of different types of social media information to the recommendation performance, we investigate the performances of MRH on four different subsets of social media information. The first subset only contains listening relations (i.e., R_3), which is considered as the base relations. The second subset contains listening relations and social relations (i.e., R_1, R_2). The third subset contains listening relations and tagging relations on tracks (i.e., R_4). The fourth subset contains listening relations and inclusion relations (i.e., R_7, R_8). From Table 6, we can see that inclusion relations significantly improve the recommendation performance. By using inclusion relations among resources, we can recommend music tracks in the same or similar albums, as well as the tracks performed by the same or similar artists. As can be seen, there is slight improvement at low recall region by using social relations. Intuitively, the users' preferences may be inferred from friendship and membership relations. Tagging relations do not improve the performance. That is because people usually bookmark music tracks they have already listened to. Therefore, there is strong correlation between listening relations and tagging relations, and thus the usage of tagging relations is limited.

7 Conclusions and Future Work

We address the music recommendation problem in music social communities, and focus on combining various types of social media information and music acoustic signals. We model the recommendation problem as a ranking problem on a unified hypergraph and propose a novel algorithm for music recommendation via hypergraph (MRH). MRH constructs a hypergraph to model the multi-type objects in a music social community as vertices, and the relations among these objects as hyperedges. Similarities among music tracks based on acoustic signals are treated as one kind of relations. In this way, the high-order relations in social information can be naturally captured. In addition, collaborative filtering and acoustic-based music recommendation is combined in a unified framework. Based on the constructed hypergraph, we then use a regularization framework to derive the ranking results for query vertices. We treat a user as the query and recommend the top ranked music tracks to the user. The experiments on a data set collected from the music social community Last.fm have demonstrated that our proposed algorithm significantly outperforms traditional recommendation algorithms and the rich social media information is very useful for music recommendation.

MRH can also be used for recommender systems in other kinds of social media communities, such as movies and pictures. In this work, we treat all types of social relations (except music similarity relations) equally. However, in practical applications, different types of relations may have different importance. For example, in some pure social networks such as Facebook[5] and LinkedIn,[6] the preferences of the users can be affected by their friends significantly. In this case, we should assign relatively higher weights to social relations such as friendship and membership relations. On the other hand, for special interest social media communities (e.g., Last.fm and YouTube), the unified hypergraph model should put more emphasis on the users' actions on resources (e.g., rating and tagging) and the relations among resources (e.g., inclusion relations).

Moreover, as mentioned in Sect. 5.4, our approach is not limited to music track recommendation. We can exploit it in different applications, such as friend recommendation and personalized tag recommendation. These problems are left for our future work.

---

[5]http://www.facebook.comu.

[6]http://www.linkedin.com.

References

1. Adomavicius, G., Tuzhilin, A.: Toward the next generation of recommender systems: A survey of the state-of-the-art and possible extensions. IEEE Trans. Knowl. Data Eng. **17**(6), 734–749 (2005)
2. Agarwal, S.: Ranking on graph data. In: Proc. the 23rd International Conference on Machine Learning, Pittsburgh, PA (2006)
3. Agarwal, S., Branson, K., Belongie, S.: Higher order learning with graphs. In: Proc. the 23rd International Conference on Machine Learning, Pittsburgh, PA (2006)
4. Aucouturier, J.-J., Pachet, F.: Scaling up music playlist generation. In: Proc. IEEE International Conference on Multimedia and Expo, Lausanne, Switzerland (2002)
5. Berenzweig, A., Logan, B., Ellis, D.P.W., Whitman, B.: A large-scale evaluation of acoustic and subjective music-similarity measures. Comput. Music J. **28**(2), 63–76 (2004)
6. Breese, J., Heckerman, D., Kadie, C.: Empirical analysis of predictive algorithms for collaborative filtering. In: Proc. the 14th Conference on Uncertainty in Artificial Intelligence, San Francisco, CA (1998)
7. Bu, J., Tan, S., Chen, C., Wang, C., Wu, H., He, X.: Music recommendation by unified hypergraph: Combining social media information and music content. In: Proc. the 18th ACM International Conference on Multimedia, Florence, Italy (2010)
8. Bulò, S.R., Pelillo, M.: A game-theoretic approach to hypergraph clustering. In: Advances in Neural Information Processing Systems 22, Vancouver, Canada (2009)
9. Cai, R., Zhang, C., Zhang, L., Ma, W.-Y.: Scalable music recommendation by search. In: Proc. the 15th International Conference on Multimedia, Augsburg, Germany (2007)
10. Cano, P., Koppenberger, M., Wack, N.: Content-based music audio recommendation. In: Proc. the 13th ACM International Conference on Multimedia, Singapore (2005)
11. Celma, Ò.: Foafing the music: Bridging the semantic gap in music recommendation. In: Proc. the 5th International Semantic Web Conference, Athens, Georgia (2006)
12. Celma, Ò., Lamere, P.: If you like the beatles you might like... : a tutorial on music recommendation. In: Proc. the 16th ACM International Conference on Multimedia, Vancouver, British Columbia, Canada (2008)
13. Chen, S., Wang, F., Zhang, C.: Simultaneous heterogeneous data clustering based on higher order relationships. In: Proc. the 7th IEEE International Conference on Data Mining Workshops, Omaha, Nebraska (2007)
14. Diederich, J., Iofciu, T.: Finding communities of practice from user profiles based on folksonomies. In: Proc. the 1st International Workshop on Building Technology Enhanced Learning Solutions for Communities of Practice, Crete, Greece (2006)
15. Donaldson, J.: A hybrid social-acoustic recommendation system for popular music. In: Proc. ACM Conference on Recommender Systems, New York, NY (2007)
16. Guan, Z., Bu, J., Mei, Q., Chen, C., Wang, C.: Personalized tag recommendation using graph-based ranking on multi-type interrelated objects. In: Proc. the 32nd ACM SIGIR Conference on Research and Development in Information Retrieval, Boston, MA (2009)
17. Guan, Z., Wang, C., Bu, J., Chen, C., Yang, K., Cai, D., He, X.: Document recommendation in social tagging services
18. Harpale, A.S., Yang, Y.: Personalized active learning for collaborative filtering. In: Proc. the 31st ACM SIGIR Conference on Research and Development in Information Retrieval, Singapore (2008)
19. Herlocker, J.L., Konstan, J.A., Borchers, A., Riedl, J.: An algorithmic framework for performing collaborative filtering. In: Proc. the 22nd ACM SIGIR Conference on Research and Development in Information Retrieval, Berkeley, CA (1999)
20. Knees, P., Pohle, T., Schedl, M., Widmer, G.: Combining audio-based similarity with web-based data to accelerate automatic music playlist generation. In: Proc. the 8th ACM International Workshop on Multimedia Information Retrieval, Santa Barbara, California (2006)
21. Konstas, I., Stathopoulos, V., Jose, J.M.: On social networks and collaborative recommendation. In: Proc. the 32nd ACM SIGIR Conference on Research and Development in Information Retrieval, Boston, MA (2009)

22. Li, Q., Myaeng, S.H., Kim, B.M.: A probabilistic music recommender considering user opinions and audio features. Inf. Process. Manag. **43**(2), 473–487 (2007)
23. Lin, Y., Sun, J., Castro, P., Konuru, R., Sundaram, H., Kelliher, A.: Metafac: community discovery via relational hypergraph factorization. In: Proc. the 15th ACM SIGKDD International Conference on Knowledge Discovery and Data Mining, Paris, France (2009)
24. Liu, N.N., Yang, Q.: Eigenrank: a ranking-oriented approach to collaborative filtering. In: Proc. the 31st ACM SIGIR Conference on Research and Development in Information Retrieval, Singapore (2008)
25. Logan, B.: Music recommendation from song sets. In: Proc. the 5th International Conference on Music Information Retrieval, Barcelona, Spain (2004)
26. Logan, B., Salomon, A.: Music similarity function based on signal analysis. In: Proc. IEEE International Conference on Multimedia and Expo, Tokyo, Japan (2001)
27. Lovász, L.: Random walks on graphs: A survey. Combinatorics, Paul Erdos is Eighty **2**(1), 1–46 (1993)
28. Ma, H., King, I., Lyu, M.R.: Learning to recommend with social trust ensemble. In: Proc. the 32nd ACM SIGIR Conference on Research and Development in Information Retrieval, Boston, MA (2009)
29. McKay, C., Fujinaga, I.: Combining features extracted from audio, symbolic and cultural sources. In: Proc. the 9th International Conference on Music Information Retrieval, Philadelphia, PA (2008)
30. Pauws, S., Verhaegh, W., Vossen, M.: Fast generation of optimal music playlists using local search. In: Proc. the 7th International Conference on Music Information Retrieval, Victoria, Canada (2006)
31. Ragno, R.J., Burges, C.J.C., Herley, C.: Inferring similarity between music objects with application to playlist generation. In: Proc. the 7th ACM SIGMM Workshop on Multimedia Information Retrieval, Hilton, Singapore (2005)
32. Resnick, P., Iacovou, N., Suchak, M., Bergstrom, P., Riedl, J.: Grouplens: An open architecture for collaborative filtering of netnews. In: Proc. the ACM Conference on Computer Supported Cooperative Work, Chapel Hill, NC (1994)
33. Rho, S., jun Han, B., Hwang, E.: Svr-based music mood classification and context-based music recommendation. In: Proc. the 17th ACM International Conference on Multimedia, Beijing, China (2009)
34. Rubner, Y., Tomasi, C., Guibas, L.J.: The earth mover's distance as a metric for image retrieval. Int. J. Comput. Vis. **40**(2), 99–121 (2000)
35. Sarwar, B., Karypis, G., Konstan, J., Reidl, J.: Item-based collaborative filtering recommendation algorithms. In: Proc. the 10th International Conference on World Wide Web, Hong Kong, China (2001)
36. Sen, S., Vig, J., Riedl, J.: Tagommenders: connecting users to items through tags. In: Proc. the 18th International Conference on World Wide Web, Madrid, Spain (2009)
37. Song, Y., Zhuang, Z., Li, H., Zhao, Q., Li, J., Lee, W.-C., Giles, C.L.: Real-time automatic tag recommendation. In: Proc. the 31st ACM SIGIR Conference on Research and Development in Information Retrieval, Singapore (2008)
38. Sun, L., Ji, S., Ye, J.: Hypergraph spectral learning for multi-label classification. In: Proc. the 14th ACM SIGKDD International Conference on Knowledge Discovery and Data Mining, Las Vegas, Nevada (2008)
39. Svizhenko, A., Anantram, M.P., Govindan, T.R., Biegel, B., Venugopal, R.: Two-dimensional quantum mechanical modeling of nanotransistors. J. Appl. Phys. **91**(4), 2343–2354 (2009)
40. Symeonidis, P., Ruxanda, M., Nanopoulos, A., Manolopoulos, Y.: Ternary semantic analysis of social tags for personalized music recommendation. In: Proc. the 9th International Conference on Music Information Retrieval, Pennsylvania, USA (2008)
41. Tao, D., Liu, H., Tang, X.: K-box: a query-by-singing based music retrieval system. In: Proc. the 12th ACM International Conference on Multimedia, New York, NY (2004)
42. Tiemann, M., Pauws, S.: Towards ensemble learning for hybrid music recommendation. In: Proc. ACM Conference on Recommender Systems, New York, NY (2007)

43. TsoSutter, K.H.L., Marinho, L.B., Schmidt-Thieme, L.: Tag-aware recommender systems by fusion of collaborative filtering algorithms. In: Proc. the 2008 ACM Symposium on Applied Computing, Fortaleza, Brazil (2008)

44. Yoshii, K., Goto, M.: Continuous pLSI and smoothing techniques for hybrid music recommendation. In: Proc. the 10th International Society for Music Information Retrieval Conference, Kobe, Japan (2009)

45. Yoshii, K., Goto, M., Komatani, K., Ogata, T., Okuno, H.G.: Hybrid collaborative and content-based music recommendation using probabilistic model with latent user preferences. In: Proc. the 7th International Conference on Music Information Retrieval, Victoria, Canada (2006)

46. Zhang, Z., Zhou, T., Zhang, Y.: Personalized recommendation via integrated diffusion on user-item-tag tripartite graphs. Physica A **389**(1), 179–186 (2009)

47. Zhou, D., Bousquet, O., Lal, T.N., Weston, J., Schölkopf, B.: Learning with local and global consistency. In: Advances in Neural Information Processing Systems 16, Cambridge, MA (2003)

48. Zhou, D., Huang, J., Schölkopf, B.: Learning with hypergraphs: Clustering, classification, and embedding. In: Advances in Neural Information Processing Systems 19, Vancouver, Canada (2006)

49. Zhou, D., Weston, J., Gretton, A., Bousquet, O., Schölkopf, B.: Ranking on data manifolds. In: Advances in Neural Information Processing Systems 16, Cambridge, MA (2003)

Using Geotags to Derive Rich Tag-Clouds for Image Annotation

Dhiraj Joshi, Jiebo Luo, Jie Yu, Phoury Lei, and Andrew Gallagher

Abstract Geotagging has become popular for many multimedia applications. In this chapter, we present an integrated and intuitive system for location-driven tag suggestion, in the form of tag-clouds, for geotagged photos. Potential tags from multiple sources are extracted and weighted. Sources include points of interest (POI) tags from a public Geographic Names Information System (GNIS) database, community tags from Flickr® pictures, and personal tags shared through users' own, family, and friends' photo collections. To increase the effectiveness of GNIS POI tags, bags of place-name tags are first retrieved, clustered, and then re-ranked using a combined tf-idf and spatial distance criteria. The community tags from photos taken in the vicinity of the input geotagged photo are ranked according to distance and visual similarity to the input photo. Personal tags from other personally related photos inherently carry a significant weight due more to their high relevance than to both the generic place-name tags and community tags, and are ranked by weights that decay over time and distance differences. Finally, a rich set of the most relevant location-driven tags is presented to the user in the form of individual tag clouds under the three mentioned source categories. The tag clouds act as intuitive suggestions for tagging an input image. We also discuss quantitative and qualitative findings from a user study that we conducted. Evaluation has revealed the respective benefits of the three categories toward the effectiveness of the integrated tag suggestion system.

1 Introduction

The popularity of digital cameras and the proliferation of online communities have led to an explosion in the number of personal and Web images. It has become a serious challenge to manage such an overwhelming amount of image data. Commercial search engines and Web albums rely heavily upon text annotations associated with images for indexing and retrieval tasks. Recognizing the need for semantic annotation, the latest version of the Google™ Picasa™ now enables users to label images

D. Joshi (✉) · J. Luo · J. Yu · P. Lei · A. Gallagher
Corporate Research and Engineering, Eastman Kodak Company, Rochester, USA
e-mail: dhiraj.joshi@kodak.com

S.C.H. Hoi et al. (eds.), *Social Media Modeling and Computing*,
DOI 10.1007/978-0-85729-436-4_11, © Springer-Verlag London Limited 2011

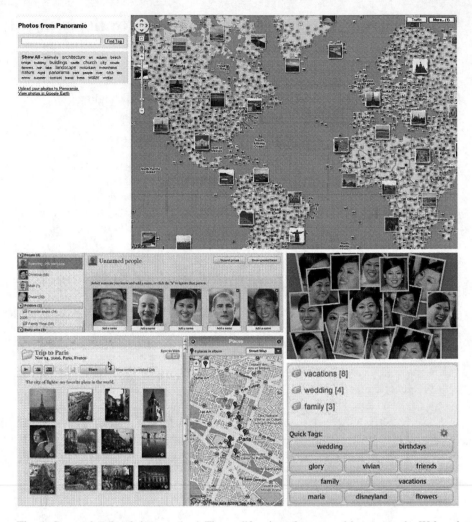

Fig. 1 Personal and web images: (*top*) The proliferation of geotagged images on the Web and (*bottom*) Personal images often described in terms of people, places, and events

in terms of faces, places, and user-specified tags (Fig. 1). However, text annotations associated with Web pictures are free-form in nature and therefore can be very noisy. One potent form of noise is incorrect or alternate spellings associated with certain place names (e.g., Eifel tower and Eiffel tower are both popular). Another form of noise occurs because of the inherent polysemy and synonymy of words in the English language. While there is a significant effort toward building richer and more accurate semantic annotation models for image applications, there is also a push to leverage large-scale crowd-sourced information for improved annotation. Trust in the collective wisdom of the crowd is a driving factor behind the latter school of approaches. Regardless of whether the former or the latter approach is adopted, machine annotations are far from perfect and can best be used as plausible suggestions to users that they can then choose to accept or refine.

A valuable piece of information that has recently become available with pictures is geographic information. Photo-sharing sites such as Yahoo! Flickr also tap into geographic information for search, sharing, and visualization of multimedia. Flickr allows users to provide geo-location information for their pictures either as exact or approximate geographical coordinates with the help of a map interface or as geographically relevant keywords. This process, referred to as geotagging, has generated a wave of geo-awareness in multimedia. During the month this chapter was written, Flickr had collected about 4.5 million geotagged entities. Google Panoramio™ now uses Google map interface to depict geotagged pictures on the globe (Fig. 1). Geotagging can also be performed by using a digital camera equipped with a GPS receiving sensor or by using a digital camera that can communicate with a standalone GPS receiver (e.g., through a Bluetooth® link). Photos can also be synchronized with a GPS logging device. Capture of geo-coordinates or availability of geographically relevant tags with pictures opens up new data-mining possibilities for better recognition, classification, and retrieval of images in personal collections and on the Web. This information can be used alone or in conjunction with pixel data for better inferencing of people, places, and events, much of which is either directly linked to or intimately associated with the picture-taking location, which provides important and more relevant (compared to time context alone) context. Consequently, we refer to the collection of tags that can be derived from the location as "location-driven" or "location-oriented" tags. The enormous amount of geotagged data on the Web thus calls for intelligent systems that can help make sense of the world and realize the vision of a geo-aware community.

2 Survey of Geotagging Related Work

Content understanding in multimedia has been studied extensively for decades in the vision research community [13, 21, 23]. With rapid advances in technologies related to digital imaging, digital cameras also bring with them a powerful source of information little exploited previously for content understanding: camera metadata embedded in the digital image files. Camera metadata (or "data about data") record information related to the image capture conditions and includes values such as date/time stamps, subject distance, and GPS coordinates. They contain rich contextual information that is usually complementary to the image features and provides an opportunity to derive more leverage from data than pixels alone can provide. In the last several years, there has been an increased emphasis on modeling and using contextual information [9, 24, 31–33]. Although metadata captured with pictures or videos are a primary source of contextual information [24, 30], relationships between spatio-temporal segments in multimedia data [24], or patterns in multimedia collections as a whole [3, 4, 35] also provide a basis for modeling broad context.

Geographic information has been embraced by multimedia and vision researchers within a contextual modeling framework.

Research in event and scene detection has benefited from the presence of geotagging information with images. In [35], the authors use geographical trace information in association with certain informative compositional visual features to detect event types such as hiking, skiing, party, etc. Clearly, the inherent information that is tapped here is the motion patterns of the photographers and the photographed. Another source of derived knowledge is geographical information systems databases. Points-of-interest (POI) summaries were used to find associations between places, picture semantics, and location in [14]. The aforementioned work models salient geographical descriptive words or geotags with respect to generic event categories such as vacation, beach, hiking, etc. Aerial images have been employed in [25] for event recognition. The cited work illustrates how ground images and the co-located aerial images complement one another for event recognition. Another work [34] acknowledges seasonal and geographic differences for improved scene understanding. The basic motivation lies in the fact that seasonal and geographic information with pictures can help improve region labeling.

While analyzing an image is an indispensible part of the event detection process, patterns mined from image collections as a whole can often shed additional light onto the events captured in them. In this respect, [3] incorporates (i) the relationship between collection-level annotations (events) and picture-level annotations (scenes), and (ii) the time-location constraints into the modeling and annotation process. In a similar vein, [4] exploits image-collection-level semantic coherence for label propagation. Another work [28] uses visual, textual, and spatial information to perform object and event mining on a large-scale geotagged image collection. The work derives its novelty from linking semantic image clusters to articles in Wikipedia and reaffirming cluster assignments using content in Wikipedia pages.

Image annotation or tagging research has also focused increasingly upon geotagging. Naturally, annotation models require establishment of structure or association among words or tags, and hence natural language processing is often necessary. A location-dependent probabilistic Latent Semantic Analysis model (LD-pLSA) was proposed for joint modeling of visual and geographical information in [8]. The model attempts to extract two different kinds of latent classes, visual topics and geo-topics (the latter influencing the former), underlying the observed data. The work aims to perform a geo-visually coherent image categorization automatically using the dual topic modeling approach. Annotation of pictures using very large collections of community geo-referenced pictures is becoming vastly popular in multimedia research. In [19], a 1.2 million Flickr image collection is used to build a geo-profile, which is then employed to annotate images. The first step involves prediction of geographic coordinates of the input image using the K-nearest-neighbor approach as in [11] that the user can choose to refine. The geographic location is then used to suggest likely tags in the identified location as learned from the image collection. In rhyme with the above work, [26] presents a Spirit-tagger tool that mines tags from geographic and visual information. The sheer volume and diversity of geotagged images on the Web have been used to explore and exploit deeper correlations between visual features and their annotations using Logistic Canonical Correlation Regression (LCCR) in [5]. There have also been research efforts to understand user image-tagging behavior [2] and to characterize this behavior over time [10].

The emergence of very large Web image repositories such as Flickr has opened yet new doors for image understanding research. It is now realized that large-scale user participation can generate valuable metadata. The Web has witnessed a surge of collaborative tagging from users, resulting in folksonomies. At the same time, such repositories provide very large datasets for learning and search. Recently, brute-force searches using massive image databases have been shown to be useful for image understanding tasks [29]. Geographical landmark recognition from the Flickr dataset was studied using a combination of visual features and geotags in [17]. Of late, emphasis has shifted to landmark recognition in very large image datasets [7, 37]. While location context has been used for image understanding, the inverse problem of inferring location from image content, using very large image collections, has also been studied in recent years [11, 12, 14, 20]. Taking encouragement from some recent image-tagging research [1, 18], we develop and evaluate a tag-cloud-based personal picture tagging system. A preliminary tag-cloud suggestion system was introduced in [16]. The key difference between our work and the cited literature in image tagging lies in the construction and evaluation of multisource location-driven tag-clouds as tag suggestion systems. Our work falls in the confluence of mining geographical context, community-contributed information, public information databases, and personal information for image tag suggestion.

3 Tag-Clouds

A tag-cloud is a visual depiction of the word content of a document. A tag cloud can provide a quick word-content summary of large documents or collections (see Fig. 2). The most appealing aspect of tag-clouds is the ability to present the relative emphasis or importance of different words or concepts in a seemingly simple manner that a human eye can quickly discern (in contrast to listing numeric weights against different words). Here we explore tag-clouds as tag visualization and tagging interfaces for variable-sized tag-sets.

A tag-cloud can be constructed by tag-frequencies or derived from an ordered tag-set by using tag-weights. In our framework, tag-clouds are constructed and used to describe a given picture with tags from three different sources. Because the vocabularies of the information sources differ and their relevance to users may also differ, for this work we display three different tag-clouds for a given picture. Moreover, it helps us to differentially evaluate the verity, appeal, and significance of tag-sets obtained from the different sources. As the chapter progresses, readers will be able to appreciate the varied nature of content in the three tag-clouds.

Fig. 2 Examples of tag-clouds depicting (*top*) Popularity of Flickr tags, (*bottom*) Comparing Republican (first) and Democratic (second) Convention speeches in 2008 US Presidential Elections

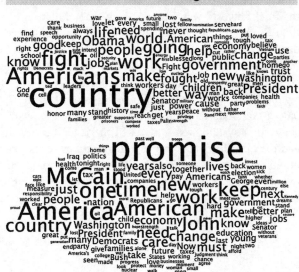

In our system:

- Tag suggestions are obtained from three sources of information, Geographic Names Information System (GNIS) points of interest (POI) (public source), tags from Flickr (large-scale community source), and personal tags (personal source). The three sources are generally complementary in terms of the description and detail that they can provide about a picture.
- We incorporate tag uniqueness, distance, visual coherence, and personal value into the tag-weighting process to form an effective and integrated personal picture tag suggestion system.
- Instead of providing flat (albeit rank-ordered) tag lists such as in Zonetag™ [1], we explore the usability of tag-clouds in our tag-suggestion system where the tag-sizes are proportional to their likelihoods given the picture content, geographic location, and time. Besides providing an intuitive, easy-to-use interface, tag-clouds can facilitate evaluation of the tag-suggestion system.

3.1 Cloud of Geotags from Points-of-Interest Databases

Points of interest (POI) or Geographical Information Systems (GIS) databases provide useful geographical knowledge about important landmarks or points of interest. A GIS database typically consists of detailed geographical information about places, such as latitude, longitude, country, population, and other demographics. Geonames is a GIS database available free of charge and contains over 8 million geographical names and associated information collected and compiled from multiple sources. The process of querying a POI database given a GPS co-ordinate is known as reverse-geocoding. POIs can be used to provide geo-location-based services to travelers [36], perform intelligent actions based upon location demographics [22], summarize the location with nearby POI tags to assist image understanding [14], or identify persons in images [27].

Place-names and corresponding demographics, as purely textual or numeric entities, can inherently be handled using text or data analysis techniques. At the same time, GIS databases contain fairly reliable data collected professionally with serious human effort. Intuitively, reverse geocoding through entries in a GIS database should be specific enough to identify the location environment and help summarize a location. However, certain limitations to acquiring complete semantic knowledge through this process are: (1) a place is represented as a point (e.g., the central office in a zoo) in the database without any definition of the actual spatial extent; (2) multiple environments can potentially co-locate in close proximity of each other—such as cemeteries, churches, schools, etc.

For our work, we treat each POI in Geonames as a bag of geotags where geotags constitute its basic building blocks. Although a reverse geo-coding Web service has been provided by Geonames, we decided to download the raw geographic data and write our own procedure for reverse geo-coding because of our specific needs. Besides being scalable (as a local database is searched versus a remote one if a Web service were to be used), our program returns a list of POIs that summarize a spatial neighborhood of the input latitude-longitude pair. In an earlier work [14], we incorporated a place-names bag of geotags approach for learning event-level geotag saliency. Here, we extend that work to obtain generic geotag saliency using a combination of place category (filtered for photographic interest), distance, and uniqueness criteria.

The main components of the procedure include (1) obtaining POIs ranked by their distance from the location of a query image, (2) clustering POIs into *near* and *far* POIs using K-means clustering and distance as the feature, and (3) estimating the discriminative saliency of individual *near* place-names bags by analyzing the uniqueness of geotags in the bag. Note that the (relatively) *far* POIs are discarded from further consideration although they are in the proximity. We rely upon the natural clustering (considering atmost 50 POIs within 5 miles of query) into *near* and *far* POIs, to reduce the number of place names.

Suppose $N = \{g_1, g_2, \ldots, g_K\}$ denotes a bag of place names or geotags where g_i is a geographically relevant tag or geotag. We compute two weights $W_{\text{Dist}}(N)$ and

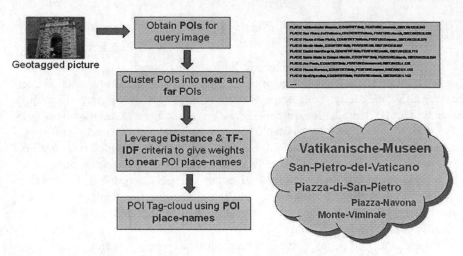

Fig. 3 Construction of cloud of geotags from points of interest (POIs)

$W_{\text{Unique}}(N)$ for each place-name bag that falls in the *near* cluster around the query location as follows:

$$W_{\text{Dist}}(N) = 1 - (d_N/D)^{0.2},$$

$$W_{\text{Unique}}(N) = \max_{g_i}\big(\textit{tf–idf}(g_i)\big)/M.$$

Here D is the set as 5 miles and M is a normalizing factor so that $W_{\text{Unique}}(N)$ lies between 0 and 1. The term $\textit{tf–idf}(g_i)$ is the term frequency–inverse document frequency weight of term g_i. Finally, the two weights are combined as $W(N) = W_{\text{Unique}}(N) + \alpha W_{\text{Dist}}(N)$ where α is 10. Intuitively, close-by POI names can serve as useful tag suggestions. However, for points roughly equally distant from the location of the query image, we give higher weights to place names that contain more unique geotags. Therefore, in our formulation, distance plays a higher role than uniqueness of a place name. In other words, $W_{\text{Unique}}(N)$ plays the role of tie-breaker for ranking place names. The composite weight of a place name $W(N)$ determines its size in the POI tag-cloud (Fig. 3).

3.2 Cloud of Community Tags from Flickr Pictures

In order to tap community effort in image tagging, we rely upon a database of generic Flickr images that contain geo-location metadata that we constructed in [15]. Our collection contains about 1.2 million images downloaded from Flickr as follows: We observed that geo-located images are *nearly always* also annotated with user-tags. We queried Flickr for the 2500 most interesting geo-located images captured on a specific day, and repeated this process for 503 specific days. We have no requirements for user-tags except for a set of negative query terms that prevent low-quality (e.g., camera phone) or otherwise objectionable images from being gathered in our query. Note that using the interest level as a filter ensures that the quality and content of the images in the collection are reasonable thanks to the implicit human filtering by Flickr users.

To obtain region-level geographic annotation, we employ a mean shift algorithm to perform clustering on the GPS locations of pictures [5, 6]. One advantage of mean shift is that it does not require specification of the number of clusters, which is usually unknown in practice. We only need to specify a parameter bandwidth (bw), which denotes the bandwidth for neighborhood search. Another advantage is that for clustering low-dimensional data, mean shift is much faster than the popular k-means algorithm. In this work we set $bw = 0.05$, and obtain a total of 59654 clusters. Figure 4 shows the geographic clusters of images over (top) the entire world, (bottom) North American continent. Construction of a tag-cloud from community pictures is a two-step process:

- For a given input image that contains GPS information, we focus upon pictures taken in the vicinity of the image. In order to do this, we first find its nearest geographical cluster and narrow the search to images in that cluster. If the cardinality of the nearest cluster is smaller than 100, we include the next-nearest cluster(s) to form a searchable set of pictures. A preliminary tag-cloud is first constructed strictly from geographical information using frequency of tags that occur in a subset of 100 geographically closest neighbors (Fig. 5).
- The above tag-cloud is enhanced by contribution from visually similar pictures of the query image that lie within the cluster(s) identified in step 1. While the geographical tag-cloud summarizes the location, visual information can help construct a visual profile from among pictures in the cluster(s) (see Fig. 5). To this end, the visual K-NN approach as described in [15] is adopted. This tag-cloud is constructed from tags strictly in the tag-set identified in step 1 with the frequency of tags from visual sources enhanced by a factor of 60 (a parameter that we settled upon using controlled experiments).

The advantage obtained from using visual information is evident in Fig. 5 using a schematic from a real example in our dataset. For the picture of Jesus in Florence, tags such as Jesus, Jesuschrist, Duomo, and church become prominent in the integrated tag cloud.

3.3 Cloud of Tags from Personal Photos

For online photo sharing, users tend to provide annotations that describe that event or scene depicted in the images. However, it is tedious for the users to annotate every image in his/her collection. Usually, tags are only available for selected images. We have observed that the images in the same user's collection have a strong semantic relationship. Specifically, the images taken in the same time period are usually

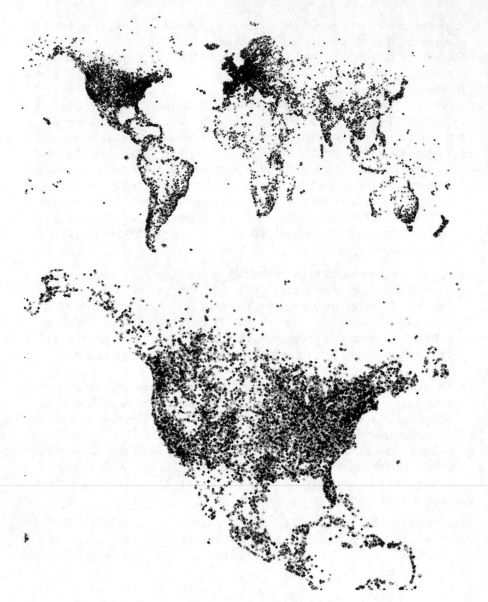

Fig. 4 Geographical clusters of pictures in our 1.2 million Flickr collection: (*top*) pictures in the entire world, and (*bottom*) North America

related to the same event and the ones taken in the same location can be labeled with the same geographical names. It is desirable to leverage the time and location similarity and propagate the user's annotations of the selected images to other images in the same or related collection (Fig. 6). Without loss of generality, we model the images in the user's collection as nodes in a graph. The edges between any pair

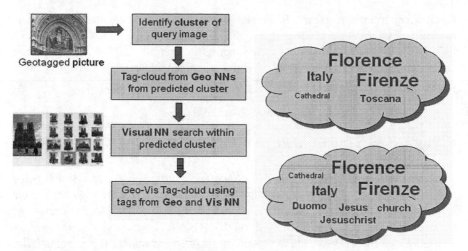

Fig. 5 Construction of cloud of community tags from Flickr pictures

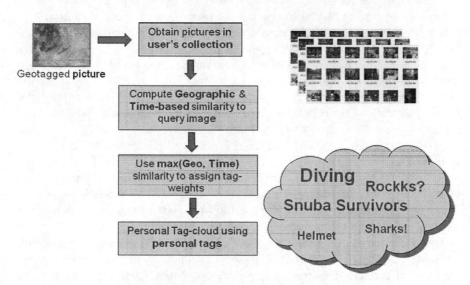

Fig. 6 Construction of cloud of personal tags from personal photo collections

of nodes are weighted by the proximity in time and location. Specifically, we use the following function to calculate the weight because of the satisfying performance in experiments: $w_{i,j} = \max(\frac{1}{1+e^{\lambda_t(\Delta t_{i,j} - \varepsilon_t)}}, \frac{1}{1+e^{\lambda_l(\Delta l_{i,j} - \varepsilon_l)}})$. Here $\Delta t_{i,j}$ and $\Delta l_{i,j}$ are the time and geographic location distances between the i-th and j-th images, respectively. λ_t, λ_l, ε_t and ε_l are the parameters that define the slopes of the sigmoid functions.

Let us suppose a user annotates a collection of N_{img} images with N_{tag} tags. We can calculate an $N_{\text{img}} \times N_{\text{tag}}$ occurrence matrix O in the following way: the element of occurrence matrix $o_{i,t}$ is defined as the number of times the i-th image is annotated by the t-th tag. Clearly, the initial occurrence matrix is sparse because only a few images are annotated. Considering the proximity of the images in time and location domain, the occurrences of the tags from the annotated images can be propagated using the affinity matrix W: $O' = W \times O$.

4 Tag-Cloud Visualization Tool

We have developed a graphical user interface application (Figs. 7 and 8) that helps visualize our three tag-clouds and allows users to add or remove tags from their images with tag-cloud suggestions. We chose to leave three tag-clouds separate as opposed to somehow merging them through a fusion process because the criterion for doing so is unclear and each tag-cloud offers different values. The merging issue can be a topic of future work, preferably with the aid of psychophysical studies. The users can load their images via an Open Folder dialog box. The tool displays the thumbnails on the bottom tray where the user can then select any image with which he/she wants to work. Upon selection, the application displays the image on the right, and the three tag-clouds appear on the left-hand panel. User tags already assigned to the image are displayed below the image in the tag session located immediately beneath the displayed image. Each time a tag is selected, the application writes it to the tag session area. Tags can be added or removed from an image by simple user clicks. The application also allows the user to enter additional new tags manually. We use a sigmoid mapping from a tag-weight to its displayed font size. If w is the weight of a tag and T is the maximum weight assigned to any tag, its displayed tag font size is given by $f(w) = 36/(1 + e^{-5(w/T-0.3)})$. To increase tag visibility, smaller tags are enlarged when a user mouses over them. For the purpose of evaluation, we categorize tags into *big-tags* and *small-tags* where *big-tags* constitute tags for which $w \geq 0.3$ or $f(w) \geq 18$. We do not display tags with $w \leq 0.1$ to avoid unnecessary clutter in the tag clouds.

One characteristic of a generic tag-cloud is the random arrangement of tags with the salient tags standing prominently against the others. To facilitate efficient user-tag scanning and selection across large picture collections, it was suggested to us by a user that an alphabetical rather than purely random arrangement of tags would be more beneficial. We incorporated this suggestion into our system.

5 Results and User Study

In order to quantitatively assess the usability of our tag-suggestion system, we conduct a user study. Our target picture dataset consists of a set of 54 image collections with the number of pictures per collection varying from about 8 to 137. These collections were gathered by five users who took pictures with GPS-equipped cameras

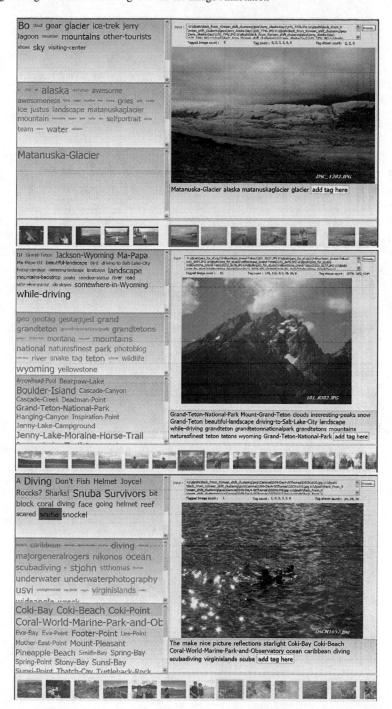

Fig. 7 Personal (*black*), community geo-vis (*green*), and points of interest (POI) (*red*) tag-clouds for pictures taken in Alaska (*top*), Grand Teton National Park (*center*), and St Thomas, Virgin Islands (*bottom*). Note that user-selected tags are shown in the area below the pictures

Fig. 8 Community geo-vis (*green*), and points of interest (POI) (*red*) tag-clouds for pictures taken in Florence (*top*), Vatican City (*center*), and Rome (*bottom*). Note that user-selected tags are shown in the area below the pictures

in their work or vacation trips in and around the USA and Europe. Some of the collections have personal tags assigned by their owners while some do not. The study consists of asking users to look at their respective collections and choose appropriate tags from the three tag-clouds based upon their best memory of the location and the trip. Figures 7 and 8 show six noteworthy examples from the user-study and the associated tag-clouds. In Fig. 7, all three tag-clouds have been shown while in Fig. 8, the personal tag-cloud is absent due to the unavailability of user-assigned personal tags to images. Notice the salient tags from different tag-clouds and the user selection. We invite the readers to assess the semantic diversity and appropriateness of the different tag-cloud suggestions themselves.

In Fig. 9, we plot the statistics of our user study. Figure 9 (top) shows percentage distributions (as pie charts) of tags-displayed (in tag-clouds) and tags-selected (by users) from different tag-clouds. One can notice that while tags-displayed distribution is more or less uniform (with a slight dip for POI tags), the tags-selected distribution is heavily biased toward community (geo-vis) tags (59%); personal tags come second (35%), while POI tags form a mere 6% of the selections. Figure 9 (center) compares the proportions of big-tags from all tag-selections among different tag-clouds. The percentage profiles are computed across all participants. It is evident that big-tags form a large proportion of the user selection, thus validating our tag-weighting schemes as well as the usefulness of tag-cloud suggestions. However, small-tags are also selected by users across all tag-clouds. This plot corroborates the earlier finding that comparing across tag-modalities, community tags (geo-vis) and POI tags have the largest and smallest percentages of selection. POI tags are location specific and precise. Most users tend to remember and choose only the most salient point of interest around their picture. However, community tags have a wider semantics than POI tags or personal tags and therefore form the most widely chosen set. Personal tags from other related photos inherently carry a significant weight due to their high relevance, although they are not always available. In Fig. 9 (bottom), we show the tag-selection rate, computed as the percentage of tags displayed that were selected for different tag-clouds. As observed before, selection rate is highest for community (geo-vis) tags (24.8%), followed by personal tags (14.4%) with the POI tag-selection rate being relatively low (3.9%). We again refer to the above reasoning for POI tags to explain these numbers. While the selection rate measures the usability of tag-clouds in some proportion, we would like to mention here that readers should not be deterred by low numbers obtained in our study. The whole philosophy of tag-clouds is the ability to present the user with a wide variety of tags ranging from very relevant to irrelevant and a soft suggestion conveyed in the form of tag-sizes. Thus tag-clouds form excellent and user-friendly tag-suggestion systems with low cost for errors or redundancies in suggestions.

6 Conclusion

In this chapter, we developed an integrated and intuitive system for suggesting location-driven tags for geotagged pictures. Tag suggestions in the form of three

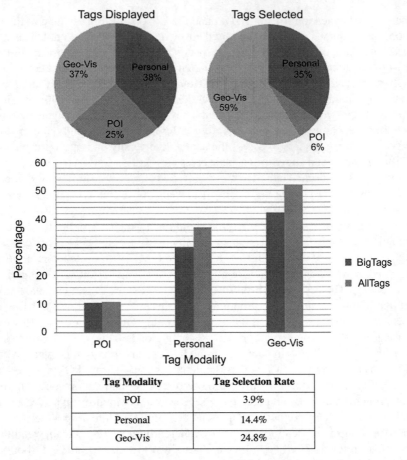

Fig. 9 Results from user study: (*top*) Pie charts depicting percentage distributions of tags-displayed (in tag-clouds) and tags-selected (by users) from different tag-clouds; (*center*) Comparing the proportions of big-tags from all tag-selections among different tag-clouds; (*bottom*) Tag-selection rate computed as the percentage of tags displayed that were selected among different tag-clouds

tag-clouds from diverse information sources were presented. A user study was conducted to evaluate the benefits of the proposed system. Several interesting and useful suggestions were offered by some of our study participants and can form future work directions, which we discuss below.

A user can benefit from real-time mining and tag propagation. Tags selected frequently within a windowed time-line can be automatically propagated to images, perhaps reducing the number of user clicks. The user can then deselect unwanted tags that were propagated. Real-time tag-cloud adjustment as a response to user participation would also be beneficial. Tag selection by users can act as authoritative input thus reweighting the appropriate tags based on location and/or user in order to assist the current and future users of our system. Furthermore, the new tags that were manually added should be dynamically incorporated into the tag-clouds perhaps with higher weights.

At a higher level, it would be interesting to investigate ways to combine the three individual tag-clouds. Moreover, it would also be interesting from a user attention perspective to implement "floating" tag-clouds that dynamically evolve.

References

1. Ahern, S., Davis, M., Eckles, D., King, S., Naaman, M., Nair, R., Spasojevic, M., Yang, J.: Zonetag: Designing context aware mobile media capture to increase participation. In: Proceedings of Workshop on Pervasive Image Capture and Sharing (2006)
2. Ames, M., Naaman, M.: Why we tag: Motivations for annotation in mobile and online media. In: Proceedings of ACM SIGCHI Conference on Human Factors in Computing Systems (2007)
3. Cao, L., Luo, J., Kautz, H., Huang, T.: Annotating collections of geotagged photos using hierarchical event and scene models. In: Proceedings of IEEE CVPR (2008)
4. Cao, L., Luo, J., Huang, T.S.: Annotating photo collections by label propagation according to multiple proximity cues. In: Proceedings of ACM Multimedia (2008)
5. Cao, L., Yu, J., Luo, J., Huang, T.S.: Enhancing semantic and geographic annotation of Web images via logistic canonical correlation regression. In: Proceedings of ACM Multimedia (2009)
6. Comaniciu, D., Meer, P.: Mean shift: A robust approach toward feature space analysis. IEEE Trans. Pattern Anal. Mach. Intell. **24**(5), 603–619 (2002)
7. Crandall, D., Backstrom, L., Huttenlocher, D., Kleinberg, J.: Mapping the world's photos. In: Proceedings of World Wide Web Conference (2009)
8. Cristani, M., Perina, A., Castellani, U., Murino, V.: Geo-located image analysis using latent representations. In: Proceedings of IEEE CVPR (2008)
9. Divvala, S., Hoiem, D., Hays, J., Efros, A., Hebert, M.: An empirical study of context in object detection. In: Proceedings of IEEE CVPR (2009)
10. Dubinko, M., Kumar, R., Magnani, Novak J., Raghavan, P., Tomkins, A.: Visualizing tags over time. In: Proceedings of World Wide Web Conference (2006)
11. Hays, J., Efros, A.: IM2GPS: Estimating geographic information from a single image. In: Proceedings of IEEE CVPR (2008)
12. Jacobs, N., Satkin, S., Roman, N., Speyer, R., Pless, R.: Geolocating static cameras. In: Proceedings of IEEE International Conference on Computer Vision (2007)
13. Jain, V., Singhal, A., Luo, J.: Selective hidden random fields: Exploiting domain specific saliency for event classification. In: Proceedings of IEEE CVPR (2008)
14. Joshi, D., Luo, J.: Inferring generic activities and events from image content and bags of geotags. In: Proceedings of ACM CIVR (2008)
15. Joshi, D., Gallagher, A., Yu, J., Luo, J.: Inferring photographic location using geotagged web images. Multimed. Tools Appl. J. (2010)
16. Joshi, D., Luo, J., Yu, J., Lei, P., Gallagher, A.: Rich location-driven tag cloud suggestions based on public, community, and personal sources. In: Proceedings of ACM Int. Workshop on Connected Media Mining (2010)
17. Kennedy, L., Naaman, M., Ahern, S., Nair, R., Rattenbury, T.: How Flickr helps us make sense of the world: Context and content in community-contributed media collections. In: Proceedings of ACM Multimedia (2007)
18. Kennedy, L., Slaney, M., Weinberger, K.: Reliable tags using image similarity: Mining specificity and expertise from large-scale multimedia databases. In: ACM Workshop on Web-Scale Multimedia Corpus (2009)

19. Kleban, J., Moxley, E., Xu, J., Manjunath, B.S.: Global annotation on georeferenced photographs. In: Proceedings of ACM CIVR (2009)
20. Kosecka, J., Zhang, W.: Video compass. In: Proceedings of European Conference on Computer Vision (ECCV) (2002)
21. Lazebnik, S., Schmid, C., Ponce, J.: Beyond bags of features: Spatial pyramid matching for recognizing natural scene categories. In: Proceedings of IEEE CVPR (2006)
22. Liao, L., Fox, D., Kautz, H.: Extracting places and activities from GPS traces using hierarchical conditional random fields. Int. J. Robot. Res. (2007)
23. Li, L.-J., Fei-Fei, L.: What, where and who? Classifying event by scene and object recognition. In: Proceedings of IEEE ICCV (2007)
24. Luo, J., Boutell, M., Brown, C.: Pictures are not taken in a vacuum: An overview of exploiting context for semantic scene content understanding. IEEE Signal Process. Mag. 23(2), 101–114 (2006)
25. Luo, J., Yu, J., Joshi, D., Hao, W.: Event recognition: viewing the world with a third eye. In: Proceedings of ACM Multimedia (2008)
26. Moxley, E., Kleban, J., Manjunath, B.S.: SpiritTagger: A geo-aware tag suggestion tool mined from Flickr. In: Proceedings of ACM Multimedia Information Retrieval (MIR) (2008)
27. O'Hare, N., Smeaton, A.: Context-aware person identification in personal photo collections. IEEE Trans. Multimed. (2009)
28. Quack, T., Leibe, B., Van Gool, L.: World-scale mining of objects and events from community photo collections. In: Proceedings of CIVR (2008)
29. Torralba, A., Fergus, R., Freeman, W.T.: Tiny images. Technical Report MIT-CSAIL-TR-2007-024 (2007)
30. Toyama, K., Logan, R., Roseway, A.: Geographic location tags on digital images. In: Proceedings of ACM Multimedia (2003)
31. Tsai, C.-M., Qamra, A., Chang, E.: Extent: Inferring image metadata from context and content. In: Proceedings of IEEE ICME (2005)
32. Wei, X.-Y., Jiang, Y.-G., Ngo, C.-W.: Exploring inter-concept relationship with context space for semantic video indexing. In: Proceedings of ACM CIVR (2009)
33. Wolf, L., Bileschi, S.: A critical view of context. Int. J. Comput. Vis. 68(1), 43–52 (2006)
34. Yu, J., Luo, J.: Leveraging probabilistic season and location context models for scene understanding. In: Proceedings of ACM CIVR (2008)
35. Yuan, J., Luo, J., Kautz, H., Wu, Y.: Mining GPS traces and visual words for event classification. In: Proceedings of ACM Multimedia Information Retrieval (MIR) (2008)
36. Zheng, V.W., Zheng, Y., Xie, X., Yang, Q.: Collaborative location and activity recommendations with GPS history data. In: Proceedings of World Wide Web Conference (2010)
37. Zheng, Y.-T., Zhao, M., Song, Y., Adam, H., Buddemeier, U., Bissacco, A., Brucher, F., Chua, T.-S., Neven, H.: Tour the world: Building a webscale landmark recognition engine. In: Proceedings of IEEE CVPR (2009)

Social Aspects of Photobooks: Improving Photobook Authoring from Large-Scale Multimedia Analysis

Philipp Sandhaus and Susanne Boll

Abstract With photo albums we aim to capture personal events such as weddings, vacations, and parties of family and friends. By arranging photo prints, captions and paper souvenirs such as tickets over the pages of a photobook we tell a story to capture and share our memories. The photo memories captured in such a photobook tell us much about the content and the relevance of the photos for the user. The way in which we select photos and arrange them in the photo album reveal a lot about the events, persons and places on the photos: captions describe content, closeness and arrangement of photos express relations between photos and their content and especially about the social relations of the author and the persons present in the album. Nowadays the process of photo album authoring has become digital, photos and texts can be arranged and laid out with the help of authoring tools in a digital photo album which can be printed as a physical photobook. In this chapter we present results of the analysis of a large repository of digitally mastered photobooks to learn about their social aspects. We explore to which degree a social aspect can be identified and how expressive and vivid different classes of photobooks are. The photobooks are anonymized, real world photobooks from customers of our industry partner CeWe Color. The knowledge gained from this social photobook analysis is meant both to better understand how people author their photobooks and to improve the automatic selection of and layout of photobooks.

1 Introduction

Since the broad availability of consumer photo cameras, photos have been a means to capture important moment of anyone's life and to preserve them for personal usage and to show them to others. However, having only simple prints or files on a computer in a digital is not sufficient for many. Thoughts and memories connected

P. Sandhaus (✉)
OFFIS – Institute for Information Science, Oldenburg, Germany
e-mail: sandhaus@offis.de

S. Boll
University of Oldenburg, Oldenburg, Germany
e-mail: susanne.boll@uni-oldenburg.de

S.C.H. Hoi et al. (eds.), *Social Media Modeling and Computing*,
DOI 10.1007/978-0-85729-436-4_12, © Springer-Verlag London Limited 2011

to events can far better expressed by taking the raw photo content as a means to design semantically rich multimedia presentations. Besides Web Galleries, travelblogs and other possibilities a popular way to do this are photobooks. Even in the analogue days photobooks were used to structure and enrich memories by arranging pictures in an album and enriching it with additional information and content. In the digital age this has become even easier: Service providers like CeWe Color[1] enable users to design photobooks on a home PC and transfer these presentations into a physical product. The digital way provides the user with additional means: Photos are sorted, clustered, resized, cropped, rotated and the pages are decorated with textual annotations, background and content from different sources, e.g. a geographical map to illustrate a hiking trip.

The sources for the photobook contents are not only the users' own harddisks anymore. With the growing success of photo sharing platforms and photo sharing in social networks, photobooks are more and more getting a representation of the users' social interactions: Important photos not only sit in the users' personal accounts, but are spread widely over their social network [17]. This social aspect is also present in the users' photobooks: Typical events seem to incorporate people to a quite large degree, and photobooks are often a reflection of the authors' social life.

With CeWe Color as a project partner we have access to a large number of structural representations of photobooks as well as their pixel-based content. These representations allow for an analysis of photobooks on a large scale. By exploiting large numbers photobooks we can strive to understand the structure and types or categories of albums. Furthermore, we can learn what kind of photos actually find their way into the album.

In this chapter we will analyze and discuss the social nature of photobooks. We aim to find out if and how social aspects are reflected. Additionally, we analyze the expressiveness of photobooks, i.e. we explore how explicit different events are described and how emotional this is done. The third aspect we analyze is the vividness of photobooks, i.e. are photobooks designed very colorful and lively or rather uniform and factual.

The remainder of this chapter is organized as follows. We start by giving an overview over relevant related works and then introduce the data model and characteristics of our test set. For further analyses of the data set we first describe the development of semantic classifiers for photobook classes. These classifiers are used in the photobook analyses regarding socialness, expressiveness and vividness.

2 Related Work

Research in the context of personalized multimedia presentations has been an active topic in the multimedia community for over a decade now. However, most works are

---

[1]CeWe Color is Europe's leading photo finisher.

focusing on the generation or authoring part. For this several frameworks and systems such as the Cuypers Multimedia Transformation Engine [25] and the SampLe System [9] have been developed. Important file formats for the representation of multimedia presentations are the W3C standardized SMIL [28], SVG [27] or Flash [1] format. The analysis of such multimedia presentations has only been addressed rarely. However, some works have approached the problem of missing semantic annotation from another perspective by giving support for semantic annotation during the creation of these presentations. One example is the SemanticMM4U Framework [20] which adds semantics support to personal multimedia presentations. It also became clear that different kinds of semantics can occur in the context of multimedia and that semantics are not static but vary according to multiple dimensions, like time, place and person. One attempt to structure the different types of semantics in MIR is given in [21]. The emergent character of semantics in personalized multimedia content is described in [22].

On the other side, several works are aiming to better, how people manage, share and interact with their digital photographs. An early work from an anthropologist's perspective analyzing the use of home videos and photos was done in [6]. A more practical study was done by Frohlich et al. [10] with the goal to find requirements for photoware, which the authors define as technologies enabling photo sharing. Van House [24] has done some early works in studying the uses of digital photos in general. One of the most prominent means to share photos are online communities. However, some works have explicitly focused on studying the way people share photos in such communities. A recent study analyzes different factors which impact the sharing of photos in online communities [16]. As activities before sharing, but after capturing Kirk established the terminus photowork [12]. An older, but still relevant study aiming at finding out how people manage their digital photographs was carried out by Rodden [18] by observing and analyzing the management habits of 13 participants over a period of 6 months. Crabtree [7] has analyzed the way people naturally collaborate around photos and share collections of photographs. Bentley [2] has studied the similarities between consumer photo usage and music usage.

The interest in understanding the human usage of photos has also led to dedicated workshops clustering different aspects of photo usage. In [11] the boundaries between activities regarding preparation of photo for sharing (photowork) and actually using these photos to communicate with others (phototalk) are challenged by analyzing means of collaborative photowork. Another workshop [14] has focused on the analysis of co-located photo sharing activities. These are sharing activities which take place at the same place and at the same time, e.g. watching a photo slide show together with friends.

Looking at works dealing with the semantic understanding of photos in general we see this has been a prominent topic for several years now. Starting with pure content analysis [23] more recent works have a stronger focus at combinations with context-based methods [4, 15]. [8] and [13] give a good impression over approaches of the last years. With MetaXa [3] the authors of this article have developed a semantic photo analysis library and framework which combines content- and context-based analysis methods semantic image annotation.

Fig. 1 Examples of typical photobook pages

3 Digital Photo Books

Personal photobooks have always been a popular way for organizing photos in a pleasant way and to preserve memories and share them with others. For this, people do not only place photos in a book, but decorate them with additional snippets like text annotations or page decorations. Have glue, scissors, and pencils been the tools in the analog days to assemble a photobook, the process has become digital nowadays. The user gets support by authoring tools like the one in [5] to digitally master photobooks. Such authoring software allows one to arrange digital images on the pages of an album, add textual annotations, and design the book with the preferred colors and style. In the end the user can order a print from a photo finishing company. Examples of photobook pages designed with such an authoring tool are shown in Fig. 1.

Creating a photobook is a form of digital story telling that reveals much about the user, the album and the different parts of the album. By authoring the photobook the user has implicitly enriched the photos, the single pages and the book as a whole with different kinds of semantics: She or he has established relations between photos, texts and pages. Photos and text become more prominent than others by their size and placement in the book, which may reflect their importance for the user. Some photos are clustered into groups or put on special pages, which might allow to draw conclusions about relations between photos and their semantics. We aim to reveal these hidden semantics by analyzing authored photobooks and the contained photos. Basis for this are the CeWe photobook software and photobooks which have been digitally authored and ordered.

To present the potential that photobooks offer for semantic analysis, we describe in the following the structure of photobooks and our data set.

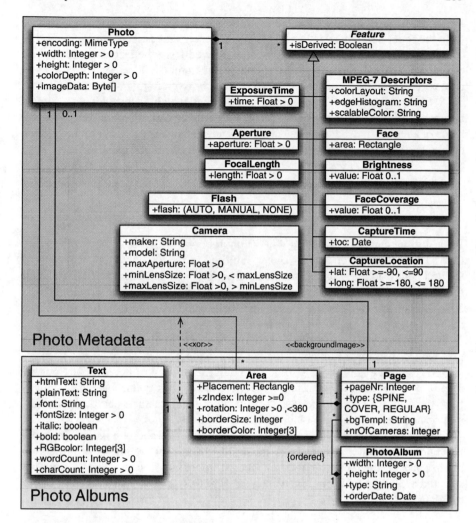

Fig. 2 Photo Album Model (UML class diagram)

3.1 Photobook Structure

Photobooks are represented by a structural model capturing their content and layout over the pages of the book. This model serves as the input for the semantic analysis and directly represents the structural representation of photobooks ordered at CeWe Color. Figure 2 illustrates this structure in a UML model. It is divided into two parts, representing the photo album as a whole, the contained photos and their associated metadata.

A photo is defined by a number of features which stem from the photo's content and context together forming the *Photo Metadata*. These features are either directly extracted from the photo or derived by analyzing and combining other features.

Extracted features are, e.g., the capture time and location or the camera extracted from the photo's Exif header. Derived features are, e.g., the percentage of photos that contain faces or the brightness of the photo derived from the brightness histogram of the photo. A more thorough description of our framework for content-based and context-based metadata enhancement for photos is given in [3].

A *Photo Album* consists of one or more pages which each holds an arbitrary number of photos and text areas. A page can either be an album cover, the book spine or a regular page. It may hold a single image acting as the background. Photos and text areas can be of arbitrary dimension and can be rotated and overlap.

3.2 Test Data Set

Basis for our analysis are about 44,000 photobooks which have been ordered at CeWe Color. The photobooks have been authored and ordered by users with the help CeWe Photo Book software [5] in the time period from 3/2008 to 8/2010. From all orders in this time period, a portion of the daily orders of the day is selected and added to our test data set. The photobooks originated from all over Europe but the majority of orders come from Germany.

For our analysis, the photobooks have been completely anonymized, which means that all information about the person having placed the order has been removed from the photobook. Also, to maintain the privacy of the test data, our semantic analysis runs only on photo features, the photos themselves are removed from the data set. Thus, our test data set consists of all structural photo album information and the extracted photo features.

CeWe Color offers a wide variety of different kinds of photobooks ranging from low budget soft cover albums for a couple of Euros to premium books printed on photo paper in linen or leather cover. The photobooks of our test data set are not selected according to this criterion and therefore this variety is also reflected in our test data set.

4 Concept for Social Photobook Analysis

In this section we further explain the goals and concept of our social analysis of photobooks. Additionally we describe the development of semantic photobook classifiers to be able to distinguish different types of photobooks.

4.1 Goals

Our aim is to gain more knowledge about the social aspects of digitally authored photobooks. Specifically we are seeking to answer three questions.

4.1.1 How Social Are Photobooks?

We are interested in the question of how social aspects are represented in photobooks. Thus, how are social relations between people reflected in the photobook, how prominent are people shown in the book and are there differences for different types of photobooks.

4.1.2 How Expressive Are Photobooks?

By expressive we mean, how explicit is an event of a story documented in photobooks. A photo may, e.g., be not much more than a sole collection of photos, or it may be a detailed documentation of a specific event.

4.1.3 How Vivid Are Photobooks?

Photobooks can be either quite uniform and factual in their overall impression or more vivid and informal. One might suspect that this is different for different purposes or classes of photobooks, e.g. a book documenting a party might be more vivid than a professionally designed photobook of a wedding.

In the remainder of this chapter we will approach these questions.

4.2 Album Classification

One goal of our analyses is to detect differences between different types of photobooks. As shown in Sect. 3 these semantics are not directly present in the photobooks' structure of our test collection. Thus, we need a way to automatically extract these semantics for a large set of photobooks. In the following we describe the development of such classifiers by using a small portion of photobooks as a training data set.

The main requirement for the reliable derivation of characteristics for a specific semantic label is the availability of a sufficient large, labeled data set. This labeled data set is the ground truth for our analysis. Our problem is that we are equipped with a quite large quantity of data, but this data set is not semantically labeled in any sense. E.g., we do not know if a photobook is documenting a holiday or a wedding without looking at the book manually.

To compensate for this, we opted for a quite pragmatic method: We choose those samples from our test data set for which we are quite sure about their semantics according to the values of one or more features. By this we select only a small portion of the test data set as training samples. Samples of this labeled set are manually inspected to avoid wrong labels. With the help of these labeled samples we determine additional features discriminant for the respective semantic label. By this we are able to derive rules for the semantic annotation of book parts, also for samples not fulfilling our initial characteristics. We are aware that this approach has two major drawbacks: The labeled training samples are not evenly distributed over the test data set and therefore we cannot be sure that derived rules for this labeled set can be used for labeling the rest of the data set. On the other side we cannot be sure whether or not the automatically determined ones do contain wrongly labeled samples. However, the manual inspection of samples of the automatically labeled data set determined by our approach has shown that our method is feasible.

From our and CeWe Color's experience we know that there exist some typical types of photobooks which are often ordered. Our goal was to determine features to distinguish between these different kinds of albums. For this we determined a set of labeled albums by selecting them by characteristics typical for specific kinds of photobooks. We then analyzed these labeled photobooks for additional discriminative characteristics.

4.2.1 Assumptions on the Data Set

The most typical albums according to CeWe Color are travel albums and albums documenting a party-like event, e.g. a birthday party or a wedding. Thus we opted to analyze our data set according to these typical events. Specifically, we chose three event types: a wedding and a birthday party and photobooks documenting a journey. We assume that we can select a considerably large subset of all albums belonging to these classes by looking for typical keywords in the title of the photo albums.

4.2.2 Ground-Truth Determination

We chose a quite pragmatic approach to select albums documenting such an event: We looked for typical keywords of on the title pages of the photo albums. Photobooks ordered at CeWe Color originate from countries all over Europe, but the majority of albums is ordered from Germany. We therefore restricted the input data set to albums ordered from Germany and selected albums that contained typically German keywords on the title page of the album. The selected keywords were *Hochzeit* (Wedding) for the wedding class, *Urlaub* (Holiday) for the travel class, and *Geburtstag* (Birthday) for the birthday class. We only looked for one very typical keyword for every class, as our goal was not to select as much albums as possible but to select the albums that quite reliably belonged to the respective class.

4.2.3 Analysis

Our goal was to find additional features which significantly differ when looking different classes of albums. For the classification of albums we opted to chose the following features:

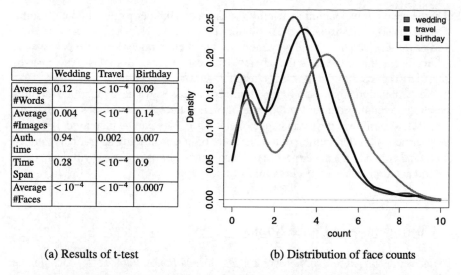

	Wedding	Travel	Birthday
Average #Words	0.12	$< 10^{-4}$	0.09
Average #Images	0.004	$< 10^{-4}$	0.14
Auth. time	0.94	0.002	0.007
Time Span	0.28	$< 10^{-4}$	0.9
Average #Faces	$< 10^{-4}$	$< 10^{-4}$	0.0007

(a) Results of t-test   (b) Distribution of face counts

Fig. 3 Results (p-values) of Student's t-test for the significance of different features to decide about different album classes

- Average *number of words* per page
- Average *number of images* per page
- *Album authoring time*
- *Time Span* of the album
- Average *Number of Faces* per photo

We chose these features as we assumed that they would significantly differ for different classes. E.g., we assumed that a wedding album would show significantly more persons than a travel album.

Figure 3a shows the result of our analysis for the classification of albums. As in the determination of sub albums we performed a t-test for every album class and feature. A p-value lower than 0.05 designates a significant difference in the respective feature values.

4.2.4 Discussion and Classifier Training

One can see that most of the p-value are smaller than 0.05 which means that they are suitable to differentiate between the different classes of photobooks. The only feature that is significantly different in all classes is the average number of faces shown in a photo. Figure 3b shows the distribution for the respective classes. The average number of faces is 4 (wedding), 2.6 (travel), and 3.1 (birthday). The album time span is only significantly different for the travel class. This seems reasonable as journeys usually cover time periods of several days or weeks, while birthday and wedding events are only single day events. Another discriminative feature to distinguish between travel and other album classes is the number of words per page. We observed that a travel album on average consists of 10.3 per page, while a wedding album consists of 6.3 and a birthday album of 6.5 words. This, again, seems reasonable as we observed that travel photobooks often contain rather long text passages in a diary-like manner. We used the labeled data set to train a Multiclass Naive Bayes classifier. The resulting multi-class classifier showed an accuracy of 79.46%.

We can conclude that, for a limited number of classes, we have identified features which quite reliably determine the type of a photobook. The results show that our approach is feasible and we can expect that the accuracy can be increased by tuning the parameters for the training of the classifier or by considering additional features. On the other hand we may expect that the accuracy of our classifier will decrease if we add additional classes of photobooks to it.

5 How Social Are Photo Books?

To answer the question if a photobook is also a *social* photobook or to which degree it is, we first have to define what makes a photobook social or how we can measure the *socialness* of a photobook. The common understanding of social is referred to as the kind and degree of interaction between two or more individuals. Thus, the socialness of photobook can be described as the degree of social relations shown in the photobook. In addition, we can also differentiate these social relations on their degree of intimacy: How close are the relations of people in the photobook? Are they only strangers to each other or are they intimate friends or a couple?

We are aiming to at least to some extent find answers to these questions by analyzing the contents of the photobooks of our test collection. As indicators for the degree of socialness we have identified a number of indicators which will be further explored in the following.

5.1 Number of Persons

The presence of persons in a photobook is generally a good indicator that the photobook has a social aspect. The more people are shown, the more social the underlying event or story is. E.g. if a photobook shows many photos with people one may generally conclude that the photobook has a strong social aspect. However, if looking on a photo level, thus how many persons are shown in the photo, one may also be able to decide how much the people are related to each other.

In Fig. 4 the distribution of number of faces in a photo is shown. For this we employed the face detection algorithm proposed in [26]. We found out that over 85% of all photos in our test collection contain faces. The presence of persons in a photo is usually a sign that it is a quite personal and emotional photo. Knowing how many photos in an album contain faces can in turn tell us more about the type of the album. One may assume that a rather emotional event such as a wedding would also contain a lot of photos showing persons. Figure 4 shows the distribution over

Fig. 4 Distribution of average number of faces per photo per photobook

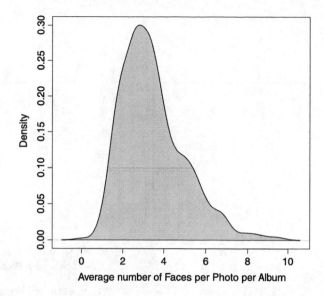

all photobooks for the average number of faces per photo. Obviously the majority of photobooks show an average of nearly two persons per photo.

Looking again at the results of our initial analysis of features for the development of a classifier for photobook types, we are also able to derive semantics for different kinds of photobooks. Figure 3b shows that the number of faces significantly differs for different photobook types: On average, travel photobooks show less people (2.6) in the contained photos than photos in birthday (3.1) or wedding photobooks (4). This backs up the common intuition that, e.g., weddings in general incorporate much more social aspects than e.g. a holiday trip. Also our manual inspection showed that almost all photos show people and often large groups of people e.g. in the wedding ceremony or at an evening party. On the other side, photobooks documenting a journey also show people, but to a much smaller extent, as not only the social relations are documented, but often the main topic are, e.g. a nice landscape or famous landmarks or buildings. Thus, we can conclude that there is a significant difference between different kinds of photobooks regarding the presence of social aspects.

5.2 Person Dominance

Not only the number of persons in a photo is an important indicator for the socialness of a photobook, but, perhaps more important, how dominant they are shown in the photo or the photobook. Thus, one person who occupies a large portion of a photo could indicate a portrait shot which would be considered as much more social than a photo which shows a large group of people, but only in the background.

Fig. 5 Face coverage and portrait shots

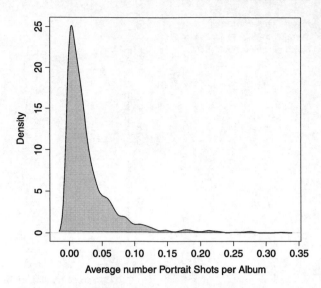

(a) Fraction of Portrait Shots of albums

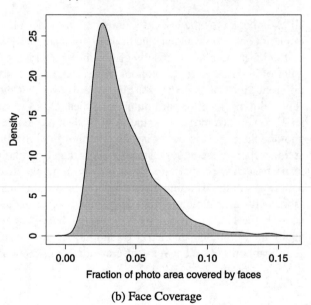

(b) Face Coverage

To cope with these differences we additionally determined the fraction of portrait shots taken over all photos in out test set. As portrait shots we have defined photos which show a single or two faces which occupy at least 20% of a photos' area. The result is depicted in Fig. 5a. The majority of photobooks does not have more than 10% of photos showing portraits. Giving the average number of faces per photo (nearly 2) per photo photobook, this seems to be not much, but backs up

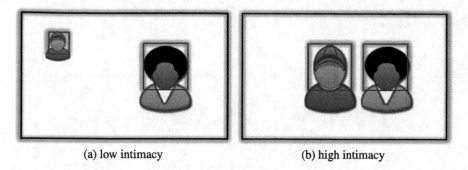

|(a) low intimacy|(b) high intimacy|

Fig. 6 Examples showing high and low levels of intimacy in a photos based on the size and closeness of shown faces

our visual inspection of the photobooks: Most photos showing people are showing their full body or additional objects besides the person itself. Typical examples are, e.g. photographs with one or two persons in front of a landscape or a famous building. Figure 5b shows an overview over the area in photos showing faces which are covered with faces.

5.3 Intimacy

Besides the dominance of persons in photos another interesting indicator for the socialness of photobooks is the degree of intimacy of people shown. The level of intimacy of people shown in a photo can partly be decided by their spatial closeness. This is especially true for only small groups of people (2–3). An example is shown in Fig. 6. Thus, the distance can be seen to be proportional to the level of intimacy in the photos. In most cases this is not true for large groups of people, e.g. group shots, as here people tend to gather to fit on the photo regardless of their intimacy to each other.

As depicted in Fig. 6 we see the distance of people in photographs as an indicator for their intimacy. Thus, if two persons are placed very near, we see this as an indicator for a quite intimate relation. We formally express this by the following formula:

$$intimacy(f1, f2) = \frac{area(f1) + area(f2)}{dist(f1, f2)} - \alpha |area(f1) - area(f2)|. \quad (1)$$

We set the distance of two faces in relation to their size in the photo: If two faces are rather small, then a large distance indicates a less intimate relation than the same distance for larger faces. Additionally, if one face is depicted a lot larger than the other this also indicates a large spatial distance i reality as one face is placed in the foreground while the smaller is placed in the background. This is expressed by the right part of the formula above.

Fig. 7 Degrees of intimacy
for different album classes

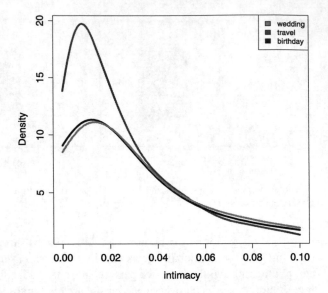

We have analyzed all photos of our data set showing two persons according to
this formula and have distinguished the photos regarding different classes of albums.
The result is depicted in Fig. 7. Interestingly, especially travel photobooks show a
high level of intimacy compared to wedding and birthday photobooks. A further
manual analysis of these travel photobooks showed that the photos showing two
persons are mainly photographs where two people took a shot of themselves in
a rather informal and intimate situation. Wedding photos with two persons were
comparably formal, e.g. taken at the reception of an evening party or formal photos
of the wedding couple.

5.4 Photo Origin

Besides at looking at the content of photobooks, one may also consider the origin of
the contained photos as an indicator of the socialness of a photobook. If the photos
in a photobook only originate from a single person, supposedly the author of the
photobook, this can be an indicator of lesser social involvement than if the photo
originate e.g. from a two or more people.

As a measure for the diversity of origins of photos in a photo the number of
different cameras can be taken. To a certain degree we can derive the number of
people having contributed photos to the photo album when assuming that every
person only owns one camera or one camera is not shared among a group of people
like a family. We know that this is a strong assumption, but from our own experience
and from interviewing people in our group we found out that people rarely own more
than one camera. The presence of more than one camera in an album therefore at
least seems to be a good indicator if more than one person was involved contributing

photos to the photo album. To determine the number of cameras we looked at the number of distinct values for the camera information in the photos' Exif headers of one album. To minimize the error we preprocessed the data set by removing photos without an Exif header or a missing value in the camera field, which, from our analysis of the data sets, is usually an indicator that it has been edited or scanned from a print.

The mean number of cameras over all photobooks in our test set is 2.8, which is a strong sign that not only one's own photos are used for an album but photos are shared among others. The photobook could be a compilation of photos from attendants of a holiday trip or the author of the photo could have added single photos from photo sharing sites or other sources to enrich his album.

6 How Expressive Are Photobooks?

Often photobooks are not only a means to preserve the memory to events for only the owner and creator, but can also act as vehicle to express one's feelings and thoughts to others. This can be done in various ways, either rather factual or more emotional. E.g. a photobook could have a very strict visual layout with none or only a few, but very precise and emotionless descriptions for the photos (like a photo of the Eiffel Tower with only the words *Eiffel Tower* as a description). A more emotional photobook would e.g. have a more casual layout (like tilted photos) and a more slang-like language (*Wow, what a cool view of that old tower!*).

In this section we are aiming at analyzing this expressiveness of real world photobooks. For this we will mainly focus on the text portions of photobooks.

6.1 Image–Text Ratio

In a first step, we analyze the ratio of text and image items in the photobooks of our test set.

Text Items per Page The mean number of text items per page in our test set is 0.5. Only about 30% of all pages do contain text. This may be hint that only special pages are annotated with text and these pages may be a way to identify the beginning of a semantic unit in a photo album. Also, only 10% of the pages do contain more than one text item. This may be a hint that people tend to annotate pages as a whole rather than annotating single photos.

Images per Page The mean number of photos per page is 2.9 and the majority of pages do not contain more than 3–4 images. This shows us that users, despite having the possibility to place much more photos on a page, prefer to have their photos being shown comparably large in a photo album.

Fig. 8 Distribution of font
sizes and text lengths over all
photobooks

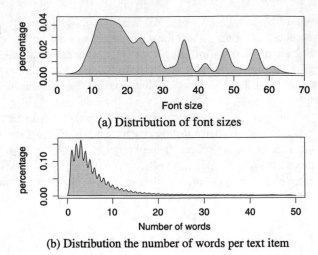

(a) Distribution of font sizes

(b) Distribution the number of words per text item

6.2 Text Lengths and Font Sizes

Besides photos the pages of an album can contain one ore more text items which
further describe one or more photos or one or more pages. We have already shown
that only about 30% of the pages contain text, which is a strong sign that such a
text description is a way to emphasize special parts of a photobook. One of the
main characteristics of text descriptions is their length in words and their font size.
Knowing these features may be a way to further semantically categorize text items
as, e.g., a page or image description. Thus we analyzed the text items in our test data
set regarding these two features.

The median number of words over all text items in our test set is five and 30% of
the text items contain up to three words. Thus, descriptions seem to be rather short
in albums and only very briefly give additional information to the album contents.
Text items with more words may designate a different kind of annotation, e.g. diary
type text describing a specific day or place of a holiday but not solely describing a
single photo. The distribution of text lengths is depicted in Fig. 8b.

In this context it may also help to take the font size of the text into account. We
found that the median text size is 22 and that 30% of the test items have a font
size of at most 16. Thus, these seem to be typical sizes for general annotations in
a photobook. A text with a font size significantly exceeding these values may be a
candidate to be a more important annotation such as an album title or the title for an
event in an album. The distribution of font sizes over all text items in our test set is
depicted in Fig. 8a.

7 How Vivid Are Digital Photobooks?

So far we have analyzed the degree of socialness and expressiveness of photobooks. Another interesting characteristic is the vividness: Photobooks can be de-

signed rather factual and *cold* or more lively, e.g. by the use of many colors or strong variations in the visual layout. To some degree this is strongly related to the expressiveness of photobooks. However, unlike in the last section, we will focus more on the overall visual impression of photobooks rather than on the photobooks' textual contents.

As indicators for the vividness we have chosen two features, the diversity of colors and the intensity of the photobook pages. We have derived these features for the same photobook classes as in the last section.

7.1 Color Distribution

A way to rate the vividness of a photobook from a visual perspective is to determine how diverse the colors of the photos throughout one page are. E.g. a photobook with sepia or gray photos or photos which often show the same scene would be perceived as much less vivid than photos with very diverse colors. We have analyzed all pages of our photobooks regarding this diversity in colors and have compared this to different classes of photobooks with the help of our photobook classifier. For the comparison of photos we have employed the Color Distribution Descriptor defined in the MPEG-7 standard. For every album we have determined the average pairwise similarity of photos on a page.

The result is depicted in Fig. 9. Compared to travel and birthday photobooks, wedding photobooks show a much lower variation in their color layout throughout a page. This seems reasonable and backs up the impression from the manual, visual analysis of a number of wedding photobooks. These photobooks usually mainly incorporate very light and non-intensive colors and are limited to only a couple of colors. Thus, we can conclude that wedding albums are visually less vivid than other types of photobooks and create a rather calm, romantic and perhaps more intimate impression.

7.2 Intensity

As a second indicator for the vividness of photobooks we have identified the degree of smoothness or the intensity of the individual photobook pages. Thus we determined how many strong edges are present in the photos: A layout aiming at a more romantic style will often contain quite uniform areas with a strong use of depth-of-field smoothness. This effect is e.g. often used in professional portrait shots. Thus, we similarly analyzed our test set regarding the sharpness or contrast of contained photos and compared different classes of photobooks. For this we employed the MPEG-7 Edge-Histogram Descriptor and determined the percentage of non-edged pixels for every photobook page for different classes of photobooks.

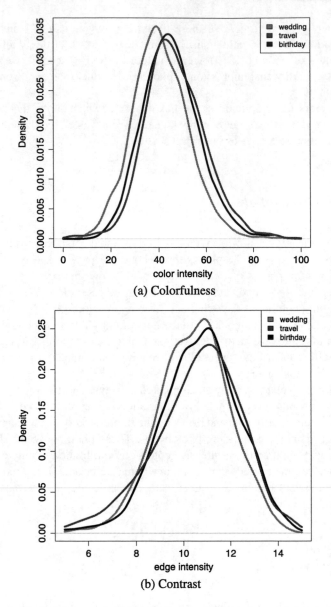

Fig. 9 Degrees of colorfulness and number of edges for different classes of photobooks

The result is depicted in Fig. 9b. Interestingly the degrees of edge intensity have a stronger variety in the travel photobooks compared to wedding or birthday photobooks. This can probably be explained by the variety of different events for travels. E.g. one could be on a winter skiing trip with a lot of smooth white areas in the photos or on a city trip where there are a lot of strong edges in the photos due to a lot of buildings. Also, again, the wedding photobooks shows significantly less strong edges than the other photobook types, which also backs up our visual impression of wedding photobooks, which usually create a more intimate, less vivid and romantic impression, which is in line with the results of the color distribution analysis.

8 Conclusion

In this chapter we have presented the results of a large-scale analysis of real-world photobooks regarding the presence and degree of socialness, expressiveness and vividness. For this we have distinguished between different types of photobooks and have developed a classifier to automatically decide on the type of a photobook. In conclusion we can say that photobooks are showing very strong social aspects and persons are very prominent in most photobooks. However, we have also observed significant differences for different types of photobooks. One example is that wedding photobooks aim to create a much more intimate and calm atmosphere than other types. Although we limited the categorization to only three important photobook types, our analyses have shown that photobooks are a very interesting means to reveal more about peoples' incentives to design photobooks and how they express semantics and emotions for different types of events documented in these photobooks. We see the results in this chapter only as a first step. In the future we aim to identify additional photobook types and their special characteristics.

The main incentive for our analysis, besides to better understand peoples' behavior in photobook design, was to develop methods for automatic photobook design which take characteristics and implicit rules of real world photo books into account. The main conclusion of our analysis is that a meaningful layout system has to take into consideration the type of photobook which has to be created. E.g. different kinds of photos should be selected and a different layout should be chosen when designing a wedding photobook compared to a book documenting a journey. We will take this into account for future versions of our automatic photobook layout system [19].

References

1. Adobe: Flash file format specification 7. http://www.adobe.com/licensing/developer/ (2004)
2. Bentley, F., Metcalf, C., Harboe, G.: Personal vs. commercial content: the similarities between consumer use of photos and music. In: CHI '06: Proceedings of the SIGCHI Conference on Human Factors in Computing Systems, pp. 667–676. ACM, New York (2006). http://doi.acm.org/10.1145/1124772.1124871
3. Boll, S., Sandhaus, P., Scherp, A., Thieme, S.: Metaxa—context- and content-driven metadata enhancement for personal photo books. In: Cham, T.J., Cai, J., Dorai, C., Rajan, D., Chua, T.S., Chia, L.T. (eds.) Advances in Multimedia Modeling. LNCS, vol. 4351, pp. 332–343. Springer, Berlin (2007)
4. Boutell, M.R., Luo, J.: Beyond pixels: Exploiting camera metadata for photo classification. Pattern Recognit. **38**(6), 935–946 (2005)
5. CeWe Color: CeWe Photobook (2007). http://www.my-cewe-photobook.com

6. Chalfen, R.: Snapshot Versions of Life. Bowling Green University Popular Press, Bowling Green (1987)
7. Crabtree, A., Rodden, T., Mariani, J.: Collaborating around collections: informing the continued development of photoware. In: CSCW '04: Proceedings of the 2004 ACM Conference on Computer Supported Cooperative Work, pp. 396–405. ACM, New York (2004). http://doi.acm.org/10.1145/1031607.1031673
8. Datta, R., Ge, W., Li, J., Wang, J.Z.: Image retrieval: Ideas, influences, and trends of the new age. ACM Comput. Surv. **40**, 51–60 (2008). http://wang.ist.psu.edu/survey/analysis/
9. Falkovych, K., Nack, F., van Ossenbruggen, J., Rutledge, L.: Sample: Towards a framework for system-supported multimedia authoring. In: Proceedings of 10th International Multimedia Modelling Conference, p. 362. IEEE, New York (2004)
10. Frohlich, D., Kuchinsky, A., Pering, C., Don, A., Ariss, S.: Requirements for photoware. In: CSCW '02: Proceedings of the 2002 ACM conference on Computer supported cooperative work, pp. 166–175. ACM Press, New York (2002). doi:10.1145/587078.587102. http://portal.acm.org/citation.cfm?id=587102
11. Frohlich, D., Wall, S., Kiddle, G.: Collaborative photowork: Challenging the boundaries between photowork and phototalk. In: Proc. of CHI Workshop on Collocated Social Practices Surrounding Photos (2008)
12. Kirk, D., Sellen, A., Rother, C., Wood, K.: Understanding photowork. In: CHI '06: Proceedings of the SIGCHI Conference on Human Factors in Computing Systems, pp. 761–770. ACM Press, New York (2006). http://doi.acm.org/10.1145/1124772.1124885
13. Lew, M.S., Sebe, N., Djeraba, C., Jain, R.: Content-based multimedia information retrieval: State of the art and challenges. ACM Trans. Multimedia Comput. Commun. Appl. **2**(1), 1–19 (2006). doi:10.1145/1126004.1126005
14. Lindley, S.E., Durrant, A.C., Kirk, D.S., Taylor, A.S.: Collocated social practices surrounding photos. In: CHI '08: CHI '08 Extended Abstracts on Human Factors in Computing Systems, pp. 3921–3924. ACM, New York (2008). http://doi.acm.org/10.1145/1358628.1358957
15. Luo, J., Boutell, M., Brown, C.: Pictures are not taken in a vacuum. IEEE Signal Process. Mag. **23**(2), 101–114 (2006)
16. Nov, O., Naaman, M., Ye, C.: Motivational, structural and tenure factors that impact online community photo sharing. In: Third International Conference on Weblogs and Social Media (ICWSM), San Jose, California (2009)
17. Rabbath, M., Sandhaus, P., Boll, S.: Automatic creation of printable photo books out of your stories in social networks. In: 2nd SIGMM Workshop on Social Media (WSM2010), Florenze, Italy (2010)
18. Rodden, K., Wood, K.R.: How do people manage their digital photographs. In: Gilbert Cockton, P.K. (ed.) Proceedings of the Conference on Human Factors and Computing Systems, pp. 409–416. ACM, New York (2003)
19. Sandhaus, P., Rabbath, M., Erbis, I., Boll, S.: Employing aesthetic principles for automatic photo book layout. In: Proc. of International Conference on Multimedia Modelling, Taipei, Taiwan (2011)
20. Scherp, A.: Semantics support for personalized multimedia content. In: Proceedings of the IASTED International Conference on Internet and Multimedia Systems and Applications, pp. 57–65. ACTA Press, Innsbruck (2008)
21. Scherp, A., Jain, R.: Towards an ecosystem for semantics. In: MS '07: Workshop on Multimedia Information Retrieval on the Many Faces of Multimedia Semantics, pp. 3–12. ACM Press, New York (2007). http://doi.acm.org/10.1145/1290067.1290069
22. Scherp, A., Boll, S., Cremer, H.: Emergent semantics in personalized multimedia content. In: Fourth Special Workshop on Multimedia Semantics (WMS), Chania, Greece (2006)
23. Smeulders, A.W., Worring, M., Santini, S., Gupta, A., Jain, R.: Content-based image retrieval at the end of the early years. IEEE Trans. Pattern Anal. Mach. Intell. **22**(12), 1349–1380 (2000). http://doi.ieeecomputersociety.org/10.1109/34.895972
24. Van House, N., Davis, M., Takhteyev, Y., Ames, M., Finn, M.: The social uses of personal photography: Methods for projecting future imaging applications. University of California, Berkeley, Working Papers 3, 2005 (2004)

25. Van Ossenbruggen, J., Hardman, L., Geurts, J., Rutledge, L.: Towards a multimedia formatting vocabulary. In: Proceedings of the 12th International Conference on World Wide Web, pp. 384–393. ACM, New York (2003)
26. Viola, P., Jones, M.: Rapid object detection using a boosted cascade of simple features. In: Proc. IEEE Conf. on Computer Vision and Pattern Recognition (2001). citeseer.ist.psu.edu/article/viola01rapid.html
27. W3C: Svg. http://www.w3.org/TR/2004/WD-SVG12-20040510/ (2004)
28. W3C: Smil. http://www.w3.org/TR/2005/REC-SMIL2-20051213/ (2005)

Index